HIDDEN MEMORIES

HIDDEN MEMORIES

VOICES AND VISIONS FROM WITHIN

ROBERT A. BAKER

PROMETHEUS BOOKS
59 John Glenn Drive • Amherst, New York 14228-2197

Published 1996 by Prometheus Books

00 99 98 97 96   5 4 3 2 1

Library of Congress Cataloging-in-Publication Data

Baker, Robert A. (Robert Allen), 1921–
    Hidden memories : voices and visions from within / Robert A. Baker.
        p. cm.
    Originally published: Buffalo, N.Y. : Prometheus Books, 1992.
    Includes bibliographical references and index.
    ISBN 1–57392–094–0
    1. Subconsciousness. 2. Memory. 3. Hallucinations and illusions. I. Title.
[BF315.B35   1996]
154—dc20
                                                                    96–8961
                                                                        CIP

Printed in the United States of America on acid-free paper

This book is dedicated to
my mother, Audrey Belle Thurmond,
and
my wife, Rose Elizabeth Paalz,
two of the world's greatest mothers.

Contents

Preface   9

Acknowledgments   11

Introduction   13

1. The Search Within   31
2. Cryptomnesia and Other Anomalies of Memory   78
3. Planetary Voyages: Then and Now   111
4. Hypnosis: The Gateway to Fantasy-Land   141
5. Calling All Corpses or Dial "D" for Dead   181
6. Mediums, Channels, and Out of Body Experiences   222
7. The Little Coed Who Wasn't There:
    Hallucinations, Delusions, and Such   279
8. No, Virginia, Those Lights in the Sky Aren't Spaceships!   314
9. Toward the Year 2000: A Modest Proposal   346

Recapitulation: Questions and Answers   360

Reference List   365

Index   385

Preface

Like the White Queen, it seems that too many of our supposedly well-educated and well-informed citizens are also able to believe as many as six, seven, eight, or even more impossible things before breakfast, and a half-dozen more before dinner. If the sale of supermarket tabloids and the popularity of such books as Strieber's *Communion* and *Transformation,* Hopkins's *Intruders* and *Missing Time,* and Blum's *Out There* are indicators, the average citizen's capacity for credulity and impossible beliefs far and away exceeds anything the poor White Queen ever imagined.

Unlike the White Queen, too many of our citizens are devoting a full twenty-four hours a day to believing the impossible, and they manage to live with a world view closer to the demon-haunted world of the superstitious medieval peasant than that of a skeptical, scientifically-oriented American living in the 1990s.

If there is any truth to this statement (and I think the book that follows will persuade you there is), then there ought to be a reason why everyone in the 1990s would accept the claims of so-called "psychics," "channeled entities," and "alien contactees" and lend credence to their stories of prophetic abilities, spirit and demon possession, the healing power of crystals, alien spaceships, and conversations with the dead. One is, by all means, fully justified in asking: Why do ordinary, seemingly sane individuals believe such things? Is there any truth at all in such apparent nonsense? What on earth would motivate people, even momentarily, to take such things seriously? And how do you explain all of the weird things that so many different people say has happened to them—especially when so many different people describe exactly the same experiences?

In the pages that follow, I have made an attempt to answer these questions. To what extent I have succeeded or failed only you, the reader, will be able to determine.

Lexington, Kentucky   ROBERT A. BAKER
October 1990

Acknowledgments

I would like to thank Henry Palka of Hartford, Conn., and Hilary Evans and Lewis Jones of London, England, for some of the material included. I would also like to thank Mrs. Pam Flynn for her skill and dedication in turning my horrible penmanship into a readable manuscript.

Introduction

Last night I saw upon the stair
A little man who wasn't there,
He wasn't there again today
Oh how I wish he'd go away.

—Nursery rhyme

In March of 1974 the science-fiction writer Philip K. Dick had a most unusual experience—he met God: "Some transcendent divine power which was not evil, but benign, intervened to restore my mind and heal my body and give me a sense of the beauty, the joy, and the sanity of the world." According to Dick, it was "as if I had been insane all of my life and suddenly I had become sane." Since Dick was a highly intelligent, very sensitive individual he, too, had his doubts. "On Thursdays and Saturdays," he said, "I would think it was God, on Tuesdays and Wednesdays I would think it was extraterrestrial, sometimes I would think it was the Soviet Union Academy of Sciences trying out their psychotronic microwave telepathic transmitter. I tried every theory, I thought of the Rosicrucians; I thought of Christ. . . . It invaded my mind and assumed control of my motor centers and did my acting and thinking for me." (Platt 1980)

A year or so after Dick had his experience, John C. Lilly, the biophysicist and dolphin expert, implied he became God. "We have created several universes, have dissolved them, and have created new ones. Each universe we have created has become more complex, more amusing to us. Our control of the current universe is on the upswing; it is becoming more complex as we regulate its regulation of itself. . . . To create a universe

13

we first create light. We contain the light within the universe, within the space that we create to contain the fight. We curve the space to contain light." Lilly also communicated regularly with several extraterrestrials and discovered that he was actually a visitor here on earth from the year 3001. (Lilly 1978)

In August 1975 Miss Claudette Pierce, then in her early sixties, reported having difficulty watching her television. Since she was being treated with L-dopa for a Parkinson's disorder, along with the standard medication Artane, her physician assumed that the medication was interfering with her vision. Upon being questioned Miss Pierce said that she had no visual problems whatsoever. The reason she could not watch TV, she said, was because of her Uncle William. "Your Uncle?" the doctor asked. "Yes. He sits in my chair," Claudette replied. "Why don't you tell him to move?" "I can't." "Why not?" "He's dead. He died in 1961." (Klawans 1989)

In the western part of New York State in April 1988, a middle-aged woman reported that every time she lay down to sleep or rest, a host of demons crowded around her bed, pulled at her feet and legs, and shook her covers. If she was able to fall asleep a few minutes later, she would wake up screaming because the ghosts were tearing at her feet and legs while she also gasped for breath because of the demons who were trying to suffocate her.

In January 1988 Faye Knowles and her three sons left Perth, Australia, for a holiday in Melbourne. At 3 A.M. while driving along the Erie Highway near Mundrabilia in the southern Australian desert, they saw a strange light in the sky. This light soon became a large egg-shaped object that descended on their car, hoisted it into the air, and then dropped it onto the road. The family quickly scrambled into some roadside bushes and hid until the object departed. After changing a tire and driving to Ceduna, they reported the incident to the police. (Huyghe 1988)

Feeling somewhat tired and a little nervous, Jennifer sat down in her easy chair and closed her eyes for a moment. Immediately she was catapulted back down through the years to her early childhood when she was only four years old and was being taken to "devil parties" by her father where she watched ritual torture and the sacrifice of animals, and then, later, the torture and sacrifice of human beings—adults, children, and infants. Images of being forced to help cannibalize the corpses of the sacrificed crowded her mind. As she watched the torture of other children, she remembered being tortured herself with electric shocks, being kept in cages for long periods with nothing to eat or drink, being hung by her wrists or ankles, and being choked into unconsciousness many times. She also recalled being raped by many objects including hot pokers, burning sticks, and the leg bones of disinterred corpses—with animals, and by up to a dozen people at a time. By the time

Jennifer was five she was forced to participate in the torture and killing of animals, was given to Satan in a marriage ritual, and forced to have intercourse with a little boy whom the cult members then killed. She had to "give birth" to a disemboweled infant's corpse while being told over and over again that she was the mother of evil, that her womb was full of death, and that she would grow up to give birth to evil. She was brainwashed to believe that she belonged to Satan forever, was a "child of the devil," and would eventually grow horns and bring death to anyone she ever loved. She remembered repeatedly being fed human eyeballs and tongues, being placed in a coffin full of human organs and live snakes, and of having her eardrums pierced with hat pins while several cult members rang loud bells. The memories were so vivid that she would writhe on the floor, choke and scream and shiver and gag and throw herself around, and beat at her face until finally she was calm enough to relax and fall asleep. From June of 1988 to January of 1989, Jennifer had between three to ten such memories a week. (Peters 1990)

In 1988 Ralph Tolman, a physicist working in a supersecret Silicon Valley lab, reported that he was being controlled by the newest model personal satellite launched by a rival company to follow him around and drive him insane. This satellite transmitted detailed pictures in color and stereo directly into his brain. No matter where he went or what he did, he could not escape the broadcasts. These transmissions always began with a buzzing in his ears and a tingling in his skin followed by small luminous objects darting through his visual field. These were always followed by a series of lights pulsating with bluish colors. The bluish lights were always followed by geometric forms which soon gave way to horrible and complex visual images of blood and gore, festering corpses, and tortured children. These scenes were so vivid and graphic that Tolman was made physically ill.

A few months ago the distinguished psychologist Ronald K. Siegel went to bed one cold winter night only to be awakened at about 4:00 A.M. by the sound of his bedroom door being opened. He heard footsteps approaching his bed accompanied by heavy breathing. There seemed to be a murky presence in his room. When Siegel tried to throw off the covers and get up, he found he was pinned to the bed by a weight on his chest. The more he struggled, the more he found himself unable to move. His heart was pounding, and he was having difficulty breathing. The presence got closer, and a shadow fell across his bedside clock. Something touched his neck and arm, and a voice whispered in his ear in a strange language that sounded like English spoken backward. Soon the voice stopped, the presence left the room, and the pressure on his chest eased. At 4:30 A.M., Siegel got up and checked the house. There was nothing there.

Harry Balise talked with a long line of historical figures—from Socrates, to Joan of Arc, to the Buddha—in his skid-row hotel room in Los Angeles. Balise also believed that he had the power to levitate objects, which he proved by causing pieces of tissue paper to float in his cupped hands. Balise believed that he could move coffee cups and pencils—even when they were standing still.

Rudy, a young Californian, was convinced that he was being followed by a black hole. Rudy would be walking along the sidewalk when suddenly a black hole would start chasing him. It would appear once or twice a month in the most unexpected places: on the street, in the park, once it even popped out of a newspaper he was reading. When Rudy would run to the hospital or the police station for help, the doctors would give him tranquilizers while the police would simply laugh at him. When Rudy went to Dr. Siegel's office for help, the black hole waited for him outside Siegel's door. One morning in the company of Dr. Siegel, Rudy started back to his apartment when he suddenly turned and saw a giant funnel sixteen feet in diameter following him. The outside of the funnel was covered with a black lacework while the inside was lined with geometrically arranged girders. At the very center of the hole was a very bright light.

According to Whitley Strieber, the novelist:

Sometime in the night I awoke and found myself unable to move or even to open my eyes. I had the distinct impression that there was something in my left nostril. . . . I tried to struggle. . . . The next thing I remembered, it was morning. . . . There are six figures standing at the end of the bed looking right at both of us. . . . They're menacing looking. Strange. . . . I feel like I've just gotten some kind of weight on me. I want to get up. I want badly to get up. . . . They're just standing there.

(Strieber 1987)

In another context Strieber reports another experience:

In the wee hours of the night I abruptly woke up. There was somebody quite close to the bed. . . . I caught a glimpse of someone crouching just behind my bedside table. . . . I could see by the huge dark eyes who it was. . . . I felt an absolutely indescribable sense of menace. It was hell on earth to be there, and yet I couldn't move, couldn't cry out, couldn't get away. I lay as still as death, suffering inner agonies. Whatever was there seemed so monstrously ugly, so filthy and dark and sinister. . . . I still remember that thing crouching there, so terribly ugly, its arms and legs like the limbs of a great insect, its eyes glaring at me. . . . Every muscle in my body was stiff to the point of breaking. I ached. My stomach felt as if it had been stuffed with molten lead. I could hardly breathe.

(Strieber 1988)

In the early 1960s, Ed Duvall, a roving mechanic at a mine, worked the night shift. After most of the routine work was finished, Ed would often drive to an isolated area, park, and catch a wink or two of sleep until he was needed. A two-way radio in his truck made him accessible to anyone who called. One night Ed had been napping in his truck when,

> I awoke completely paralyzed. I was wide awake but the only thing I could move was my eyes. My first thought was that I had gotten carbon monoxide in the cab. My second thought was to try to reach over for the radio mike to call for help. It was within easy reach, but I couldn't move. It seemed like I lay there for a long time, but it probably wasn't more than a couple of minutes. The paralysis left. I got out and had suddenly had an extreme urge to get away from there. I jumped in my truck and hurriedly left that area. I never slept in that area again.
>
> (Hopkins 1987)

After undergoing regressive hypnosis Ed remembers seeing a very bright light, getting out of his truck to look at it, and then being kidnapped by little gray aliens from a UFO, taken aboard their spacecraft, and forced to copulate with female aliens.

> Llanca struggled to get up. . . . but his muscles wouldn't respond, his body being paralyzed. Then, hovering just off the ground, near his truck, there was a dome-topped disc and standing near him, under the UFO were the creatures from it. . . . He tried to scream at them, to make them go away, but he couldn't speak. The paralysis was spreading by then, making his body weak while the creatures just stood near him, studying him. . . . Panic spread; he wanted to run or fight but couldn't do either. He tried to scream but there was no sound. . . .
>
> (Randle 1988)

What the fourteen foregoing stories have in common is that all of these people suffered from a false perception, or a *hallucination*. The major characteristic of hallucinations is that they appear to be very real, and they can have all the sensory qualities of our everyday and ordinary perceptions including sight, sound, smell, taste, and touch. These hallucinations consist of previously stored memories or imagined fantasies or dreams that are tied together by our brain and projected onto the eye of the mind. Another common aspect of the fourteen false beliefs is that none of the people who had these experiences were in any way, shape, form, or fashion crazy or psychotic. At the time they had their unusual experiences they were, indeed, delusional, that is, suffering from a misperception and confusing their seemingly real experiences with that of consensual reality. Although

I have provided only fourteen examples of the kinds of hallucinatory experiences that ordinary, sane, and rational individuals occasionally undergo, I could well have provided a thousand or more gleaned from psychological and psychiatric literature, or from examples furnished by friends, students, and clients. What is not generally known and accepted is that ordinary, perfectly sane and rational people have many such delusional, hallucinatory experiences similar to those just reported. Moreover, such individuals who do are in no way "crazy," or psychotic, or in need of confinement in a mental hospital. They are, in no way, dangerous to themselves or others. This is not to say that at the time the foregoing individuals were having their hallucinatory experiences there was not a specific cause for it—there most certainly was. They were, at the time, mentally disturbed, and there were quite specific reasons for the disturbance in each instance. Let us look at the reasons:

(1) Philip Dick's experience began while he was under the influence of sodium pentothal, while undergoing an extraction, given by his dentist. When he reached his home after the extraction, he had a sudden flood of memories about having lived a "past life" in ancient Rome. For weeks thereafter other memories about other past lives came back to him repeatedly, in intervals between sleep and wakefulness. Other visions involved his being in contact with extraterrestrials. Another even stranger vision was that of being in contact with another Philip K. Dick in a parallel universe where the United States did not exist. These visions were followed by experiences of channeling in which he "knew" ancient languages he had never studied, and other feelings that he was somehow or other picking up transmissions from Russian parapsychologists or extraterrestrial telepaths. But by far the most powerful and transformative visions Dick experienced were those of encountering a vast, alien, living intelligent source that he believed was God, and this contact left him with the strong intuition that a divine being of some sort—a new Buddha or Christ—was about to appear on our planet. There seems to be little question but that Dick's encounters were brought on by stress, self-imposed psychological pressures, excessive alcohol consumption in the form of wine with a consequent build-up of uric acid in his system, along with a steady diet of amphetamines. "I did sixty finished pages a day," Dick stated, "and the only way I could write that much was to take amphetamines, which were prescribed for me." The fact that the creative pressures were mounting was shown by the fact that a few years later, in 1981, Dick wrote and distributed to about seventy of his friends a letter in which he claimed that Jesus had been reborn and was currently living on the island of Sri Lanka. Dick died a year later, at age fifty-three, of a cerebral hemorrhage.

(2) John Lilly's experience of becoming God, and of meeting and conversing with extraterrestrials was the result of the ingestion of 150 milligrams of ketamine or vitamin K followed by immersing himself in his sensory-deprivation flotation tank. Once the effects of the ketamine wore off and he left the tank, his perceptions returned to normal.

(3) In the case of Miss Claudette Pierce, she knew it was a hallucination she experienced and that her dead uncle was not really there. She also suspected that the hallucination was due to the L-dopa she was taking for Parkinson's disease, but she didn't want to give up the drug since it had helped her so much. Approximately half of the patients who take L-dopa for many years do have hallucinations. Although the hallucinatory phenomena vary greatly from patient to patient, in any one patient they tend to become fixed or stereotyped, occurring over and over. The hallucinations are almost always nonthreatening, often occur at night, and seem to be precipitated by a bright light that contrasts with the prevailing darkness. Every night that Ms. Pierce went into her darkened den and turned on the TV, the light of the bright screen would precipitate the same visual hallucination: her favorite uncle seated in her favorite chair. (Klawans 1988)

(4) The woman who had demons pulling at her feet and legs every time she lay down was suffering from a neurological condition known as "restless legs." Some unfortunate people experience involuntary jerking motions of their legs periodically throughout the night which either keep them awake or disturb their sleep without their awareness of being wakened. This form of myoclonus, or "muscle jerks," may also cause hypersomnolence—sleeping too much—during the day in some people. A number of drugs can cause this effect also. It may be helped by the use of benzodiazepines (valium and other tranquilizers) but there is no known cure. Getting out of bed and walking, or continually changing position, are ways in which relief can be obtained until diagnosis and treatment begins. The woman's fundamentalist religious belief in demons, along with a neurological disorder was sufficient to convince her she was being bothered by demons. Along with the restless legs her condition was complicated by *sleep paralysis* (hypnopompic hallucinations) which is accompanied by a sensation of weight pressing on the chest, difficult or labored breathing, and visual hallucinations—all normal accompaniments of sleep paralysis.

(5) In the case of the Knowles family in Australia, according to Keith Basterfield, a field investigator for UFO Research—the Knowles told "the truth as they saw it." What really happened was that the Knowles saw a bright light in the sky, most likely from a plane moving toward them.

Since the family had been driving nonstop for several hours, they were suffering from highway hypnosis. Suddenly a blowout occurred while Sean was driving. Then the family heard a thump as the luggage on the roof jolted loose. The right rear end of the car struck the ground, and Sean hit the brakes hard. The car vibrated as he tried to pull it off the road. The dogs barked. The Knowles rolled down their windows and smelled the nasty smoke from the strained front brakes. The frightened family then headed for the bushes. Although the light remains a mystery, no one ever saw an alien spaceship.

(6) Jennifer's memories of Satanic abuse and torture perpetrated by her father at an early age are classic examples of *confabulation*, that is, making up stories to fill in gaps in one's memory. Jennifer herself had trouble believing her own stories. In her words, "What I could not explain to myself or to her (her therapist) was why these pictures felt so real, exactly like the other memories I had been working on; why I could not only see but feel and smell these scenes. . . . My biggest task was just to believe that what had happened to me was real—even though the memories *felt* utterly real, they seemed so outrageous that I was hard-pressed to believe them. Also, more importantly, it would have been easier for me in some ways to believe that I was crazy than to believe that my childhood was as bad as it was." At another point in her narrative Jennifer expresses amazement that no one noticed her abuse, and at still another point she reports stopping all contact with people who refused to believe her fantasies. More to the point there was no corroboration of any kind coming from members of Jennifer's family, or neighbors, or friends. This is an excellent example of "hidden memories" or cryptomnesia, a series of false memories hanging together to form a pattern or story that is pure fantasy, fabrication, or fiction with a few minor elements of fact or truth included.

In another classic example of this confabulatory phenomena, Dr. George Ganaway, an expert in the treatment of multiple personality disorders (MPD), reported the case of a young mother who reported to a number of therapists before she saw Dr. Ganaway that she had been sexually molested and abused by her grandmother on numerous occasions when she was a child. Following treatment by Dr. Ganaway, the young woman admitted openly that none of the stories she told were true. When questioned as to her motives, she stated that she wanted people to feel sorry for her, and to give the love, affection, and attention she needed and felt she deserved.

(7) When Ralph Tolman was taken into Dr. Ronald Siegel's laboratory and given a number of physiological and psychological tests, it was discovered that Tolman was under a great deal of stress and was also suffering

from high blood pressure which created the buzzing, tingling sensations he experienced. This was what caused the panic, anxiety, bluish lights, and bloody images he saw. The original source of the bloody images was a Mexican film he had seen a few weeks before. Tolman's brain was reacting to a simple trigger: high blood pressure induced by extremely high job-related stress. Siegel stopped the high blood pressure with antihypertensive medication. With the drop in blood pressure, Tolman's visions disappeared. The medication was so effective he didn't even need psychotherapy.

(8) Dr. Siegel's own experience of the ghostly intruder was the well-known phenomena known as *sleep paralysis,* and he suffered from an incubus attack, a type of nightmare once believed to be caused by a female monster or spirit that sat upon the dreamer. The attack usually occurs when the rapid eye movements (REM) associated with dreams intrudes in periods when you have just been aroused from sleep. The brain is unable to switch instantly from dreaming to a waking state so the dream extends into the waking period. During dreams the brain circuits send signals—an image of the incubus for example—to the cerebral cortex where the signals are processed just as if they came from the outside world. Ergo the feeling of hard cold reality. Dr. Siegel's experience with meeting the Buddha came following a long session in John Lilly's sensory-deprivation tank. Both Lilly's ETs and Siegel's Buddha were products of the same brain mechanism: stored visual images from memories, dreams, and fantasies now projected onto the mind's eye as a result of the drugs and isolation tank.

(9) Harry Balise's hallucinations are easily explained. They were simply caused by his overdosing on crack. Sensations of motion in the visual field are a common result of excessive cocaine usage. When Balise focused on specific objects they did, indeed, seem to him to be moving. Since he was so high—so awake and so alert—he felt that his perceptions must be real. But when Balise was examined by Dr. Siegel, it was quite evident that the levitations were only in Harry's mind, which was deluded by the drug.

(10) Rudy's black hole turned out to be one of the hallucinatory geo-metric forms first described by the psychologist Heinrich Kluver in 1926. Kluver found these forms to be common in a variety of conditions including drug intoxication. Dr. Siegel discovered that thirty minutes prior to Rudy's attack he had chain-smoked ten cigarettes. Moreover, Rudy had seen a similar funnel years before when he tried LSD. When Siegel used a photostimulator on Rudy, bathing him in bright, pulsating light, Rudy again saw the black hole. Further study by Siegel revealed that Rudy's visual hallucination of the black hole could be triggered by cigarettes, coffee,

or flickering neon lights. Siegel assured Rudy that the black holes would disappear provided he changed his lifestyle by giving up coffee, cigarettes, and his stressful night life under the neon lights.

(11 and 12) Whitley Strieber's experiences with the aliens are, again, typical of sleep paralyses and most characteristic of the *hypnopompic dream,* a hallucinatory condition in which the sleeper is suddenly awakened but finds himself paralyzed, unable to move, and in the presence of a ghost, a demon, or an extraterrestrial. Strieber's accounts of these experiences in his *Communion* are classic: he wakes up from a sound sleep; there is a strong sense of reality and of being awake; paralysis (due to the fact that the body's neural circuits keep our muscles relaxed and help preserve our sleep) and the encounter with strange beings occur. Following the encounter, instead of jumping out of bed and going in search of the strangers he saw, Strieber typically goes back to sleep. He even reports that his burglar alarm is still working—more proof that the intruders were mental rather than physical. On another occasion Strieber reported awakening and believing that his house was on fire and the aliens were threatening his family. Yet his only response was to go peacefully back to sleep. Again, evidence of a hypnopompic dream. Strieber, of course, is convinced of the reality of these experiences. This, too, is expected. If he was not convinced of their reality, then the experiences would not be hypnopompic or hallucinatory. In the second example, the similarity between Strieber's experience and that of Dr. Siegel is so evident, it needs no further elaboration because it would be repetitive.

(13) Ed Duvall's experience with sleep paralysis and, following regressive hypnosis, an imagined encounter with a UFO are, again, typical of the reports elicited from individuals having "missing time" experiences who are then "hypnotized" by people who have not been sensitized to the fact that their suggestions—albeit unwittingly given—pretty much determine the UFO reports, especially if this possibility has been suggested to the victim anytime prior to the "hypnotic regression." Such suggestions are the key to the gates of the memory bank, and once that key is turned the present is inundated with wave after wave of fantasies, dreams, and confabulations pouring out in a cryptomnesiac flood.

(14) Dionisio Llanca's encounter with the UFO and the golden-haired extraterrestrials is, of course, quite similar to that of Ed Duvall. In Llanca's case as well, his encounter with the UFO and the ETs emerged only after regressive hypnosis was carried out by two psychiatrists unfamiliar with people claiming UFO encounters. Llanca's case also involved sleep paralysis

and its usual accompaniment—encounter with strange beings. In this case the aliens were beautiful, golden-haired humanoids rather than ugly little slant-eyed grayskins. Maybe South American potables are more potent than their North American counterparts.

The fourteen cases just reviewed, bizarre as they are, are all easily explained and understood in terms of contemporary psychology and what is currently known about the functioning of the human nervous system. They are, nevertheless, but a small sample of the many unusual behaviors and beliefs that have haunted and bedeviled human beings over the centuries. In earlier centuries anything odd and unusual about human behavior was usually attributed to the presence of spirits or demons. With the growth and development of science, and a better understanding of human anatomy, physiology, and psychology, such occult and supernatural explanations were discarded for the most part. This sentence must be qualified, however, because even in the early years of the last decade of the twentieth century—today—there are still many people—even some medical men and scientists—who cling to occult and supernatural explanations in matters related to human psychological behavior. They have, moreover, helped to publicize and popularize these medieval beliefs under such labels as "the New Age," "metapsychiatry," and so forth. While it is true that in the public eye extraterrestrial aliens, ghostly hauntings, phone calls from the dead, pictures of the dead on the TV screen, houses with flying furniture and crockery, and other such improbable occurrences make spectacular headlines and are very entertaining—can such improbable reports be true? Did these events really occur as reported or was something significant left out, or some elements of the story exaggerated? Were some of the happenings due to misperception? Was the story received first-, or second-, or even third-hand? Were perfectly natural and normal events misinterpreted? All of these questions need to be asked about every highly unusual media event, no matter where it is reported. The daily competition for the attention of the average person is both ferocious and frenetic. The medium that is successful in grabbing your attention will not only survive, it will prosper. In the high-powered world of commerce, time is definitely money! In such a competitive and rapacious environment it is certainly not improbable that close attention to factual details and opposing points of view will fall by the wayside. The bizarre, the incredible, and the spectacular are certainly much more entertaining than the dull, mundane, or run-of-the-mill ordinary facts. "Man spots meteorite" is not news. "Man spots UFO" is.

In the pages that follow, we will look closely at a number of specific sorts of paranormal and supernatural behavior that have gained a considerable amount of media attention within the last decade, and attempt to determine to what extent these phenomena are, indeed, truly supernatural or unexplainable, and to what extent they are due to the operation of well-known and well-understood (yet seldom publicized) psychological principles. Or even in the event that the psychology is not well-understood at this time, the odds are overwhelming that the behavior falls within the domain of the natural, is amenable to the methods and techniques of scientific psychology, and does not require the invocation of a paranormal or supernatural explanation. In other words, although no one has *personally examined* John Doe's alleged poltergeist, it is highly unlikely that Doe's poltergeist has done or can do anything more than what hundreds of other noisy ghosts have done that *have* been scientifically studied and explained. Indeed, although you have never jumped off the roof of a twelve story building before, we can predict with a considerable amount of confidence what will happen if you do. Although if you insist you can fly minus a hang-glider, parachute, or wings, we could not confidently predict that the law of gravity would be repealed just to save your hide. Sadly enough, last October a Soviet psychic named Frenkel, flushed with pride from his successful efforts in stopping bicycles, automobiles, and streetcars, thought he was ready for something bigger and stepped in front of a freight train; unfortunately, emergency braking didn't help. According to the daily *Sovietskaya Rossiya,* Frenkel was buried on the outskirts of Astrakhan. In the fight between you and the physical laws of this world, it pays to back the world!

Although it is little known and poorly publicized, the term "cryptomnesia" embraces a wide range of supposedly abnormal and paranormal behavior that is currently claimed to be "unexplained," and is allegedly due to "supernatural causes." Bypassing the issue of just how anything within nature or the universe can be above or beyond it, i.e., *super* for the moment, it can be said here and now that the phenomena known as past-lives regression, future lives progression, channeling and mediumistic phenomena, alien encounters and abductions, and dissociative phenomena such as multiple personalities, fugue states, and glossolalia—all involve aspects of what is generally considered to be hidden, remote, or unconscious parts of the human mind, and all have a known or well-understood psychological explanation. A better understanding of cryptomnesiac psychology and of how the human memory works, as well as a better understanding of the reputed conscious, preconscious, and unconscious aspects of normal human behavior, can be quite helpful in simplifying the complexity and reducing the mystery surrounding these supposedly unearthly and supernatural marvels. The purpose of *Hidden Memories* is to provide readers interested in these matters with a rational, credible explanation of such affairs couched in simple, easy-to-understand language that requires no vast or arcane knowledge of either science or psychology or, for that matter, knowledge of the supernatural, or parapsychology.

A second purpose of *Hidden Memories* is to offer a response to recent efforts on the part of a number of psychiatrists and psychologists who are trying to persuade the public that: (1) we have all lived before and reincarnation is a proven scientific fact; (2) hypnosis provides us with the ability to see and accurately predict the future; (3) it is well established that the spirits of the dead return to earth and take over the minds of the living; (4) some rare and gifted individuals are able to contact dead and discarnate intelligences from both the past and the future as well as from other planets in the universe, and glean from these non-existent brains wisdom and guidance for humanity today; and, finally, (5) exotic and occult forces are, on selected occasions, able to invade the bodies of chosen religious fundamentalists and give them the ability to "speak in unknown tongues," i.e., to converse at length and fluently in languages unknown to linguistic scholars on Earth today. What strikes the impartial observer as exceedingly strange is the fact that these supposedly educated, degreed, and licensed mental healers and helpers apparently have abandoned the banner of science and are urging a return to the pre-scientific days of warlocks and witches, amulets and spells, conversations with the dead, and spirit possession. It is a curious situation indeed to find men and women with Ph.D.s and medical degrees, from some of the best universities in the nation, sitting down in front of their word processors in air-conditioned rooms with tele-visions blaring in the background as they write long tracts arguing for the curative power of crystals, past-lives therapy as a cure for present neuroses, and the use of exorcistic rites for psychotic patients.

In the chapters that follow, you will encounter a considerable amount of bias and personal conviction having to do with what is and what is not possible, what is and what is not probable, and what is or what is not silly, inane, foolish, or even ridiculous. These biases and convictions are, like all such things, based upon faith. Because of the complexity of human behavior, the extraordinary complexity of the human mind and central nervous system, as well as the fundamental mysteries surrounding human existence, faith is all we have. But the faith is in the explanatory power of science and scientific reasoning, and in the patience, persistence, and creative ingenuity of human beings who have, over thousands of years, constructed a lawful and orderly civilization based upon logic and reason and other humane considerations aimed at making this planet a better place to live. Although life may be brutal and short for many, indeed, too many at the moment, it is not only possible but probable that the basic intelligence of the human species and a basic scientific education will not only, as Faulkner said, guarantee our survival, but it will also insure that we will prevail.

Some while ago Albert Einstein remarked that, "God doesn't play dice with the universe," to which another scientist added, "No, but he sometimes throws them in the corner where they can't be seen." We take this to mean that although nature is subtle, she is never malicious. The universe, we believe, is lawful, and order can be found even in chaos. There are patterns everywhere, and while some are simple, others are extraordinarily subtle and complex. As individual human beings we err and are far from infallible, but enmasse, and in the long haul, perfection may be attainable even though it may require eons of time.

With regard to much simpler and more mundane beliefs and convictions, and despite our recognition that it is very difficult to prove a negative[1] (Pasquarello 1984), we firmly and emphatically state that in the 1990s on the planet Earth:

(1) There are no extraterrestrial or interdimensional spaceships with either big or little hominid-like aliens kidnapping human beings;

(2) There are no demons, apparitions, spirits, or genies of either the dead or the living in possession of the bodies and minds of human beings in the past, in the present, or in the future;

(3) There is no firmly grounded, scientifically acceptable evidence for the existence of ghosts, apparitions, demons, fairies, elves, gremlins, or extraterrestrial living beings at this time or in the past;

(4) People's minds do not physically leave their bodies and roam around the countryside, nor do they voyage to distant planets or other civilizations in the universe;

(5) People cannot accurately and reliably predict the future with tea leaves, tarot cards, crystal balls, or any other sort of artifact nor can they do so by way of imaginary trips into the future via hypnotic progression;

(6) People cannot go into a trance—hypnotic or otherwise—be seized with religious fervor and instantly acquire or "channel" complete knowledge or another unknown or known foreign tongue;

---

1. According to Pasquarello, "It is always possible to prove the nonexistence of something."

(7) People cannot communicate with the dead via mediums, telephone, TV, radio, or through human channels or any other communication means known to man;

(8) People have not lived before in another lifetime no matter how real or vivid their memories of these past lives may be. Past-lives memories brought into consciousness via hypnotic regression are excellent examples of cryptomnesia, confabulation, and imaginative fantasy production and nothing else. None of this material brought up to the light of consciousness offers any proof whatsoever of reincarnation. Reincarnation may or may not be a fact, but past-lives hypnotic regression is neither a reliable nor a convincing way to determine it.

All of the foregoing beliefs are creations of the fertile and imaginative human mind. All are explainable in terms of known psychological principles, and in terms of human needs and motives, as well as recent discoveries about the operation and functioning of the brain and central nervous system. With regard to item #3 there is, of course, no evidence for the existence of the Tooth Fairy, the Easter Bunny, the Great Pumpkin, or even, sadly enough, for Santa Claus with his flyaway sleigh and reindeer. For these entities, however, it will be best to keep this information away from all children under eight years of age.

There will be, of course, a number of individuals who will disagree and take strong exception to these statements. Many people will insist they have proved otherwise. For all such individuals, the burden of proof rests upon their shoulders not mine. If any of these paranormal or supernatural claims can be validated under the appropriate and unbiased conditions, the scientific world will be the first to champion the fact. In presenting evidence in support of such claims, however, the proponent must be prepared to present evidence before a panel of scientific peers who, acting in the manner of a grand jury, will determine whether there is or is not sufficient evidence to warrant subsequent follow-up investigations. All proponents of these supernatural or paranormal claims will be required to show by replication and demonstration the truth of their contentions and claims under carefully controlled experimental conditions with legitimate experimental controls. Until these conditions are met, none of the paranormalist's claims, no matter how loud or long, will be considered worthy of the time or attention of the scientific community.

Advocates and proponents of occult beliefs, those who make a living off of the credulous or those who have made a reputation and gained some measure of wealth and fame from their essays in printed paranoia, may protest and continue to raise an endless stream of specific cases, e.g.,

"Well, how do you explain this?" or "What about this friend of mine who. . . ." Science, obviously, cannot respond to every human instance of delusion, illusion, hallucination, misperception, nor can it investigate every urban legend, false report, or unfounded rumor—every error made by the normal and abnormal operations of the human mind—the acknowledged most complex mechanism in the universe. What science and scientists study must be carefully selected since science's and the scientist's time and money are limited. If, however, sufficient justification exists for a thorough scientific exploration of any given phenomena, and such an investigation is carried out with regard to the paranormal or occult phenomena referred to earlier, the odds are heavily stacked against the discovery of any startlingly new and revolutionary findings. It is for this reason that the majority of scientifically trained remain skeptical.

On this planet at the moment we have over five and a half billion individual universes—sentient minds made up of a complex nervous system that, only in rare instances, functions perfectly. Each of these mental universes is unique in its experiences and interpretations of the world around it. Each of the human heads containing these universes sees the world in terms of its own unique beliefs and assumptions. These beliefs and assumptions, in turn, are based upon our personal experience, i.e., what we experience first or second hand. In certain circles of polite society, many children and adolescents are traumatized to discover that their elders and their parents actually engage in acts of sexual congress. Even in today's permissive society it is possible to grow up never having personally witnessed an act of sexual intercourse and thus conclude that sex doesn't exist. The rationale is: I have never experienced it; I have never seen it; therefore it doesn't exist. Because of such possibilities, there is some danger in being overly skeptical and there are definite limitations on the range of any human's experience. Moreover, no matter how sophisticated or worldly we become, truth continues to be elusive and is not easily gained. People we trust implicitly lie and deceive us. Paragons of honesty and probity cheat and betray us. On occasions we even find that we are lying to ourselves. It is even more disconcerting to find that we cannot even trust our own senses and perceptions. As for our memories, these too prove to be faulty and unreliable. Then we find ourselves perceiving as true things that we wish to be true and perceiving as false things that we so earnestly desire to be untrue. The discovery that our beliefs and wishes, that our feelings and emotions can affect the way we think and perceive can also be disconcerting and lead us to that ancient paradox: Only one thing is certain, and that is that nothing is certain! And if this statement is true, it is also false. The mental discomfiture this situation engenders recently led Dennis Flanagan, editor of *Scientific American* for thirty-five years, to remark:

If someone believes something that on the face of it is unbelievable, he is a crank. Among people I have known well there are none who did not believe something unbelievable, and whereas I believe I do not believe something unbelievable, others have informed me I am quite mistaken. . . . If it can be said that one of the main requirements of human life is distinguishing the signal of the true from the noise of the false, then noise that interferes with the signal is a serious matter. Moreover, if tolerance of noise becomes a habit, it can become a very serious matter.

(Flanagan 1989)

For this reason it behooves us not only to subject the "apparently" unbelievable to careful scrutiny, but to do our best to separate the signal of the truth from the noise of the error.

In the chapters that follow we will look first at what is currently known about human mental operations and particularly the nature of what has been referred to as the "unconscious mind." Then we will examine briefly what is known about the nature of human memory and hidden memories specifically. Following this we will study some of the mental aberrations that can mislead and confuse us with regard to the differences between reality and fantasy. Next we will look into the phenomena of channeling, past lives regression, future lives progression, and spirit possession, as well as some of the more serious and perplexing disorders such as schizophrenia and multiple personality that have been in the past, are in the present, and can be in the future very destructive to individual lives. Then, for those who are interested in acquiring personal experience in the art of channeling and exploring their own past lives or speaking in tongues, we will provide specific instructions so that you, too, can share in the fun. Finally, we will look at some of those areas of anomalistic psychology that are far more deserving of the researcher's time and attention than merely demonstrating to the believers in the unbelievable that their beliefs are, in the long run, unsatisfactory, unhealthy, and counterproductive. Let us begin.

1

The Search Within

Past lives, spirit possession, near death experiences, psychic powers, and so on are part of a vast psychic *terra incognita* like lost temples in South America that have been overtaken by centuries of jungle growth. . . . In common with many a lone explorer, I have become accustomed to my stories of fabulous discoveries being scoffed at a little. Nevertheless, to be fair to my more skeptical colleagues, I will admit that it is quite easy, to stay with the metaphor, to get lost in the jungle of occultism and to hallucinate things that are not really there.

—Roger J. Woolger, *Other Lives, Other Selves*

Anyone who undertakes the exploration of the depths of the human mind is fully justified in comparing the trip with exploring the depths of either a swamp or a jungle. Moreover, nearly every therapist who has used either hypnosis or psychoanalytic approaches soon finds himself hip-deep in what Freud called "the black tide of mud—occultism." Except for a few brave and curious amateurs, few of our citizens ever dare to dabble with the inside of their heads or play around with their minds. Their attitudes are like that of the legendary Sam Goldwyn who supposedly remarked, "Anyone who goes to see a psychiatrist ought to have his head examined." Also, unfortunately, there is still quite a bit of social stigma attached to the fact that one has undergone mental therapy, and the fear of "losing one's mind" or being thought "crazy" is still a cross no one wants to bear. Although a good number of years have elapsed since Thomas Szasz first called our attention to the possibility that mental illness does not exist and is nothing more than a social myth or useful fiction (Szasz 1961), and thousands of psychologists, psychiatrists, and mental health workers have done their utmost to inform the general public that having "a nervous breakdown" is no worse than having the flu or appendicitis, Mr. and Mrs. John Doe have not been convinced. Most people would, given a choice, rather be dead than be considered "nuts." Moreover, the average man or woman has only the most rudimentary knowledge of or understanding of either "normal" or "abnormal" human behavior. Despite the fact that more and more people are graduating from college every year, and in spite of the almost universal requirement for courses in the social sciences before one can receive a BA degree, even if one had a course in General Psychology most of what was learned was either forgotten or never applied for it to become useful knowledge. The philosopher John Searl pinpointed the problem several years ago:

> There is nothing more mysterious or mystic about the mind than there is about digestion. What the brain does for the mind is what the stomach does for digestion. We have got to start treating mental life and consciousness as just an ordinary part of the physical world like anything else. I think of the mind not as a separate kind of thing or arena, but rather as the sequence of thoughts, feelings, experience, and so-called mental phenomena that go on in it. "Mind" is the name of a process, not a thing. We've got to demystify it. We have this tradition that makes it seem spooky, but there's nothing spooky about it. It's part of our biological life. We can give up our thumbs, or in a pinch our eyes. But if we give up our consciousness, that's it. We're dead.
>
> (Searl 1988)

There are some fairly elementary principles and facts, however, that everyone needs to be aware of if he or she expects to make sense of human behavior, which is certainly complex enough and strange enough on certain occasions to baffle even the most astute professional psychologist. One of the more important of such principles is the need to recognize that our emotional lives play a very significant role in our perceptions (what we believe is real) and our thinking. The old adage, "Love is blind," is, literally, true. Our emotion of love blinds us to the flaws in the beloved that everyone who is not in love with him or her can plainly see. Fear of a ghostly attack literally converts the rattling of a window into a full-scale attack by our deceased enemy. To a much, much larger degree than most suppose, we, literally, do see and hear what we expect to see and hear. Most of the tales of haunted houses, cemetery ghosts, noises made by the dead, and so forth are directly due to suggestion, fear, and expectation. If one is told that a dark, run down, old, unoccupied farm house was the scene of several horrible and bloody murders, and that passersby had seen strange lights in the house at night, this is all the suggestion needed to arouse a feeling of uneasiness and to prime any visitor to the farm to the point that any stimulus of any sort—e.g., a flash of light from a passing car, rat noises coming from the cellar, noises made by settling floor beams, the creaking of floors, stray dogs or cats who came in out of the cold—any of these natural and normal nocturnal events is immediately translated into horrible apparitions and demons dead set on the imminent destruction of the intruder. Love and hope and desire are also powerful emotions that, once amplified by suggestion and belief, quite literally dam floods and move mountains. Belief, or the need and will to believe, is another human element that must never be underrated or neglected in any investigation into the hidden springs and motives of human behavior. Jastrow remarked long ago, "When human interest enters, pure reason is a figment of an abstracting philosopher." (1935) Jastrow also observed that in human beings there are seven inclinations that lead us into serious error. First, *credulity* or the will to believe; second, the thrill of *marvel,* which is bound up with magic—the primitive explanation for how things happen; third, *transcendence*—the crediting and claim of supernatural powers; fourth, *prepossession,* i.e., the mentally-set mind finds what it looks for; fifth, *congeniality of conclusion*—the human tendency to believe in those things that give us emotional support and comfort; sixth, *fanaticism* or vagaries—the human tendency to blindly pursue a goal with single-minded purpose even to the point of self-destruction; and seventh, *rationalization* or pride of intellect in which our wishing destroys all wisdom. Jastrow has also provided us with a useful analogy of the stream of belief in which there are two main currents: *folklore,* as handed down by tradition, and the systematized body of *doctrine.* Over the centuries folk beliefs have given us werewolves and witches, haunted houses and ghosts, premonitions and prophecies, curses and blessings, the evil eye and protective amulets, mascots and hoodoos, signs and magic spells, and customs and superstitions. Its tools are the logic of analogy, resemblance, hidden connections, and congenial conclusions. Jastrow gives us the example of the Adirondack guide who trolled for the body of a drowned man by means of a floating cork, which "by the power of the human brain" he believed would be drawn downward when it passed over the corpse. The folk mind—though it works mostly via recipes—also creates doctrine, i.e., a principle to go by, e.g., "the power of the human brain." These primitive doctrines also follow folklore clues; they deal with common hopes and fears and the desire for understanding. Those people who become adept at manipulating these hopes and fears acquire prestige and authority while they find allies in ignorance and credulity. The manipulator then creates a profession of pondering, explaining, advising, and through the use of rites, symbols, and mystical routines bolsters and supports the convert's belief. Astrology, for example, is a product of the doctrinal mind and the horoscope is the material proof of the doctrine. From this comes dogma— the dogma of vested interest which blocks inquiry, delays, and misleads. It enlists the instituted powers to enforce opinion or to lend prestige to the doctrine, and further complicates and confuses the general public. In our own time we have seen the triumph of folklore in prime time on the TV networks which prominently feature programs such as "Unsolved Mysteries," "Psychic Detectives," "UFO Conspiracies," and the like. Additionally we find one of the major popular publishers, Time-Life, Inc., promoting a series of slick and attractive books extolling the paranormal and supernatural and advertising the product in all of their major magazines and on all the television networks. Here we find the new occultists presenting new varieties of ancient fantasies in modern dress. In its conflict with science, superstition may lose the battle, but in the long run it may win the war. Sad as it is to say, Jastrow was both perceptive and prophetic when he wrote in 1935:

> If we could assemble and gauge the total mass of thinking that has gone on through the ages, shaping belief and behavior, hopes and fears, institutions and ways of living, by far the greater volume of it would be the product of the feebly tutored, strongly traditioned folk-mind with its predilection for guess and fantasy and faith.
>
> (Jastrow 1935, p. 12)

Nothing could more aptly describe the modern phenomena that has captured the attention of tens of thousands of curious citizens from coast to coast and, in its various occult and paranormal manifestations, is collectively known as "The New Age." Interestingly enough, the one thing it truly is not is "new." Rather than being novel, it is nothing more than the exaltation and enhancement of the folk-mind and the folk systems of belief.

In the pages that follow, we will look at some of the unusual beliefs that were commonly held centuries ago but faded from view until they were recently resuscitated, given new clothes, a new name, and presented to the public as the latest scientific achievements of the New Age—a social phenomenon which is designed to propel the entire human race into a transcendent state of spiritual enlightenment.

To understand this phenomenon in its fullest and broadest aspects it is necessary that we look briefly at several different areas of everyday human psychology: particularly at the difference between normal and abnormal behavior, and the difficulties we have in discriminating between them, at the brain and human nervous system, at the concept of the unconscious mind and psychoanalysis before examining in depth the efforts on the part of many mental health professionals to see the entire human race as mentally ill and in dire need of their services.

What is Normal? What is Not?

Students of human behavior have known for a long time that the difference between normal and abnormal, i.e., between non-pathological and pathological behavior is only a matter of degree. It is not categorical and there are no sharp dividing lines separating the sane or non-psychotic individual from the insane or psychotic person. Indeed, it is very difficult to discriminate "well" behavior from "sick" behavior despite what the general public has been led to believe. Ironically, people in the mental health professions know well how easy it is to be fooled into believing that a client has recovered when he or she is still extremely ill. The news media are filled with hundreds of stories of psychotic patients who fooled institutional examining boards into releasing them so that they could subsequently rape or kill again. Within the institution and on the wards they are models of reason and decorum. No one could ask or expect any better behavior. Why should such people as these be kept in confinement when bedspace is so much in demand? Psychiatry, however, is far from being (or perhaps ever becoming) an exact profession. No better illustration of this occurred a few years ago when *Science* published a report of an experiment in which eight normal and sane individuals gained admission to twelve different and well-respected psychiatric hospitals by feigning mental illness. Included among the pseudopatients were four psychologists, a psychiatrist, a pediatrician, a painter, and a housewife. Each used a false name, false vocation, and a false employment record and each claimed the same symptom—hearing voices saying things like "hollow" or "empty." None of the twelve had any difficulty in being admitted and, with only one exception, all were diagnosed as being "schizophrenic."* Shortly after being admitted all of the patients reported that their symptoms had gone and they felt normal. These statements were uniformly ignored by both physicians and staff. While in the hospital, all the pseudopatients acted and talked nominally with the staff and other patients and all spent a lot of time openly taking notes about their experiences. The note-taking, however, was considered by the staff as a symptom of their abnormality. Each of the twelve had to get out of the hospital as best as he

---

*Technically the term means "split mind" but in practice among the cognoscenti it means: "This person is mentally ill and I have no idea on Earth what to do about it." It is, essentially, a wastebasket term. Treatment consists mainly of drugs to keep the patient tranquil and hallucinations under control. Prognosis is very poor and little can be done. Research is, as always, promising, i.e., always promising more than is delivered.

or she could by convincing the physicians they were normal, and there was nothing wrong, and they no longer needed any therapy. All but one of the pseudopatients asked to be discharged immediately after being admitted, yet their confinements lasted from seven to fifty-two days with an average stay of nineteen days. In none of the cases was the person's sanity discovered by either the staff or the physicians, and all twelve were finally discharged, because in the opinion of the doctor their illness was "in remission."

After the study was completed, one of the hospitals involved publicly denied that it was possible. This same hospital was then told that a second study was underway and that within the next three months other pseudopatients would try to gain admittance. The hospital then had all of their staff members whose duties required close contact with the patients rate every new patient on a "sanity scale" so they could detect the poseurs. Out of 193 patients admitted during the period, 41 were identified by at least one member of the staff as being pseudopatients. Unfortunately, no pseudopatients tried to get in. Rosenhan's study (1973) has been replicated a number of times and, despite a massive wave of protest from the psychiatric profession, no one who knows the current status of conditions in our mental institutions, the problems of correctly diagnosing mental illness, or the social and behavioral milieu of the psychiatric profession has any doubts as to the authenticity of the findings.

Although Rosenhan's study was carried out in the early seventies, little has been done to improve the diagnostic problem in the intervening years. In fact, more recently experts have noted that the problem of false psychiatric diagnosis is broader than might have been supposed. Currently, schizophrenia is diagnosed in approximately 1 percent of the general population. At some time one out of every hundred persons will be diagnosed as being a schizophrenic. The bigger problem is that many, many times that number go undiagnosed. The difficulties in diagnosis are legendary and there are a number of amusing stories told about schizophrenic behavior. One has to do with a motorist whose car broke down close to an asylum and who was told how to patch it together by three of the inmates who were leaning against the wire fence surrounding the institution. The driver was taken aback when he realized that the ingenious suggestions had come from the three crazies. The patients were also perceptive enough to understand his feelings. "Remember," one of the patients told the driver, "we're here because we're nuts, not because we're stupid." Another variation on this tale has to do with one of the schizophrenics who engages the psychiatrist in a chess game and beats him three times. As the doctor walks away frustrated, the patient reminds him, "I may be crazy but I sure ain't stupid."

The serious side of this issue is the fact that undiagnosed schizophrenics, especially those suffering from paranoid schizophrenia, can cause a great deal of irreparable harm to themselves and others with their delusions of persecution and evil influences long before their disordered thinking is detected. A recent example of this, with its horrible repercussions, was the McMartin child sex-abuse case in Manhattan Beach, California. This led to the longest and most expensive trial in U.S. history and was triggered by one Judy Johnson who complained in August of 1983 to Manhattan Beach police that her son had been molested by a man named Mr. Ray at the McMartin Preschool fourteen times over a three-month period. The child, however, had been in Raymond Buckey's class no more than two afternoons. Mrs. Johnson's complaints against Buckey grew increasingly bizarre as time went on. She accused him of sodomizing the child while he stuck the boy's head in a toilet, of making the child ride naked on a horse, and of tormenting him with an air tube. Moreover, she made almost the same accusations against her estranged husband and three health-club employees. Despite these outlandish charges, Mrs. Johnson was used by the prosecution as their first witness in July 1984. The next year Mrs. Johnson had to be hospitalized and was then diagnosed as an acute paranoid schizophrenic. In 1986 she died of an alcohol-related liver disease. Not only have Buckey and all of the other teachers originally charged with sexual abuse been exonerated, but the handling of the case and the manner in which the children were interviewed and interrogated were shown to be almost as horrendous as the original charges. The case was, in every sense of the term, an out-and-out "witch hunt" triggered initially by an undiagnosed mentally ill mother with strong delusions of persecution and abuse not only of herself but of all those around her.

The McMartin case is, however, by no means new. Over the last decade, we have experienced what a number of child experts have referred to as "The Sexual Abuse Crisis." In 1967 only about 160,000 incidents of child abuse were reported. In 1972, 610,000 were reported nationally, and by 1985 the number had exceeded 1.7 million! Interestingly enough, 65 percent or more of these reported cases were unfounded, and every year more than 500,000 families are needlessly investigated. Why? Has human nature somehow or other suffered a revolutionary turn to produce a startling increase in the number of pederasts? Has satanism broken out across the land with more and more children being captured and abused in satanic rituals? With the increase of working mothers, and the sudden growth in day care centers, is the placing of thousands of children in the care of strangers —all of whom may suffer from pedophilia—to blame? Aha, here in the latter category may lie the answer. Reports of mass abuse in day care centers from Maine to California have appeared over and over again. What we have witnessed is *an increase in the rumors of sexual abuse, an increase in anxiety about sexual abuse,* an *increase in the expectation of sexual abuse,* an *increase in the reporting of sexual abuse,* and a *subsequent increase in suspicion of sexual abuse,* and with this increased awareness of sexual abuse there have been dramatic changes in the attitudes of all people who deal with children. More than at any time in history, children are now being told about sexual abuse, how to identify it, and they are even being encouraged to report it to their teachers and parents—whether it happens or not. According to Mary Ann Mason Ekman:

> Through videotape, storybooks, and presentation children are encouraged to report sexual abuse to their teacher and parent. And in increasingly large numbers children do. Teachers, nurses, and mental health workers are often now legally required to report a reasonable suspicion of sexual abuse, where before they had no such obligation.
>
> (1989)

In a brilliant review of the so-called "sexual abuse crisis," Mrs. Ekman notes that there are three major categories of sex abuse. First, there are the *mass abuse cases*; next, *abuse allegations against one parent in custody* disputes; and, last, the abuse of a single child, often by a family member or close friend. Two well known examples of *mass abuse* are the Jordan, Minnesota, case and the McMartin Preschool case. The Jordan case involved two dozen men and women (most of them married and upright citizens) who conspired to sexually abuse and torture their own children, to arrange parties where parents had sex with each other's children, and where, *finally,* several children claimed they witnessed the torture and murder of one little boy and other children as well. Despite intensive investigations to locate the bodies, nothing was turned up. Shortly after the trials of the defendants began, all charges were dropped. In their testimony, the children began to admit they had made up the murder stories and had lied about most of the other claims. Further investigation turned up not one shred of evidence to support either abuse or child murder. Medical evidence regarding sexual abuse can be very ambiguous and even when such evidence as ruptured tissues are found, those do not tell who did it or how it was done.

Interestingly enough, in investigating the McMartin preschool the prosecution used the services of one Kee MacFarlane, "an administrator turned therapist" at Children's Institute International, who, after interviewing 400 children, concluded that 369 of them had been abused. MacFarlane's interviewing techniques were models of how *not* to obtain the truth: emotional rewards were granted to those children who accused the teachers and there was rejection for those who didn't. To one child who confessed ignorance of the game "Naked Movie Star" MacFarland said, "What good are you?

You must be dumb." She also elicited stories of children digging up dead bodies at cemeteries, jumping out of airplanes, and of killing animals with baseball bats. Incredibly, the accuracy of these fabrications was never questioned. When asked to point out molesters while driving around the city, the children fingered community leaders, store clerks, and gas-station attendants. One child identified a photograph of the actor Chuck Norris and the Los Angeles City Attorney James Hahn as molesters at the school. As the interviews wore on, some of the older children told tales of Satanic rites—ritual abuse with black robes, black candles, and the drinking of animal blood. Ray Buckey supposedly supervised the exhumations and then hacked the bodies with knives. According to the prosecution, child pornography was Buckey's motive. Yet, despite an intensive international search for evidence by five government agencies including the FBI, no pornographic photos of any McMartin children were ever found.

The pretrial hearing—not an actual trial but a step in the judicial process where the judge decides if there is enough evidence to send the defendant to trial—lasted twenty months and was the longest in California's history. Although forty-one witnesses were scheduled to testify against seven defendants, after the first witness was cross-examined for a week and the second testified for sixteen days, it became apparent this trial could take years, which of course it did.

For our purposes the major question is the children's credibility, the spread of misinformation, and the gullibility of the public. Studies by Jean Piaget (1975), Michael Hoyt (1978), and Lewis, Stanger, and Sullivan (no date) have shown clearly that even very young children are capable of telling outright lies. As far back as 1891, the Belgian psychologist Varondeck was called upon as an expert witness to defend an accused murderer. The only witness to the murder was an eight-year-old child. When Varondeck asked twenty eight-year-old children to identify the color of the beard of one of their teachers, nineteen of the eight-year-olds obligingly replied with a color. Only one student made the correct observation that the teacher in question had no beard.

In both the Jordan and the McMartin cases, many of the children either admitted that they had lied, or they were caught in contradictions that showed they had lied. Some of the bizarre testimony elicited in the McMartin case included one child's claim that children at the school were beaten regularly with a ten-foot bullwhip, taken to an Episcopal Church where they were slapped by the priest if they did not pray to three or four gods, and were forced to participate in Satanic rituals held in the Episcopal churchyard. Moreover, children's reports of satanic rituals associated with sexual abuse have sprung up all over the country. John Crewdson in his book *By Silence Betrayed* (1988) shows that the descriptions children give of rituals, chants, being forced to drink strange liquids, the killing of small animals, and the murder of children and babies are very similar. Yet police investigations of such charges have yielded nothing. Despite intensive searches with dogs combing woods, excavating fields, and draining ditches in search of bodies, nothing has been found.

There is no question but that children—even very young ones—create fantasies and, obviously, many of them are dark ones. The popularity of horror and fantasy films, TV series involving the occult, comic books and magazines, and even the same themes in cartoons are all rich enough and lurid enough to supply any child with any imagination at all enough themes to last a lifetime. Both Freud and Piaget seriously questioned children's ability to separate fact from fantasy. Freud felt that children's tendency to fantasize reduced the reliability of their assertions while Piaget believed all children have difficulty separating fact and fantasy up until ages seven or eight. While these observations are debatable, current research still shows that children are more likely to fail to separate fact from fantasy than adults. (Lindsay and Johnson 1987) If adults have difficulty in separating fact from fiction, and if they are notoriously bad observers and prone to delusions and hallucinations of various sorts, why would we assume children to be less so?

The most difficult problem of all the many problems in the area of sexual abuse is the problem of children who are caught up in a custody dispute. Anytime a child in this situation accuses a parent of sexual molestation the legal community immediately assumes the other parent put him up to making the accusation. And rightly so. Not only has the Family and Law program at the University of Michigan found that more than half of the allegations of sexual abuse in custody cases are untrue (*New York Times,* November 14, 1987), but sexual abuse is now alleged so often that it is now "looked for" in just about every divorce case involving children and custody. This crisis is due to four factors: (1) greater public awareness of sexual abuse; (2) laws that require teachers and doctors to report even unsubstantiated accusations; (3) careless counselors who interview purported victims with leading questions; and (4) joint custody laws that often lead mothers to fight harder for sole custody of their children. All of these things are responsible for the crisis we face.

There are undoubtedly specific instances of sexual abuse just as there are a *few* specific and isolated instances of satanic rituals and cults among the deranged elements of our vast and heterogenous society. But this in no way supports the claim that every adult who is placed in close proximity to a child is either a sex abuser or a satanist as the rumor-mongers and petty paranoiacs would have us believe. This is nonsense belonging in the same category as claims of alien abduction, or claims of out-of-body trips to Venus. And hardly less absurd are the claims of many psychiatrists and other mental health professionals who say they can accurately distinguish between a child who is lying about sexual abuse and one who is telling the truth. In most sex abuse cases, unfortunately, there are rarely any eyewitnesses, and resort to the so-called "child molestation syndrome" is far too unreliable a criterion for the determination of truth. As for the testimony of mental health "experts," we need to remember the work of Faust and Ziskin (1988) who showed that clinician's judgmental accuracy does not surpass that of lay persons, and to recall also a study that showed that high school students could predict violent behavior in an individual just as accurately as mental health professionals. Why should we believe, therefore, such experts can tell us when a child, or anyone else for that matter, is lying?

More disturbing yet are the statistics from the U.S. National Center on Child Abuse and Neglect (USNCCA), which show that approximately 65 percent of the reports of child abuse and neglect are unfounded. We have good reason to believe that many children are lying about being abused. So many parents have been falsely accused of child abuse that Douglas Besharov, the first director of the USNCCA, now argues that the cry to "do something about child abuse" has succeeded so well that overreaction to sensational media coverage has led to counterproductive effects. In 1975 about 35 percent of all reports turned out to be "unfounded." In 1985 about 65 percent were dismissed after investigation. The flood of unfounded reports is now overloading the system and endangering the children who really are being abused. Besharov reports that each year over 500,000 families are put through investigations of unfounded reports. This amounts to a massive and unjustified violation of parental rights. Predictably, parents have struck back and have formed a national organization, Victims of Child Abuse Laws (VOCAL), to protest and to protect their rights. We must never forget that being accused of such a crime is viciously destructive, and it can cost the victim his or her child, their career, their reputation, and their rights. A few years ago in St. Petersburg, Florida, an assistant school superintendent committed suicide before learning that the fifteen-year-old girl who had accused him of lewd and lascivious acts had retracted her story two days earlier (*New York Times* 1988). Exactly how devastating to an individual such accusations can be is shown most graphically in Lawrence D. Spiegel's *A Question Of Innocence* (1986). Spiegel, a psychologist, was charged by his wife of sexually molesting his 2½-year-old daughter. She was first asked to testify at age 3½. As a result of the charges, Spiegel was forced to resign his professorship, denied access to his daughter, arrested, betrayed by his business partner, and it required over three years of legal assistance and a small fortune to prove his innocence and regain his daughter. As Mary Ann Mason Ekman notes, "A false accusation of sexual abuse can ruin the life and reputation of an innocent victim more predictably than a false accusation of almost any other kind of crime." (Ekman 1989, pp. 177–178)

Psychologically, the most serious problem in all such cases is the naivete of the interrogators when questioning the victims. Young children have great difficulty with full recall and the younger the child the greater the difficulty. To tap their memory the interrogator needs to aid the child's recall, and unless the questioners are well trained, cautious, and skilled at the task, they can easily contaminate the information they obtain. The ease with which the questioner can lead his witness to believe things happened that did not happen and vice versa is mind-boggling. Though children as young as four can give reliable testimony, they are poor at recalling details, especially about novel or unfamiliar events. But the biggest problem is the child's inability to recall without help. To sample their memory the interrogator has to guide the recall process, and in doing so it is difficult to avoid influencing the child's memory by suggesting things the child will believe must have happened when they didn't or vice versa. In general, children are much more vulnerable to misinformation than adults and adults are far from being immune themselves. Loftus has shown in a number of studies that suggestion is a subtle and powerful force that can easily destroy the validity of eyewitness testimony (1979). Children under seven are particularly vulnerable to misinformation about details but less so about the main event, and preschoolers are even more vulnerable to influence by the person questioning them. (Ceci et al. 1987) Even well-trained interviewers can easily or unwittingly mislead a child. Mrs. Ekman gives the example of the standard interviewing use of two anatomically correct dolls and to ask the child to show what happened. One study, for example, that compared twenty-five abused with twenty-five nonabused children found little or no differences, but a second study of 100 nonabused children showed that half of them interacted with the dolls in a manner that suggested evidence of sexual abuse. For young children the orifices and sex organs possibly suggest a play pattern. As a result of such studies, many experts in the area of children's suggestibility recommend doing away with such dolls in interviews and they say one should assure the child it's perfectly all right to say "I don't remember." (Ceci et al. 1987) As Mrs. Ekman summarizes it:

> Many experiments have been done in which the interviewer provides misinformation about an event after a child has witnessed it. A clear pattern of suggestibility evolves. Children are most susceptible to misinformation if their original memory of the area of misinformation is weak; the misinfor-

mation deals with a peripheral, not central, event; and the interviewer who provides is an adult they respect. In one experiment, when the misinformation was provided by a child rather than an adult it was accepted half as often.

("Age Differences in Suggestibility," p. 82)

While I was writing this chapter, the results of Raymond Buckey's final trial were announced. The jury was out for nearly two weeks and was hopelessly deadlocked; the judge declared a mistrial; and the prosecution threw in the towel stating that they would not pursue the matter further. In Manhattan Beach the parents of the children were outraged and believed their children were violated and that justice had not been served. The most glaring aspect of the trial is the difficulty of getting at the truth. This is how urban legends are born. The parents in the McMartin case are also victims of suggestibility and are suffering from the delusionary belief shown also by believers in the threat of satanic cults and alien abductors.

Margaret Carlson summarized the McMartin case most effectively.

If the McMartin children were not robbed of their innocence by sexual abuse, it was stolen from them by a legal system that took more than six years to bring their case to a conclusion. One child witness was four when the abuse allegedly occurred, seven when she first told a social worker about it, eight when she told her story to a grand jury, ten when she told it to a judge, and eleven when she finally told it to a jury that rendered its verdict last Thursday (January, 1990). Perhaps the only thing of value that has come out of this case is the determination to ensure that such a fiasco can never occur again.

(Carlson 1990, pg. 27)

The fact that all of these problems began with the paranoid delusions of one disturbed mother underlines most emphatically just how dangerous paranoid schizophrenics can be. It should also be stressed that they are doubly dangerous because in most every aspect of their lives—except in one area of their delusion—they appear to be sane, mentally balanced, and behaviorally normal. It is this mask of sanity that makes them appear to be so ordinary and normal that they have, on many occasions, managed to convince boards of psychiatrists that their delusions are over. Upon their release they have immediately returned to their old haunts and have murdered innocent people their deluded thinking has convinced them were mortal enemies.

Difficult as it is to believe, the McMartin case was barely concluded before an almost identical case was brought to trial in Framville, N.C. Robert F. Kelly Jr. of Edenton, N.C., age 43, former owner of the Little Rascals Day-Care Center has been charged with 248 counts of sexually abusing more than two dozen children. He has already been in jail for over two years unable to post the $1.5 million bond. Six other defendants whose trials have not been scheduled face about 200 additional charges. Kelly has been accused of raping children, having oral and anal sex with them, forcing the children to have sex with one another, and having sex with day care workers in front of the children. Kelly's attorneys have noted that Kelly has never been given details of the allegations such as where and when the offenses are supposed to have occurred and the indictments do not specify any such details.

In May of 1991 a two-hour PBS "Frontline" documentary about the case was viewed by some as so sympathetic to the defendants that it unleashed a storm of protest against the Little Rascal parents. The "Frontline" producer Ofra Bikel told the *Washington Post* she did not think the abuses occurred. In a review of the show *The Wall Street Journal* called the case "a frenzy to convict" and also stated "We are about to see McMartin II take place in Edenton."

As in the McMartin case some of the charges were so flimsy that before the trial started the presiding judge threw out well over a hundred of them. For the fate of the rest we will have to await the outcome of the trial.

In April 1991 in Mission Viejo, California, Ellen Roe, a 76-year-old widow wound up as the center of a landmark ritual-abuse trial. Incredibly, Grandmother Roe was accused by her two daughters, Bonnie, a 48-year-old Ph.D., and Patti, a 35-year-old businesswoman, of indoctrinating them into a satanic cult when they were still infants. The women claimed that their mother and father forced them to join in group sex, animal mutilation, cannibalism, and the stabbing of kidnapped transients. Roe insisted her family was a normal, healthy one until her daughters started psychotherapy three years ago. According to Roe, therapists at a Huntington Beach counseling center planted the idea of Satanic abuse and, according to the daughters, they had repressed their memories of ritual abuse until they underwent the therapy. Roe insists that no abuse occurred and that the therapists were responsible for planting the idea and memories of satanic abuse. The motive behind all of this was to bilk Mrs. Roe of her savings. The daughters were suing her for a total of 7 million.

As a number of lawyers, journalists, and therapists have noted, such delayed lawsuits of sexual abuse are on the rise with the alleged victims basing legal action on memories which may well have been implanted— intentionally or accidentally by untrained and unskilled therapists now so sensitized to the possibility of childhood sexual abuse they now see it everywhere they turn. Already this year three books have been published warning psychotherapists of the dangers of seeing sexual abuse as the causative factor in every clinical problem. In late spring the American

Psychological Association published *The Suggestibility of Children's Recollections* (1991). In this work several experts have questioned the truthfulness of children's testimony, stating "there are definite limits to our knowledge about whether children are telling the truth." For the child the truth can be blurred, especially in periods of stress, such as during a trial (Cramer, 1991). To protect children from sex crimes and adults from unfounded accusations—child-welfare workers, prosecutors, and therapists should be *very* careful when searching for the truth. A second book, *The Clinical Detective: Techniques in the Evaluation of Sexual Abuse* by A. N. Horowitz (1991), shows how to carry out a sexual abuse evaluation and helps one figure out whether or not an abuse actually occurred. The third book, *Sex Abuse Hysteria: Salem Witch Trials Revisited* by Richard A. Gardner (1991), is also designed to prevent the unleashing of false allegations of sexual abuse which Gardner sees as now approaching a state of "mass hysteria."

The problem of delayed civil suits is so prevalent that in the last few years at least nine states have passed laws making sexual abuse lawsuits a separate category of personal injury suits and extending the length of time victims have in which to sue. Under the old law, in California for example, adults had one year from discovery of the abuse; now, it's three years from the discovery of the harm caused by the abuse. In our litigious society, more and more often civil suits claiming sexual abuse are being filed. Civil cases are much easier to prove than criminal cases since the plaintiff needs only to convince a judge or jury that his allegations are probably true. In criminal cases the defendant must be guilty beyond a reasonable doubt. Moreover, civil plaintiffs can use evidence barred in most criminal cases, e.g., memories recorded under hypnosis. Filing a lawsuit gives the abused victim legal redress in the form of money and the satisfaction of confronting one's abuser.

The crux of the problem arises when the alleged victim goes to a psychotherapist and here, for the first time, discovers they have been abused. Then the critical question becomes: Are such memories of sexual abuse true or false? Therapists, expectedly, disagree. Therapists unfamiliar with the phenomenon of cryptomnesia and with only a hazy notion of how the human memory works are convinced that no one could fabricate memories with such rich detail as those found in the memories of adults who have suffered sexual abuse and that no therapist is capable of implanting such fantasies. Repressed memories, they argue, stem from psychological denial and the resulting dissociation when the child cannot believe a person he loves would hurt him. Violation of such trust is, indeed, a horrifying event. Certainly such emotional traumas can and do cause significant psychological damage *if* they occur.

Unfortunately, on the contemporary stage sexual abuse is seen everywhere and in most every case coming in the clinical door. The result has been that, at the moment, more and more psychiatric patients are being diagnosed as having multiple personality disorders (MPD). They, in turn, report satanic cult abuse stories to their therapists and the therapists believe them because: (1) the patient's stories are internally consistent; (2) the stories are told with obvious emotional pain; (3) the same stories are revealed under hypnosis; and (4) clients from different parts of the country tell similar stories. This "evidence" however is that of the typical urban legend. In a two-year study of MPD psychotherapists Sherrill Mulhern discovered that the key factor in the acceptance of satanic cult "survivor" stories is the predisposition of psychotherapists to accept them as a result of the social process called "groupthink," i.e., a collective response to conformity pressures. Also discovered was the fact that MPD patients fed the therapists the kind of stories they felt the therapists wanted to hear. (Mulhern 1991) The process by which satanic cult survivors recall unverifiable experiences with the help of their therapists is exactly the same way in which alien abductees remember their UFO abductions. As Bill Ellis has noted, "Organizations armed with such 'memories' have been able to inflict considerable social and mental harm on patients and innocent parties named by them." (Ellis 1988)

The process by which the therapist uses his influence on a client has been outlined by a number of psychologists and psychiatrists interested in the influence of suggestion on memory. Psychologist Elizabeth Loftus states, "When you say to a patient, 'You've got the symptoms, I think you were sexually abused, think hard,' a lot of people don't remember at first." Soon thereafter, however, "The next thing they start having dreams and nightmares." And it is then, of course, that the fantasies and dreams become the "reality." Since controlled studies of memories that recur decades later are virtually impossible, we are forced to fall back upon the fact that we do know how false memories are created and how confabulation and cryptomnesia can turn dreams, fantasies, and fictions into assumptions of actual occurrences.

Stephen J. Ceci, in his studies of how suggestion affects recall, also questions the accuracy of long-repressed memories that are the result of outside influence. When someone recalls something with a lot of perceptual detail, we assume it is veridical. This is deceptive because through intensive and repetitive suggestion, coaching, bribes, threats, and inducements by people in a child's life all of the details can easily be implanted. Ceci reports a story told by Jean Piaget who, as an adult, remembered when he was only 20 months old a red-haired man assaulted him and his nanny and the nanny saved him. Fifty years later the nanny confessed it never happened.

She had made up the story and retold it so often the young Piaget processed it as fact. "How could someone at a later age report something in great detail that was not born through experience?" Ceci replies, "The answer is through suggestion. It is difficult to distinguish between what is real and what is repetitive suggestion. . . . By its very nature therapy tries to bring to fruition psychically rich material. Overlain on the therapeutic context is people's hypotheses about what might have happened. That process can be contaminating." (Oldenburg 1991)

Ralph Haber, a psychologist specializing in memory and eyewitness behavior, also warns us about the unreliability of memory. While our reports of past events appear to be organized and accurate, this is not how either our brain or our memory work. What is reported from memory is altered through the normal passage of time. Haber also notes that many long-repressed, childhood memories are expressed in adult contemporary language rather than the words of the child at the age of the alleged abuse. Thus the memories have been reinterpreted. It would be easy for emotionally troubled adults to mistake memories of childhood sexual fantasies or fears for fact. People's memories also tend to produce self-serving rationalizations. Haber points out people aren't necessarily dishonest but their memories are fallible and the idea that they could make up complex tales of sexual abuse out of whole cloth "is not more difficult to understand and is no more fantastic than that they could retrieve it after 30 years." (Oldenburg 1991)

Richard Mikesell, a Washington, D.C., psychotherapist, also argues that the current wave of long-repressed memories of sexual abuse is "socially contagious." Once publicity is given to one or two cases everyone comes down with it and every therapist sees it in every client. According to Mikesell, this is the current "in" mental health issue. "It may be an epidemic we're uncovering," Mikesell reports, "but if a therapist goes looking for something, it is more likely they'll find it whether it happened or not." (Oldenburg 1991)

Lenore Terr, Professor of Psychiatry at the University of California School of Medicine in San Francisco, has carried out studies of the memories of traumatized children. Terr notes that childhood memories do recur in adulthood but they are not reliable and need to be confirmed. In a recent "false memory" case where a 14-year-old girl accused her male therapist of sexually abusing her when she was between ages 5 and 9, Terr found the accusations were baseless. The girl's parents being concerned about her had questioned her extensively and made scripts and transcripts of the interrogations. Terr noted:

I could see it was like brainwashing that had planted a memory. The child sincerely believed the doctor had done her this harm. But she could not describe the sex act and there was nothing that could be described as fears. There is no way to be sexually abused repeatedly and not have signs and symptoms, like a fear related to that kind of behavior. Some of them are sexually anesthetic, some become over-aroused. You also see repetitions—people who were victimized as children will also be in abusive situations as adults . . . they'll marry an abuser and become victimized again.

Terr adds that other significant signs include perceptions that have been trying to emerge for a long time and a pessimistic attitude toward the future that terrible things will happen. According to Terr:

This is one of the most literally specific conditions in psychiatry that we have. It creates symptoms that are perfectly recoverable parts of the puzzle. If you see more of these, there's a good chance the person has been told a memory and thinks it is a real event.

(Oldenburg 1991)

Sexual politics also play a role in all those cases because the alleged victims are usually children and women. Being highly skeptical of charges of sexual abuse and molestation (especially if you are an adult male) according to Lee Coleman, a California psychiatrist who feels the courts give too much credence to all these clinically obtained memories, can be politically dangerous and is seen in some quarters as being supportive of child molestation. According to Coleman, accepting repressed memories as evidence in court cases is nothing but "a witch hunt."

Again, we must remember that many—if not most—of the sexual abuse allegations turn out, upon careful investigation, to be unfounded. Researchers are increasingly sure that children, particularly those who have been extensively coached, give inaccurate testimony far more often than previously imagined. Just as in the case of allegations of satanic ritual cult abuse, for every single true incidence of abuse there are hundreds of unsubstantiated claims. What we have witnessed recently is an increase in *rumors* of sexual abuse, an increase in the *anxiety* about sexual abuse, an increase in the *suspicion* of sexual abuse, and an increase in the *publicity* about sexual abuse, but the *amount* of sexual abuse has remained relatively the same over the centuries.

Obtaining the truth is never very easy, but claims of childhood sexual abuse that emerge only after psychotherapy are particularly suspect and both judges and jurors should be made fully aware of the unreliability of such memories and the everpresent possibility of memory contamination and confabulation. Prosecutors should be advised of the need to seek out and find additional supportive material evidence, which is harder and better, before filing their charges and bringing such cases to trial. Both steps are badly needed if justice is to be properly served.

If, as a society, we want to insure that such social tragedies as the McMartin and Farmville cases do not recur it is necessary that we understand much better how these social anomalies arise and why the parents of these young California and North Carolina children became captives of their fears and imaginations, fell under the influence of mass suggestibility, and finally developed full-blown delusions of persecution and mistreatment taken out on their children.

But how, pray tell, do such hallucinations, delusions, and the more benign illusions arise, and what role does suggestibility and expectation play in their genesis? To answer these questions we will have to look a little more closely at human psychology as well as at the human brain and how it works and what can, on occasion, go wrong with it.

A Little Physiology

A few years ago Emerson Pugh stated, "If the human brain were so simple that we could understand it, we would be so simple that we couldn't." There is much truth in this statement and no one would argue that we do fully understand the human brain at the moment. We do, nevertheless, have a general idea of how it is put together and how the brain works. One of the better theories, the tribrain theory, argues that the modern human brain is actually three brains laid atop each other.

First and oldest is *the reptilian brain,* which regulates and maintains the body machinery: growth, tissue regeneration, movement, respiration, circulation, and the other physical systems. It is the brain of habit and a survival tool. In the course of evolution when the requisites for survival became more complex, the brain increased in size a hundredfold and *the limbic brain* was born. Bearing the emotions, over time the limbic brain became the driving force behind all human behavior and gave rise to the "four Fs" of human motivation: fear, feeding, fighting, and fornicating. These four drives have controlled human behavior ever since. With the advent of the limbic brain humans began to develop the concepts of territory and property, and tribes and villages were created, followed by social rituals and laws.

Next, approximately 100,000 years ago, the brain of *homo sapiens* again expanded and nearly doubled in size. Another 1,000 years, however, was required in order for the human race to learn to use this "new" brain, *the neocortex.* This new brain proved to be exactly the organ humans needed in order to deal with the superstitious and ritualistic thinking of the limbic system. The left and right hemispheres of the neocortex were found to control language, and spatial and abstract thought. The forebrain was found to control planning, foresight, imagination, reflection, and looking forward and backward in time. The neocortex is the seat of the "mind" and the intellect.

Though seldom considered as such, the brain is a gland. Dr. Richard Bergland, in his fascinating and informative book *The Fabric of Mind* (1985) shows that the brain not only produces hormones, it also has hormone receptors, it is constantly bathed in hormones, and hormones run up and down the fibers of individual nerves. In fact, every brain activity involves hormones. The role played by various regulatory hormones in our behavior and the bodily functions influenced by regulatory hormones are listed in Table 1. Little wonder that alcohol, drugs, and other chemical agents have such tremendous mind-altering effects on our behavior. Not only is opium a hormone-like substance but the brain is also a producer of this hormone. In fact the enkephalins were the first brain hormones discovered with the endorphins being the second. Several years after these initial discoveries more than forty-five different brain hormones have been discovered. A partial list is provided in Table 2.

It is also known that various combinations of these hormones combine in various ways to do the brain's work. Neuroendocrinologists are well aware that various parts of the brain convert the electrical signals they receive into endocrine messages that can be carried to the body. Coded chemical messages are thus constantly flowing between the body and the brain. Not all of these chemical codes are understood yet, but one of the best known is the 31-K hormone released by the pituitary gland. The brain releases 31-K from the pituitary by first releasing two other hormones, *vasopressin* and the *corticotropin releasing factor* (CRF). When the pituitary cells receive the coded message from the brain, they, in turn, release 31-K into the bloodstream. It is also known that both vasopressin and two of the 31-K components—ACTH and MSH—are linked to or play a role in memory. Dutch researchers have shown this conclusively in animals, and synthetic preparations of these hormones are now being widely used to treat people with amnesia.

Many psychologists now hypothesize that memory is stored in the brain in somewhat the same way that photographic information is stored in a hologram—since there is no one single site or locale in the brain for specific memories. Karl Lashley's (1890–1955) failure to find a "memory-site" in the brain in his animal work led him to conclude, "I sometimes feel that in reviewing the evidence on localization of the memory trace that the necessary conclusion is that learning is not possible." Recognition that memories are diffused and stored everywhere and focused nowhere, as in a hologram, seems to have solved Lashley's problem. Thus, if memory is dependent on hormones, and is

TABLE 1*

Regulatory Hormones, Behavior, Bodily Functions Influenced by Regulatory Hormones

REGULATORY HORMONE	BEHAVIOR	BODY FUNCTION
Acetylcholine	Memory	Sleep
Adrenaline		
Noradrenalin		
Serotonin	Joy	Pain
GABA		
Dopamine	Thirst	Blood pressure
Muscarinic Neurophysin		
Nicotinic Neurophysin	Hunger	Digestion
Vasopressin		
Angiotensin	Satiation	Blood coagulation
Thyroid Hormone		
Thyroid Releasing Hormone	Orgasm	Immunity
Luteinizing Hormone		
Gonadotropin Releasing Hormone	Sleep	Sexual function
Growth Hormone		
Somatostatin	Addiction	Reproduction
Corticotropin Releasing Hormone		
Prolactin	Opiate overdose	Temperature control
Substance P		
Neurotensin	Sorrow	Bowel motility
Vasoactive Intestinal Peptide		
Gastrin	Rage	Gastric acidity
Cholecystokinin		
Bombesin	Depression	Skin rashes
ACTH		
Pro-opiomelanocortin	Suicide	Asthma
Lipotropin		
Endorphin	Fear	Ageing
Dynorphin		
Enkephalin	Peace	Obesity
Melanotropin Stimulating Hormone		
Insulin	Pain	Arthritic stiffness

holographic, finding memory hormones in many sites outside the brain moves Lashley's engram outside the brain and into other glandular organs. If electricity can carry messages from the brain to the body, then why can't the electricity produced by the body hormones carry messages to the brain? It is well established that both the ovaries and the stomach have all the required equipment to do this since they produce the same hormones—vasopressin and CRF—that the brain does, and they make 31-K just like the pituitary gland. Also 31-K molecules are specifically linked to specific kinds of thoughts—pleasure,

*Tables 1, 2A, and 2B have been adapted from *The Fabric of Mind* by Richard Bergland (Viking Penguin Books, Australia Ltd., 1989). Used with permission.

TABLE 2A

Brain Hormones

REGULATORY HORMONE	ABBREVIATION
Acetylcholine	ACh
Adrenalin	EPI
Norepinephrine	NE
Serotonin	5-HT
Histamine	H
Dopamine	DA
Gamma Aminobutyrate	GABA
Glutamate	GLU
Glycine	GLY
Melatonin	MEL
Muscarinic Neurophysin	NP (Mus)
Nicotinic Neurophysin	NP (Nic)
Arginine Vasopressin	AVP
Lysine Vasopressin	LVP
Angiotensin	A2
Thyroid Hormone	TH
Thyroid Releasing Hormone	TRH
Luteinizing Hormone	LH
Gonadotropin Releasing Hormone	GNRH
Growth Hormone	GH
Growth Hormone Releasing Hormone	GHRH
Somatostatin	SRIF
Corticotropin Releasing Hormone	CRH
Prolactin	PRL
Substance P	SUB-P
Neurotensin	NTSN
Vasoactive Intestinal Peptide	VIP
Gastrin	GAST
Cholecystokinen	CCK
Bombesin	BOMB
Adrenocorticotropin	ACTH
Pro-opiomelanocortin	31-K
Lipotropin	LPH
Endorphin	ENDO
Dynorphin	DYN
Enkephalin	ENK
Melanotropin Stimulating Hormone	MSH
Insulin	INS

pain, memory, appetite, and stress. These are all modified in certain specific ways by the 31-K pieces. The implications of this for theories of mental functioning are profound. It means the mind can best be understood by looking at the biochemical intracellular molecular events rather than at the brain's superficial electrical noise. Moreover, the mechanisms that drive thought are found all over the body, and no matter where they are located they function at this high level by recognizing the molecular patterns of

TABLE 2B

Sites of Hormone Production Outside the Brain

REGULATORY HORMONE	OTHER ORGAN SITES				
	Brain	Pituitary	Adrenal	Gut	Gonads
Acetycholine	x	x	x	x	x
Adrenalin	x	x	x	x	x
Noradrenalin	x	x	x	x	x
Serotonin	x	x	x	x	x
Histamine	x	x	x	x	x
Dopamine	x	x	x	x	x
GABA	x	x	x	x	x
Glutamate	x	x	x	x	x
Glycine	x	x	x	x	x
Melatonin	x				
Muscarinic NP	x	x			
Nicotinic NP	x	x			
AVP	x	x	x	x	
LVP	x	x	x	x	
Angiotensin	x	x			
Thyroid Hormone	x	x			
TRH	x	x			
LF	x	x			
GNRH	x	x			
Growth Hormone	x	x			
GHRH	x	x			
SRIF	x	x			
CRH	x	x	x		
Prolactin	x	x			
Substance P	x	x	x		
Neurotensin	x	x	x		
VIP	x	x	x		
Gastrin	x	x	x		
Cholecystokinen	x	x	x		
Bombesin	x	x	x		
ACTH	x	x	x		
31-K	x	x	x	x	x
Lipotropin	x	x	x	x	x
Endorphin	x	x	x	x	x
Dynorphin	x	x	x	x	x
Enkephalin	x	x	x	x	x
MSH	x	x	x	x	x
Insulin	x	x			

the combination of hormones that modulate thought. Thus the mind is made pattern-dependent and also shares in the secret of evolutionary survival: pattern recognition is the *sine qua non* of the genetic code and the DNA/RNA interactions which underlie all immunology and are basic to all the hormone/hormone receptor interactions of cell regulation. Pattern recognition is also the highest form of thought. Bergland's speculations are most provocative.

Bergland's thinking is also in line with the results of the best contemporary brain research that shows very clearly that the human brain is not like a computer in any way. It is also a very "worldly" brain, i.e., an organ designed with specific human needs and human-world interactions in mind.

With regard to memory, some of the mind's most important hormones, vasopressin, ACTH, and MSH, have all been shown to be necessary for learning in animals. If these hormones are important to normal memory processes, they are almost certainly important to disorders of memory as well. Further work is needed to determine what role they might play in senile dementia and other diseases that cause memory loss.

Whether we like it or not, humans are primarily physical beings, and physical factors trigger and control our mental state. For centuries men have altered their mental states by subjecting their bodies to fasting, flagellation, beatings, fatigue, unusual breathing techniques, exposure, as well as by the ingestion of various and sundry mind-altering substances. The resulting mental states depended, of course, upon the type of physical assault made or the kind of chemical substance that was consumed. Prolonged dancing, for example, causes hyperventilation followed by a high degree of blood alkalosis, leading to brain alkalosis. Brain alkalosis, we know, tends to produce suggestible behavior and a trance-like state. Although the excessive use of the muscles would create more lactic acid which could counteract part of the alkalosis, the total effect would lead to brain alkalosis and trance-like behavior.

Protein and vitamin B deficiencies can also cause hallucinatory states and in 1937 the German researcher Schmeing claimed to have discovered that all so-called "second sight," i.e., ESP and clairvoyance, was due simply to calcium deficiency, and that by adding calcium to the body it could be erased. If Schmeing is correct in this claim, maybe all so-called "psychic abilities" could be eliminated by a quick visit to the nearest vitamin and health-food store. In 1958 the American pharmacologist Cedric Wilson discovered that the ergotropic drugs such as dexamphetamine and caffeine depress ESP ability whereas trophotropic drugs such as the major tranquilizers appear to slightly enhance "psychic abilities." As mentioned earlier, the anesthetic ketamine also produces out-of-body and near-death experiences. To what extent *all* of a human being's paranormal or supernatural encounters and experiences are due to malfunctions or disorders of normal body chemistry, which, in turn, have profound effects upon our perceptions and cognitions, remains to be determined.

Although it is not generally known nor well publicized, there is now good evidence that schizophrenia is neither a genetic nor a brain disease

(Sarbin and Mancuso 1980 and Modrow 1992). Recent evidence shows that schizophrenics—long believed to be incurable—can, when provided with long-term supportive milieu therapy involving cognitive restructuring and the acquisition of new coping skills, be released from the hospital. Moreover, when schizophrenics are taken off debilitating neuroleptic drugs which, in many patients, induce incurable neurological disorders such as tardive dyskinesia (delayed abnormal movement), tardive akathisia (hyperactivity), and tardive dementia, as well as many other behavioral symptoms much worse than schizophrenia, improvement following cognitive therapy can be quite dramatic (Harding 1987 and Podvall 1990).

In fact, there are few, if any, genuine *psychiatric* illnesses other than purely neurological ones where organic damage has been done to the brain and nervous system by bacilli, viruses, other pathogenic agents, physical trauma, or developmental disorders. Physicians, neurologists, and general practitioners, as well as psychiatrists, can treat dementia, delirium, and mental retardation, i.e., clear-cut organic impairment. All of the remaining disorders found in the American Psychiatric Association's *Diagnostic and Statistical Manual* do not represent "true" psychological illnesses. They are not, in other words, the kind of illnesses or diseases that require the specialized services of a psychiatrist. What we normally consider to be a neurosis is in no way an "illness," nor do the many and varied practitioners of "talk therapy" have any major impact whatsoever on the true organic illnesses cited above. Further investigation of the facts behind these statements will be discussed in the following section.

Where Oh Where Is the Unconscious Mind?

John Locke, the English philosopher, assumed that we come into the world with a mind like a *tabula rasa*—a blank slate upon which experience writes messages enabling us to think and act. We know now that Locke's assumption is only partly true, and that we come into the world already equipped, i.e., with a brain already equipped with a number of hard-wired cognitive skills that are too difficult or technical to learn from trial and error. The perception of objects, vision, recognition of speech, sounds, and the human face, and the ability to understand the syntax of our native language as well as an implicit understanding of cause and effect—are all things that infants know almost at birth. These processes are not only necessary for our very survival, but also go on below the level of awareness. In fact, these items are so important that nature cannot afford to let us learn them haphazardly from experience. They are part of the human continuum and our adaptation to the world. Even those basic skills such as talking and walking, that we have to learn through practice, quickly become automatic and unconscious so that we do not have to devote much conscious effort and attention to them. Tying one's shoe is slow and difficult for a three-year-old but an automatic act for an adult.

In other words there are a number of self-contained schemes or modules that are innate and unconscious from birth to death. There are even other mental systems that begin by being conscious but are then pushed down into the unconscious, not due to Freudian repression, however, but simply because of the need for mental economy. We simply cannot waste the time, attention, and effort required to perform a number of simple mental tasks. We simply can't afford to have to think deliberately about every move and step along the way. Learning to read is, at first, slow and arduous and is done in word-by-word fashion; but in order to make progress, the entire process must become automatic, i.e., unconscious. We have to learn to read in phrases, then sentences. Catching and throwing a ball, hitting a golf ball or a baseball—little athletic skill is possible until all of the activities become automatic. If one has to think about what one is doing or how to do it—as professional athletes know—one is in deep trouble. For all mastered skills the mind has to remove learned routines from the field of immediate awareness so that our limited attentional capacity is free to deal with the new and unlearned and ever-changing world of harsh reality. In fact, the failure to make consciously learned skills automatic, or making them only partly automatic, is the major problem with "slow learners." Once these skills have become automatized, then not only are they independent of their origins, but they have a life all their own.

We must also recognize that a very great deal of our behavior has a firm physiological basis and depends entirely on wholly self-regulatory internal processes of which we are totally unaware or unconscious. We are referring, of course, to the *autonomic* or automatic *nervous system.* We don't have to consciously breathe, beat our hearts, regulate our body temperature, stimulate the digestive system, form urine, and so on. None of these things require our awareness or any focus of our mental powers. The autonomic nervous system is, therefore, an integral part of a large number of neurological and physiological forces that go on either partially or entirely outside of our normal field of awareness.

With regard to consciousness or awareness, it is well known that the Reticular Activating System (RAS) in the mid-brain furnishes the indisputable substratum for conscious experience. Sleep is the only time in the organism's life when there is little or no activity and the organism is comatose and the cerebral cortex is generating slow waves like those of deep sleep. Although it would seem evident that the cortex is involved in awareness since cortical slow waves also occur during wakefulness, we know that cortical activation is regulated by mechanisms in the RAS. The brain lesions which most dramatically abolish conscious awareness are lesions not to the cortex but to the arousal system of the brain stem.

Recently there have been a number of experiments that bear on the relationship between awareness and repression and the unconscious. Benjamin Libet carried out a series of experiments on patients being treated for Parkinson's disease and intractable pain in the 1970s. By applying an electrical stimulus to the skin of one hand—which the patient could feel and report—and applying a second stimulus directly to the neocortical area governing skin sensation, which the patient felt as a somewhat different tingling sensation in the skin of the same hand, Libet demonstrated that in order for a sensation to become conscious processing was required somewhere in the brain, and that this processing took about one-half of a second. Ordinarily this would result in a bizarre condition; our skin would be touched and we would not feel it for one-half second. To maintain the normal simultaneity, however, that we sense between the touching of the skin and the subjective feeling that it is being touched, Libet found that the brain registered the subjective event as occurring one-half second earlier than when the processing of the subjective sensation was completed. That is, the brain mechanism producing conscious sensation corrected for its own processing time in order to attain subjective simultaneity. (1979, p. 193)

These experiments are significant since they point to consciousness as the result of a distinct neural process. The one-half second required for a sensation to become conscious provides a neuropsychological basis for repression in that there is time for other associative processes in the *preconscious* part of our mind to analyze events, thoughts, and memories, and repress them if their content is too painful. Freud, along with many other psychologists, assumed there were three distinct parts to our mental apparatus: *conscious* awareness of the here and now; the *preconscious,* a repository of thoughts and ideas reachable whenever they were necessary, and the *unconscious,* thoughts and ideas beyond our reach even if we wanted to recall them. Are these assumptions correct? We shall see.

Of further relevance are the experiments carried out by Shevrin at the University of Michigan Medical Center (1988). When a word like *fear* is flashed on the screen for a thousandth of a second, too fast for conscious perception, the watching subjects show a brief response to the flashing of *fear,* and then a quarter of a second later, a sharp burst of activity. When the word is flashed at a much slower rate, however, slow enough for conscious perception, it takes twice as long for the brain to react. Shevrin concludes from this difference in reaction time that all messages to the brain are selectively transmitted first to the unconscious in a filtering process. It is this filtering process that causes the delay. When the words are presented above the threshold so that the subject can actually see them, there is some kind of inhibition or delay of the brain's responses to those words. These experiments indicate that we all take in a lot more information than enters our conscious level of awareness, first into the unconscious and then, only selectively, into consciousness. This process takes time. According to Shevrin, what is meaningful to the mind has an existence in the brain and it isn't simply a matter of electrical or biochemical activity. Interpretation is critical and what is going on is a part of what is meaningful in our lives. It seems very clear that we all know far more than we think we do. Our conscious minds know only a fraction of what the entire network of the mind knows.

Whereas the computer goes one step at a time in serial fashion and proceeds in logical fashion, the computer is so poor at something like simple perception it can literally take days to tell the difference between a dog and a cat. The brain, by contrast, sees a cat as a cat in half a second because it juggles tremendous amounts of evidence simultaneously and the decision is over so fast that the conscious mind cannot detect it. Only the final decision "a cat" is ever dumped into our conscious apprehension. When our thinking is difficult or slow we are well aware of it, but when it is easy and fast the conscious mind has to stand by and wait for the result. One of the reasons why so much of this processing is unconscious is that not only does it happen fast but also there is active suppression of knowledge. Ideas compete with the stronger ones or the ones most appropriate winning the struggle. The brain must have some way to get rid of information that is not relevant at a particular moment and pull together the elements that *are* relevant. It is these relevant items that are the only ones we become aware of from moment to moment. As Jeremy Campbell suggests, these sorts of memories are content-addressable and they are the natural "emergent" properties of a "parallel distributed" network. They also manage to fill in the missing parts of information that is incomplete. Because of their very nature and the nature of this process, the version of the truth that does appear in conscious awareness may be largely false or fictitious. Because we only observe the *product* not the process by which the decision was reached in wholly unconscious decision-making, we have no way of separating the true from the false or fact from fiction. Unconscious processing is, therefore, not a very reliable source if one is after the truth.

In Freud's view the unconscious was also seen as unreasonable, disorganized, and irresponsible, as well as being powerful and indestructible. He also saw it as a repository of information that the conscious mind doesn't want to know about, and therefore is pushed as far away as possible. Memory, according to Freud, was the agent that accepted or rejected ideas, thoughts, and feelings according to the meaning they might have for the individual. Memory is the active agent that pushes the unwanted material into the unconscious and would like to banish it altogether but has to accept the fact that it is still there but hidden from awareness. Neurosis, according to Freud, occurs when some of this information escapes. To get rid of the neurosis the conscious mind has to get rid of these banished memories through the use of reason. Although this concept of the unconscious is a little dated, it does foreshadow the modern view that a great deal of highly intelligent thinking goes on below the level of conscious awareness. William James called the unconscious "a tumbling ground for whimsies." Around the turn of the century there was a great deal of interest in unconscious thought and a number of psychologists studied it in the form of automatic writing, crystal gazing, and hypnotic trances. In Jeremy Campbell's words:

> Crystal gazers "saw" scenes in their glass globes and automatic writers penned messages that were interpreted as visitations from the spirit world, or as intimations of the future. In the light of what we know today, these pictures and words were almost certainly fragments of past experience lodged in the mind that had never entered conscious memory. At the time, however, since the relics of the past were not part of the gazer's or the writer's known autobiography, it was tempting to assume that they appeared from nowhere, which was an invitation to conclude that they were otherworldly.
>
> (Campbell 1989, p. 205)

In our own time cognitive researchers are well aware that hidden memories, unconscious thinking, and learning without awareness are commonplace. One of the mind's most basic operations—that of creating categories and prototypes—is in large part wholly unconscious. Not only does the mind categorize but it also reasons, remembers, and solves problems. We also know that it suffers somewhat from conscious reasoning. Studies at Cambridge University following up on Shevrin's work have shown that when words are flashed on a screen so quickly no one could read them and then followed by an abstract pattern, human subjects could still form mental categories of the words even though they were unaware of having seen them. If *queen* is flashed on the screen and the viewers are then asked to guess what the word is, they will often respond with *king*. Or if the flashed word is *yellow* they will guess *blue*. Even though all they have seen is an abstract pattern they still classify the words on the basis of meaning. Evidence from cryptomnesia also shows that accurate records of many objects and events will enter our minds completely unawares and can show up in the form of intuition, likes and dislikes of which we are totally ignorant of their origin. Anesthetists and surgeons have often reported the fact that many patients supposedly drugged into unconsciousness often remember and report what was being said during their surgery.

We also know that knowledge consciously acquired and thoroughly assimilated can become so unconscious and automatic that it is almost impossible to ever make it conscious again. Moreover the unconscious mind seems to be able to consider many more and a wider range of alternatives than the conscious mind which has a considerably narrower focus. What we call "intuition" is probably nothing more than the conscious mind's dim awareness that the unconscious mind has already solved a problem and is trying to provide an answer. The psychologist Kenneth Bowers calls this feeling "the presentiment of coherence," which is the surfacing of these hidden memories. John Kihlstrom is able to explain this presentiment in terms of a connectionist network in the brain. In his view the intuitive computer, which is distributed and parallel, is able to connect ideas and find chains of associations much easier than the conscious computer which has a much more restricted capability. Also in connectionist networks an item of knowledge is not in one place but it is distributed over many units and is superimposed on other items. Since knowledge is wide ranging, and interacting with other knowledge, an exact description of how the answer was achieved is out of the question. The psychologist James Anderson, a connectionist pioneer, points out that this situation is both an asset and a liability. In his words:

> You really don't know why the network ended up where it ended up. The reason is that so many different things are going on at the same time. And just as accurate knowledge is spread out over the system, so too is erroneous knowledge. Error is as robust as truth in these networks, which makes it very difficult to remove. Since error is distributed, unpredictability is built in, and that is both an asset and a liability.
>
> (Anderson 1989)

The philosopher Jerry Fodor says that since so much is going on out of the field of awareness, perhaps we should treat the unconscious as normal and consciousness as a sort of mental aberration, i.e., a pathological mental condition. As mentioned earlier, there are many different systems of interactions going on in the brain at any given time and the total amount of knowledge in the system always exceeds that which is able to work its way into conscious awareness. Bowers believes that these unconscious systems are much richer in knowledge of the world than the conscious systems, so that people are always much closer in touch with reality than they realize. Moreover, they always know much, much more than they are able to convey to themselves or to others.

Nevertheless, there is a problem here that we need to come to terms with—the problem of making the unconscious conscious. If, as Freud argued, the unconscious is unreachable, how does it ever surface? What are the mechanisms that make the forgotten unforgettable? If something is truly forgotten, how do we get it back? This raises the possibility that there are actually only two mental states: processes that are in the field of awareness, and processes that are out of the field of awareness. Nevertheless, both are mental states that are in the brain and all are subject to recall. If they are not in the brain and have never been in the brain, then they are forever beyond recall. There are many, many things that we have apprehended in our lifetimes that have long faded from the mental systems of our brain and that are, consequently, absolutely and forever irretrievable. They are gone forever. If we are asked to remember them we can, of course, bring our imagination into play and create a pretty good replica of those things we *believed* that happened. But this is not the same thing as a reinstatement of what *did* happen. Similarly, all of our memories are just this: *recreations,* not reinstatements.

Therefore, as Campbell comments, if there are networks in the brain that know more than they can tell, there are other conscious systems that are in the opposite predicament: they tell more than they can know. In other words, they make up the very best story they can out of the partial, incomplete, and distorted information they get from within. They put together the best story possible under the circumstances. Whether it is or is not accurate is not as important as the fact that *it does make a good story!* Little wonder that our memories are so unreliable and that the nature of eyewitness testimony is so notoriously undependable.

The Freudian Fallacy

So much has already been written about Freud and his contributions to psychology that it is difficult to add to what has already been said. Nevertheless, there are aspects of the man and his work that need to be aired; aspects that are seldom mentioned or discussed in the glare of adoration surrounding the great mental emancipator. Certainly one of the most enduring contributions of Freud's personality theory is the concept of the unconscious—the part of the mind that is hidden. Freud believed, as we have seen, that all behavior, no matter how trivial, was motivated more often than not by unconscious processes.

Exactly how this works is supposedly illustrated by a conversation Freud had with a young man who, in expressing his pessimism about the state of the world, quoted a line from Virgil: "Let someone arise from my bones as an avenger." But the young man could not remember the Latin word for "someone" and asked Freud to supply it. He then challenged Freud to show how this trivial memory lapse could have been motivated by unconscious processes. Freud took the challenge and had the man concentrate on the word *aliquis* (someone) and report every association he had to the word with no censoring of any kind.

The man's associations to the word included fluidity, fluids, relics, and idiosyncratically, to St. Januarius, whose blood was kept in a vial in a church in Naples. On a particular holy day, the blood liquefies. If this event is delayed for any reason, the people of Naples are aroused and wait for a miracle to happen. At this point the man blushed and said he had an association too intimate to express. When Freud reminded him that complete candor was required, the man alluded to some information a woman might pass along. Freud then floored the man by correctly telling him he was worried that his girlfriend had missed her period and might be pregnant. Freud's clues, embedded in the association, were: blood flowing on a particular day, a calendar saint, and the hope that the miracle of blood flow would take place.

Freud tried to explain the complex workings of the mind by dividing it into levels of consciousness. *Conscious* thought is concerned only with material of which we are momentarily aware. Mental work or knowledge that is available to our awareness, but that the person is not immediately thinking of, is part of the *preconscious*. We all know what a tiger looks like but until it is referred to and brought to awareness it is part of our preconscious. Most, or at least a large part, of our mental life is *unconscious*. People are normally unaware of material in or at the unconscious level of awareness—even though much of our behavior is influenced by it. The young man's inability to remember the word *aliquis* was influenced by those unconscious mental forces Freud believed in. Much of the pathological behavior that Freud treated with psychoanalytical methods was behavior determined by unconscious thought. When things too unpleasant, emotion provoking, or anxiety arousing occurred, Freud believed these were repressed, that is, barred from conscious thought and shoved down into an unconscious level. Since so much relating to sex was disapproved or anxiety arousing, it is no wonder, in Freud's view, repressed sex was such a driving force in human affairs. Freud's theory was not only strongly deterministic, but he also held that human behavior was under the control of strong instinctual pressures over which people have little or no control; in fact, he believed people are largely unaware of the reasons for their behavior. Personality, he also believed, was formed in early childhood through interaction in the family, and through modification of the sexual instinct.

The *id*—the primal, driving, instinctual forces—is joined in childhood by the *ego* (sense of self), and later by the *superego,* or conscience. This theory has had, over the years, a stupendous impact on our thinking about man's mental life. Yet, astoundingly, there is not one smidgen of scientific evidence to support any of it. Every experimental effort to validate any of its essential elements has ended in failure. Moreover, and even more startling, is the fact that none of the ideas expressed or elaborated upon by Freud were novel or new—even his most celebrated notion of the unconscious.

The Unconscious Before Freud

A number of writers have gone to great lengths to trace the concept of the unconscious mind from its beginnings in the distant past up to Freud. Three of the most prominent efforts have been Lancelot L. Whyte's *The Unconscious Before Freud* (1960), Henri Ellenberger's monumental *The Discovery of the Unconscious* (1970), and D. M. Klein's *The Unconscious: Invention or Discovery* (1977). As Whyte points out very emphatically, Freud did not discover the unconscious mind. His writing about it was the culmination of a cultural process that extended over centuries. Nietzsche expressed several of Freud's insights twenty or more years earlier. Though ideas come suddenly to individuals, they usually have a long history, there is seldom a monopoly in great ideas, and every generation exaggerates the achievements of its own era's heroes. This was certainly the case with Freud. Men have known for a very long time that their field of awareness is quite narrow and that much of what we know is hidden. What we know about our mental life today, however, is considerably greater than what Freud knew, and in fifty or one hundred years it will be much greater still. The central principle of the history of ideas is that all of them are partial. In Whyte's view, Freud's true contribution lay in the fact that he compelled modern man to find a more adequate concept of the mind and its operation and forced us to face up to the fact that hidden mental forces are very powerful in determining our behavior. When we first became aware that many of our mental processes are hidden is unknown. Nevertheless, it soon became apparent that we needed to infer from our direct and immediate experiences that other things were going on inside. Also it soon became clear that our mental lives were dynamic, i.e., constantly fluctuating and changing. In William James's term, "consciousness was an everflowing stream" and each of us as infants came into a "world of booming buzzing confusion" that we soon learned to order and make sense of.

Descartes was perhaps the first thinker to separate mind from matter and to argue for two separate realms of being—an idea that Whyte believes was one of the fundamental blunders of all time. Although Descartes recognized the "union of soul with body," he said this was an illusion resulting from some sort of parallelism between the two modes of being. Prior to Descartes there was no reason to consider the possible existence of unconscious mentality as part of a separate realm of mind. Until *awareness* was considered, the hallmark of an independent mode of being called mind, there was no need to invent the idea of an unconscious mind as a correction. Thus, it was only after Descartes that the term "unconscious mind" came into being.

There is no doubt whatsoever that our experience is split into two aspects: our individual awareness and the world itself. It is also most likely that the individual only performs the mental act of separating himself from everything else when the world of reality forces him to do so. Intuitively, however, each of us as part of our normal course of development creates a persisting experiencing self and each of us attributes to that self permanence, unchanging identity, and continuous awareness. We do this in spite of the facts of growth, and change, and aging, and death. And the ever-changing, easily altered character of awareness makes it difficult to see "mind as either stable or permanent. It is of considerable interest that some of our more primitive cultures see reality—not as a material world out there—but as merely a series of mental events." For most of us the separation of a conscious self from an objective universe was inevitable. This divorce Whyte sees as a tragedy of immense proportions and it has led to the dilemma of self-conscious man: a creature eternally discontented and neglectful of his own biological perfection in process. Life develops, mutates, evolves, and—if left alone—can develop fully and naturally in terms of species and race. When we become too self-aware, we go to any length to escape it, even to recognizing the primacy of the unconscious mind, and to losing our "self in a larger source of being."

Whyte sees the discovery of the unconscious by self-conscious man—who still does not know how to properly define "mental"—as taking two centuries, roughly from 1700 to 1900. The idea of unconscious mental processes was, in many of its aspects, conceivable around 1700, topical around 1800, and it became effective around 1900, thanks to the imaginative efforts of a large number of many individuals of varied interests in many lands. While the existence of the unconscious mind was being established during these two centuries, the discovery of its structure only began in the twentieth.

In the post-Cartesian period increasing attention was paid to different aspects of unconscious mental processes beginning with unconscious memory, perception, and ideas. Speculation regarding therapeutic applications came much later. Nevertheless, even in the seventeenth and eighteenth centuries many thinkers were interested in mental therapeutics for mental and physical pathologies as well as dreams, hallucinations, somnambulisms, suggestion, hypnosis, dissociation, alcoholism, drugs, diseases, hysterias, obsessions, collective myths, religions, and perversions. But no one bothered to consider all of the known aspects in a comprehensive and scientific manner. It is to Freud's credit that he knitted together in a comprehensive and systematic manner many of these loose and scattered mental threads.

More than anything else it was the German Romantic movement that had the greatest impact upon Freud and this thought. The fundamental principle here was that in the unconscious mind lay the tie of the individual to the universal powers of nature. Thus, the wellsprings of human nature lie in the unconscious, and here the individual is linked with the universal. it can be the union of the individual soul with the divine, or a perfectly natural linkage of moments of human awareness with organic neurological processes within which they begin. From the eighteenth century on there was an increased interest not only in the normal aspects of mental life (sleep, dreams, reveries, etc.), but also in the unusual or pathological states (hypnosis, hallucinations, fainting, ecstasy, dissociation, drugged states, epilepsy, etc.) and in the processes that underlie ordinary thought (imagination, judgment, selection, diagnosis, etc.). Although many of these things appeared to fall into the realm of the irrational, this interpretation was an error. All sustained mental processes—including those of which we are aware—are primarily unconscious and are regulated by unconscious factors. Moreover, there is no reason to regard unconscious processes as basically irrational and in opposition to rational analysis. In fact, the little empirical research that is available suggests otherwise. Simply because we do not fully comprehend exactly how the mind is organized and functions does not mean that we should think of unconscious aspects as either irrational or pathological. Because Freud demonstrated that unconscious factors can sometimes lead to behavior contrary to reason, this is not sufficient cause to assume that every unconscious aspect is always irrational. Nevertheless, from 1750 to 1950 too many thinkers tended to regard the unconscious as the source of all the irrational forces in man and an ever present threat to social and intellectual order.

Whether he intended it or not, Freud's emphasis on the pathological aspects of human behavior cast an unfortunate pall over most of our thinking about mental processes. What little understanding we do have about our mental life has come about primarily through speculative philosophy at first, then through clinical and laboratory studies, and only in the last few years through physiological and psychological studies of the brain and nervous system. It wasn't until the last decades of the nineteenth century, however, that the first systematic professional efforts to base curative procedures on theories of the structure of unconscious mental processes were made. Despite the brilliance of the Freudian theories and ideas, "cures" for mental pathologies were not an immediate outcome. In Whyte's words:

> Freud did not regard the benefits of psychoanalysis to the neurotic individual or even to the analyzed analyst as normally complete or permanent, and his own techniques have not yet led to important discoveries improving and extending them.
>
> (Whyte 1960, p. 74)

It seems clear now in the fifty years that have elapsed since Freud's death that he contributed few wholly satisfactory techniques for therapy. Although a number of important cumulative advances in the treatment of psychoses and neuroses have been made, they have not been based on any solid physiologically or psychologically experimentally established theory. Certainly not Freudian theory. The few attempts and experimental efforts to determine the validity of certain Freudian ideas and hypotheses have been negative. Most of these efforts to empirically establish the truth or falsity of the Freudian dynamic took place shortly before and shortly after World War II and gave little support to Freud's major assumptions.

The early rumblings of discontent and disillusion with the Freudian edifice came to full fruition in the early 1980s. While reading Ernest Jones's biography of Freud, E. M. Thornton, a lay Fellow of the Royal Society of London, was struck by a passage quoted from one of Freud's letters written in the 1890s. Because it sounded like the imagery used by drug addicts, she wondered if Freud was under the influence of some powerful drug when the passage was written. Her curiosity aroused, Ms. Thornton began an intensive inquiry into the rest of Freud's life and career. The resulting book, *The Freudian Fallacy* (1983), has been called in some circles "The Demolition of Sigmund Freud." Those who have managed to resist his canonization and elevation to secular sainthood have long found it difficult to understand his influence and prestige because his teachings and his theories are totally lacking in scientific support, and few, if any, people have ever been cured of any psychosis or neurosis by psychoanalysis. Other forms of therapy, drugs, and shorter therapeutic regimens—all of these are vastly more effective for nearly any class of mental disorder than any Freudian methology or technique. As Dr. Raymond Greene noted, Freud undoubtedly believed in the truth of his hypotheses when he pronounced them, but his scientific training should have prevented him from committing the sin of explaining one mystery with the substitution of another.

In subjecting the Freudian structure to the cold glare of logic and content analysis, only those who have been totally brainwashed would deny the truth of Thornton's findings. No doubt the publication of her book took a large amount of courage. No one has had a more profound effect on twentieth-century thought than Freud. His work has influenced psychiatry, psychology, anthropology, sociology, penology, and all of the arts; he has, literally, changed the face of society. Psychoanalytic terms have become part of the language of everyday life, and many writers and thinkers have described Freud as a genius—one of the great thinkers of all time— and in a class with Newton, Einstein, Darwin, and Copernicus.

Yet Freud's central postulate—*the unconscious mind*—does not exist; it is a function with no scientific support whatsoever, and a contradiction in terms. More damaging yet, as Thornton has shown, Freud's theories were baseless and aberrational, and when he formulated them he was under the influence of cocaine, which specifically affected his brain. This latter fact is known by his own admission, as is his use of the drug from 1884 to 1887 during his medical practice and his resumed use of cocaine in the latter half of 1892—the year, incidentally, in which his revolutionary new theories emerged. In her book Thornton shows, most convincingly, that his theories were the direct outcome of his cocaine addiction. The cocaine addiction also accounts for Freud's delusions of persecution, memory lapses, suspicions, and denunciations of his disciples, as well as the incompatibilities and discrepancies in his work.

Although Freud's definitive biographer, Ernest Jones, discusses some of Freud's behavioral eccentricities, they are dismissed as the harmless peccadillos of a man of genius. Now they are seen for what they were: a dramatic picture of a tormented genius wrestling with the demons of his "unconscious mind" and following the classic course of the cocaine addict. Freud's rapid mood swings from elation to depression, episodes of clouded consciousness, periods of hyperactivity, paranoid mysterious heart symptoms, were all not the "creative neurosis" that Jones described, but symptoms of the paranoid delusions peculiar to the later stages of cocaine addiction.

We must not, however, judge Freud's work on such grounds. It should stand or fall on its own merit. Many works of creative genius have come from those who have managed to probe the depths of human imagination, and Freud could have gained invaluable insight into his own mind from such "consciousness expanders." Unfortunately, as Thornton points out, such drugs act not on the mind but on the brain and affect most strongly the brain centers where sense data are interpreted and memories are stored. The false perceptions so vividly described in the drug literature, which the deluded users interpret as emanations from the "deeper levels of the mind," are the "distortions arising from poisoned brain cells." It was, unfortunately, these drug-induced misperceptions that plagued Freud and produced his neurotic symptoms.

Brainwashed as we have been by the thousands of writers and intellectuals paying Freud tribute, it is still difficult for us to realize how, in just a few decades, psychoanalysis became such a dominating force in psychiatry. Though much less so in psychology, it was nevertheless a major force. Thornton does, however, show how this came about. Not only did Freud hide his psychosis from his followers for a while (one by one his early disciples left him), but he selected his champions carefully, picking intellectuals with a philosophical rather than a scientific education, and those people who valued ideas for their own sake rather than for their factual value. They were very good, however, at propagating and publicizing his theories and ideas to a lay public and in dealing with criticism by calling it old-fashioned, rigid, or inhibited. The climate of the times was also in Freud's favor. Along with Darwin and rapid advances in medicine and biology, the ground was ready for, and receptive to, new—even bizarre— ideas. Freud's theories were also helped along by exaggerated claims of innumerable "cures" obtained through psychoanalysis. G. Stanley Hall, in the American edition of Freud's early work, testified to "thousands of cures," which was, of course, impossible. In his practice Freud saw every patient for an hour each day, six days a week, and their analysis continued for years. Later in his career he devoted most of his time to training other analysts. Therefore, the total number of patients he analyzed in his entire career were probably numbered in tens rather than thousands. Moreover, few—if any at all—were or could have been "cured" by his treatment. Even his most famous patient, Anna O., was still ill at the end of her treatment. Even analysts now concede psychoanalysis has little or no curative value. The practicing analyst Anthony Storr, in his 1968 essay on "The Concept Of Cure," stated, "The evidence that psychoanalysis cures anybody of anything is so shaky as to be practically non-existent." When the American Psychoanalytic Association took a survey to test the efficacy of analysis, the results were so disappointing they were withheld from publication. (*Psychoanalysis Observed,* edited by C. Rycroft, 1968)

Although Freud's theories, particularly those of the unconscious mind, are generally hailed as "discoveries" and accorded the status of established fact, more discerning critics see them primarily as inventions (Klein 1977), and a number of medical historians (Whyte 1960 and Ellenberger 1970) have shown most of Freud's thinking about unconscious mental processes can be traced back to the "Romantic" phase of German medicine, and specifically to Johann Friedrich Herbart (1776-1841) whose system is almost identical to that of Freud. Ellenberger in his history, *The Discovery Of The Unconscious,* states, "There is hardly a single concept of Freud or

Jung that had not been anticipated by the Philosophy of Nature and Romantic medicine." (p. 68)

It is also interesting to note that Freud's fundamental hypotheses about repression and the unconscious mind grew out of Mesmerism and animal magnetism, which in the early nineteenth century were taken more seriously in Germany than anywhere else in Europe. Since strange aberrations of memory showed up in "hypnotized" people who recalled long forgotten events of childhood in the waking state, the concept of repression was born. And since "hypnotized" patients would occasionally be subjected to a flood or even a panorama of childhood memories so sharp it seemed they must have occurred the day before, it seemed there must be a reason for this. And there was. Penfield found that when the temporal lobes of his patients were physically stimulated, similar panoramic memories occurred. It is also well known that the temporal lobes are primarily affected in states of drowning and suffocation because their structure and peculiar vascular supply makes them much more susceptible to anoxia, hypoglycemia, and drugs than other parts of the brain. They also have the lowest seizure threshold of all parts of the brain and, consequently, the most rapid spread of an epileptic discharge. Wilson, in 1928, reported the case of a sailor who fell into the ocean and was under the water for approximately two minutes. Although his senses were deadened, he felt his mind begin to race and every past incident of his life appeared before him. In short, he reported that the whole period of his existence seemed to be placed before him "in a kind of panoramic review; indeed, many trifling events which had been long forgotten then crowded into my imagination, and with the character of recent familiarity." (Wilson, p. 173, 1928). Wilson also reported the case of another patient who tried to commit suicide by hanging himself. Even though he had been suspended for only a few seconds, he also reported that nearly every incident of his early life in their most minute particulars suddenly appeared before him. Incidents connected with the school where he received his earliest instruction showed up in crystal clarity. Faces he knew as a child that he thought were completely obliterated from memory were restored in a remarkable and vivid manner. Every trifling and minute circumstance connected with his past life was presented in his memory in sharp clear pictures during these moments when he struggled with death.

Wilson also tells the story of a friend's son who choked on a piece of meat in a restaurant and he was able to observe an instance of panoramic memory first hand. Wilson reports the time that had elapsed since the son had become semiasphyxiated and his father extracted the meat from the upper larynx was only one minute at the most. The boy reported, however, that in that brief period he went back in time to scenes and incidents of his earliest childhood. Trifling events of his nursery life, his childhood and school days passed before him in a succession of vivid pictures. He reported seeing again the furniture of his nursery, its paper and carpet, his nurse, and so on. And he also told Wilson how amazed he was to see these things so clearly.

Panoramic memories also occur during the aura of epileptic attacks, and many patients report that their seizures are accompanied by a string of old memories. One of Wilson's epileptic patients reported that he wandered back down through the years and wondered how he could remember all those "forgotten" things. "It is like a vision. It seems as if I had gone right back and become part of the scene again." Another patient reported that during her auras she would go into a curious state in which she would suddenly remember all sorts of things that happened when she was a child. Most were stupid, silly, trivial, old-fashioned things of her childhood she reported. She remembered things like swinging, playing with her toys, and other children.

Although the events recalled by Penfield's patients when stimulated by his electrodes involved more recent memories, they, too, were similarly unremarkable. One patient reported while the electrode was in place he saw a Seven-Up bottling company and a local bakery. Another patient when stimulated reported seeing a man and his dog walking along a road near his home. Another patient reported hearing a telephone conversation while another saw a man coming through a fence at a baseball game.

Under so-called "hypnosis" the memories reported are evoked by an analogous mechanism although it is not due to anoxia or electrodes. It is, however, due to relaxation and suggestion and getting the individual into *a frame of mind that is conducive to recall*. In a series of experiments on hypnosis in which subjects' memories were tested while under hypnosis and while awake, during the awake and control condition the subjects had to do nothing but sit relaxed in an easy chair and try to recall as much as they could about their early childhood, beginning with the first thing they could remember up until the present. They were required to do so for an entire hour. What was most surprising was that, without exception, all of the 120 subjects participating in this exercise produced literally reams of material, and hundreds of memories of both significant as well as trivial events. Invariably, the comments of the subjects after the hour was over were like "I hadn't thought of those things in years," or "I thought I had forgotten all about that cat I had in the first grade," and so on. Once these associational chains are started they quickly reveal a veritable ocean of experiential material. Once begun it becomes very difficult to stop. Most of the student subjects were perfectly ready to continue the recall much beyond the hour provided. Many had only progressed through the fifth or sixth grade before the hour was over. If you have any doubt as to the richness of human memory and the total number of events one can recall when one approaches one's past in a systematic and associative manner, try this exercise yourself. What you will discover is that each of us is another Proust, and everyone of us is capable of writing another *Remembrance of Things Past.* Since there is no real alteration of consciousness, none of these memories are of a *repressed* nature or even of a *suppressed* nature, albeit some of them were definitely unpleasant, and even if they were not verbalized they *were remembered.* There is, in fact, no known mechanism by which memories can be *repressed* by the conscious mind or ego as Freud imagined. In Thornton's words, and she is quite correct, "Painful and distressing events are, as common sense tells us, those that most clearly *stand out* in our memory. We may 'put them out of our head,' i.e., turn our attention to something else, but they will return unbidden when some chance association recalls them to mind." Moreover, the recovery of memories under any of the above conditions is essentially an involuntary process. Individual memories cannot be recalled at will. Occasionally, the memories recalled under hypnosis may have been of greater significance than the trivia mentioned. This probably occurred often enough to credit the process with the power of widening the field of consciousness to reveal *all* forgotten material. But for the most part so-called "hypnotic regressions" are nothing more than suggestion and compliance along with the ingenuous use of the subject's imagination. Thornton is also correct in calling attention to the fact that any and all regressions to the first years of life, and even to birth, are especially suspect. At this stage of development the brain is still so immature that large tracts of nervous pathways are still unmyelinated; the brain mechanisms for establishing long-term memory have not yet developed. For this reason alone, Thornton points out, contrary to psychoanalytic theory, the first years of life are probably the *least* important for the development of future personality!

As for the topic of past-lives regression, despite the hysterical claims of so-called psychotherapists like Fiore, Goldberg, Bernstein, and all the other psychics, these productions are nothing more than the exercise of the subject's imagination and, if they are not outright frauds and hoaxes, they are excellent examples of cryptomnesia. As for panoramic memories, it is particularly interesting to note that these are also common accompaniments of people undergoing near death experiences (NDEs) and, rather than having an otherworldly or unearthly basis, it should now be clear that many or most are the standard neurological accompaniment of temporal lobe anoxia.

Returning to Freud and his system, it is important to remember that his entire theoretical edifice was more or less a regurgitation of old theories he had read many years before. In one sense of the word, Freudian theory is, itself, a beautiful example of cryptomnesia. That all of these concepts and ideas flashed into his head as new and original concepts is, of course, not only completely compatible with his cocaine usage but as excellent an example of cryptomnesia as can be found anywhere. This conclusion is also in line with Edmund Bergler's theory regarding writers.

According to Bergler in his classic work, *The Writer and Psychoanalysis* (1986), every writer is a would-be, if not already a practicing, plagiarist. Even though the writer may not *believe* he wants to steal the work of others, he still does want to *unconsciously*. Bergler sees all of us as putty in the hands of unconscious forces. In chapter 10 of Bergler's book, for example, he lists twenty-four types of literary theft including "Plagiarism as a substitute for a cover memory," "Plagiarism of people in love," "the plagiarist hunter: the man who is always compulsively searching for plagiarisms of others." The latter type is one of those paranoids "who write books about somebody else's plagiarism, real or imaginary." According to Bergler, all of us are helpless pawns and no more than "the ground on which the various psychic forces do battle." The "I" in Bergler's view is impotent and helpless. The book, according to Bergler, that was written to help other writers would in actuality drive anyone reading it stark raving mad. In Bergler's own words:

> The idea that the writer is objective and the highest representative of his time or the culture in which he lives is, politely speaking, ridiculous. Of course, writers often proclaim that slogan as an inner rationalization, but why should he believe that rationalization *any more than that of any other neurotic.* . . . No, the writer is not the objective observer of his time. He is just a neurotic operating his defense mechanism without knowing it.
>
> (Bergler 1986, p. 111)

What is difficult to conceive is how anyone in his right mind could take this sort of utter nonsense seriously. It is almost as bad as some of the other extremist views of the Freudian apostles who see the man watering his thirsty lawn with a garden hose as a closet masturbator. Following this same line of thought, the man who uses an automatic sprinkler is, in actuality, impregnating the universe!

Although Thornton has done a masterful job of poking holes in the Freudian curtain she is far from being the last to do so. Garth Wood, in his book *The Myth of Neurosis* (1987), compares psychoanalysis with a cure for cancer. If one proposes a new treatment for cancer then it must be scientifically validated, shown to be at least as effective as other methods, prove that it will at least do no harm, insure that there is some scientific mechanism by which the cure works to diminish the cancer, and so on. If no one bothered to test the cure, to check its efficacy, to quantify its negative effects, to compare it with other treatments, and to determine whether it was the pill *per se* or merely the passage of time that brought about the cure, what then? Suppose the person proposing the cure then proceeded to hire a group of supersalesmen and flood the land with these dedicated peddlers

> possessed of an almost messianic belief in my pill's efficacy, wearing the cloak of science to cover their scientific poverty, peddling it to those whose judgment the disease had weakened in the desperation of their desire to be made whole. Live through the nightmare and experience a whole industry profiting from and preying on the gullible, the disappointed, the weak, as they sell shamelessly their snake oil equivalent, their "guaranteed" restorer of hair. Now, as you wake in a cold sweat to the reassuring familiarity of reality, consider Freudian psychoanalysis.
>
> (Wood 1987, pp. 268–69)

Wood goes on to point out that it is well over eighty years since the psychoanalytic "pill" was invented, and yet, in 1985, Arnold Cooper, a past president of the American Psychoanalytic Association, was quoted in the *New York Times* as saying, "Psychoanalysis has been enormously successful clinically and vastly important culturally . . . but the time has come to recast psychoanalytic assumptions *so that they can be tested scientifically.*" Yet in the same article, Adolf Grünbaum, a Freudian critic, stated, "Its scientific foundations are impoverished. To say that the theory is ill-founded does not mean it is false. I'm trying to lay bare the logical structure of the theory, and to show what must be done if suitable evidence is to be found." To these comments Wood adds,

> The situation is mind-boggling. The psychoanalysts are admitting openly that the theories on which psychoanalysis is based have never been validated by the scientific method, and this despite the constant assertions of Freud that it was above all else a scientific discipline. Of course, many of us have known all along that psychoanalysis was scientifically bankrupt, a mythical creation rather than the science it pretends to be. But how many patients, who have spent small (and frequently large) fortunes on the "treatment," know that it is not scientifically respectable? Do the analysts who take their money tell them? Do *they* know? Do they care? And if not, why not? . . . Untested and unproved, it is dispensed by the unscientific for the consumption of the unhappy.
>
> (p. 269)

Wood also points out that although many have objected to the psychoanalytic claims, these objections have been studiously ignored. In 1953,

Sir Karl Popper examined a number of theories that were having an impact on man's thinking. Included in the study were the theories of Einstein, Adler, Marx, and Freud. Popper felt that the theories of Adler, Marx, and Freud were in a different category than those of Einstein. What was most noteworthy about their theories was their enormous *explanatory* power. They explained everything that happened. Whatever happened always confirmed it. In Popper's words,

> A Marxist could not open a newspaper without finding on every page confirming evidence for his interpretation of history. . . . The Freudian analysts emphasized that their theories were constantly verified by their "clinical observations." . . . I could not think of any human behavior which could not be interpreted in terms of either theory. It was precisely this fact—that they always fitted, that they were always confirmed—which in the eyes of their admirers constituted the strongest arguments in favor of these theories. It began to dawn on me that this apparent strength was in fact their weakness.
>
> (Popper 1962, p. 212)

In other words, Popper was pointing out that it is easy to find confirmations of theories if all we look for is confirmations. To confirm the theory that all crows are black, we can rush about discovering large quantities of black crows. But even very large numbers of black crows are not sufficient to prove the theory. Just how many black crows do you need to convince yourself of the theory's truth? A million? A billion? It will depend on the psychology of the person being convinced. If, however, just one white crow were to turn up, it would destroy the theory completely. The theory that says: All crows are black forbids the existence of white crows, and as Popper knows, the more a theory *forbids,* the better it is. In sum, every genuine test of a theory is an attempt to falsify it, not to confirm it, and any theory that is not refutable by any conceivable event is nonscientific, or pseudoscientific. The irrefutability of both Marxism and Freudism is not a virtue; it is a vice. Nothing can prove psychoanalysis false. Everything confirms it and nothing denies it. Simply said, scientific inquiry doesn't matter to psychoanalysis; it is simply not relevant.

Both Sir Aubrey Lewis and Ernest Nagel also agree with Popper. Lewis pointed to what he called "an unabridged gap" in psychoanalysis between what could be checked and observed experimentally, and the ambiguous concepts such as "instincts," "unconscious fantasies," etc., which purported to explain them (1949). Nagel noted that though it is permissible for a theory to be based on entities that cannot be directly observed, e.g., protons and electrons, there must, however, be a demonstrable link between those entities and their observable effects in the world of the senses. Psychoanalysis fails to provide this link. Perhaps the one individual who has done the most to leave the psychoanalytic edifice in ruins is Sir Peter Medawar. Medawar picked several samples of psychoanalytic writing from papers presented at the 23rd International Psychoanalytic Congress held in Stockholm in 1963 and let the authors' own words damn them. Two samples should suffice. One analyst wrote about one of his patients, who suffered from ulcerative colitis and who dreamed of snakes, and reported:

> The snake represented the powerful and dangerous (strangling), poisonous (impregnating) penis of his father and his own (in its analsadistic aspects). At the same time, it represented the destructive, devouring vagina. . . . The snake also represented the patient himself in both aspects as the male and female and served as a substitute for people of both sexes. On the oral and anal levels the snake represented the patient as a digesting (pregnant) gut with a devouring mouth and expelling anus. . . .
>
> (Medawar 1972, p. 72)

The second example is another analyst's explanation for the etiology of anti-Semitism:

> The Oedipus complex is acted out and experienced by the anti-Semite as a narcissistic injury, and he projects this injury upon the Jew who is made to play the role of the father. . . . His choice of the Jew is determined by the fact that the Jew is in the unique position of representing at the same time the all-powerful father and the father castrated. . . .
>
> (Wood 1987, p. 274)

Medawar's comment on these and other examples was that he did not intend to poke fun at them, ridiculous though he believed them to be. Rather his purpose was to illustrate the olympian glibness of psychoanalytic thought. Though the contributors to the congress were concerned with very real and serious problems, problems more difficult than those scientists face in the laboratory, there was never any hesitancy whatsoever, no admission of ignorance or incompleteness, no expression of any doubt about any pronouncement, no questions and no humility—none of the attitudes and expressions commonly found at similar gatherings of physiologists, biologists, or biochemists. In his words, "A lava-flow of *ad hoc* explanation pours over and around all difficulties, leaving only a few smoothly rounded prominences to mark where they might have lain." (Medawar 1972, p. 87)

Wood is even more scathing in his denouncement of the analysts, and feels that Medawar let them off much too easily. In Wood's words:

The effrontery of these brazen pseudoscientific poseurs takes away the breath. It is surely one of the most amazing phenomena of the twentieth century that such absurd and disgusting psychofilth is regarded as credible by so many. Sir Peter says that it is not his purpose to poke fun at them, but is not that what they deserve? If the scientific method is not sufficient to discredit them, then what is left in the armory of the commonsensible but the weapon of ridicule? Will laughter and scorn weaken the stanglehold of psychoanalysis on the culture of our age? We shall see.

(Wood 1987, p. 275)

Unfortunately, what we have seen since Wood published his book is scarcely any dimunition in the pronouncements of the credentialed but obtuse pseudoscientific psychoquacks. If anything, we are currently witnessing at the beginning of the 1990s a resurgence, if not a veritable renaissance, of psychotherapeutic garbagology. While it is true that we have always had it amongst us, it has certainly seemed to have picked up speed in the last few years with the advent of the so-called "New Age" with its own peculiar brand of degreed but irresponsible and anti-scientific zealots. Admittedly, it may be hard to top that very dandy fellow Francis I. Regardie, M.D., of Los Angeles, who in the 1950s introduced his revolutionary new treatment called *Vomit Therapy*. Dr. Regardie, using a tongue depressor, cures his patients of whatever ailment they may have by having them regurgitate into a kidney pan. If the patient is puzzled at the request and resists the suggestion, the therapist provides a brief explanation and tells his client this is not the time for intellectual discussion. Regardie's procedure is to have the patient gag ten or twelve times. The gagging style itself provides an index to the client's level of inhibition. Some gag with finesse, others with delicacy, some without noise, whereas others will cough and spit. Still others will scoff and sneer. Those who gag without sound are the most difficult to deal with, and their character-armor is almost impenetrable and their personalities rigid. Others will retch with horrible completeness. This is a very, very literal application of the Freudian notion of catharsis.

On the other hand we have Arthur Janov, the inventor of Scream Therapy, who believes devoutly that man's search for meaning in life is, itself, most neurotic. The cure for everything is, of course, to scream your little head off and get rid of all that bottled up anger. On the other hand, Viktor Frankl's logotherapy rests on the assumption that man's search for the meaning of his existence and his failure to find it *is* the basis of his neurotic discontent.

Much of the foregoing information is neither well known nor understood by members of the helping professions—clinical psychologists, psychiatrists, social workers, etc. As a result, when these professionals encounter strange and unusual phenomena such as past lives, alien abductions, multiple personalities, or contact with the dead they, too, yield to the transcendental temptation and invoke a religious or supernatural explanation. This we will discuss at length in later parts of this book.

2

Cryptomnesia and Other Anomalies of Memory

Theodore Flournoy (1854–1920) is important to mention here because he established a skeptical paradigm, namely cryptomnesia, which remains to this day one of the positivist's most devastating weapons in dismissing the claim that past life memories are in fact derived from historical events unknown to the subject. The theory of cryptomnesia claims, simply stated, that the unconscious mind has recorded all sorts of overheard conversations, pictures, stories from books, and nowadays, films and television programs, that are now forgotten. These forgotten stories or images, it is claimed, become the basis for historical romances that mature in the unconscious and later emerge disguised as fully elaborated past life "memories."

—Roger J. Woolger, *Other Lives, Other Selves*

Cryptomnesia, the power of the mind to recall things of which there is no conscious memory, is much more common than most people realize.

The phenomena of experiencing, i.e., seeing complex visual images in one's head that you cannot remember ever having seen before or, in a similar fashion, suddenly hearing voices from unknown and unrecollected sources is not only a much more common occurrence than is generally known but is also one of the more interesting and intriguing anomalies in the field of "normal" human behavior. While the "hearing of voices" is one of the most frequent hallmarks of psychosis or "insanity," it is not generally known that this symptom is an experience that literally hundreds of perfectly normal and rational people experience from time to time, and does not in any way indicate or imply that they belong in a looney bin.

In most instances these "voices" are heard only infrequently and they last for only a moment or two. They are also usually of an unknown origin. Sometimes the voice is heard in the form of a command or a request for information. On other occasions the voice is that of a friend, an acquaintance, a close relative, or a spouse. Only if the voices persist and begin to take control of one's thinking and behavior and cannot be controlled or turned off are they indicative of a sickness or mental illness.

In a similar fashion, mentally healthy individuals who are neither intoxicated by alcohol or drugs also may see things that others cannot see, or have experiences with so-called "entities" in the form of ghosts, dead people, spirits, fairies, demons, and extraterrestrial aliens that, as far as they are concerned, are very "real" and no different from their ordinary, everyday other perceptions and experiences. While such experiences and "encounters" are definitely unusual, they are in no way either supernatural or beyond the explanatory powers of modern psychology despite the efforts of many amateur psychiatrists, psychologists, and sensation-minded journalists to prove otherwise.

Early in the beginning of the present century members of the British Society for Psychical Research were called upon to investigate a woman who, under hypnosis, became a medieval lady named Blanche Poyning. While in a hypnotic state the woman had remarkable and detailed memories of every aspect of the Countess of Salisbury and her husband and family. Every detail of life in the medieval period seemed accurate. Finally one of the investigators, G. Lowes Dickinson, had the idea of asking her "How can we prove what you are telling us is accurate?" She replied, "Read his will." "Whose will?" "Wilshere's." "Where is it?" "Museum. On a parchment." "How can we get it?" "Ask, E. Holt." "Where is he?" "Dead. There is a book. Mrs. Holt." "Do you know where she lives?" "No. Wrote a book. *Countess Maud* by Emily Holt." When aroused from hypnosis the woman could recall nothing about the book except the title, and the fact that she had read it. When G. Lowes Dickinson found the book and read it, every fact relating to Blanche Poyning was also found in the book about the nineteenth-century Countess Maud.

One day when Dr. Erika Fromm of the University of Chicago was regressing one of her patients for a demonstration in a psychology class, a twenty-six-year-old man named Don suddenly began speaking fluent Japanese. It seems that when she regressed him back to three years of age he began to speak the language that he and his family spoke while they were interned in a California camp during World War II. When the patient was progressed to age seven, he spontaneously reverted to English. Japanese was the language of the camp, but he had not spoken it since his release at age four.

Henry Freeborn, a Scottish doctor, in 1902 was treating a seventy-year-old patient with pneumonia when in a delirium she suddenly started speaking Hindustani, and talking to her *ayah* or nursemaid, begged to be taken to the bazaar to buy sweets. She had left India sixty-six years earlier where she had been born and had been cared for by a native servant. She was totally unaware of being able to speak the language. Dr. C. A. Mercier, in a comment on this case published in the June 1902 *Lancet,* noted, "it was not the forgotten language alone whose memory was so strangely revived. Her whole personality was transported back. She spoke to friends and relatives of her girlhood and asked that she might be taken to the bazaar." Dr. Mercier also reported on a case described by Coleridge in which an illiterate maid-servant, when delirious, was able to recite Greek and Hebrew for hours, languages she apparently acquired from a person for whom she had worked some years before. It appears as if the person was in the habit of reading Greek and Hebrew books aloud to himself in her presence.

In his *The Interpretation Of Dreams* Freud observed:

> It is a very common event for a dream to give evidence of knowledge and memories which the waking subject is unaware of possessing. One of my patients dreamt. . . that he ordered a "Kontuszowka" while he was in a cafe. After telling me this, he asked me what a 'Kontuszowka' was, as if he had never heard the name. I was able to tell him in reply that it was a Polish liqueur, and that he could not have invented the name as it had long been familiar to me from advertisements on billboards. At first he would not believe me, but some days later, after making his dream come true in a cafe, he noticed the name on a billboard at a street corner which he must have gone past at least twice a day for several months.
>
> (Modern Library Edition, p. 477)

Cryptomnesia is also the key to the so-called "past lives" phenomena. What is not well known is the ability of the human mind to store and retrieve with complete accuracy huge amounts of information at the same time that many other memories turn out to be pseudo-memories, and that what seems so utterly factual and true to the individual doing the remembering turns out—after checking—to be wholly imaginary.

When in 1976 twenty-seven-year-old Michelle Smith suffered a miscarriage, she called her former psychiatrist, Dr. Lawrence Pazder, to help her cope with her feelings of emotional loss. Since Dr. Pazder had treated her earlier for some phobias and other problems, he was shocked when in Michelle's first session she entered the office in a trance-like state and proceeded to scream at the top of her voice for the first half hour. After calming down, Michelle began to recall long lost childhood memories—

memories of torture and ritual abuse by members of a Satanic cult that included her parents. She also recalled being forced to participate in ritual murders, drink blood, and sacrifice animals. Finally, she remembered a ceremony called the Feast of The Beast at which Satan himself appeared. Finally, Michelle was saved at five years of age by a heavenly figure called Ma Mere. The precise details of Michelle's ordeal are provided in the book she wrote with Pazder titled *Michelle Remembers*. Unfortunately, there is nothing whatsoever in the way of facts to corroborate the authenticity of her story or her memories.

Why would these memories be hidden all these years if they were true? Once one understands the mind's natural tendency to reconstruct, reorganize, and confabulate, we can be quite confident that Michelle's memories are a blend of both fact and fiction. What is interesting is that these sorts of memories of murder, rape, torture, abuse, etc., are really quite common among people who have had very ordinary, prosaic, and protected childhoods.

In many instances such memories, rather than pointing to mistreatment or parental abuse, reflect the rage, anger, frustration, resentment, and powerlessness of children in a world dominated by larger and much more powerful adults. Rather than being *real* memories of *real* events in the lives of those who report them, they are, for the most part, inventions and fabrications, cryptomnesic memories of horrors and hurts experienced vicariously. In the rare instances in which children were subjected to all these aforementioned indignities, the most natural response was to protect themselves by repressing and suppressing the horror. To avoid being paralyzed by their painful recollections they doctor their memories, making them less terrible, less traumatic than the reality. Often the horror may take on a bizarre and different aspect or form, and children rewrite their punishment and abuse at the hands of parents they love in the form of torture by satanists, or abduction by aliens. In this fashion they protect themselves from the terrible pain of the truth—punishment at the hands of those they love. Cryptomnesia is one of the human mind's most common and universal protective mechanisms. The term cryptomnesia itself we owe to the Swiss psychologist Theodore Flournoy and his investigations of Mlle. Helene Smith, fully recounted in his book *From India To The Planet Mars*. A full account of his work with Ms. Smith will be discussed in the following chapter.

While the phenomenon of "hidden memories" was well known to the "Mesmerists" and "animal magnetists" much earlier as a product of the "hypnotic trance," it had not been carefully researched or identified as a purely *psychological* phenomenon. The fact that a person can, especially in the hypnotic regression state, remember and report facts that the normal waking self had forgotten completely was, in a sense, Flournoy's discovery. Flournoy also emphasized that cryptic memory was much much more extensive than anyone had realized before.

Following his publication of *From India To The Planet Mars* in 1899, Flournoy felt that the subliminal psychology of Myers and the abnormal psychology of Freud needed to be merged. He also strongly believed that most, if not all, of the alleged "spiritualistic" or "spiritistic" phenomena were "easily explained by mental processes inherent in the mediums and their associates." Flournoy was careful to distinguish *spiritism,* which is an assumption that certain phenomena are due to the intervention of dead spirits, from *spiritualism,* which is a religious-philosophical belief.

As Flournoy saw it, the medium's entire attitude of expectancy, belief in spirits, state of relaxation, suggestion, and imagination all combined to put a person into a state of:

> . . . mental dissociation and a sort of infantile regression state, a relapse into an inferior phase of psychic evolution where the imagination naturally begins to imitate the discarnate, utilizing the resources of the subconscious, the emotional complexes, latent memories, instinctive tendencies ordinarily suppressed, etc. for the various roles it plays.
>
> (Flournoy 1911, p. 205)

In 1911 Flournoy published *Spiritism And Psychology* in which he examined several other cases of the alleged supernormal. One was the case of Madame Dupond of Geneva, a sixty-three-year-old matron who, after reading a great deal of spiritistic literature, attending a number of seances, and engaging in automatic writing, began to make contact with the spirits of the departed. One evening while doing automatic writing, she came up with the name of a M. Rudolph, a young Frenchman of her acquaintance. She was not aware that he had died, but as her hand continued to write the message from M. Rudolph proceeded to give the specific details surrounding his demise. For several days following Mme. Dupond continued to receive spiritistic messages from Rudolph.

A few days later, however, she received a letter in the mail from a M. Rudolph who was still very much alive. When Flournoy investigated this case and looked at all of the extenuating circumstances surrounding the event, it became evident that Mme. Dupond was very fond of the young man in question, was concerned about his welfare, and she feared for his health. Out of this multitude of thoughts and fears she and she alone created his discarnate state. The fact that Rudolph eventually became a priest deeply upset her, and his entry into holy orders deepened the gulf between them and led to almost an end of correspondence between them after a period when they had been corresponding almost daily. The sudden cessation in real correspondence plus her disappointment and anger with the young man led to her secret desire for his death—hence his "dead" spirit and, to boot, a communicating and "repentant" spirit.

A number of other similar cases led Flournoy to the conclusion that the play of imagination in the medium leads the medium to believe that his creations have a reality and an origin completely independent of himself. The creation of spirit protectors, guardian angels, demons, spiritual guides, etc., are all given the name of *teleological automatisms*. These beneficent spirits also often served as a secondary personality for the medium and as such they could be very helpful and protective in times of stress.

Flournoy then discussed a number of other "hidden psychological mechanisms" which he called *cryptopsychisms*. The two most important are *cryptaesthesia*, "hidden or latent feelings or perceptions," and *cryptomnesia*, "hidden or latent memories." Flournoy believed that all of our psychic functions—association, reasoning, imagination, etc.—can contribute to these strange and unusual behaviors. As a classic example of cryptaesthesia Flournoy gives the example of the hysteric in whom the tactile excitation of an anesthetized finger, although not felt by the subject, was nevertheless seen by her as a visual image of this finger. One could say, generally, that cryptaesthesia is the process by which an afferent sensation which remains unperceived and ignored by the subject provokes an efferent phenomena which seems to arise spontaneously by itself without apparent cause. It must be understood, Flournoy says, that a production of this kind, of which the subject has no awareness of being the author, might easily be attributed to spirits—no matter how little it appears to deserve such an explanation. Flournoy also calls attention to the subconscious functioning of a number of our mental faculties, memory, imagination, will, etc.

Many of our everyday behaviors are so automatic that we are astonished when they occur, and we are unsure they were willed by ourselves.

Forgotten memories, returning at a favorable moment, repartees which are *à propos,* and which surprise us ourselves, suppressed after-thoughts, inexplicable hesitations preventing us from action, or, on the contrary, obscure impulses which we are glad we have followed, good ideas, illuminating thoughts, inspirations of genius which flash into our heads and bring us unexpected help; in fact, all that we call "tact," "presence of mind," "inspirations," or "intuition," all that is at the basis of teleological automatisms and fill our whole lives—the study of all this is well worth the most painstaking research and analysis.

(p. 115)

Flournoy gives, as an example, his looking for a book in his library. He starts to leave to see if he can find it in another room but finds there is something holding him back. Turning around he sees the sought for book buried under some others on a table. The latent memory of the misplacing of the book subconsciously stops him from leaving the room and steers him to the table. Yet he had no memory of putting it there originally. This is another simple and common example of cryptomnesia. Flournoy says if he were a medium, or hysterical, this little incident would take on the character of a psychic phenomenon. He would have heard a voice say, "Look on the little table," or he would have seen its location in a dream or a crystal ball, or his guardian angel would appear and lead him to the table, or through typtology or automatic writing he would be told where to look.

Flournoy also gives an interesting example of cryptoaesthesia in which subconscious perceptions provided a premonition that saved the experiencer's life. It seems that a merchant travelling in South America heard a mysterious voice giving him a warning. In two separate cases the mysterious voice saved not only his life but the lives of his companions as well. On one occasion the traveler's party had just halted under a tree to prepare a meal. Suddenly, the traveler heard a voice command him: "Save yourself." He forced his men to break camp at once. Scarcely had they done so when the tree they had been camped under came crashing down on the spot they had been in only moments before. All of the men would have been killed had not the premonition occurred. An examination of the tree trunk showed it was rotten and had been hollowed out by termites. On another occasion, floating down the river in a canoe, they were approaching a promontory when this same voice commanded them to immediately cross the river and go ashore as quickly as possible. This seemed so unnecessary and so ridiculous that the traveler had to threaten his guides to make them comply. They had scarcely gotten halfway across the river before the promontory suddenly toppled into the river causing a whirlpool in the river that would undoubtedly have capsized their boat and swallowed them up had they continued.

Mystical? Supernatural? No, far from it. The traveler felt that the voice was so imperative that he had to obey it and make his men obey it, too. Analyzing the events later, the traveler began to realize that on approaching the tree, he had noticed that the base of the tree was rotten, and he also noticed termites on the trunk, as well as mentally noting the size of the tree. These visual perceptions set off internal alarms and aroused presentiments of danger and panic which aroused the warning voice. In the case of the promontory, he remembered having heard grinding and cracking noises that could only have come from the promontory that was ahead of them. Again, the visual perception of the size of the cliff, and an awareness of what would happen to their little boat in the event of a rock fall teetering on the edge—conscious awareness of this triggered the presence of danger and motivated the internal voice to scream a warning.

Another similar case involved a very nervous and sensitive Austrian lady who experienced many things she felt were truly psychic manifestations. This woman usually spent her winters on the isle of Madeira. One year when she went down to the dock and boarded the ship, she suddenly saw the ghost of one of her absent physicians whose expression gave her to understand that she was in great danger. The figure seemed to be urging her to disembark immediately. This the woman did in a sort of dream-like state. A few days later she learned that not only was her boat ship-wrecked, but that a deadly plague was ravaging the island of Madeira. Although at first she attributed her experience to some supernormal faculty of precognition, a little investigation turned up a much more mundane and natural explanation. First of all, it turned out that the ship was never shipwrecked after all. As for the plague, it turned out that the lady had read about it a few days earlier but had filed it away and forgotten about it until she boarded the ship. After realizing her destination, she associated it with the plague and thus her vulnerability. The result was the warning figure of her protector—the physician who fends off death and disease.

Flournoy also told the story of his mother, who, while giving him birth, suffered a hallucination in which she saw an elderly gentleman dressed in blue and gold lean over her bed and tell her that she was in no danger and would recover. When she described this man to her mother, Flournoy's grandmother told her that it was a perfect description of her father who died before she ever saw him. While the spiritists would see this incident as proof of the dead father returning to comfort his daughter in distress, psychologists see in the hallucination a dramatic combination of long-forgotten auditory memories, "some descriptions formerly heard and then completely forgotten toward which the thought of his daughter would turn in the crisis through which she was passing." The American researcher Morton Prince fully agreed, and in an article in the 1908 *Journal of Abnormal Psychology* told the story of how such things can happen. According to Prince:

> A lady of my acquaintance gave me a very exact description of a person whom she had seen in a dream, whom she had never met in reality. She had completely forgotten that I had described that person to her a few days before. The description which she gave me after her dream was an exact reproduction of mine, and in the same terms.
>
> (p. 265)

Such concrete representations, once activated, may exist in the latent memory and suddenly reappear even when one can no longer remember the occasion which first of all provoked them.

Another class of such phenomena are those cases in which automatic memory processes provide us with information we already have but of which we're totally unaware and don't realize that we have. A classic example is a dream we have in which we are able to locate a ring that we had lost. In the dream it was on a shelf in the bathroom—the place where we had forgotten we put it in the first place. Upon awakening, sure enough there it is on the bathroom shelf! The paranormalist will insist that something supernatural has occurred. Psychologists see it simply as a case of an individual being distracted or thinking of something else when the ring was placed on the shelf. Nevertheless, the action was noted and filed away in memory. Then, when in a more relaxed state, this memory was reinstated. It is, admittedly, strange that something as important would be forgotten, and that putting the ring on the shelf does not register in the immediate memory but is, instead, filed away at a lower level and forgotten until a later time when it can be clearly and easily recalled. Personally, I have witnessed the same phenomena on numerous occasions when friends and students have lost and misplaced a number of valuables and I have used relaxation and suggestion to help them recall, in step-by-step fashion, what happened to the missing item. So much of our ordinary behavior is done without our full attention, it is surprising that even more of our belongings do not magically disappear.

Although cryptomnesia is usually classified as one of the several disorders of memory, its universality and frequency of occurrence in the general population ought, perhaps, to cause us to reconsider our classifying it as a "disorder." As we will see in the case of Helene Smith, this gifted young woman not only was able to remember just about everything that she ever read or heard, but she also was able to use her imagination and story-telling skills to weave truly marvelous tales of past lives and planetary visits. It is also important to note that Mlle. Smith did not require the services of a hypnotist to go into her so-called trance state. She was perfectly capable of doing this on her own merely by using her imaginative skills. This ability, although most people are not aware of it, is far from rare. People who are highly susceptible require little or no effort on the part of the hypnotist to enter fully and completely into bizarre flights of fantasy. Time and time again in working with so-called "hypnosis," therapists have noted how easily and quickly certain clients went into a so-called "trance" with hardly any effort at all on their part. I have seen this over and over again in my own work with experimental subjects. Roger Woolger, in his book dealing with past-lives therapy specifically states that not only has he had a 90 to 95 percent success rate in teaching past-life remembering, but he also says, "what past-life remembering entails is a kind of deep identification with an inner or secondary personality, an identification which does indeed involve imagination, as all remembering does, but in the fullest sense." Woolger is also quick to note that "in our deeper or fuller consciousness *we are multiple beings,* that we have many personalities within us. Some of these other selves are surprisingly close to consciousness and can be awakened quite easily. . . ." Morris Netherton, another past-lives therapist, has also remarked about how easy it is to move his clients into a past-life fantasy. Without the use of hypnosis, and without needing a patient's belief in reincarnation, Netherton, through the simple device of asking his client's questions, sends them back into their past where their imagination takes over. (1979) In Netherton's own words,

> Reaching the unconscious mind without hypnotism is quite simple. I do not use any relaxing exercises with my patients, nor do I use sensory awareness techniques to make the body, or eyelids, feel heavy. There is nothing trancelike, in fact, about a Past Lives Therapy session. At the beginning the patient may have some trouble getting the unconscious memories to flow, but this difficulty is usually eliminated as the patient sees the therapy beginning to work. Once a sense of trust is established between the patient and his own unconscious mind, reaching back to the past becomes a very simple matter.
>
> (p. 215)

Helen Wambach, also an investigator of past-lives experiences, admitted to Dr. James Alcock that reports she gathered from hypnotized subjects who had been regressed to past lives do not differ in any way from those of unhypnotized subjects. Dr. Wambach interprets this as clear evidence that one can have access to past-life material without being hypnotized. (Alcock 1986, p. 167)

Carl Jung, in his *Memories, Dreams, Reflections* (1973), tells the story of one of his practical demonstrations of hypnosis when he was a lecturer at the University of Zurich. Jung's patient for the demonstration was a fifty-eight-year-old woman who arrived on crutches, led by her maid. For seventeen years the woman had suffered from a painful paralysis of her left leg. Jung had her sit in a chair and tell the audience about her illness. She not only did so but she began to tell a tale of such length and woe that Jung was afraid she would consume the entire lecture period. Jung interrupted her and said, "We have no more time for such talk. I am now going to hypnotize you." At this point the woman closed her eyes and fell into a deep trance with *no hypnotic induction whatsoever.* Jung was taken aback but could say nothing because the woman continued to talk, but this time she talked about her dreams for another half hour. Jung then decided to wake her but he couldn't since she droned on. Finally, when she did come to, she was giddy and confused. Jung then told her, "I am the doctor and everything is all right." At this point the woman called out, "But I am cured!" She stood up, threw away her crutches, and demonstrated that she could walk unaided. Disconcerted, Jung turned to his students and said, "Now you have seen what can be done with hypnosis!" But in the book he admitted that he had no idea about what had happened, and this incident was one of the reasons he gave up using hypnosis in his clinical practice. Incidentally, the woman was indeed permanently cured of her ailment. (pp. 117-118)

The above examples clearly substantiate the fact that "hypnosis" is, after all, nothing more than highly imaginative role playing—the sort of thing that anyone can engage in with sufficient motivation.

Whereas most people have assumed that "hypnosis" is a prerequisite condition for any and all psychological regressions, it may come as a surprise to find that not only is "hypnosis" not necessary, but that what we have called "hypnosis" is nothing more than the use of suggestion by the therapist or hypnotist to arouse the imagination of the patient or client. That this can be done with only a few well chosen words, or that the client can do it to him or herself without the need of external assistance lends further support to the wonders of belief, suggestion, and the power of the human imagination. The recent discovery by the UFOlogist community that many victims of alien abductions did not have to be hypnotized in order to remember their abductions is considered proof that the abductions were real. Unfortunately for them, it only substantiates the power of the human imagination.

Cryptomnesia is also the fundamental psychological phenomena underlying what is nowadays called "trance channeling," but around the turn of the century was called "a seance" or "spiritualistic readings." Yet, as its proponents are quick to point out, channeling is as old as religion, and even the Bible is purported to have been "inspired by God" and channeled through the prophets. This is also held to be true of the Koran, and the Book of Mormon, channeled through Mohammed and Joseph Smith respectively. It is also estimated that well over one hundred thousand channeled books have been self-published or published by vanity presses by a number of true believers in the United States alone over the past hundred years. As Ted Schultz has remarked, "a good case could be made that channeling is an essential element in the formation of any new religion." Again, the channel supposedly goes into a "trance," and some other other-worldly personality takes possession of the channel's mind and body and gives advice and counsel. Usually when this occurs the channel's voice, facial expressions, gestures, etc. undergo a remarkable alteration, and the audience to this phenomenon is struck by the difference between the original personality and the one who has assumed control. Unfortunately for the believers in this drama, just about anyone with the time and money can take a channeling workshop and with a little practice can learn to simulate almost any sort of entity from Alexander the Great to Dagwood Bumstead or Peter Piper or Elvis Presley. One is, however, much better off if one decides to channel a less well-known entity—one that is closer to being a non-entity will enable you to rattle off facts and figures that no one can or would be interested in checking. Biographies of Napoleon are plentiful but who has ever written one about Harold, the sixteenth-century hod-carrier, or Sam, the fourteenth-century shepherd?

There are, of course, a number of other occasions in which our "hidden memories" show up and can cause no end of embarrassment and difficulty. George Harrison, one of the Beatles, innocently rewrote the Chiffons' song "He's So Fine" and called it "My Sweet Lord"—totally unaware of its origin in his forgotten memory. The same thing happened to Helen Keller who published a story in 1892 called "The Frost King," completely unaware of the fact that Margaret Canby's story "The Frost Fairies" had been read to her via braille in 1888. The two stories were almost identical, but Helen Keller had no memory of ever having known it before and she was convinced it was her own creation. Nietsche's masterpiece *Thus Spake Zarathustra* includes details contained in the work of Kerner which the philosopher had read at the age of twelve. Melvin Harris, in his *Investigating The Unexplained* (1986), reports that many other authors have been trapped in the same way. Samuel Rosenberg, a literary consultant on plagiarism cases for Warner Brothers Pictures, advises,

> Don't be fooled by the sometimes astonishing resemblances you will find when you compare *any two* films, plays, stories, books, or film scripts. During the past twenty-five years we have made hundreds of such comparisons in preparation for court trials, and in a great many cases we have found that *both* of the quarreling authors—each convinced that *he* was honest and the other writer was an idea-thief—had copied their plots, ideas, sequences from an *earlier* literary classic or from the Bible or some "forgotten" childhood story.
>
> (Harris 1986, p. 150)

Similarly, a number of cases of automatic writing, supposedly from discarnate spirits, have been traced to published works. The famous "Oscar Wilde" scripts of the 1920s were gradually shown to have been derived from many of Wilde's own published sources including *De Profundis* and

"The Decay Of Lying." S. G. Soal, one of the writers of the automatic scripts, remarked, "the variety of the sources from which the script is drawn is as amazing as the adroitness with which the knowledge is worked up into sentences conveying impressions of the different mannerisms of Wilde's literary style." If one understands the nature and operation of human memory, such findings are far from surprising.

Instances of cryptomnesia in academic circles are also quite common. In an atmosphere where ideas are continually interchanged and problem solving is important, it is easy for one to forget the source of an idea that for him has a novel flavor. Since the cryptomnesic cannot acknowledge his source, cries of plagiarism are common. Where it is important to be first with a scientific breakthrough, and in an experiement where so many people with similar background, training, and experience are working toward the same ends with the same knowledge-base and with the Nobel prize as a possible reward, it is easy to understand why cries of theft are frequent. What Graham Reed calls "cryptomnesic chains" are often found. The graduate student excitedly announces a brand-new discovery to the irritation of his supervisor who suggested it to his student months before but failed to realize that he himself had heard it from a colleague, who in turn heard it at the last professional meeting. . . . Ironically enough, however, the originator of a subsequent cryptomnesic idea is often the individual himself. Reed states that he got very excited about a new idea he had only to discover that he had written this new idea down in his notes two months earlier. What is so fascinating, however, is the fact that cryptomnesia is an everyday example of *recall without recognition* and is best considered as a *failure of recognition.*

That such failures of recognition are truly common and much more frequent than most people realize is not a well-known fact. One of the most dramatic and fascinating examples of cryptomnesia was reported recently by Harold Rosen. In his introduction to Kline's 1956 follow-up on the Bridey Murphy case, Rosen told the story of one of his patients who when hypnotized suddenly began speaking a language called Oscan that was current in third century B.C. Italy. Since Rosen did not understand what the patient was saying, he asked him to write it out. Rosen took the written words to a language expert, who identified it as a magical curse in Oscan. Since the patient was unfamiliar with Oscan and was completely unaware of the meaning of what he had said and written, everybody was baffled until it was discovered that a few days before the hypnotic session he had gone to the university library to study for an economics exam. Seated at the library table, instead of studying his textbook, he began daydreaming about his girlfriend while looking at a 1904 book called *Grammar Of Oscan and Umbrian,* which was opened at a page displaying on a medallion below the name "Vibia" (which looked like his girlfriend's nickname) a magical curse. Without being aware of it, the student photographically imprinted in his memory the Oscan curse that emerged during the hypnotic session.

Similar sorts of occurrences have even been produced in the laboratory. In 1958 Dr. Edwin Zolik of Marquette University hypnotized subjects and instructed them to "remember previous existences." His subjects obliged by providing convincing accounts of "past lives." Everything was tape-recorded, and every subtlety and nuance of the voices was preserved as the tales were told. Next the recordings were listened to by the subjects in their waking states. Nevertheless, their verdicts were clear—they knew nothing about these "past-lives" and their disclaimers were sincere.

When Zolik re-hypnotized and reexamined the subjects, however, they all were able to remember the fictitious sources they had used in constructing their past-life scenarios. Zolik clearly demonstrated that past-life memories were nothing but a mixture of remembered tales and strong symbolically colored emotions. For anyone interested in the truth, Zolik's method is one way to get it. Most of the regression enthusiasts, however, are not interested in getting at the source of these fantasies. The Finnish psychiatrist Dr. Reima Kampman, in the 1960s, also carried out many investigations of so-called "past lives" with one major difference. Kampman tracked down the sources of these alleged "past lives."

Using volunteers from the three highest grades of the secondary schools of Oulu, and picking good hypnotic subjects, Kampman told them to "Go back to an age before your birth, when you are somebody else, somewhere else." Nearly all of his subjects produced past lives, and one of his stars created eight different past lives! In one of these lives she lived in ancient Babylon, another was lived in China, a third in Paris, another in England, and a final one in Russia during the time of the revolution. One of her lives was that of a seven-year-old girl named Karen Bergstrom who died in an air raid in 1939. The regressee knew everything about Karen—her address, names and occupations of her former parents, etc. Kampman's research revealed that there was an air raid on the date given, and the addresses given had actually been bombed. Population records, however, showed there was no Karen Bergstrom, and neither she nor any of her relatives had died in the raid. Kampman then re-regressed his star to the time when she had first heard of the Bergstroms and the bombing, and the subject then remembered herself as a small girl leafing through the pages of a book about World War II. The book contained pictures of streets and houses hit by bombs, and stories about some of the people who were made homeless. On one of the pages there was a picture of two of the victims who were killed that day—a mother and her seven-year-old daughter. In other words, the complete regression was put together from nothing more than this disjointed material found in this one book.

Of even greater interest was this regressee's thirteenth-century English life as an inn-keeper's daughter. She amazed Kampman by singing a song called "The Summer Song" in old-style English—a language that not only meant nothing to the regressee, but that she had no memory of ever having heard the words or music before. Kampman solved the riddle in a later study in which he sent the regressee back to a time when she might have seen and heard the words and music, or might have even heard it sung. When regressed to the age of thirteen, she remembered taking a book from the library shelves, casually flipping through it, and stopping at the famous "Summer Is Icumen In" with words provided in a simplified medieval English. Kampman followed up his "past lives" and in nearly all of his cases he was able to track down the present life sources of all the so-called past-lives of his regressees. Kampman concluded from his work that

> . . . the experiences of the present personality were reflected in the secondary personalities, both in the form of realistic details and emotional experiences. The recording of a song from a book simply by turning over the leaves of a book at the age of 13 is an outstanding example of how very detailed information can be stored in our brain without any idea whatever of it in the conscious mind, and how it can be retrieved in deep hypnosis,
>
> (Kampman 1976)

i.e., via relaxation and suggestion.

Before proceeding, it might be wise to pause and consider what we currently know about our memory, and some of the things that can and do go wrong with it.

Memory and Some Anomalies of Memory

Although a full and complete understanding of human memory is not yet in, over the past decade a number of important discoveries have been made that provide us with explanations for many of memory's most common functions. First of all, human memory is not like that of a computer. The major outcome from several decades of research on artificial intelligence is the discovery that, aside from the fact that it processes information, a digital computer bears little resemblance to the human brain. Computers work serially, manipulating symbols in step-by-step fashion under the control of a central processing unit following explicit logical rules. The brain, on the other hand, has literally billions of processing units and has millions of connections acting in parallel. These connections, as a whole, define the information content of the system. The brain can bring a vast amount of knowledge to bear when a decision needs to be made. In fact, the brain can perform as many as two hundred trillion operations in a second; not serially, but simultaneously! The brain is a parallel device without programs in which massive amounts of knowledge, implicit in the connections that make up the bulk of the brain's volume, are brought to bear upon a problem simultaneously.

Recent research in cognitive psychology has shown that we do not think logically at all; we are "logical" in only a superficial sense. At a deeper level we are systematically illogical, and biased as well. Our everyday reasoning depends to a surprisingly large extent on what we know, on the way our knowledge is organized in memory, and on how this knowledge is evoked. When very intelligent people are asked to solve simple problems in logic, they often act like morons unless the problem is framed in such a way that networks of knowledge, organized in logical fashion, are triggered. In deciding whether we think rationally or not, *content* is of critical importance, whereas in logic exactly the reverse is true—content is unimportant and form is crucial.

The brain is, in other words, not a logic machine but a knowledge *medium* in which large amounts of knowledge are active simultaneously, and so much happens in such a short period of time that we are not even aware of it happening. We now know that many complex forms of thought go on below the level of awareness, and that conscious deliberation is only a very small part of our intelligence. The conscious part of thinking has been compared to the tip of a huge iceberg whose very existence we overlook because we are so seldom aware that it is there. Moreover, in this very complex mental system we call the mind, learning goes on continuously. Rather than being programmed, our mental system is always in a state of change and is always becoming ever more complex.

Further, whenever a complex new skill is learned and learned well, it is performed almost unconsciously, leaving the conscious mind free to attend to other matters. This is why we can drive a car and carry on a conversation with a companion at the same time, or type fifty to sixty words a minute at the same time we are listening to the news on the radio. As long as one of the things is automatic, i.e., unconscious, and is thus undemanding of our full attention, we can easily do two things at once. But often, by merely turning our attention to an activity, we lose the ability to perform. For example, if you concentrate on where each of your fingers should be while typing, you become almost paralyzed.

With regard to memory, the difference between humans and computers is even more dramatic. Human memory, though much less reliable than a computer's memory, is millions of times larger and more flexible. Since human memory is associative by its very nature, it naturally connects one thing it knows with something else it knows. This is highly unnatural for a digital computer. Rather than having programs in our heads, cognitive theorists know that humans think by means of knowledge patterns or modules given the general name *schemas*. These schemas are the building blocks of thought, and are as fundamental to human reason as cells are to biology. Schemas are not, however, actual physical units like groups of neurons in the brain. They are, instead, units of existing knowledge which we use to process and interpret new incoming information. In other words, the mind, by its very nature, is a knowledge device and not a logic machine. It uses its schemas to tell us how the world works, what is usually true or not true, and what is real. We see and interpret the world we live in through our schemas.

Henry Head, the English neurologist, came up with the notion of schemas in 1932. Following up on this idea, Frederic Bartlett, an English psychologist, proposed that memory is not a precise reinstatement of the past exactly as it happened. Instead, according to Bartlett, memory organizes the data stored in our heads, and whenever the mind remembers, it actually reconstructs the most plausible story it can from the "bits and pieces" of past information it has as well as the "networks" of preexisting knowledge (schemas). Unfortunately, in this "memory" process of rebuilding, the schemas not only manipulate reason but they also bias our understanding. The schemas resolve ambiguities; they make "reasonable" connections between facts even when the connections are neither reasonable nor clear; they may even be missing entirely. They, in a word, dote on imperfect information; they find links, fill gaps, round off corners, and do their damnedest to make the illogical logical. Memory, in sum, is most often a plausible reconstruction of the reality, never an exact copy of it. The human mind is essentially metaphorical, whereas the computer is essentially literal.

As many cognitive theorists have observed, the human mind is a very worldly device designed to function efficiently in the world we inhabit. Thank God this is so! Our mind works to maximize exactly those qualities that insure its adaptation and survival. It is able to make the unfamiliar familiar through its basic ability to generalize. It can take just a tiny bit of information and make it go a very long way. It can bypass logic when necessary, and thrive on information of very poor quality. These are all important survival skills. Remembering, thus, is not essentially different from solving everyday problems. Each time we remember, fragments of information activate networks of interacting knowledge, which results in a pattern of activity representing a memory, an answer to a problem, or whatever happens to be the most consistent with the initial trigger. The network that is the human mind, rather than operating in a *serial* fashion, considers hundreds of pieces of evidence simultaneously—all at the same time—and at tremendous speed in what is called a *parallel* fashion. To understand this we need to look at how the brain is organized.

Cerebral Organization

Early in the 1960s neuroscientists made three major discoveries about the way in which the brain is organized. *First,* the major brain structures— notably the cerebral cortex—were found to be composed of multiple, repli- cated, more or less similar *modules,* each of which contained hundreds of thousands of neurons. In the cortex these modules are organized in vertical columns, extending from the surface down through six layers of cortex. *Second,* the connections between the cells within the cerebral cor- tex were found to be far more numerous and specific than previously be- lieved. *Third,* the total set of processing modules within the cortex is divided into subsets. Each of these modular subsets is linked to similar subsets in other brain structures and areas. According to Dr. Vernon Mountcastle, one of the discoverers, these connective subsets form *distributed systems,* each composed of modular elements in several or many brain regions, con- nected in both parallel and serial arrays. They thus form the neuronal pathways for *distributed* and *parallel processing* within the brain.

Older conceptions of the brain and memory assumed there were specific areas of the brain where certain memories and functions were localized— places from which specific actions emanated. A distributed system, however, has no "center" from which the action issues. There is no master or controlling neuron, no controlling "ghosts" within the neuronal works. Instead, in a distributed system the so-called *motor* and *sensory* areas are only terms of convenience. According to Mountcastle, it is their extrinsic connections— the inputs they receive and the connections they make to other brain areas— that make them uniquely motor or sensory. Mountcastle also believes that if we understood exactly how a single area of the cortex, or even a single vertical column, operates, we could probably figure out how other areas or even the entire brain operates. So far a large number of cortical areas corresponding to each of the major sensory systems have been identified. There is not just one "auditory center," there are four auditory areas; nor do we have a solitary "visual center"—instead there are twelve visual areas. Moreover, all of these sensory areas impose their own abstractions and syntheses upon the representations that reach them, and they also further function as distribution centers.

All of these ideas have dramatically changed our thinking about the nature of memory. In the past it was assumed that we remembered people, places, and things because images of them have been imprinted and permanently stored in our brains, and though we may not be conscious of them, such images are the basis of recognition and thus of thought and action. Obviously we recognize people and things because we match what we see and hear and feel with what is stored in our brains, and we recall them by activating the permanent images stored in our brains. Although there are moments when we don't remember some particular fact, eventually it does come to mind so we know that it was always there. So there can be little doubt that there are permanent memories stored in our brains. Until recently, most neurologists took for granted the notion of permanent memories. It was also generally assumed that the brain was made up of a collection of highly specialized functional regions which controlled various activities like speech, movement, vision, etc. Not only was function localized and specialized, but memory also was of the same nature. We had memory centers for "visual word images," "auditory word images," and so forth. Failure to remember was due to damage to these specific areas. This view was called the doctrine of localization of function, and the belief in permanent memories supported it. The general unreliability of memory, however, troubled a number of theorists, including Sigmund Freud.

To Freud's way of thinking, since so many of our memories were fragmentary, recognition could not be simply a matching of perceived with stored images. He noted that bits and pieces of a person's past often showed up in dreams and were only recognized as "memories" when linked to the emotions. Freud argued that it was the emotions, therefore, that structure our recollections and perceptions. What he was doing here was describing the limbic system long before it was discovered to play a crucial role in emotional behavior. More recently limbic structures have been found to affect memory as well. Perhaps the biggest boost that believers in localization of function received was from the work of Wilder Penfield, who showed that the electrical stimulation of certain areas of the brain in conscious patients elicited what he thought were recollections of "forgotten" experiences. Here was positive proof to believers in permanent memory traces. Recent work, however, has shown that all Penfield's memories were but fragmentary impressions, like pieces of a dream, and they contained elements that were not part of the patient's past experience. In fact, of the 520 patients who received electrical stimulation in the temporal lobes, where Penfield believed the memories were stored, only forty produced what he called "experiential responses." Subsequent studies revealed that such experiential responses occur only when the limbic structures—generally thought to be essential for emotional experiences—are activated. Gloor and his colleagues in 1982 confirmed this with epileptic patients and reported that "unless the limbic structures are activated, either in the course of a spontaneous seizure or through artificial electrical stimulation, experiential phenomena do not occur." It seems clear, therefore, that emotions are essential for creating and categorizing memories, and that sensations of both perception and recollection also require limbic activity. Neurologists also know that inactivation of limbic structures will produce amnesia, confusion, and automatisms.

Activation of the limbic system alone, however, is not sufficient for a true sensation of memory; the establishment of an immediate here-and-now context is also required. Without the context, the recollections remain vague and fragmentary. As Rosenfield states,

> Limbic system activity (emotions) links the ambiguous fragments of "memory" into more coherent wholes that can be related to the immediate setting. There are no symbols in the brain; there are patterns of activity, fragments, which acquire different meanings in different contexts.
>
> (Rosenfield 1988)

Within the brain it has been assumed there are one or more memory systems holding information organized in permanent categories, and that these memory systems can be brought to consciousness in ways similar to the memory searches in a computer. The processes that are responsible for our recognition of categories, however, do not seem to depend upon such fixed mechanisms. Instead, if we are to function with maximum efficiency in a constantly changing world, we must be able to react to it not in terms of previously stored and fixed images that no longer match anything in our surroundings, but in a way that will take account of the new and unexpected as well as of our individual past experiences. *What we need is not stored images, but procedures for dealing with the world as it is right now!* In other words, we need a theory of the brain that can account for how we can give a sense to stimuli in terms of their present context and our individual experiences. It is obvious that the environment doesn't teach the organism what it should know; it has to make its own sense of an ever changing, very confusing place, and there is no *specific* way in which this can be done.

Clearly what is needed is a theory of the mind and memory that can knit together the past and the present, taking into account that some schemas or modules are provided for us at birth. One such theory is that of Gerald Edelman and his concept of Neural Darwinism. Not only does this theory stress the categorical nature of recognition and its strong ties to motor activity in the form of past and present environmental exploration, but it also suggests that perception and recognition are not independent brain functions. Edelman also believes that the Darwinian principle of selection can help explain the perceptual categorizations that form the basis of memory and recognition. The selected structures, Edelman claims, are groups of neurons that react more strongly to particular groups of stimuli than to some other groups. There can, however, still be considerable overlap in the way they react to environmental stimuli. Edelman sees these neuronal groups organized into sheets called *maps*. Not only are there many interactions between various maps, but the maps are connected to both the initial sensory inputs and the motor outputs, and they also categorize information. Their most important role, however, is to restructure the past in terms of the present and, furthermore, to make perception and recognition also a part of this same unitary process.

As for the physiological basis of the storage theory of memory there has been a tendency recently to combine the three best established theories: the electric, synaptic, and molecular processes which are all triggered by repeated external stimuli. (Adams, *Consciousness, Memory: Reflections of a Biologist,* 1980) These, it seems clear, are dependent upon one another and occur in succession as follows.

First, a series of sensory impulses arranged in a frequency code start a reverberating activity in a self-stimulating circuit. The reverberating digital signals represent, as an overall effect, information stored in an analog manner. These memory traces are labile and only last for a short time.

Next, in the case of very intense, frequently repeated, or emotionally strongly motivated stimuli, the rhythmic changes in membrane potential— by a presently unknown process—accelerate the intercellular protein synthesis. The reproduction of RNA in the neurons is nonspecifically stimulated, resulting in an increased rate of protein synthesis. This process leads to an increase in the size of the synaptic interface between the cells. From the cybernetic viewpoint, this too is an analog process. Information, rather than being carried by a single neuron, is contained in the neuronal network interconnected by the synapses whose functional capacity has increased. The memory traces established this way are fairly stable.

Finally, with impulses of long duration or intensity a qualitative change in the RNA-protein system of the neuron cannot be ruled out. Similarly, in the DNA-RNA system of the genetic code, the incoming electric impulses may lead to the formation of a quantitatively different RNA. This RNA could then control the synthesis of a specific protein carrying the memory code.

The possibility of a memory code similar to the genetic code has led some theorists to postulate a uniform system of memory for the entire living world. The coding of information passed down from generation to generation seems well established and, as well, the memory system of the body's defense mechanism, i.e., the antigen-antibody reaction or the immune response which lasts a lifetime. Perhaps the genetic memory of the species is merely another aspect of a larger biological law. Time and the advance of knowledge perhaps will tell.

Although the concept of memory as procedure and perceptual categorization were implicit in the old idea of localization of function, no one questioned the existence of a number of specialized centers. It turns out that the specialized centers are actually just part of the procedures of the brain. Their activity makes sense only in terms of the activity of other centers, and the present setting in which the organism happens to be. Rosenfield, a strong supporter of Edelman's theory, has observed, "Even some of the computer simulations used in the computational approaches to brain function captured the need for procedures that can make sense of stimuli; rather than stimuli that could tell the brain or the computer what to do." (Rosenfield 1988, p. 10) Edelman, guided by fundamental biological principles, sees memory not as an exact repetition of an image in one's brain, but rather as a recategorization. And recategorizations occur when the connections between the neuronal groups in different maps are temporarily strengthened. Recategorization of objects and events depend upon motion as well as sensation, and this is a skill acquired in the course of experience. We recollect information in different contexts; this requires the activation of different maps interacting in ways that differ from those of our initial encounter with the information and this leads to its recategorization. We do not simply store images or bits; instead, we deepen and we enlarge our ability to categorize. Memory considered as recategorization is also integral to Bartlett's theory that was mentioned earlier. In 1932, Sir Frederic pointed out that remembering is not essentially different from solving everyday problems, because in each case fragments of incoming information arouse maps of interacting knowledge, resulting in a pattern of cortical activity that represents a memory or the answer to a problem— a memory or an answer that is the most relevant or consistent with the evidence. In his words:

> Remembering is not the re-excitation of innumerable fixed, lifeless and fragmentary traces. It is an imaginative reconstruction or construction, built out of the relation of our attitude towards a whole active mass of organized past reactions or experiences and to a little outstanding detail which commonly appears in image or in language form. It is thus hardly ever really exact, even in the most rudimentary cases of rote recapitulation, and it is not at all important that it should be so.
>
> (Bartlett 1964, p. 213)

Because we are not used to thinking of memory in this way—having become so inured to the idea of fixed stored images in our heads—this new look may still be hard to comprehend. Therefore, let us review what we have said so far, and use a perhaps weird analogy to make it clearer how the brain remembers.

Let us assume that right at this moment you are on the stage of a vast auditorium, and filling up the seats in front of you are hundreds of exact duplicates of yourself. Out there in the audience is one you for each and every day of your life thus far. If you were only ten years old, then there would be 10 × 365 or 3,650 "yous" sitting in the seats before you. If you were fifty years of age, there would be 18,250 "yous" looking at you up on the stage. Now let each of these duplicates represent all of the past experiences you had on that particular day of your life in the past. Each head of all the "yous" before you contains the experiences accumulated on that one particular day. Now, let us imagine that each of the "yous" has available to it all of the experiences that all of the other "yous" before it have accumulated. Only the "you" on the very first day of your life would have nothing before it to count on. Even here we do know, however, that a number of "maps" are hard-wired into our brains even while we are still in the womb. The "you" who is standing on the stage facing all of the other "yous" in the audience obviously has the greatest number of "maps" or accumulated experiences to draw on. In this vast collection of "yous" all connected to each other in a very large network of all the knowledge in your life, the major problem that the "you" on the stage has is that of retrieving what it knows from all of the "yous" with all of their maps sitting in the audience before you. Now let us imagine that in this audience of "yous" all of these independent entities are doing all of the various things that human beings do. Some are asleep, some are talking to each other about the weather, or what they ate earlier, others are watching TV or daydreaming. Suddenly someone in the wings asks the "you" on the stage, "Who is the author of the novel *Les Miserables*?" The "you" on the stage has not seen, heard, nor thought of this today or anytime within the last two years. The "you" on the stage hollers out to all the yous in the audience, "Hey, who wrote *Les Miserables*?" This question now becomes a problem for all the audience "yous" to solve. Suddenly a "you" from your grade-school days pipes up, "I know; it was Paul Muni in a movie I saw!" Another one of the high school "yous" shouts him down, "No, you fool, Muni is an actor. He wants the writer." Next one of the "yous" from your freshman year in college wakes up and says "Hey fellows, what gives?" Another "you" from last week answers, "The guy up front wants to know who wrote the novel *Les Miserables*?" The college frosh "you" speaks out, "Oh, that's easy. I had to read the damn thing in French class and the author's name was Victor something, Victor Thingamuhbob." Then a "you" from your high-school days contributes, "Well I do know he was a French writer and he was one of the big ones." "That's it," shouts the freshman "you,"—"Victor Huge, i.e., VICTOR HUGO!!!" And joy and pandemonium breaks out all across the entire audience. The parallel distributed network of independent processing units has done it again. It has recreated the author of the novel and solved the problem of who wrote that long ago read and long-forgotten book.

As Jeremy Campbell describes the process in human memory as distinct from computer memory,

> Nothing could be more unlike the digital view of a memory as a piece of information, encoded in symbols, either correct or incorrect, stored in one specific place. In a standard computer, information sits there, waiting to be used, and is the same entity while it is waiting as it is while it is being used. Something far more exotic and ethereal is going on in a connectionist network (*human brain*). The information cannot really be said to exist at all when it is not being used. It is only potential, latent, a wraith implicit in a myriad connection strengths which are simultaneously engaged in representing other kinds of information by patterns of activity. It is a ghost in the machine. . . . When that information is not in use, the pattern is nowhere present in the system. Information is not stored as data structures. The only symbols ever present in a connectionist system are active representations. . . . Memories are not stored, they are recreated over and over again in response to whatever reminds you of them. Information that is not presently active—not in use—is only in the system potentially. . . . All this means that in a connectionist network memory becomes interpretation. It is not a filing cabinet, nor a set of index cards, but a hermeneutical system. A cue that triggers a memory is a sort of puzzle that has to be solved, a riddle with multiple possible answers that must be disentangled so that the right answer pops out. The network constructs a pattern of activity that fits the cue most plausibly. . . .
>
> (Campbell 1989, pp. 163-164)

Campbell also makes the very important additional point that a machine may be able to store and manipulate a large number of facts and symbols and combine them in various ways, but if it does not know what the facts and symbols are about, and what they *mean* in terms of the real world, then the system is not *intentional* or purposive. Humans behave because they have intentions (goals and purposes) in mind, i.e., humans know what they are doing. The brain does not rely on preprogrammed representations in its processing units. It constructs representations as responses to incoming information and it develops networks and adjusts the importance of the information in such a way that it categorizes it on its own instead of letting a programmer do it for it. The brain is a device that adjusts itself to its environment or attempts to—always.

With regard to Edelman's theory, Oliver Sacks, the neurologist, observes:

Edelman's theory provides a detailed picture of how neuronal "maps" can be formed, which allow an animal to adapt (without instruction) to wholly new perceptual forms and categorizations, new orientations, new approaches to the world. This is precisely the situation in the deaf child; he is flung into a perceptual (and cognitive and linguistic) situation for which there is neither genetic precedent nor teaching to assist him; and yet, given half a chance, he will develop radically new forms of neural organization, neural mappings, which will allow him to master the language-world, and articulate it in a quite novel way. It is difficult to think of a more dramatic example of somatic selection, or neural Darwinism.

(Sacks 1989, p. 22)

Anomalies of Memory

If, as we have seen, all of our memories are recreations and are subjectively biased recreations at that—it is easy to understand why so many things can go wrong with recall and recognition. Cryptomnesia, as we have also seen, is usually defined as the revival of an experience without the attributes of memory. It is, in other words, *recall without recognition* and, as we noted, is very common particularly where integrative ideas and the solutions of problems are concerned. For most of us, cryptomnesiac experiences are everyday occurrences but we never have to face the fact that what we thought was a new or original idea we had heard somewhere else. Most of these things are so ordinary we fail to get excited about them. Although psychologists still argue about how many different kinds of memory there are, most agree the three major kinds are: *episodic* memory, which is for specific events; *semantic,* for knowledge and facts; and *implicit* memory, for skills that we exercise automatically, such as speaking, riding a bicycle, or swimming. We also know that semantic memory—the most robust— and implicit memory do not decline with age. Episodic memory, which deals with specific events, such as what you ate for breakfast yesterday, does decline somewhat with age, although not very much. Cryptomnesia is experienced most commonly, it seems, with semantic memory, i.e., in association with formal knowledge, and this is because formal knowledge is not richly personalized. Or, in terms of what we have just discussed, it has not been incorporated into as many "maps," or modules, or "yous" as other things. Therefore, its thinness does not favor an emotional sense of familiarity which is, of course, what determines recognition.

Another quite ordinary but interesting memory anomaly is that of *checking*. This shows up most commonly as our inability to remember whether we did or did not lock the door, turn off the basement light, put the butter back in the refrigerator, let the cat out, mail the letter, return the library book, etc. The result of this inability to remember is that we have to go back and "check." There are, it seems, two types of checkers: the *insightful checker* who knows that he has put the cat out before since it is a routine act. But what he can't recall is whether it was last night or *tonight* that he did it. These doubts have to do with the *temporal ordering*. The second type of checker is the type that isn't sure if it happened at all! This type has trouble with the *memory image,* and what is unsatisfactory is not *what* he recalls, but the quality of recalling itself. Whatever its cause the phenomenon of "checking" is one that is very common.

Another very fascinating and very common experience is that of *déjà vu,* a French term meaning "already seen." As typically reported, one visits a city in a foreign land for the very first time and is immediately overwhelmed with a haunting and powerful feeling of familiarity. Usually this feeling only lasts for a few seconds, but in its pathological form the sensation may be prolonged or even continuous. It is often accompanied by the sensation that you are positively certain that you know what is going to happen next. Though it has been experienced by nearly everyone at one time or another, and has even been attributed to the fact of reincarnation and the Eastern myth of "the eternal return," i.e., that the entire universe recycles itself every several billion years, the phenomenon is also often reported by psychiatric patients and is known to be associated with temporal lobe lesions and focal epilepsy. Extreme fatigue or exhaustion is also known to bring this sensation on. While attempts to explain *déjà vu* have been many and various, most see it as a failure to recall, and as a failure to remember something that we did experience before, and why we should think that we did not is considered *paramnesia.*

A first occurrence is assumed and the postulated forgetting is explained in terms of the repression of a painful or ego-threatening experience. Other explanations have been that the "first" experience took place in a dream and this is why the *déjà vu* often assumes a dream-like quality. Much more prosaic explanations involve the idea of *partial* recall, or *restricted paramnesia.* Though the individuals have never walked down this particular street before, they have walked down a number of streets having a great number of common features—so many in fact that they are reminded of them, i.e., they have partial recall. The confusion arises from our inability to construct the *whole context* of the previous experience or experiences. There is also a neurological theory that says the cerebral hemispheres may temporarily lose synchronicity. The result is that one side of the brain is receiving input, i.e., the original event, a microsecond before the other side registers the second occurrence. Reed and others prefer to deemphasize the recall aspect, and to interpret the phenomenon as an example of *false recognition.* From this aspect the question is "Why does the person think he recognizes the present situation?" not "Why isn't he able to recall where he saw it before?"

My personal experiences with the phenomenon should help to illustrate and clarify precisely how it works. During World War II I was stationed in southern France, in the Rhone River valley outside of Marseille. A fellow airman who had been an art instructor at NYU before the war took me for a Sunday drive up the valley near Arles. After several miles he pulled the jeep over at the side of the road and pointed to the landscape which included a distant hill, a valley, and a number of trees and buildings. My friend said, "Have you ever seen this before?" To my amazement I was suddenly overcome with the most powerful feeling of familiarity—the strongest *déjà vu* experience I have ever had. Of course I had never been there before, never that far up the valley, and never on that road. Yet the sense of having been there before was overpowering and I said so. My friend was delighted and returning to our barracks, he trotted out a dozen art books featuring the work of French artists and proudly showed me painting after familiar painting of the famous Mont Sainte Victoire outside of Arles. We had stood where the many artists had sat and painted the landscape, particularly Van Gogh, who creatively thrived in the region and painted the mountain several times.

A psychiatrist friend also told me about one of his patients, a young New Yorker suffering from agoraphobia. As part of his treatment, my friend would drive the young man to various parts of Manhattan and walk him across its open areas. On one occasion he took the young man to the entrance to the Holland tunnel. When they got out of the car, the young man turned to the psychiatrist and said he was undergoing an overpowering *déjà vu* experience, yet he had never been to this entrance before in his life. Looking at the tunnel, the psychiatrist burst into laughter and told his patient, "Wait till we get back to the office." On their return my friend took the patient to the waiting room and lifted from the table a large volume titled *Manhattan Views*—large color photographs of city scenery. Opening the book to one plate, my friend showed it to his patient and said, "Ever see this before?" The picture was, of course, a panoramic view of the entrance to the Holland tunnel where they had stood a few minutes earlier. The patient, waiting for his appointment, had thumbed through the picture book many times before and had seen the tunnel entrance many times.

Similarly, it is frequently reported by European travelers that on their first visit they are continuously having *déjà vu* experiences as they move from place to place. If we recall that nearly all travelers, months before they make their maiden voyage abroad, pour over travel books, travel guides, and other pictures of the places they intend to visit on arriving at their destination, we can easily understand why so many sights and places witnessed in person for the first time evoke deep feelings of great and intimate familiarity. They have, indeed, been witnessed before—but vicariously.

Another memory anomaly is *jamais vu*, the converse of *deja vu* in which the individual reports a feeling of unfamiliarity about a situation or a scene that is well known and very familiar. Because it is a much rarer phenomenon it is seldom mentioned, and while it does occur with many disturbed persons, it is rare among normal people. On occasions when a slight change has been made in a familiar room, someone might feel that something is "different," but as soon as the change has been identified, the sense of unfamiliarity disappears. It is, of course, a classic example of recall without recognition, and where cryptomnesia is a failure to recognize known ideas, *jamais vu* is a failure to recognize regularly experienced perceptions. Unlike people experiencing cryptomnesia, the *jamais vu* sufferer is fully aware of what has happened before.

Some individuals suffering from paranoia have on occasion experienced something called *l'illusion des sosies*. In this instance the paranoid person does not recognize a well-known person as being who he or she is. For example, the paranoid will agree that this woman looks, acts, and dresses like his wife but he is convinced that she is an impostor, and no amount of evidence or argument can persuade him otherwise.

Some other memory anomalies that occur in anxiety and phobic states particularly are *depersonalization* and *derealization*. In the former case the individual has a feeling of being detached from his physical self. Though aware of what he is doing, and knowing the environment is unchanged, he still feels different and unreal. In the *derealization* experience the individual feels that he is unchanged but that the environment is unreal. These sort of reports are also quite common in normal people who are subjected to great stress or fatigue, and they also can accompany the use of alcohol or drugs. Even states of elation, happiness, or stage fright can bring on feelings of depersonalization and derealization, and they are considered disorders of recognition since the crucial characteristics of familiarity and personal reference are either absent or distorted.

Déjà vu is the classic example of faulty recognition, i.e., recognition being reported in response to a situation *not* previously encountered, or a case of *false positive* responding. On the other hand, both cryptomnesia and *jamais vu* are cases of *false negatives,* i.e., no recognition in situations that *have been* previously experienced. Common experiences such as "I can remember the face but not the name" or "I know I've seen him but can't remember where" are examples of mixed recognition wherein recognition is reported but recall is fuzzy. Most psychologists believed for a long time that recall and recognition were equivalent, but differed in degree with recognition, of course, being easier. Recently, however, psychologists have shown that *recall* involves two separate mental processes—search or retrieval, and decision making, whereas *recognition* involves the decision process only.

More recently, however, Reed has shown that in terms of Bartlett's assumptions the paramnesias can be explained very easily. Anomalies of memory, whether in recall or recognition, are the product not of the input into the system, but rather of how that input is organized or schematized *within* the neuronal system. Reconstructed schemas or maps are seldom precise copies of the original input. Except in very, very familiar or repeatedly practiced tasks, the material to be recalled will undergo condensation, reordering, distortions, interpretations, or elaborations. Bartlett demonstrated that these changes are accentuated during a series of recalls or reproductions. Thus, in a series of recollections we are not recalling the original event at all, but rather our last recollection of it. The longer the series the more the remembered version will differ from the original because each further recollection will involve elaborations of the elaborations. Recognition, therefore, involves the acceptance of "a good fit," or a match of currently perceived material with the recalled, imagined material. The better the subjective match then, the more pronounced will be the accompanying sense of familiarity. So the more that the original event has been recalled or reminisced about, the more changes will have been brought in and, therefore, the weaker will be the "fit" between our current reconstruction and any re-presentation of the original. On occasions we may even fail to recognize the original because in many ways it will no longer match our reconstruction. The psychologist Belbin carried out a study confirming this in 1950. Unsuspecting subjects were left in a waiting room for two minutes; on the wall facing them was a poster. Their task was to recall later as much as they could about the poster. Control subjects in the same room for the same period of time performed an unrelated task. All subjects were much later shown the original poster and asked if it was the one they saw in the waiting room. Only four of the sixteen experimental subjects recognized it, whereas fourteen of the sixteen control group subjects did so. Conversely, it is equally possible that a feeling of familiarity could be evoked with material that differs radically from the original, assuming that the differences happen to be in line with the modifications developed during reconstruction.

Here lies the explanation for the *déjà vu* experience. Our reconstructive remembering of a street scene, for example, may provide a close match with the scene currently perceived. If we know for certain that we have never been on this particular street before, then the feeling of familiarity that comes with the match will be highly perplexing. Most likely this perplexity *is* the feeling of *déjà vu,* and it is due to the discrepancy between the objective knowledge and our subjective response in a situation of heightened affect. It is appropriate here also to recall that pieces of our past are only recognized as "memories" when linked to our emotions. It is important to remember that a number of other cognitive states or processes are accompanied by the experience of recognition or familiarity. When we meet someone new we don't ordinarily say, "Hey, I recognize that, it's a FACE!" Instead we run through a series of categorizations; for example, it's old, it's weatherbeaten, it's ruddy, it has a long nose with thin lips, it has squinty eyes, the eyebrows are white, etc. Only after all of this do we suddenly rejoice, "Hey, I recognize that old puss! Why it's old Uncle Harry! Gosh man I haven't seen you in twenty years and I hardly recognized you!" According to Reed (1979) the intensity of the familiarity is related to the level of conceptualization, the higher the level in the hierarchic organization, the more schemata have been involved. Moreover, the degree of familiarity experienced is proportional to the number of schemata or maps contributing to the match. Reed also argues that the richness of the personal quality of remembering is also a function of the level of schematic synthesis, leading to more satisfactory reintegration.

Repression and the Unconscious

We have, thus far, purposely avoided discussing the anomaly of *repression,* or the act of deliberate or purposive forgetting. According to the great novelist (and lay psychologist) Fyodor Dostoevsky, there are secrets every- one is afraid to tell, even to themselves, and every decent person has a number of such things stored away in his or her mind. Not only is the concept an emotionally loaded term, but it also is the foundation stone on which the entire structure of psychoanalysis rests. Since there is a good question as to the validity of psychoanalysis as a useful or viable system, most cognitive psychology texts ignore the subject of repression altogether. Turning to Freud we find that he defines repression as "simply in the function of rejecting and keeping something out of consciousness." (Freud 1915, p. 105)

Although many others did, Freud himself did not specifically distinguish between unconscious and conscious forms of consciousness rejection by using "repression" for the former and "suppression" for the latter. The idea has been called, however, many other names: "inhibition," "exclusion," "dis- sociation," "intentional forgetting," "removal," "resistance," "forcible repudi- ation," "defense," "censorship," and so on. The evidence for its existence is of two kinds: clinical and experimental. The clinical data is so voluminous that it would be impossible to summarize and shows up in subjects who are in therapy, subjects who are drugged, subjects under so-called hypnosis, or in subjects who with just the passage of time manage finally to remember some heretofore inaccessible and painful idea. This is, perhaps, the most straightforward proof of the concept. It has also been commonly observed that patients experience great anxiety in achieving hypermnesia of traumatic material, and struggle against recollection as, for example, in men suffering from combat neuroses. Many people have argued that the latter constitute unambiguous corroboration of the reality of repression. It is also certain that most people, inside or outside the clinical setting, can recall material they had previously excluded from consciousness in order to avoid psychic pain. It is also evident that they can remember how they rejected or expelled the memories from consciousness. We must always keep in mind, however, that we have a serious problem with all of these self-reports of "paramnesias or false reports." There is the strong and ever-present possibility that people purportedly recovering lost memories are in fact generating not memories of true events, but rather fantasies and confabulations, i.e., creations of their imagination. This is certainly the case in most of the memories uncovered from studies using so-called "hypnotic regression." Failure to recognize this possibility is a major unrecognized problem with most clinicians, doubtless because clients will frequently generate false memories which they will then proceed to believe in themselves. Freud himself was trapped by many of his early patients' hyperamnesias of infantile seductions, which led to his hurried theory of hysteria which he had to recant in short order. As Erdelyi and Goldberg (1979) note:

> Hypnotic hyperamnesias are similarly suspect. . . . Those not inclined to dismiss reincarnation out of hand may well have to contend with time travel or clairvoyance as well, for experiments have shown (Kline 1958; Rubenstein & Newman 1954) that subjects imaginatively responding to hypnotic suggestions will confidently recall events not only from the past but from the future as well. As Bernheim used to warn his students, "when a physician employs hypnosis with a patient it is wise always to be. aware who may be hypnotizing whom."
>
> (p. 370)

As noted earlier, even Penfield's dramatic hypermnesia brought on by temporal lobe stimulation turned out in many cases to have been highly elaborate fantasies. It is also, of course, most difficult, if not impossible, to obtain independent verification of the memories. Even when this is done it is often impossible to determine whether the subject is actually *recalling* more or merely *reporting* more. What we desperately need is some ESP or clairvoyance so we can read our clients' minds!

On the experimental laboratory side, studies of word-associations, memories for unpleasant or anxiety-provoking events, the issue of perceptual defense and the question of whether perceptual defense is or is not the same thing as repression, and hypnotic studies of intentional forgetting—all have been remarkably inconclusive and have led Erdelyi and Goldberg to conclude with regard to work in this area:

> Ponderous experiments, bristling with technical competence, continue to be churned out at an ever greater pace, fostering the illusion of a scientific enterprise. . . . The laboratory data tend to prove nothing anymore; they are mere anecdotes from Shakespeare or some telling case. The pathetic faddishness of contemporary cognitive psychology, remarkably unremarked, is the clearest proof of the breakdown of its methodological underpinnings. Roughly every five years (the approximate lifespan of the average graduate student), the "facts" of the field change. Short-term memory is in, short-term memory is out; imagery is a true phenomenon, no its an epiphenomenon; psycholinguistics is in, psycholinguistics is out; depth of processing is the new metaphor of information processing, but by the time that this chapter appears in print, it will already ring with time.
>
> (p. 385)

Nevertheless, out of the experimental chaos of claim and counter-claim we can confidently conclude that people do reject information from awareness on a selective basis, that people do tend to avoid aversive or unpleasant stimuli and situations, that people do work to defend themselves against pain, and that there are a number of psychological processes that do occur outside of our immediate awareness. All of these processes can result, at a later date, in the production of memories that appear to be not memories at all, but experiences that are fresh and new and have never been encountered before.

The topic of cryptomnesia cannot be abandoned, however, without raising another fascinating possibility. Lewis Jones, an English skeptic, has suggested that many of the claims of inability to remember are fraudulent (1990), especially those memories that suddenly appear when the subject is supposedly "hypnotized." Since it is now well known that no such state of awareness as "hypnosis" exists, all such claims of cryptomnesia—all "hidden" memories suddenly emerging when the narrator is "hypnotized"—are particularly suspect. In such cases it is highly likely that the subject does remember the event but, for one reason or another, does not want to admit it. Jones suggests that in the case of Dr. Reima Kampman's subject—the innkeeper's daughter who sang "The Summer Song" (Summer Is Icumen In), but had no memory of ever having learned it—the most parsimonious explanation is that she either knew the song, or at the very least she remembered coming across it. The fact that she said she "had no memory of ever having heard the words or the music" is not convincing. The only evidence we have that this is true is the subject's own word—a very questionable and unreliable source.

Similarly, in the case of Virginia Tighe's Bridey Murphy, Mrs. Tighe is using the same loophole when she insists that she has no memory of where the information about Bridey and all the other folks in the old country came from. In Jones's words, "You can't be held responsible for what's in your subconscious." Can you? Again, in the case of Bloxham's Jane Evans, we have the same possibility. Jones argues:

> How do we know that Jane Evans knew nothing of Jacques Coeur, nothing of Carausius and his times and nothing of the massacre of the Jews at New York? Simply that Jane Evans in her unhypnotized state was adamant. . . . Harris (1986) claims that Jane Evans inevitably has the ability to subconsciously store vivid accounts, though he doesn't present any evidence for preferring this explanation over simply reproducing the information from memory. I find it ominous that Graham Huxtable proved unable to help in any constructive way, while Jane Evans flatly refused to cooperate. We all at times come up with bits of information that we didn't realize we had absorbed, but I find it totally implausible that subjects should have totally forgotten the acquisition of every single detail of their often lengthy and intricate accounts.
>
> (Jones, personal correspondence, 1990)

Since it is, admittedly, singularly difficult to determine the truth and almost impossible to know when someone is or is not lying, we are left on the horns of a dilemma: Was the *source* of a person's memories truly remembered or not? If people say they know something but *don't know* how or why they know it, it is, literally, impossible for us to prove that they *do know*. In such situations what we can do is examine the claimant's motives, study the situation they are in, and look at all of the relevant background factors that could play a role in the act of telling the truth or lying. If the claimant has little or nothing to gain from being deceitful and has a prior history of honest behavior, we can place some trust—some credence—in his or her claims of unknown or forgotten sources of the memory.

If, on the other hand, the claimant has much to gain by insisting the source was unknown—as in the case of a plagiarized song or a plot for a novel—then the probabilities are clearly on the side of an act of prevarication.

3

Planetary Voyages: Then and Now

"I think all psychical researchers should devote themselves to the unmasking of the crooks and tricksters proliferating in this field. . . ."

"And if they find something that they consider genuine?" Anatole France was asked.

"Then they should be investigated themselves. . . ," laughed the great writer.

—Paul Tabori, *Pioneers of the Unseen*

Spiritism (*or assumption that certain phenomena are due to the intervention of dead spirits*) as I understand it, is a complete error.

—Theodore Flournoy, *Spiritism & Psychology*

Ever since man looked to the heavens on dark nights and saw a number of bright moving points of light that returned night after night and named these wonders "planets," he has wondered what life on these worlds might be like and what forms of life they might hold. Frustrated perhaps, because he could not visit them physically, he decided to visit them mentally— using his imagination. One of the first visitors who travelled to the planets in a trance-like condition was the Swedish seer Emmanuel Swedenborg (1688-1772). In a sense Swedenborg was also the first spiritualist in that those who went before him did not commune with the spirits of departed men. In April of 1744, however, in an altered state of consciousness, Swedenborg wandered in the spirit world and conversed with its inhabitants as freely as with the living. It was Swedenborg who bridged the gap between life and death and insisted that death brings no immediate change, and that the spirit world is a mere counterpart of this world below. During his many trips to the spirit world, Swedenborg also visited the various planets and described conditions there. According to him, the people of Mars are the best in the universe. Not only are they God-fearing, but the Lord sometimes walks among them. With Martians, physiognomy is an expression of thought and they judge each other by it.

The Venusians, however, come in two types: some are gentle and benevolent, while the others are wild, cruel, and of gigantic stature. The latter Venusians are evil, and live by robbing and plundering, whereas the former are kind and gentle and worship the good. To them the Lord often appears in their own form.

Inhabitants of the Moon are small, the same size as children six or seven years of age, yet they have the strength of fully grown men. Moon people have voices that roll like thunder with a sound that wells up from their bellies because of the moon's radically different atmosphere—completely unlike that of the other planets.

Though Swedenborg was the first, he was—by no means—the best of the spiritualists. That honor belongs exclusively to Mademoiselle Helene Smith (1861–1929), the pseudonym of Catherine Elise Muller of Geneva whose mediumistic travels were made internationally famous by the Swiss psychologist Professor Theodore Flournoy in his brilliant work *From India to the Planet Mars* (1899). Flournoy not only analyzed, but also convincingly disproved Helene Smith's supernormal claims. Were it not for this debunking, Mademoiselle Smith would, undoubtedly, have been acclaimed as the greatest medium who ever lived, and the first person to establish intelligent communication with Mars. Moreover, in so doing she also revealed the language and the writings of the red planet's inhabitants. Helene was also a woman of considerable physical beauty.

According to Flournoy,

> I found the medium in question to be a beautiful woman about 30 years of age, tall, vigorous, of a fresh, healthy complexion, with hair and eyes almost black, of an open and intelligent countenance, which at once evoked sympathy. She evinced nothing of the emaciated or tragic aspect which are habitually ascribed to the sybils of tradition, but wore an air of health, of physical and mental vigour, very pleasant to behold and which, by the way, is not often encountered in those who are good mediums.
>
> (Flournoy 1963, pp. 1–2)

Helene's father, a merchant, was a Hungarian who had a remarkable gift for language; her mother had occasional visions, but showed no other mediumistic talent. As a young girl Helene was fond of daydreaming and she also saw multitudes of brightly colored landscapes, animal figures carved of stone—a lion with a mutilated head on one occasion—statuary on pedestals, and so forth. The visions left her vaguely unhappy and discontented, and she secretly fancied herself of royal birth. Once she even asked her parents if she really was their child. When she was in her early teens, she saw a bright light filled with strange and wonderful creatures shining on the wall of her room.

In the winter of 1891–1892 it seems a friend lent Helene Smith a copy of Leon Denis's book *d'Apres la Mort (After Death)*, and after reading the book she became fascinated by spiritualism and joined one of the neighborhood groups. During the second séance she attended, she saw her hand move automatically, and then the table moved, and she knew from this moment on she had mediumistic powers. In April of 1892 Helene made contact through *typtology,* i.e., reception of message through table-tapping, with a spirit who claimed that he was Victor Hugo, and that he was Helene's guide and protector. His reign as protector and control lasted for approximately six months when suddenly another control named Leopold showed up and begin to struggle with Hugo for dominance. The fight for control of Helene lasted for nearly a year before Leopold won and completely ousted the novelist. Leopold was most adept at forcing Helene into trances. With Leopold in charge, Helene was at the peak of her mediumistic powers. Not only did she evince telekinetic powers, but she produced strange reports, found lost objects, predicted future events, saw spirit visitors, clairaudiently heard their names, and received the explanation of her visions by means of powerful table raps.

Her mediumistic skill improved and her fame spread. Then in the winter of 1894–1895 a stubbornly rational professor of psychology at the University of Geneva heard about her prowess, and being very skeptical nevertheless got himself admitted to her circle. For the next five years Flournoy attended her séances, which she also gave for several other members of the Geneva Society For Psychic Studies.

In describing Helene's triple mediumship—visual, auditive, and typtological—Flournoy was very impressed and he admitted:

Speaking for myself alone I was greatly surprised to recognize in scenes which passed before my eyes events which had transpired in my own family prior to my birth. Whence could the medium, whom I had never met before, have derived the knowledge of events belonging to a remote past, of a private nature, and *utterly unknown to any living person*?

(Flournoy 1963, p. 2)

Upon later analyses, however, it became clear that Helene did have access to information about Flournoy's ancestry, and the remaining material was due to her skill as a "cold reader," i.e., using vague general statements and having the client himself tell you what you need to know.

During the séances, Flournoy became good friends with Leopold, who also claimed to be the spirit of Guiseppe Balsamor, alias Cagliostro. Everyone—except Flournoy—believed this although Flournoy did admit "it would be impossible to imagine a being more independent and more different from Mlle. Smith herself." When Leopold wrote with Helene's hand, she held the pen in a different way and her handwriting differed significantly from her usual style, and when he spoke through her he had a deep bass voice with an Italian accent.

Flournoy was not fooled, however, and said "there is no reason to suspect the real presence of Joseph Balsamor behind the automatisms of Mlle. Smith." Moreover, he was able to trace Leopold's origins to a trauma Helene had suffered when she was ten years old and was attacked by a large dog. She was rescued by the miraculous appearance of a man in a long brown robe with a white cross and flowing sleeves who chased the dog away and disappeared before she could thank him. According to Leopold, this was his first appearance. Helene also said that Leopold always showed up anytime she was in danger. Further investigation on Flournoy's part uncovered a number of discrepancies between Leopold and Cagliostro. Leopold did not know any Italian, and refused to answer if anyone addressed him in his language. His handwriting was not at all like that of Cagliostro. He was unfamiliar with critical facts about his own life, and he could not furnish a single name, date, or precise fact about it. His answers were always evasive and vague, and his therapeutic skills were minimal and antiquated. His love for Helene was only, he claimed, a continuation of what Cagliostro had for Marie Antoinette.

And it was Marie Antoinette who composed the first of Helene's four major romantic cycles: the Royal Cycle, the Oriental Cycle, the Martian Cycle, and, finally, the Religious Cycle. The Marie Antoinette romance was outlined in séances beginning in December 1893. At one o'clock, on 30 January 1894, Helene Smith announced that she was the reincarnation of Marie Antoinette, although she earlier had claimed to be the reincarnation of one of Dumas's fictional characters. Upon learning that character was fictional, Helene dropped the claim. When Helene was Marie the queen, she put on a good show, but not nearly as fanciful as her next reincarnation during the Hindu dream in which Flournoy himself played a major role.

This Oriental Cycle began on 16 October 1894, and the Martian romance started at this time as well. In the Oriental Cycle Helene was Simandini— the daughter of a sixth-century Arab chief who was married to Prince

Sivrouka. According to Helene, Flournoy was his reincarnation. After many years of married life, Simandini was burned alive on her husband's funeral pyre. In acting out her role as the princess, Helene spoke Hindustani and wrote a few words in Arabic, a language she couldn't speak.

Flournoy could find no historical record of either Sivrouka or Simandini, and he was baffled as to where Helene had obtained this knowledge because he was convinced her séances were nothing more than "a resurrection of latent memories and faded daydreams." Yet he was forced to admit that the precise historical information given by Leopold and the language spoken by Simandini defied normal explanation. Then one day Flournoy came across a six-volume history of ancient India written by De Marles. Lo and behold it contained all of the information found in Helene's oriental fantasies. Although De Marles was considered to be a very unreliable historian, it was clear this was the source of Helene's information.

While the Oriental Cycle was fascinating, the Martian romance was by far the most impressive of the four. In November 1894, the spirit of the entranced medium journeyed to Mars. Not only did she visit there nightly and describe the human, faunal, and floral life of the plain, but she supported her story by speaking and writing in the Martian language. For example, "Dode ne ci houdan te mess Astane ke de me vedi" meant "This is the house of the great man Astane, whom thou hast seen."

Helene, floating through a dense, technicolored fog—a sequence common to the hypnotic, so-called "trance"—saw strange moving vehicles without horses or wheels that emitted sparks as they glided over the landscape. She also saw houses with fountains on their roofs, a bridge with transparent sides, and a man carrying an instrument that enabled him to fly. After Flournoy patiently analyzed Helene's alphabet and vocabulary, he concluded its source dated back to her childhood, that the language bore a strong structural resemblance to her native French, and that her Martians acted much too earth-like. As for the language, Sanskrit professors at the Sorbonne supported Flournoy's conclusions and showed how all except two percent of Helene's Martian words were derivable from known words in French. "All things become wearisome at last," Flournoy reported, "and the planet Mars is no exception." Flournoy was tired of her extraterrestrial flights although Helene was not. Nonplussed, she dipped into her subconscious and took off for a still more distant planet, Uranus. When Flournoy told her he considered her subconscious construction of the Martian language infantile and her descriptions childish, she really let her imagination go and came up with highly grotesque descriptions of the Uranians and a Uranian language totally different from Martian, and with apparently no relationship to any other earthly dialects. Flournoy was impressed not with her creations but with her extraordinary feats of memory. On one occasion he remarked:

No one dares tell her that her great invisible protector is only an illusory apparition, another part of herself, a product of her subconscious imagination; not that the strange peculiarities of her mediumistic communications—the Sanskrit, the recognizable signatures of deceased persons, the thousand correct revelations of facts unknown to her—are but old forgotten memories of things which she saw or heard in her childhood.

(Flournoy 1963, p. 44)

This process of remembering long forgotten experiences Flournoy named *Cryptomnesia,* i.e., *crypto* (hidden) and *mnesia* (memories).

Flournoy did not stop with pointing out that all of Helene's controls were merely secondary personalities, and that the source of her incarnation dreams could be found in her reading of the work of Allan Kardec, the popular reincarnationist. Flournoy also questioned the supernormal character of all of the rest of her fantasies. "As to the Supernormal," he said, "I believe I have actually found a little telekineses and telepathy.* As to lucidity and spiritistic messages, I have only encountered some brilliant reconstructions, which the hypnoid imagination, aided by latent memory, excels in fabricating in the case of mediums."

Additional investigative work on the part of Flournoy turned up further naturalistic explanations of Helene's visionary productions with the end result that in the summer of 1900 Flournoy was no longer welcome at her séances. As a result of Flournoy's account of Helene's phenomenal productions in *From Here to the Planet Mars* (1901), she was inundated with letters and requests for spiritualistic sittings. A wealthy American lady provided her with a lifetime income so Helene could quit her job at a commercial house since none of her sittings provided any income.

There later was a Lunarian phase in Helene's Planetary cycle, which was also accompanied by descriptions of moon people, a lunar language, and writing. It, like the Uranian, differed little, syntactically, from her native French. The origin of the strange notion of moon people came most likely from Helene's reading of a piece about herself in *La Paix Universelle,* in which mention was also made about a group of Yogins who made psychic visits to the inhabitants of the dark side of the moon.

The Planetary cycle was, however, short-lived, and was replaced thereafter by Helene's departure from the world of séances and her entry into a religious cycle in which Christ, the Virgin Mary, the Apostles, and the Archangels played dominant roles.

In 1903 Helene had a luminous vision in which Christ appeared, and the voice of Leopold told her to draw what she had seen. Two years later

---

*Flournoy didn't really know any better at the time.

Helene began to work with crayons and oil, and in a series of trance states she began to paint a number of religious tableaus. Although some of her mediumistic communicants told her she was the reincarnation of Raphael and Michelangelo, she never really believed it. This was just as well because her artistic productions left much to be desired.

In addition to Emmanual Swedenborg and Flournoy's Helene Smith, a number of other mediums and psychics quickly got into the act. In 1813 a fifteen-year-old German somnambulist, Fraülein Romer, was seized by convulsions and turned into a medium who, while travelling in clairvoyance, was led by the spirits of dead relatives and the spirit of a living friend, Louise, to the moon. The Fraülein described the moon's flora, fauna, and its inhabitants, as well as the spirits of the dead who spend their first stage of existence there as they progress to higher and higher spheres. Andrew Jackson Davis, the great American spiritualist, followed in the steps of Swedenborg, and in Davis's book *Divine Revelations and A Voice To Mankind* published in 1847, Davis talked about *nine* planets well before the ninth planet Pluto was discovered in 1933. On the other hand, he named only four planetoids of which there are now reckoned to be hundreds. Saturn, Davis believed, was inhabited by a more advanced form of humanity, while Jupiter and Mars were inhabited by human-like creatures. On Venus and Mercury human beings were less advanced, and the three outermost planets were, of course, lifeless.

Victorien Sardon, in his mental voyages, drew automatic sketches of houses and scenes of the planet Jupiter. Jacob, the Zouave, created drawings of strange fruits and flowers which he said grew on the planet Venus. Thomas Lake Harris, in his work *Celestial Arcana,* described the inhabitants of other planets of the solar system and also of some of the more remote fixed stars. He reported his conversations with these creatures, and he further peopled space with Aromal worlds, which are generally associated with some of the material worlds, or suns, although they do not form any part of them.

In August of 1895 an American, Mrs. Smead, told of her visits to the planets Mars and Jupiter and gave detailed descriptions of planetary life which rivaled those of Helene Smith. Mrs. Smead was actually the pseudonym of Mrs. Willis M. Cleaveland who occasionally practiced planchette writing and in 1895 began a series of systematic experiments.

In August of that same year during her séances, several references were made to the planets Mars and Jupiter. These references it was believed were due to the appearance of an article by Professor Lowell in the *Atlantic Monthly* about canals on the planet Mars. According to Mrs. Smead, Jupiter was the "babies' heaven," and she drew maps of Jupiter's surface. Over the next few sittings Mrs. Smead drew maps of Mars and identified in

Martian the various geographical zones of Mars. Then, for a five-year period, nothing more was heard from her. In September 1900 the Martian communications returned. Martian men, boats, houses, and flowers were drawn, given Martian names, and written and described in hieroglyphic characters. Some of Smead's sketches were clever—a self-winding double clock—but others like a Martian airship were pedestrian and unconvincing. Many of her drawings and descriptions were similar to those of Helene Smith, and caused Flournoy to remark that "the Martian revelation of Mrs. Smead present the same character of puerility and naive imagination as those of Mlle. Smith." Undoubtedly the psychological basis of her claims was also the same.

Even fraudulent mediums got into the act. Isaac Funk told the story of a medium who impersonated a "lady eight-feet tall from the planet Mars through the use of a wire bust covered with rubber and a false face." This disguise was arranged to fit snugly on the medium's shoulders and when in use it was inflated with air. When not in use, it folded into a small easily concealed package.

Since Mars is not only close to Earth, but during the heyday of spiritualism was described by Schiaparelli, etc., as having its surface covered with markings which were obviously canals, and thus the planet had to be a harbor for intelligent life. Therefore, the number of mediums who sprinkled the red planet with people like us was considerable. In 1916 Eva Harrison's *Wireless Messages From Other Worlds* even went so far as to introduce planetary visitors from the constellation Orion. The New York medium George Valiantine predicted in the 1920s that Martians would visit Earth long before we got around to visiting them. Finally, Dr. Mansfield Robinson, working through the medium Mrs. James and her trance control Oumaruru, also was able to obtain a Martian alphabet and other fascinating facts about life on the red planet from his trance excursions.

Modern Visits: ESP and Remote Viewing

Mental travel to other planets is also common in our time. Rather than waiting for the space shuttle, the space station, and the government's progressive but much too slow *Mars mission,* many psychics in our time prefer to travel by mind rather than by rocket. Only a few years ago Charles Fair proposed a quite sensible test for believers in ESP. Fair proposed to Jose Silva that a group of Silva graduates get together and project their thoughts to the planet Mars, examine it, and compile a report describing in detail what they had seen there. Copies of the report would be filed with NASA, the *New York Times,* and the Library of Congress. If the data matched the findings made on subsequent conventional spaceflights, ESP would have proved itself, and this would open up a whole universe for study by teams of scientifically trained swamis operating from alpha or theta states. Silva, of course, would go down in history as a scientist greater than Newton. Although Jose Silva expressed some interest in the idea, other mind control graduates did not. NASA stated that some *sub rosa* work along these lines was being tolerated but it was, officially, denied. While NASA scientists are generally too busy for such nonsense, there is the issue of NASA's hard-headed scientific image to protect. When it is already difficult enough to wheedle money from congressmen who think any and all outer space research is a boondoggle anyway, asking for mental rockets would be the back-breaking straw!

Some of the nation's most patriotic psychics have gone ahead anyway with their psychic voyages of exploration despite a lack of financial support. One of the most dedicated, as well as imaginative, has gone well beyond Hoagland's *Monuments of Mars* and has buried her mind in the Martian sands. In her awesome book *Mars Underground Cities Discovered By Cosmic Visionary,* the psychic Ruth Norman, assisted by Thomas Miller, having visited and lived among them portrays the Martians as a technologically and spiritually developed people. There are no sad or weary faces among these five-and-a-half-foot tall beings, whom she describes as having jet black hair and dark eyes, while all along we had assumed citizens of the red planet would have red hair. According to Norman, the Martians live in peace with each other and share everything they have. In her words, "The exotic beauty, the heavenly loveliness related herein, all does express the love and harmonious life of the Martian people, who have created all this beauty." One of Norman's New Age reviewers stated, "I personally haven't decided what I believe about life existing on Mars, but I love the other worldly pictures that this book paints." As you might surmise, the book was privately published by the author in 1989, and can be had by writing to her at 145 S. Magnolia Avenue in El Capon, California 92020-4522 and sending her $8.95 plus $2 more for postage and handling.

In our day, however, two of the strangest and most unusual mental trips to distant planets were made by George Adamski (his real name) and Kirk Allen (a pseudonym).

Adamski was born in Poland in 1891 and emigrated to the U.S. with his parents when he was almost two. Settling in Dunkirk, New York, his very religious parents raised George to have a deep respect for nature and her laws, and despite Adamski's intellectual brilliance his parents could not afford to send him to college. In 1913 Adamski enlisted in the army and served with the 13th Cavalry on the Mexican border, receiving an honorable discharge in 1919. In 1917 he married, and for many years after he had a number of different jobs in various parts of the country. Nearing age forty, Adamski settled down in Laguna Beach, California, and through the 1920s he began to lecture and teach what he called "the universal laws of man and nature," winning air time on radio station KFOX in Long Beach and on KMPC in Los Angeles. After one of his students gave him a six-inch reflecting telescope, Adamski began to study the heavens and take photographs. It was during this period that George photographed his first UFO in outer space. Unfortunately, it was so far out that no one could identify it.

According to D. Scott Rogo, Adamski admitted to one of Rogo's friends that he had taken up "this saucer business" because the end of prohibition had put a stop to the profit from his religious cult. The cult had made religious (and opportune) use of alcohol legal and Adamski had cashed in on the profit! (Rogo 1977, p. 113)

In 1940 Adamski and a few of his students moved near Palomar Mountain and set up a small farming center. During the war, Adamski served as an air raid warden. Selling the center in 1944, Adamski moved to the base of Mt. Palomar itself, bought a fifteen-inch telescope, and built a small observatory. During the meteorite shower of 1946, Adamski and his friends spotted a large cigar-shaped craft hanging motionless in the sky at fairly close range. Then in 1947 Adamski, his wife, and a few other students watched a group of UFOs for over an hour. Shortly thereafter Adamski co-authored his first book with Desmond Leslie titled *Flying Saucers Have Landed,* in which Adamski describes his encounter with a UFO on the ground in November 1952. Adamski also produced a photograph of the UFO, complete with a dome, four portholes, and a type of ball-like landing gear. Many people observing the photograph remarked that the UFO looked amazingly like a "lampshade." Impervious to any and all criticism, Adamski insisted he had talked to the living, human-like occupants of the spacecraft. Soon after, Adamski began to take free rides with his new friends, the Space Brothers. There were three of them in particular who became his friends—a Martian called Firkon, a Saturnian called Ramu, and a Venusian named Orthon. In his second book, *Inside The Space Ship* (1955), Adamski describes a trip with his three extraterrestrial friends aboard a Venusian scout ship, which soon joins the mother ship—like an aircraft landing on an aircraft carrier—where he meets other Venusians including Kalua, a beautiful, diminutive blonde, and Ilmuth, a taller but gorgeous brunette. Later, George Adamski encounters another Saturnian scout and a Saturnian mother ship, and a group of wise beings called Masters, along with some superscientific laboratories. During his travels, Adamski visits the moon, and when they approach the side never seen from Earth, George sees snow-topped mountains, lakes and rivers, stands of heavy timber, and communities of various sizes. Not only is the moon heavily populated, but the people live there pretty much like we do here on Earth. Later on, Adamski claimed he visited Venus and walked through beautiful Venusian gardens. In 1953 he claimed he visited Mars and Saturn as well.

As amazing as this nonsense appears, what is even more incredible is the fact that some people took it seriously, and some members of the UFO community years later argued seriously that some elements of Adamski's paranoid fantasies should be given credence. After all, they argue, for some of his sightings he did have witnesses! Adamski, following the publication of his books, went on tour promoting his work and telling of his unearthly adventures. In Louisville in the late 1950s I had an opportunity to attend one of his lectures. Anyone familiar with the seriously mentally disturbed would have recognized immediately that Adamski was not in full possession of his faculties. After maintaining he had walked through beautiful Venusian gardens, in the subsequent question and answer session I asked him, "Mr. Adamski, have your feet fully healed?" He answered, "I don't know what you mean." "Well," I replied, "since scientists tell us the surface temperature of the planet Venus is well over 470° Fahrenheit, your feet must have been very badly burned." "Don't be ridiculous," he snapped. To which I replied, "I'm not. You are."

Amazingly, Hilary Evans in his excellent work *Gods-Spirits-Cosmic Guardians* raises the possibility that there could have been some "substance to the original experience." Had Evans had the opportunity to meet Mr. Adamski, this possibility would never have entered his mind, although in his earlier work, *Visions-Apparitions—Alien Visitors,* Evans states that Adamski "gives us good reason to doubt his word . . . the truth is probably more complex." That many other individuals took Adamski's fantasies seriously and saw him as a visionary only attests to the naivete and strong "will-to-believe" idiosyncrasies of other uneducated and unsophisticated believers such as the truly amazing Laura Mundo, author of the most incredible tome in the annals of UFOlogy, her own privately published *The Mundo UFO Report* (1982). To convey the flavor of its contents three samples picked at random should suffice:

> The space people have said that no sighting is accidental, but is part of Pre-Being's Plan to remove those Earth people whom they can to safety before the sunspot peak. The purpose of this is to bring the universal honor system to this planet, among Earth survivors.
>
> It may be possible that space people are not scheduled by Pre-Atomic Energy Being (beyond the center of all atoms) through Prime Atomic Energy Being (the center of all atoms) (see atomic illustrations in front of book)

to fly over the UFO observation ranch of Project Starlight International. But their intellectual egos would never consider that possibility.

Earthmen's method is to try to prove something by trying to disprove it, because their negative intellectual infrared electronic minds are overvibrating in most instances. In some other instances, the positive ultrablue protonic mind is overvibrating so that everything is believed without question. These are opposite polarities of the conscious-mind blend. The highest and third perceptive neutronic polarity is not yet able to be very active in many Earth people's conscious mind blend, as with the space people, but getting there in spite of that!

(pp. 92–93)

Desmond Leslie (who is a spaceman, if ever there was one) had an American grandmother, Jenny Jerome, who was Sir Winston Churchill's mother, which made them cousins. Leslie told me that Churchill, whom he of course knew personally, believed that flying saucers were advanced ships from outer space but never told anyone publicly for fear of being ridiculed. (He would have it to do over.) The British Air Marshal, Lord Dowding, head of their Air Force during the battle of Britain, did speak out. Leslie talked with him, also, about UFOs which he discussed publicly. Their pilots, like the United States pilots, had seen too many saucers for anyone to be able to deny them, convincingly.

Prince Philip of England, whom Leslie knows personally, told him be believes in them, too. In fact, he has a map or chart in his private suite at Windsor Castle on the wall into which he sticks brightly colored pins, locating sightings over England as they are reported. He looks forward to meeting more advanced space people sometime, he says. He might be one, himself. Elizabeth is too busy being the Queen.

Queen Juliana of the Netherlands, however, had George Adamski come to visit her because she felt there was too much to the flying saucer reports to disregard them all. Perhaps the space people will land openly in Holland or England first.

(p. 120)

As I have written, the high frequency electrons from the atmosphere and outer space used by the space people to propel the ships from other planets are downpulling. The higher frequency protons are up-pulling, and the highest radiant neutrons are stabilizing and can do both, in balance, and go forward and backwards and at angles as well. Otherwise the ships would be attracted down by gravity of a planet too quickly, and get out of control when in a planet's atmosphere or continue to go up into the atmosphere and out into space.

At the animate or living level, electrons and positrons (the positive electron) attract each other, also, just like two metal magnets of opposite polarities do. The male is predominantly electronic (aggressive, negative), the female, predominantly positronic (receptive or passive/positive), as a rule. The polarities also repel at times (or one switches), as even within marriage, at which time both polarities can become the same, temporarily (and sometimes even permanently), and repel, which unfortunately Earth marriage counselors do not know nor do physicists. On the other planets, however, mates do not change partners as rapidly as they are doing on this planet presently. As polarities reverse and repel instead of attract, more and more as the sunspots accelerate because the space people know what is happening. Earthmates fall victim to this shifting, and lose total objectivity, often, rather than go into neutral corners of the house, like boxers in the ring, or have temporary separations with understanding, even just writing notes to each other within the home.

In the first place, also, the female's loving positive positrons and the male's negative willful electrons are in better balance to each other on the other planets, where their highest wise, neutral neutronic selves-minds-bodies can hold balance; their atmosphere more balanced.

There is no battle of the sexes!

(pp. 109–110)

What else can possibly be said? *The Mundo UFO Report* must be read to be believed!

One of the most fascinating mental voyages of all time, however, was taken by Kirk Allen, the young physicist hero of Robert Lindner's story in his book *The Fifty-Minute Hour* (1955). Working in a highly classified, tightly secure, atomic energy installation in the Southwest, Allen failed to show up for work on several occasions to the chagrin of his supervisors. Since no one could leave the installation, there was a mystery of where he *could* possibly be. It seems Allen claimed he lived on another planet part of the time. Lindner, an excellent psychiatrist, was hired to help Allen out. Lindner found that Allen—to all appearances—was a perfectly average, clear-eyed, charming, and pleasant young man who looked like a junior executive. Kirk Allen had an unusual childhood and was raised by a Hawaiian nurse on an island without other white children. Because Kirk was fourteen before he saw another boy or girl like himself, this led to a sense of mental estrangement later on in his life. Allen was also seduced by an older nymphomaniacal governess when he was in his teens. As a social isolate he turned to books and read everything he could in print. Many of the things he read he considered to be written about him personally. They were *his* biographies. When he entered the university at nineteen, he became attracted to and interested in science. Gradually his fantasy life grew until he became convinced that some of the science fiction books he read had been composed in the future and sent back into the present for his personal instruction. This made it possible for Kirk Allen to live a current life, and also to *remember the future.* Becoming bored with this way of thinking he began to imagine a future for himself and then to believe in it. One night when he was working on a map of a planet he had explored in another galaxy, in trying to recall what the terrain looked like he suddenly found himself the Lord of a planet, in an interplanetary empire, in a distant universe, dressed for the role and in his office! He felt he had discovered the secret of teleportation. From this night on Kirk Allen spent more and more time being Kirk Allen of the future and living this future life. In a few Earth minutes he lived a year or more on the distant planet.

As Lindner saw it, the chief difficulty was that Allen saw himself as completely normal, although he was totally convinced of the reality of his life on the distant future world. He admitted his experiences were extra-ordinary, but he believed they were due to some unknown psychic ability or quality with which he had been endowed. Lindner points out that for the most part psychotics are aware of their disturbances because either they suffer somehow through them, or they are made to suffer for them by others. In only the rarest circumstance does a mentally afflicted person escape suffering and, hence, an acute knowledge of his own disorder. But this was Kirk Allen's problem, and moreover his very life was sustained by his madness. This not only made his case more difficult to handle, but it left Lindner with little to go on. Since every psychosis is a life-saving maneuver on the part of the victim, and is the victim's way of resolving the conflict between the world and himself, in most cases there remains some area of life that—through therapy or otherwise—can be made to yield satisfactions comparable to those available to the victim through his madness. In Kirk Allen's case it seemed to Lindner there wasn't any other outlet. Nothing could compete with the unending gratification furnished by Allen's fantasy. Allen had trunks filled with the records of his life on distant worlds. There were 12,000 pages of typescript making up his biography. Appended to these pages were 2,000 more of handwritten notes, plus hundreds of other scraps of paper covered with jottings. There was also a glossary of over 100 pages, 82 full color maps, 23 planetary bodies in four projections, 31 of land masses on these planets, 161 architectural sketches, 12 genealogical tables, an 18 page description of the galactic system containing Kirk Allen's home planet, plus a 200-page history of the empire that Allen ruled, plus a series of 44 folders from two to twenty pages each dealing with some aspect of the planet over which Kirk Allen ruled. These covered in complete and complex detail every conceivable aspect of life on this imaginary world—creatures, biology, sociology, anthropology, genetics, and the chemistry of strange life forms on this imaginary world.

Therapy began in a situation where Allen was assured of his sanity and regarded Lindner and his efforts as a joke. Allen felt also that his very life was dependent on his keeping his psychosis. Carefully, in slow step-by-step fashion, Lindner was able to uncover all of the factors in Allen's past that brought about the gigantic fantasy. This analysis took a year, and at the end Lindner felt he still had made no progress. Rather than admit failure, Lindner decided that the best way to separate Allen from his madness would be for Lindner himself to enter the fantasy.

By participating in the psychosis Lindner finally found himself so immersed in it that he was becoming obsessed and taking Allen's fantasy seriously himself! Finally, Allen confessed that he had made all of it up and that for many weeks he had been pretending because he thought Lindner wanted him to continue with the fantasy. Lindner's ploy had worked and Allen had abandoned his fantasy once and for all. For a while though Lindner actually did doubt his own stability.

Kirk Allen's type of madness is far more common than most people are aware of and, like in Allen's case, would never have been noticed had it not interfered with his work. Had he not been under such tight surveillance, his fantasy could have continued unnoticed and unchecked for years.

A classic and chilling example of a much more serious psychosis that almost escaped detection was the dilemma of a young woman called Barbara O'Brien (a pseudonym) who described her most unusual predicament in *Operators and Things: The Inner Life of a Schizophrenic* (1958). During a period of great personal tension and self-conflict, O'Brien awoke one morning to find three gray, somewhat wispy figures standing at her bedside. Rather than being aliens, or Men from Mars, they called themselves the Operators—a group in many ways much stranger than any possible aliens. The Operators consisted of a twelve-year-old boy Nicky, an elderly conservative man named Burt, and a weirdo called Hinton. They picked O'Brien to serve as part of their experiment. The experiment was to select a person like Barbara O'Brien, revealing the facts of the Operators' world to her, and observing the results. All three of the Operators could read her mind like an open book; her every thought was instantly known. Soon a fourth operator, Sharp, showed up. These operators not only knew her thoughts, but operated O'Brien—a thing—at all times. Once the Operators took over her life, she was under their complete domination and control. They informed her that if she told anyone about their existence, they would kill her instantly. In her words,

> I listened to what the Operators had to say, weighed the facts which they presented to me, and decided there was wisdom in following their directions. I packed some clothes and mounted a Greyhound bus, as they directed and followed them. Riding off in the bus, I left safely behind me a mess of reality with which I was totally incapable of coping.
>
> But what I could not face in sanity, I had to face in insanity. It became

clear in time that the problem presented to me by the Operators was exactly the problem I had left behind me. Caught up in my new world, and with the world of sanity almost wiped from my mind, the resemblance between the two worlds was not apparent until afterward—six months afterward, when I walked into a psychoanalyst's office, at the advice of my voices, and gave him the message they had told me to give him. To his trained eye, the evidences of an approaching spontaneous recovery were apparent. He sweated out a four-day period waiting for it to occur. Just as he had almost given up hope, major symptoms—"the voices"—abruptly disappeared.

(O'Brien 1958, pp. 118–119)

Barbara O'Brien created the Operators in her unconscious and the purpose of their existence—as in all hallucinations and delusions—is to help the individual survive. O'Brien, of course, was suffering from the Cinderella disease known as *schizophrenia*. The three positive facts about schizophrenia are: first, no one knows what causes it; second, no one knows how to cure it; and, third, the number of researchers looking for a cause and a cure are so small their chances for finding a solution soon is very remote. The term itself means "a split (schizo) mind (phrenia)" and it is assumed the sufferer becomes two people, two distinct personalities, or even multiple personalities. It is assumed by most psychiatrists that the so-called subconscious mind, rebelling against the repressions imposed upon it, has declared civil war, deserted the conscious authority, and in the resulting schism the new personality that emerges is composed of the parts that earlier were deliberately, consciously, and persistently repressed.

In some cases, apparently, this does occur. The "unconscious" rebels, assumes control of a mind, and creates a person it wishes to be, forcing the conscious personality into a tightly enclosed space where it has no power. In most schizophrenic cases, however, the unconscious puts on a play. Rather than create a new personality, the conscious mind is permitted to remain and watch the "unconscious" put on an elaborate drama. The principal character may or may not be an extraterrestrial alien. It might, instead, be the awesome figure of God, or the terrifying figure of Satan, or a demon. Or it might be something much more ordinary. Regardless of the shape or form, it most frequently represents authority, has superhuman powers, and its strangeness in various ways nevertheless seems both plausible and acceptable. Exactly why the unconscious suddenly takes over is unknown but it does. As the victim sits watching his (or her) demon, the unconscious mind not only flashes the demon's picture before your eyes, but also its voice in your ears, confusing and deluding your conscious mind into believing that the demon is real. If you were sane and saw the demon, you would realize it was a delusion or a hallucination. An alcoholic with DTs knows he is hallucinating and he knows the cause. But to the schizophrenic the unconscious knocks out your reasoning and then whispers in your mind's eyes and ears, "what you're seeing and hearing is real." Nevertheless, there is a small part of the conscious mind that keeps bouncing back and insisting that there is something very fishy about the unconscious mind's creations. The conscious mind is supposed to command and rule and the unconscious damn well knows it.

Barbara O'Brien was lucky. She developed the disorder abruptly, and in the way that is most fortunate for an optimistic prognosis. Her recovery from her paranoid delusions was most fortunate. Her spontaneous recovery after six months of continuous hallucinations and delusions was remarkable—a rare and infrequent event, sort of like walking out of the fourth dimension. Yet, all along, a part of her conscious mind was supplying guidance and the Operators were telling her to be cooperative for O'Brien's own sake as well as theirs—as well as telling her there was a one-in-three-hundred chance of escape. Finally they directed her to a minister, a psychiatrist, and finally to a psychoanalyst. The guidance was kind, protective, and clear. The Operators' voices even told Barbara O'Brien that she would be well in two weeks, and she was. It is of interest to note that in O'Brien's case the analyst recognized this fact but the psychiatrist did not. The analyst was also perceptive and honest enough to freely admit to O'Brien that he had nothing whatever to do with her recovery from her major symptoms.

O'Brien's case is one of the rare cases of paranoid schizophrenia with a pleasant outcome for everyone concerned. Most cases are not so fortunate. Full recovery is rare, and in the case of those individuals so disturbed they must be confined for their own as well as society's protection, prognosis is never good. As far as society is concerned, the biggest and most serious problem is the large number of undetected and un- or misdiagnosed paranoids running around loose. It must be remembered that in Barbara O'Brien's case she was under the Operator's control for six months and could not let anyone know of her dilemma for fear of being killed. She, finally, nearing complete emotional exhaustion, voluntarily got up enough courage to tell someone about her Operators. If she had not, no one would ever have known. She would have suffered and recovered all on her own—if at all.

There is every reason on Earth to believe that cases like Barbara O'Brien's are far from rare. In fact, they are much more common than even most professional mental health workers realize. This fact has been brought into sharp focus by a number of recent social anomalies, specifically wide-spread accusations of child molestation and sexual abuse, nationwide rumors of Satanism and devil worship, and a rising wave of reports of UFO attacks and alien abductions. What is even more distressing is that among the professionals who are charged with helping those individuals suffering from these delusions and hallucinations we find a number who not only accept their clients' delusions and hallucinations as realities, but also suffer from the delusions and hallucinations themselves, and find themselves unable to, or incapable of, separating fact and fiction.

Another more recent, prime-time star voyager is Greta Woodrew, a "top flight" psychic who in 1976 received a communication of hope from a civilization in another solar system: The World of "Ogatta." Greta Woodrew grew up seeing music and hearing colors. She also heard voices from age three until she was nine. As a child she routinely took trips through the solar system and beyond, visiting many other strange worlds. She was also blessed with the power of healing. When her contact with "Ogatta" resumed, they used a channel named "Tauri" because it saved energy. Tauri told Woodrew there was no need for anyone to be concerned about the UFO abductions or the aliens. According to Tauri, the aliens only send their best and most enlightened scientists to study us, and they wish us no harm. Also in 1976 Greta Woodrew hooked up with Andrja Puharich, Russ Targ, and Uri Geller for mutual support. With her husband Dick, Woodrew also publishes *The Woodrew Update,* a New Age newsletter. The two also run and administer STAR, or the Space Technology and Research Foundation, concerned with the matters mentioned above. All of this is set forth in her book *Memories of Tomorrow: One Woman's Cosmic Connection,* published by Dolphin Books in 1988.

In her first book, *On a Slide of Light: A Glimpse of Tomorrow* (1981), many future predictions were made. So far most are yet to happen. In her first book, according to Greta Woodrew, her mental "radio" is perhaps more finely tuned than most. "I therefore boldly claim that my radio receives waves whose existence is not even suspected by the average person." Sometime during 1976 this Phi Beta Kappa business woman, teacher, wife, and mother began to pick up signals from another civilization in another solar system located astronomically on the Messier List at M-92 with the name of Ogatta. It seems they chose her to be one of the channels. Why? She has no idea. Purpose? She was chosen to bear their messages to anyone who would listen. According to Greta Woodrew:

> I shall never forget my first encounter with an extraterrestrial. I was standing in a long shadowy tunnel with a manlike being who had the most marvelous eyes I have ever seen—golden, human, deeply compassionate. There were two entities with him, both with those same wonderful eyes. They all shared a rather birdlike quality, due in part to the shape of the upper lip. They seemed to be guarding the tunnel.
>
> When I tried to speak to them, to ask who they were and where they came from, the first one stepped forward. He was answering me but his

lips never moved. He was communicating telepathically and—amazingly—I could understand every word.

The being's name was Shames, he told me, and he and his companions had been sent from Ogatta, many light-ages away. As he gave me this message, he held me with his eyes. . . .

A second later, I was back in a more familiar world with a more familiar face—my husband's—at my side. We had been visiting the renowned physician and psi researcher, Dr. Andrja Puharich, and it was he who had guided me into that tunnel where I met my first visitor from the Ogatta group. We were later to learn that Shames had been sent from Ogatta, but actually came from Mennon.

(Woodrow 1981, p. 57)

How did she get into the tunnel? Well it seems that Woodrew thought she was a psychic and after she met Puharich, who hypnotized her and had her speaking Arabic, was told that she had unusual psychic abilities. Now she knew it! She had ESP and was a channel. Andrja hypnotized her and put her in contact with the aliens. According to Woodrew: "Being a channel means moving out of your body or moving over in your body and letting another being use the physical vehicle."

"Conquer fear, you conquer failure," Tauri told us.

It is obvious that both NASA and the U.S. Government are suppressing information on UFOs. . . . There are universities that are beginning to include UFOlogy in their curriculums. . . . Channeled information tells us that some UFOs do, in fact, exist. Only they are not "unidentified." They are spacecraft from other civilizations some of them *gattae* from my friends, the Ogatta group. The ETI tell us that their UFOs' use *light* for energy.

(Woodrow 1981, p. 62)

Greta Woodrew's big, big, big story, however, involves the moon. Seems that Ogatta has built a lot of gorgeous structures—landing places, homes, bridges, buildings, etc., all shiny and silvery. When she asks, "Tauri, can beings from Ogatta breathe on the moon?" Tauri's answer is: "Those from Ogatta can breathe *any* where when they wear their feathers." Seems also that Greta Woodrew, like Uri, also is able to bend spoons. Puharich is good at passing on his skills. Greta Woodrew not only bends spoons but she also shrinks them. "Shrink! I commanded mentally, not really taking myself seriously. One spoon subsequently became smaller than the others. Two other people—a professor/scientist and a physicist—were standing nearby and watched it happen." Oh joy! Oh goody! Oh will wonders never cease! We are all agog with wonder!

Tauri's final message is a real doozie: "Better a little light than no light at all," he says.

What is absolutely mind-boggling about both of these books is that two legitimate publishers had the gall to actually put this drivel between covers and publish it. Maybe her Phi Beta Kappa key was so shiny it blinded them.

Pentagon Paranoia

If remote-viewing was possible in the past, why not now? Today? Why not go to the stars mentally? Why not save all that money now spent on space shuttles and Star Wars! We can do it cheaper, mentally. Since the Russians can't afford the hardware, that's what they're doing right now.

At the height of the Cold War some very strange things went on in the higher levels of the U.S. and Soviet governments. Both showed a serious interest in parapsychological claims. Incredible as it may seem, scientists on both sides apparently believed that one side or the other possessed or were about to possess:

(1) Weapons systems that operate on the power of the mind alone, and whose lethal capacity had been demonstrated.

(2) The ability to heal or cause disease could be telepathically sent over long distances and this had been demonstrated on lower organisms such as flies and frogs. Legionnaires' disease had been induced via a Soviet "photonic barrier modulator."

(3) Telepathic hypnosis is not only possible, but has great practical and thus military potential. Agents could be planted who had no conscious knowledge they had been programmed.

(4) Psychotronic, i.e., mind-control, weapons existed and their full capabilities are yet unknown. For example, the Soviet "hyperspace amplifier" sank the U.S. submarine Thresher in 1963 merely by concentrating psychic energies on one of its photographs.

To add to the cold war paranoia a 1972 Defense Intelligence Agency study, originally classified TOP SECRET but released in 1978, concluded that the Soviet work in psychic research would sooner or later allow them to:

(1) Know the contents of top secret U.S. documents, troop and ship deployments, and the location and nature of all our military installations.

(2) Mold and control the thoughts of U.S. military and civilian leaders from a distance.

(3) Cause the instant death of any U.S. official, from a distance.

(4) Disable, at a distance, U.S. military equipment of all types, including spacecraft.

A former army intelligence analyst also reported that the Soviets had a psychic hyperspatial nuclear howitzer that "could denude the strategic capability of the free world with a single shot" by transmitting a single nuclear explosion instantaneously to a limitless number of sites anywhere in the universe.

Although it is difficult to believe, an alleged psychic was almost successful in persuading the Pentagon ARPA to invest several million dollars into research into his "psychic" powers. Defeated in his first efforts, five years later this psychic returned to the Advanced Research Projects Agency and met with naval intelligence officials around a Virginia motel swimming pool near the Pentagon. To demonstrate his powers he asked one of the commanders to think of any nearby object. No dupe, the commander thought of a bowl of grapes behind him. He picked this so the psychic would see him staring at something. The psychic scribbled something on a pad of paper and asked for the name of the commander's object. Then he handed the officer the pad, on which was written "a bowl of grapes." The stunned officials immediately recommended that an SRI (Stanford Research Institute) contract be funded. Agency skeptics, however, immediately brought in a team of magicians—James Randi, Persi Diaconis, Ray Hyman, and Marcello Truzzi—to stop the contract cold. The commander challenged the team to explain how this psychic read his mind. The team was reluctant to do so because it was not only a magician's trade secret, but also because half the time the dupe doesn't believe he was fooled. The commander, however, was an exception. He did remember that the psychic asked him the name of the object *before* he passed the pad, not *after* as he originally recalled. This difference, of course, is crucial. When the psychic appeared to scribble on the pad, he wrote nothing; after the commander said "a bowl of grapes," the psychic quickly scratched "a bowl of grapes" on the pad with a thumbwriter—a small pen concealed under the thumbnail. The thumbwriter is a device well known to all mentalists and magicians.

Despite Randi's continuing exposure of this psychic and his tricks showing that, for example, he moves the compass needle with magnets concealed on his person and in his hair, bends nails using a hidden vise built into his large bronze belt buckle, and starts old watches and clocks by merely shaking them to get them to run for a second or so—many true believers insist that although he cheats on occasion, he doesn't cheat all of the time and that for many of his feats there is just no conceivable way in which he *could* have cheated. Unfortunately, unless they are professional magicians or students of magic, people will continue to be deceived and deluded. The history of parapsychology, like the history of spiritualism, is one long account of chicanery, fraud, and deceit followed up by exposure after exposure. Despite its sorry record, faith ignores the facts and, as Randi noted about parapsychologists in general, "When facts conflict with their theories, they throw out the facts."

Though rejecting this psychic for a short period, the navy went so far as to hire a group of palm readers to track Soviet submarines; the National Security Agency used psychics to break computer-generated codes; and the army created a First Earth Battalion of warrior-monks whose leaders encouraged recruits to "Join the Army and learn ESP." When the noted reporter Jack Anderson and Ron McRae reported these unusual things in their column, supporters of such "psychic research" charged that Anderson or McRae, or both, were acting under telepathic orders from the Soviet Union to discredit American research! *Fate* magazine hinted they were unpatriotic, and their sources had "suspicious motives for wanting American psychatronic research stopped while the Soviets proceed with theirs." Critics, on the other hand, were outraged that millions were being spent on patent nonsense. *Discover* magazine urged "millions for defense but no cents for nonsense."

When the physicist Wilbur Franklin of Kent State University used the electron microscope to examine spoons and forks bent by the above-mentioned psychic and declared he saw "a different form of fracturing than is experienced when metal items are ruptured by physical force," the army believed him. Even though shortly before his death in 1979 Franklin concluded that his microscopic studies were erroneous, he was not believed. Instead rumors had it that Franklin's death (he died of natural causes) was:

(1) suicide, in remorse for having supported the psychic's ridiculous claims,

(2) due to a psychic attack by the Soviets to prevent further U.S. advances,

(3) due to a psychic attack by Americans who were being controlled by a group of Tibetan Nazis in a Sufi monastery in Afghanistan.

During this period many people argued they were the victims of "psychic bullets." Incredibly, a former head of the Naval Electonic Systems Command argued that "ESP is the way to fight submarines" and sponsored research to test its feasibility. Other special interest groups carried out research on the development of "radionic shields," which would protect the wearer from psychic attack. These shields, believe it or not, supposedly were energized when the user inserted a lock of his hair or a drop of his blood. At one time the Pentagon even purchased a "radionic multispectral image analyzer," a psychic device that supposedly tracked Soviet submarines. By far the most bizarre was the proposed "hyperspatial nuclear howitzer," which would transmit a nuclear explosion from the Nevada desert to the gates of the Kremlin with the speed of thought. To induce death or illness telepathically from thousands of miles away one would employ the reliable "photonic barrier modulator." Defenders of the money spent on these science-fiction notions argued that Admiral William Leahy declared during World War II that the nuclear weapon project was a waste of time and effort. "The A-bomb is the biggest fool thing we have ever done. . . . The bomb will never go off and I speak as an expert on explosives."

Is there any difference, for example, between the thinking behind the proposals of the Manhattan Project scientists, and the proposals of the parapsychologists to develop a psychotronic (psychological electronic) antimissile system that would throw a time warp over the North Pole and all incoming Soviet missiles would fly into the warp and explode in the past? God help us all if the differences are negligible or non-existent! Oppenheimer, Fermi, Bethe, et al., were backed by the solid, legitimate experimental science of nuclear physics. The parapsychologists have only their hopes, beliefs, and wishful thinking.

In his fascinating and incredible book *Mind Wars* (1984), Ron McRae gives an unbelievable account of a systematic effort on the part of the Office of Naval Intelligence to have psychics use their powers to track Soviet missile subs and predict their maneuvers. At least thirty-four in all were used over a period of several years. One of these psychics, Shawn Robbins, rated "in the top ten" by the *National Enquirer,* was used extensively.

Psychic research for military purposes has gone on since World War II when a small Navy project tried to train or psychically "direct" sea gulls to defecate on the periscopes of German subs. Strange as this may seem, the weirdest one of all was a machine the Navy purchased from a Virginia Beach chiropractor and self-declared psychic, Charles Whitehouse, in 1977. Whitehouse is a board member of the U.S. Psychotronic Association, an organization which builds equipment which allegedly amplifies psychic energies by means of electronic devices. In 1977 the Navy bought Whitehouse's *multispectral image analyzer* station for $5,111. To operate this device you simply inserted a photograph of the Soviet sub into the machine and in a few minutes it would indicate where the sub was located. Interestingly enough the machine also treated cancer by correcting "holes" and "imbalances" in the patient's aura by shining various combinations of colored lights on his or her body. Whitehouse also claimed it would cure people affected by both atom and hydrogen bombs. To operate it you had to work from a pedestal three feet off the ground "to avoid the polarizing influence of cosmic rays." Though the Air Force and others showed no interest in his "MIA," the Virginia Board of Medical Ethics did and prosecuted Whitehouse for fraud, which he avoided by moving to Thailand.

Silly and preposterous as these efforts seem, psychic research was funded for several years at the million dollar or more per year level. Precise figures are, of course, hidden—either classified or disguised by titles such as "Naval Biological Information Transfer."

One can flatly state with little fear of contradiction that as the 1990s begin there have been no technological breakthroughs with psychic weapons. Attempts to apply parapsychology are simply ill-founded and ill-grounded. There is simply no incontrovertible evidence that psi phenomena exist—even at the simplest and lowest energy level. Not only is such work light years from being or ever becoming a science since there is no theory, no facts, no text, and—despite the wealth of claims that are made—NO EVIDENCE. Simply put, the claims that are and have been made are difficult—if not impossible—to validate.

Attempts to make practical use of the so-called "psychic's" powers is best illustrated, however, not by the military but by the police. The recent TV special on *Psychic Detectives* and the Time-Life Series on the Paranormal in its volume on *Psi* and psychic sleuths left the impression with the public that they are very useful in solving crimes. Police officials, in general, are very skeptical and use the help of the psychics only as a last resort and to assure the public that "everything humanly possible" is being done to solve a crime. Experienced detectives and police officers who have used them on more than one occasion are far from impressed. Most often they are considered a nuisance. In the Atlanta child murders the investigating task force received over 1,300 letters from would-be psychics. When the psychic Dorothy Allison was finally called in, the police found her clues to be "vague" and "unhelpful," despite the fact that other police departments found her impressions "useful." One of the most frequently cited cases solved by a psychic is that of the Bridgewater, New Jersey, murder and the role of Peter Hurkos, the Dutch psychic-sleuth. In this case Hurkos predicted the gun was hidden in the wall at the murder site.

It wasn't, but it was found later in another wall. Hurkos also gave the police the first and last names of the perpetrator. Two years later an accomplice confessed and the suspect was brought to trial. Unfortunately for Hurkos, and fortunately for the suspect, he was acquitted because the jury found the evidence circumstantial and inconclusive.

The place where the psychics fall apart is in the laboratory under controlled conditions. A series of studies carried out by Martin Reiser of the Behavioral Sciences Section of the Los Angeles Police Department were negative. In one test, for example, psychics were asked to identify twenty-one key aspects of a case such as the victim's name or age from a personal sample such as a key chain or lock of hair. No psychic named more than six factors correctly, and the typical score was two or three. Mere guesses were as good. (Reiser 1979)

Efforts to use psychics to find General Dozier, kidnapped by the Italian Red Brigade, were equally unsuccessful.

Strangest of all perhaps were the efforts of the New York City police to employ Cleve Backster, a polygraph operator, who discovered that plants are sensitive to human emotions. When attached to the polygraph, plants—Backster claimed—show all the human signs of emotional arousal. Using a plant that had been present at a murder, the police paraded twenty suspects past the plant. Believe it or not the plant was unable to identify the murderer! Even though both the CIA and the Navy studied the Backster effect for possible military usage, it has not been employed—(Thank God), to our knowledge—as a means of gathering enemy intelligence. One can, however, question the intelligence of all of its proponents.

Though the Reagans' use of an astrologer to advise on the President's movements and arrangements of his schedule are well known, less so is the fact that the parapsychologist Barbara Honegger, an assistant to the President's chief domestic adviser Martin Anderson, worked three years in the Office of Policy Development and played a major role in the decision regarding the deployment of the MX missile. According to Honegger, psychics carried out studies which showed that Soviet psychics could determine where the MX missiles were located no matter how they were shuffled around. One of the members of the House in the Special Committee on Intelligence believed the Soviets might also use dowsing rods in satellites (SADDOR—satellite deployed dowsing rods) to locate the missiles.

Absurd as these suggestions sound, what are we to make of the attempts on the part of the CIA, according to Victor Marchetti, to contact dead Soviet agents in the hope that in the hereafter they would realize the error of their ways and defect to the West? Then we have the California company *Heavens Union* (instead of Western Union) that sends letters to the dead, one hundred words for $60, and $200 for priority service. Letters to dead pets or to hell are not accepted. A second company has a closed circuit TV link with heaven and manages to stay busy. Just as there is an evident need for fantasy, so, too, there is a need to believe. Today the United States supports 20,000 professional astrologers and only 2,000 astronomers.

As Charles Fair notes in *The New Nonsense,* however, ESP transmissions are inherently noisy and rather unreliable—100 percent reception is rare—and messages may not get through or come through scrambled. Interpreting them might be as difficult as unscrambling the verses of Nostradamus. Even if psitrons do exist, conventional methods of communication, on the whole, work much better. As Fair puts it, as a colonel in the army,

> I would much rather that my commanding general contact me via field telephone or walkie-talkie than give his orders by going into his "alpha" state and "projecting" them to me. What with the roar of battle and the static on my own ESP line, nothing might get through at all. . . . Why, as in so many everyday ESP experiments mighten the transmission fail? . . . Further evidence on ESP phenomena in general is certainly needed, but with so many of us at work on the problem, we will doubtless soon have it cracked. Either that or the other way around.
>
> (Fair 1974, p. 135)

Although we like to assume we are better educated, less credulous, and more sophisticated than people who were taken in by the mediums at the turn of the century, the alacrity with which the public accepts and pursues the nonsense of the New Age indicates we have hardly changed at all.

Mark Twain once told Rudyard Kipling: "First get the facts—then you can distort them as much as you like."

And as Ron McRae remarked,

> There is a tendency in the psychic community to distort the facts before getting them straight, sorting out the good experimental results from the discredited experiments and unreliable anecdotes. Parapsychologists often seem to think fancifully about what has been accomplished, and to ensure any new experiment against the voluminous, but uncontrolled and scientifically useless anecdotal reports of psychic miracles. Facts get ignored and even favorable facts sink into a morass of anecdotes.
>
> (McRae 1984, p. 132)

McRae goes on to state that the failures of the psychic warfare projects in the military laboratories "have often been among the most irresponsible experiments ever reported." Thinking about seances with dead Soviet agents, the multispectral image analyzer that supposedly detects submarines with a photo, the hyperspatial nuclear howitzer, and the antimissile time warp over the North Pole certainly attests to a considerable degree of irresponsibility somewhere.

Such work is also highly reminiscent of similarly misguided efforts on the part of the CIA during the 1960s and 1970s. Rather than ESP in this instance it was "hypnosis" that was going to provide the CIA with techniques for creating human automatons and hypnosis-programmed assassins whose minds were under total manipulative control. Based on Richard Condon's novel, *The Manchurian Candidate,* the CIA launched a multimillion dollar research effort over a period of nearly twenty years--involving the aid of hundreds of researchers, universities, pharmaceutical houses, mental institutions, prisons, and laboratories—to brainwash human subjects through hypnosis, drugs, and psychological conditioning techniques to create a group of mindless robots.

All things considered, this effort was, perhaps, a bigger boondoggle and even more irresponsible and misguided than the Pentagon's ESP fiascos. The primary question was: Is it theoretically possible to gain complete control over the mind of an unwilling person with exotic techniques of brainwashing, drugs, or hypnosis? Most well-trained and experienced psychologists clearly recognized that the technology of mind manipulation was much too crude for the precise control needed in order to create a human robot. Nothing we have to date—drugs, psychosurgery, behavior modification, ESB (electrical stimulation of the brain), or anything else for that matter—is sufficiently sophisticated to erase a person's will and still permit them to function in an intelligent manner. Weakest of all is the technique labeled: "hypnosis."

Nevertheless, it was hypnosis that the CIA concentrated on as the answer to their prayers. All of the blame does not belong to the agency however. Most of it is deserved by the so-called "hypnosis experts" (of which there seems to be an endless supply these days), called in by the snoops to run the show. One of the earliest of these misguided "experts" was George Estabrooks who, in 1945, penned a book called *Hypnotism.* In a chapter titled "Hypnotism in Warfare" Estabrooks suggested that hypnosis could be used to create unconscious programmed spies. Estabrooks believed that hypnosis could be used to build a double agent—a man whose unconscious mind would be loyal to his country, but whose conscious mind would be loyal to the enemy. Such a "Super-Spy" would, in a trance, reveal useful information about the enemy. The advantages of such an agent are obvious: he wouldn't know he was a spy so he would be more sincere and effective. If captured and tortured, he'd have nothing to reveal. He would be totally unaware of the secret locked up in his unconscious mind. He couldn't "confess" because he wouldn't know anything. Although, admittedly, a little difficult, Estabrooks argued it *could* be done and, moreover, such a spy could also be converted into an assassin. While the spy might not commit murder on hypnotic command, he could be given the implanted suggestion the gun was not loaded. Also all knowledge of ever having been hypnotized would be removed and his controller would also insure no one else could put him in a trance.

Estabrooks expanded and improved these ideas in a second edition of his book published in 1957 where he argued for the creation of a "Super Spy." Picking the 1 in 5 of adults who can be put into a trance so deep he would have no memory of it, this ideal subject would be coached to behave in a trance exactly as he or she behaves while awake so that no one could tell whether he or whe was asleep or awake. The subjects would also not know they had been hypnotized, and would be told no one else could hypnotize them. Estabrooks suggested such a spy would take ten months to prepare. Precisely how and what would be done was never specified. Estabrooks also stated that hypnosis would be used to create a "multiple personality," and then set up opposing loyalties in two of them. Incredibly, Estabrooks's wild speculations were swallowed whole by the intelligence agency. This entire incredible story is reported in painful and embarrassing detail in Alan W. Scheflin and Edward M. Opton Jr.'s excellent book *The Mind Manipulators* (1978). Exactly how implausible Estabrooks's ideas are can be seen from Scheflin and Opton's amusing analysis of what would be required to make Super Spy operational. The hypnotist would have to:

(1) Locate a subject capable of reaching a somnambulist state.

(2) Hypnotize that person against his or her will by a "disguised" technique.

(3) Instill a post-hypnotic suggestion that the subject will go into a deep trance wherever the hypnotist gives a special signal.

(4) Instill a post-hypnotic suggestion that the subject will act no differently while in a trance than while awake.

(5) Instill a post-hypnotic suggestion that the subject cannot be hypnotized by anyone else unless a specific command is given.

(6) Enable the subject by post-hypnotic suggestion to resist forceful interrogation and possibly even torture.

(7) Create multiple personalities.

(8) Separately program one or more of those personalities.

(9) Induce one or more of those personalities to commit crimes or act in ways that violate the person's ethical code.

(10) Instill a post-hypnotic suggestion of amnesia for all of the above steps.

(11) Ensure that these hypnotic programs last for the life of the subject.

The total ignorance of "hypnosis," as well as the lack of knowledge and understanding of ordinary human behavior revealed in these eleven bits of wishful thinking is truly mind boggling! Most of these speculations are not only contradicted by hypnosis literature, but by common sense as well. The claims in number seven for example that MPD can be created via hypnosis in another human being is without any factual basis. While it is true that hypnotic procedures have been used in the *treatment* of MPD and some authorities have argued that all cases of MPD are iatrogenic, the idea that war between two opposing personalities with differing loyalties that would hold up in practical operation during wartime without constant reinforcement and assuming that one could "program" a single personality at all—is *science fiction,* not *fact.* Every one of the eleven items is egregiously in error.

What is of greatest interest in the above example is the mountain of misinformation about what is called "hypnosis" that is revealed by Estabrooks's ravings. Not only did the CIA proceed to try to create its own Manchurian Candidate over the next decade in a series of hilarious blunders produced and directed by a number of Three Stooges-like characters, equally ignorant of what hypnosis is and what it can and can't do, but they finally gave up after concluding their goals could be obtained more efficiently in other ways than via hypnotic programming.

If the CIA learned anything at all from the fiasco it was that neither hypnosis, brainwashing, nor drugs—the only possible techniques capable of creating a Candidate—could do such a job. Hypnosis *certainly* can't do it. Brainwashing is even less likely to do so. Rather than being an irresistible method for remolding the mind, it requires extreme physical deprivation (or torture) leaving the individual open to indoctrination, and requires an environment which continually reinforces the manipulator's control over the victim's mind. Once such control is removed the brainwashing loses its effect. There is no drug at this date that can cause an unwilling person to commit or carry out specific actions. No drug exists that can erase specific memories of recent events, or erase all memories for all time. As Scheflin and Opton (1978) state:

> We believe that the ability to create Manchurian Candidates does not exist. If such a technology did exist, it would be both dangerous and unnecessary. It would be dangerous because the plot could easily unravel. "Programmed" people may not always stay programmed. Manchurian Candidates are unnecessary because the CIA has more effective ways to do its work.
>
> (p. 469)

Readers interested in the specifics of the CIA's excursions into hypnotic fantasies should consult John Marks's book *The Search for the Manchurian Candidate: The CIA and Mind Control* (1979), as well as the work of Scheflin and Opton.

Before leaving this topic and the subject of "hypnosis," we had best look a little more closely at this much-abused phenomenon and the fallacies surrounding so-called "hypnotic" behavior. To put it as bluntly and as simply as possible: there is no such thing as "hypnosis."

4

Hypnosis: The Gateway to Fantasy-Land

Hypnosis is a treatment which is principally dependent upon the doctor's authority and the patient's compliance. The hypnotized person recovers because the hypnotist tells him that he will; or recalls the remote past because the hypnotist urges him to do so.

—Anthony Starr, *Churchill's Black Dog, Kafka's Mice*

What is commonly referred to as "hypnosis" is not only a fallacy, but the very term itself is a misnomer. "Hypnosis," from the Greek word meaning sleep, is definitely not sleep. Though it is true that, on some occasions, the client or patient who is subjected to the monotonous intonations of the hypnotist may well fall asleep out of boredom, all authorities generally agree that the condition known as "hypnosis" is definitely not sleep. As for the so-called authorities on hypnosis, most of them are not fully cognizant of what is happening when they "hypnotize" another person. Many are convinced that "hypnosis" puts their patients and clients into an "altered state of consciousness," or a "trance." Careful and extensive experimental work over the last two decades has established quite convincingly that hypnosis is not an altered state of consciousness, nor are people in any sort of a "trance" state. What we call the relaxed, compliant condition seen in the laboratory or clinic is the result of role playing, social compliance, and suggestion. The experimental evidence against the notion that "hypnosis is an altered or special state of consciousness" or that people who are hypnotized are in a "trance" is now massive. For a comprehensive review of this literature and the competing theories, this author's book *They Call It Hypnosis* (1990) is recommended. Nevertheless, a summary of what is currently known will help immeasurably in our understanding of past lives regression, future lives progression, spirit possession, multiple personality disorder, glossolalia, channeling, and cryptomnesia.

While most researchers seem to judge the depth of "hypnotic trance" by how easily their subjects respond to suggestions, the problem with this method is twofold: first, the trance state is inferred from the high level of response to suggestions and, vice versa, the hypnotic state is used to account for the high level of response to suggestions from which it is inferred. Second, most people are, in most situations, quite suggestible but even a suggestibility criterion doesn't discriminate the hypnotized person from the nonhypnotized. Juhasz and Sarbin (1966) several years ago had wide-awake, unhypnotized students participate in an experiment they were told had to do with taste sensitivity. The students tasted water samples they believed had different concentrations of salt in a solution. After each taste they were to respond: salt or no salt, depending on whether it did or did not taste salty. While most subjects tasted salt about 25 percent of the time, twelve out of the twenty-eight students swore they had tasted salt in some of the solutions. Actually, the samples all contained nothing but pure water.

Suggestibility is, thus, a poor criterion for discriminating hypnotic from waking states. This also points out the significant role that internally generated imagery plays in perception. True perceptions and our internally generated "thought images" in actuality are the end points of a mental continuum. The fact that we actually "see" our internal images was shown by a classic experiment carried out in 1910 by the psychologist C. W. Perky. Perky had her subjects observe a small spot in the center of a smoky window and to try to imagine seeing different objects such as a face, a bowl of fruit, and so forth at the spot. Though the subjects didn't know it, very faint pictures of the objects they were to imagine were projected from behind the window. From the subjects' descriptions of their imaginings it was evident that they incorporated the projections into their images but had not realized it. Most subjects rigidly insisted that what they saw was the result of their imaginations. Not only do we construct our perceptions, but our perceptions and images use the same mental mechanism. Perky's studies show clearly that perceptual suggestibility is not unique to hypnosis.

Perky's work has recently been updated by Sidney J. Segal, who has also shown how readily people will assimilate projected pictures into their visual images (*Imagery: Current Cognitive Approaches*). In some of his experiments subjects were asked to imagine a skyline scene but were shown a faintly projected color picture of a tomato; several of the subjects reported imagining a skyline with a round red sunset.

Experiments have shown that most hypnotized subjects are playing a role—the role of a hypnotized person. This role is well known in our culture. The hypnotized person is supposed to close the eyes or stare blankly in space, talk in a mechanical fashion, and obey every command or request of the hypnotist. The reasons for undergoing hypnosis are to receive therapeutic help, e.g., to lose weight, stop smoking, or to help the college professor with his research.

Orne (1966) completed an experiment several years ago showing the importance of role playing. In two psychology classes, Orne gave lectures on the nature of hypnosis. In the first class one of Orne's confederates was hypnotized in a demonstration. What the class didn't know was that the confederate had been hypnotized earlier and told that whenever he was hypnotized he would acquire catalepsy, i.e., rigidity of his dominant hand, and that it would remain in whatever position the hypnotist put it. The second class received the same lecture and demonstration, except in this case the subject had not been given the suggestion of catalepsy, and thus didn't show it. Next, when students from the two classes were themselves hypnotized, members from the first class showed "dominant hand catalepsy" while those from the second class did not. As Orne concluded, when a person is hypnotized he behaves in accord with his perception of what the role requires.

According to the social-cognitive view of hypnosis, such behavior reflects goal-directed strivings and susceptible hypnotic subjects are all aware, thinking individuals acting out the appropriate social roles attending to interpersonal cues—even highly subtle ones—and doing their best to comply, and thus presenting themselves as "good" subjects. This does not mean, however, that the hypnotized subject is "putting on" or deliberately faking what he is doing anymore than we fake our behavior when we are in the presence of the President of the United States, or in the presence of our lover. We are reacting in all three instances according to "the stylized demands placed on our social behaviors by other people," i.e., expectations. According to the role playing theory of hypnosis, for the individual who submits himself for "hypnosis" the situation is rich in social demands and social cues as to what is or is not *proper* hypnotic behavior. Moreover, since subjectively our private experiences are ineffable sorts of things—things hard to remember or describe—it is quite easy to convince ourselves that we are in a trance or in an altered state of consciousness.

Let us now examine some of the objections to the social-cognitive view and the experimental evidence that supports it. Since many hypnotic subjects frequently report that their responses to suggestions are effortless and involuntary, some investigators take these reports literally and have invented a number of psychological processes to explain how the "hypnotized" subjects are transformed from "active doers" to passive observers of their own involuntary automatic behavior. Hilgard (1977) posits that the mechanisms that control responding become dissociated from conscious control during hypnosis. Consequently, hypnotized subjects are unable— as opposed to unwilling—to resist or counter the suggested "hypnotic" effects. This means that hypnotically amnesiac subjects are purportedly *unable* to recall and those give suggestions for limb rigidity are *unable* to bend their arms.

The social viewpoint, on the other hand, sees such special mechanisms as unnecessary. Instead, such reports merely reflect the interpretation made by the subjects about their own behavior. The suggested behaviors are merely strategic or goal-directed enactments that the hypnotic subjects often interpret as involuntary occurrences (Spanos 1982b). In the context of the hypnotic situation, although the hypnotic suggestions do not specifically tell the subjects to forget or not bend their arms, the suggestions foretell the occurrence of the described behavior and invite the subjects to imagine the behaviors are involuntary (Spanos 1971). When the post-test experience of the subjects was examined, it was found that subjects who defined their responses as involuntary were actively involved in thoughts that supported that interpretation. Specifically, subjects who rated the suggested behavior as involuntary were much more likely than nonresponsive subjects to become absorbed in carrying out thoughts and images that were consistent with a nonvoluntary interpretation. For example, subjects who were told their arm was rising would imagine a pulley was lifting it (Spanos and McPeake 1977). Instead of passive simple occurrences, hypnotic responses are clearly goal-directed activities. For many subjects merely defining the situation as "hypnosis" will cause them to classify almost all of their everyday behaviors such as arm-raising or opening and closing the eyes as "involuntary."

One of the most interesting aspects of hypnosis is the fact that people who are easily hypnotized often report large reductions in pain when exposed to unpleasant or painful stimulation while under hypnosis (Barber and Hahn 1962; Evans and Paul 1970). According to Hilgard (1977), however, only the "conscious part" of the subject experiences the reduction in pain in such circumstances. The pain, in Hilgard's view, continues to be felt in its full intensity by a hidden part of the subject. What happens when the subject is hypnotized and painfully stimulated is that the hypnosis causes a part of the subject's mind to become split off or dissociated. This "hidden observer" part is fully conscious and aware but doesn't report it unless asked. Hilgard and his associates argue that the hidden reports *are not* due to the experimental instructions given in these *hidden part* studies. Spanos and Hewitt (1980), however, argued that these hidden reports were directly due to the instructions given and the strategic role enactments that were expected. In a direct test of their hypothesis they divided good hypnotic subjects into two groups, and the subjects in both groups were told that they had a "hidden self." The instructions given to one group were the same as those Hilgard used, and implied that during the hypnotic analgesia their hidden part would feel more pain than their conscious part. Alternatively, the second group was told that their hidden part would feel much *less pain* than their conscious part during the hypnotic pain trials. As expected, subjects in the two groups behaved as if they had hidden parts with opposite characteristics: high sensitively to pain in group one; reduced sensitivity in group two. Another study (Spanos, Gwynn, and Stan 1983) found that the same subjects gave hidden pain intensity ratings that changed from being the same as the conscious ratings, to being *higher* than conscious ratings, or to being lower than conscious ratings depending on the information given to them in the instructions preceding the hypnosis. Clearly these "hidden observer" instructions do much more than simply set the stage for the emergence of some sort of preexisting dissociated mental subsystem. Instead, these instructions provide cooperative and compliant subjects with the information they need to present themselves, i.e., to act properly in a way that "fits" or is congruent with the expectations or demands of the role they are to play. In other words, the so-called hidden selves or observers showing up in Hilgard's experiments are socially motivated constructions. The subjects *act* as if they have hidden selves because the instructions they receive lead them to interpret their experience in these terms and to act out or show those behaviors that are congruent with this interpretation.

Hypnotic Amnesia: Achievement or Happening?

One of the classical indicators of hypnosis is hypnotic amnesia, i.e., if people are told by the hypnotist they *will not* remember, then during the post-hypnotic period they *cannot* remember. When this occurs then this is proof that "hypnosis" did occur. Numerous studies, however, have clearly shown that post-hypnotic information processing is no different from nonhypnotic information processing (Hoyt and Kihlstrom, 1986). When subjects are given a post-hypnotic suggestion that they will not remember certain key words according to their verbal reports, they do, but according to their galvanic skin resistance, they don't. Furthermore, when subjects are given a list of words to learn and then are "hypnotized" and given another list to learn (the second list is deliberately constructed to interfere with the recall of the first), and half of the subjects are then given a post-hypnotic suggestion to forget the second list and half are given no suggestions—a later test of recall shows that both groups recall the first list at the same level. Spanos and his collaborators found that between 40 to 63 percent of their so-called "amnesic" subjects later admitted that they had suppressed their reports. The skill they employ, it seems, is not reporting. Most amnesia suggestions ask subjects to forget a "chunk" of information in its entirety, as in the previous example, a list of previously learned words. Good hypnotic subjects usually meet these task demands by shifting attention away from the target recall during the amnesia test period. When informed later that the amnesia is cancelled and that they can, again, remember, they focus on the retrieval cues and thus easily recall the "forgotten" material (Spanos and D'Eon 1980).

Clearly, hypnotic amnesia is an achievement rather than a happening, and it occurs because cooperative and compliant subjects strategically change their thinking and behavior to meet the task demands that make up "being amnesiac."

More interesting is the fact that most of these alleged amnesiacs will confess to remembering more and more of the "forgotten" material under adequate pressure "to the extent that they have nothing left to remember when the amnesia is lifted" (Coe's Chapter 5; Spanos and Chaves 1989).

Other studies of post hypnotic behavior are equally revealing. For example, thirteen subjects were told that after "waking up" they would scratch their ear when they heard the word *psychology*. After waking the subjects the hypnotist gave them the impression that the experiment was over and then had an informal conversation with a colleague in which the cue word was used. Nine of the subjects failed to respond. But when the hypnotist then suggested the experiment was still in progress, seven of the previous nine began responding again. Another study showed that all post-hypnotic responding ceased as soon as the hypnotist left the room. Spanos, in a similar study, found that all subjects complied with a cough when they heard the word *psychology* in the experimental situation. But when Spanos had a colleague pose as a lost student asking for the *Psychology* Department, none of the subjects responded to the cue word (Spanos and Gorassini 1984).

Sometimes, however, subjects will maintain their amnesia despite efforts to have them try their best to remember. If they truly are unable to remember, then this is evidence that they were, indeed, deeply hypnotized. In 1984 Spanos and deGroh tested this claim with eight good hypotic subjects who were unable to remember words they had learned earlier. Spanos then taught the eight a list of three concrete and three abstract words, and they were told that the concrete words were stored in one cerebral hemisphere and the abstract words in the other. They were also told that each hemisphere had a "hidden part" that remained aware of the information in its own hemisphere, but was unaware of the information in the opposite hemisphere. After receiving a suggestion to forget, all of the subjects showed high levels of amnesia for both the concrete and the abstract words. Before canceling the amnesia, the experimenter "got in touch" with each subjects two hidden parts in succession. In this situation each subject remembered all of the words associated with the "appropriate" hemisphere, but none of the words associated with the opposite hemisphere. In other words, all of the subjects were able to remember in a two-stage sequence that showed they were truly hypnotized and in possession of some "hidden selves." Clearly, in all hypnotic contexts information about the characteristics of the dissociated selves role is provided by the experimental instructions, and subjects guide the impression they create in terms of these role prescriptions. The "dissociated self" role usually requires displays of amnesia as a central component. To successfully carry out this aspect of the role, subjects must maintain control over memory and guide their recall according to the particular "self" being presented.

This takes care of "experimental hypnosis," but what about "clinical hypnosis?" Does hypnosis—as it is touted to do—really reduce the effects of pain? Since such techniques as relaxation, distraction, placebos, positive images, etc., are also known to reduce pain, does hypnosis do an even better job? When the effects of hypnosis on pain are examined closely and under controlled conditions, we find that other than the effects obtained from relaxation, suggestion, and distraction, there are no additional effects that come from the alleged "hypnosis" per se. Interestingly enough, suggestions for reducing the perception of pain can be effective whether they are accompanied by hypnotic induction or not. Moreover, Chaves (1989) points out "a recent review of significant developments in medical hypnosis over the past twenty-five years fails to cite a single report of hypno-analgesia. . . ." Barber's research as well as that of others has shown strong analgesic effects following instructions simply to relax and concentrate on something else (1982). Hilgard and Hilgard also state:

> Yet, despite a vast amount of excellent research on the effects of hypnosis on experimentally induced pain, there is virtually no reliable evidence from controlled clinical studies to show that it is effective for any form of chronic pain.
>
> (Hilgard and Hilgard 1983, p. 90)

Some of the world's foremost authorities on pain, Melzack and Wall, for example, also agree: "It remains to be shown that hypnotic suggestion is any better than a placebo pill or encouragement and moral support from the family physician or clergyman." (1988) The authors further state that hypnosis by itself does not have a sufficiently strong effect on clinical pain to be considered a reliably useful therapy. Mersky provides an even stronger opinion. He concluded, on the basis of available clinical reports and his own personal experience, that hypnotism is not "worth using in anyone with a pain of physical origin and very rarely in patients with pain which is psychological in origin." (Mersky 1983) It must also be remembered that as far as the use of hypnosis in surgery is concerned, very few patients ever go under the knife using only hypnosis. Moreover, there are many people who are simply not as sensitive to pain as others. Even when hypnosis is used it is in many instances also accompanied by the use of analgesics. Joyce L. D'Eon (1989) reports that in childbirth "hypnotic procedures have failed to meet the grandiose claims that have sometimes been made for them." Without the presence of a control group it is easy to assume the easy childbirth was due to hypnosis when, in fact, it is well known that "anywhere from 9 to 24 percent of women experience relatively painless childbirth without any intervention." No matter what the therapy is, there are limits to its effectiveness, and none of them abolish the pain entirely. As for hypnosis per se, if it has any affect at all upon the reduction of pain, such effects are due to relaxation alone or relaxation in combination with the suggestions that excite the sufferer's imagination and divert his or her attention from the source of pain and discomfort.

A number of studies have shown that so-called hypnosis is very effective in curing warts. Sinclair-Greben and Chalmers (1959), for example, gave their patients hypnotic suggestions that their warts would disappear on one side of their bodies only. After several months nine of the fourteen patients had their warts disappear on the "treated" side but not on the other side. Remarkable though this study is, it is less evidence for the reality and power of hypnosis than it is for the precise sort of control people can exert over their "alleged" autonomic or involuntary functions. Other studies have shown that warts can be cured by painting them with vegetable dye, and telling the patient that it's powerful medicine and the warts will go away. If left untreated, the warts generally go away of their own accord in a year or two. Any treatment the patient believes in is likely to produce results just as effective and dramatic as those claimed for hypnosis.

As for the use of hypnosis to treat cancer, there is at present no support "for the claims that psychological techniques actually reject or contain cancer or otherwise lead to its regression." (Stam 1984) As for nausea and vomiting, "the available research data have yet to indicate any advantage for hypnosis over standard relaxation or systematic desensitization treatments." (Stam 1984) This conclusion is readily understood when we realize that there is no such thing as "hypnosis" per se. There *is nothing whatso-*

ever to have any effects outside of the effects of compliance, relaxation, suggestion, and distraction.

It should, therefore, not be at all surprising that people can acquire conscious control over such things as blood pressure, muscle tension, skin temperature, swallowing reflexes, heart rate, etc. What is impressive about so-called hypnotic techniques (i.e., suggestion), biofeedback research, and placebo effects in the clinic is that they all demonstrate the great potential humans have for conscious control over bodily processes of many kinds. Everything that people can supposedly accomplish under hypnosis research —Barber's in particular—has shown they can do exactly the same things without it. And why shouldn't they—since "hypnosis" per se does not exist!

Theodore R. Sarbin argued in 1962 that the term *hypnosis* should be banished from the professional vocabulary of psychology. Today we still have the misnomer with us. Only the clinicians still cling to the out-moded concept of human behavior as being due to strange internal forces and mysterious processes beyond the reach of modern science. In William Coe's words, the clinicians cling to this view because "the opaqueness and vagueness of special state concepts allow the aura of mystery and power long associated with hypnosis and hypnotists to remain alive." (1989)

Historically, one of the saddest examples of injustice due to erroneous beliefs about hypnosis occurred in 1894 in Topeka, Kansas, where a man named Thomas McDonald was acquitted of murder on the ground that a man named Gray had hypnotized him and made him commit the crime. Following McDonald's acquittal, the court ordered the arrest of Anderson Gray as the real murderer. Gray was not only tried and found guilty, but the case was upheld by the Kansas Supreme Court. According to a story in the *New York World* of April 7, 1895:

> The Kansas Supreme Court today confirmed the rulings of the District Court of Cowley County, which resulted in the conviction of Anderson Gray for murder in the first degree through *hypnotic power* which he exerted upon the actual slayer.
>
> Thomas Patton was shot and killed near his home in Summer County, on May 5 1894, by Thomas McDonald. McDonald admitted the killing, but set up a defense that he was under the hypnotic influence of Anderson Gray, and that therefore he was not responsible for the act. McDonald was acquitted and Gray convicted, although it was admitted that he was not present when the killing was done.

The primary reason for this miscarriage of justice was the fact that medical men of the time believed and led others to believe that some peo-ple had the power to dominate others and make them execute their com-mands, regardless of their own wishes, by merely concentrating on them a piercing, mind-numbing, *hypnotic* gaze. Hopefully, we are more knowledgeable and sophisticated about "hypnosis" today.

This example of gullibility is topped only by another example cited at length in Joseph F. Rinn's fascinating book *Sixty Years of Psychical Research* (1950).* Rinn, a personal friend of Harry Houdini, remarked to the magician one day that he was impressed with the work of Charcot, who kept a hypnotized subject buried in a coffin for four days with no harmful effects. Houdini laughed and said, "You Psychical Researchers are very gullible. You don't seem to be aware that hypnotism is a big fake. All these professors have subjects they work with, called 'horses,' who don't feel physical pain and can endure hardships while they pretend to be hypnotized." When Rinn protested that the feats performed by the hypnotized were indeed scientific facts, Houdini said, "Is that so? Well to convince you that you are a sucker I'll have you meet Tommy Minnock, who is on the bill at Henderson's at Coney Island next week." The following week Rinn went with Houdini and watched one Professor Santanelli "hypnotize" Tommy Minnock and have him eat plug tobacco and red pepper, and undergo all sorts of physical torture seemingly impossible for any man to endure. Houdini assured Rinn that Minnock really felt no pain. After the performance, Houdini took Rinn backstage and introduced him to the Professor as a fellow pro who could be trusted. Grinning broadly, Minnock said, "So you fell for that Antwerp story? Well, Charcot was certainly one grand old faker, but he paid me well for my part in that burial stunt." When Rinn asked if he was actually buried in a coffin for four days, Minnock replied, "I was the one that went through that test but I wasn't hypnotized." When Rinn said, "But the scientists said you were," Minnock responded, "Scientists are easy marks for a trickster. They concluded that I was hypnotized because they couldn't feel my pulse and because I showed no sign of pain when they applied a hot iron to my body."

Rinn asked, "But how could you live and breathe sealed in a coffin for ninety-six hours?"

Minnock explained, "The story, as told, made people conclude that I was sealed in a coffin without air, but the facts won't bear that out. The doctors had to watch my face to get my reactions while I was buried, so a plate of glass was put in my coffin-top and a funnel-shaped tube ran down to it to supply me with air."

"But the doctors watched you throughout the test," Rinn protested.

"It's true the doctors never left there," Minnock replied, "but they played cards most of the time, coming to look down the tube at me occasionally,

---

*My thanks are due to Lewis Jones for calling my attention to this delightful work and the amusing story of Tommy Minnock.

while a nurse, who was my confederate, stood on watch by the tube. This nurse had under her dress rubber bottles that contained liquid food and drink, which were connected to long rubber tubes. When the doctors weren't looking, she would slip the tube down the funnel to my coffin where I would slip off the glass plate and satisfy my needs. . . . Of course, the doctors didn't expect any tricks from a man in a cataleptic state."

Houdini then asked Minnock to explain to Rinn the various things he could do. Minnock then stated, "I can endure any kind of a painful test without showing signs of it, because I don't feel any pain. . . . I can stop my pulse or make it go up or down at will. . . . I can eat any quantity of plug tobacco, cayenne pepper, or other obnoxious things without any ill effect. . . . You can drive a nail into my body, or burn me with a red-hot iron, and I'll feel no pain. I can stop a wound from bleeding or make it bleed at will. Here, drive this knife through the fleshy part of my hand and I'll show you." Sure enough, Houdini did this and when Minnock withdrew the blade no blood flowed. When Rinn commented on this, Santanelli said, "That's nothing, watch this," and Santanelli then took a needle and thread and sewed Minnock's under lip to his upper lip, then sewed through his cheek, yet no sign of blood appeared. When the stitches were removed, Rinn asked Minnock to make the wounds bleed and then stop bleeding, which he did. Minnock then demonstrated his ability to raise and lower his pulse beat and respiration, and then, heating an ordinary kitchen knife in a gas flame until it was red-hot, he pressed it against his bare leg while he hummed a tune. "You see I have no sense of pain." Rinn stared in wonder. "That's enough, Tommy, I'm convinced," Rinn finally said. "You see, Joe, how easy it is for Tommy to fool those doctors and scientists," Houdini said.

Rinn then proceeded to win several bets from his doctor friends. Later Minnock and Santanelli parted ways after Santanelli had Minnock placed in a wire cage above ground with nurses and guards supplied by the physicians. Under such conditions, Minnock could not cheat and spent ninety-six agonized hours without food or drink. Minnock never forgave him. Minnock later exposed both Charcot, Santanelli, and others, with a confession published in the *New York World* on December 27, 1896. Nevertheless, according to Rinn:

It took many years of lecturing and writing on hypnosis by Professor Joseph Jastrow and other psychologists to convince the public that there was nothing occult or mystic about hypnotism and that nobody through a piercing gaze or other method could control anybody or compel one to do anything against one's will.

(pp. 124–128)

Hypnotic Regression

Nowhere is this attitude more evident than in the use of hypnosis to regress patients back to their early childhood, or even further back to a prior or previous lifetime, supposedly for therapeutic purposes. This procedure is based upon the claim that hypnosis promotes hypermnesia and cryptomnesia, or the ability to remember things we supposedly have forgotten. For a long while it was believed that hypnosis provided the person hypnotized with abnormal or unusual abilities of recall. The ease with which hypnotized subjects would retrieve forgotten memories and relive early childhood experiences was astonishing. When told to go back to his fourth or fifth birthday, for example, a young man might begin to talk in the voice of a four- or five-year-old and proceed to talk about the presents he received, the people who were present at the party, the kind of ice cream that was served, and other specific details that had long been forgotten.

However, when the veridicality of such memories was examined, it was found that many of the memories were not only false, but they were even outright fabrications. Confabulations, i.e., making up stories to fill in memory gaps, seemed to be the norm rather than the exception. It seems, literally, that using "hypnosis" to revive or awaken a person's past history somehow or other not only stimulates the person's desire to recall and his memory processes, but it also opens the flood gates of his or her imagination. Everything the person has experienced, seen, heard, or read seems to suddenly become available and is woven into a comprehensive and credible story. A story that, in many cases, the teller or narrator is convinced is something that actually happened.

Hypnotized individuals who are regressed by the hypnotist and taken back to childhood do not, however, behave like real children. Rather, hypnotically age-regressed individuals behave the way they *believe* children of that age would behave. Silverman and Retzlaff (1986) demonstrated that age-regressed adults, when given the same cognitive and intellectual tasks as children of the age to which the subjects are regressed, usually outperform the children. Barber, Spanos, and Chaves (1974) also showed that hypnotically age-regressed subjects in no way act like real children. They behave like adults playing at being a child.

By far the greatest misuse of hypnotic regression, however, is what is known as *past-life regression*. The fact that hypnotists were able to regress many of their subjects back to birth and even to the womb encouraged many of them to take it one step further and to look into preconception experiences. The hypnotists then discovered that many individuals, if properly primed with suggestions, could report events that happened to them years before their birth when they were supposedly living in another body in another time and place. These memories of other lifetimes, or of having lived before, were not only intrinsically fascinating but became even more so when follow-up in a number of the cases provided corroborating evidence for some of the claims. To those early psychologists who were unaware of the connection between hypnosis and fantasy, not only were these findings dramatic and exciting, but they seemingly offered proof of mankind's eternal hope of immortality and his dream of reincarnation.

But as we have seen, the power of the mind to recall things of which there is no conscious memory is what we call *cryptomnesia,* and it is the "key" to most of the so-called "past lives" produced in hypnotic regression. Not only is the process common and the ability to etch memories on the mind in the most fleeting of moments universal, but we also store away much more in the way of memory and memories than we will ever, ever use. Unfortunately, many of these memories also become intermixed with and confused with our dreams and fantasies, and so leave us very unsure as to whether the remembered events are true or mistaken.

According to Christie-Murray (1981), as far back as 1887 the Spaniard Colavida attempted age regression, but it was one Dr. Mortis Stark who is credited with being the first therapist to regress subjects to a life before this one. This was in 1906. Dr. Stark's work may have been preceded, though, by Colonel Albert de Rochas, who in 1911 published an account of experiments in which, over a number of years, he regressed a large number of subjects, many with multiple past lives. De Rochas used women as subjects and believed that in the process of hypnotizing them, if he used longitudinal passes, he took his subjects into the past. If, however, he used transverse passes, he took them into the future. The future lives of his subjects, he insisted, were just as vivid as the past. Unfortunately, when hypnotically revealed futures were checked years later against the real lives that had occurred, the hypnotic revelations proved to be nothing but fantasies.

In similar fashion, despite many claims to the contrary, (Goldberg, Fiore, Iverson, and Bloxham; C. E. Jay, Netherton, and Shiffrin; Wambach and Weisman, et al.) past lives also are nothing but pure fantasy and interesting examples of *cryptomnesia.* It is now well established that we— all of us—have the ability to learn, absorb, and file away large amounts of information and then, though we have forgotten the source of its origin, we are able to retrieve all or a part of it at a later time. Since, as is also well known, we add to, subtract, amplify, contract, alter, and confabulate our memories, we find ourselves hard put to determine what is the truth and memories of real events, and what is invention and fantasy or imagination.

A classic case of cryptomnesia, or "unconscious incubation," was reported in the 1906 Proceedings of the Society for Psychical Research, in which a young lady from a good family reported under hypnosis of having lived several hundred years before. She gave names and details which research found to be true, and the hypnotized girl had no memory of ever having read about them. It was soon discovered, however, that she had read a book titled *Countess Maud,* by Emily Holt, some years earlier in which every fact she reported under hypnosis was found. There were a number of discrepancies between her facts and the facts in the novel, but most were quite minor.

Perhaps the most famous hypnotic regression case of all time was that of Bridey Murphy. In the early 1950s, a Colorado businessman and amateur hypnotist named Morey Bernstein hypnotized a neighbor, Virginia Burns Tighe, who was given the name Ruth Simmons in his book *The Search For Bridey Murphy* (1956). Under hypnosis, Tighe took on the personality of a young woman named Bridey Murphy, who had lived in Cork, Ireland, in 1806. In Bernstein's book, Bridey Murphy told in many hypnotic sessions vivid details of her life in Cork. The book was an instant success, became a best-seller, went into nine printings, and sold over 170,000 hardcover copies in 1956, and many tens of thousands more in several paperback editions.

Though many readers accepted the Bridey Murphy case as positive proof of reincarnation, and hypnosis as the method of proof, experts on early nineteenth-century life in Ireland challenged the authenticity of many of Bridey's facts. A news reporter for the Chicago *American* found that a woman named Bridie Murphy Corkell had once lived across the street from Mrs. Tighe when she lived in Chicago. Other investigators argued that all of the information Bridey reported could be traced to suppressed or repressed information acquired by Tighe in her childhood from family members who had resided in Ireland years before.

The book created such a sensation, however, that it caused what *Life* magazine called "a hypnotizzy," an intense vogue of hypnosis and hypnotherapy among a large segment of the general population.* A later corrective volume was titled *A Scientific Report On "The Search For Bridey Murphy,"* edited by Milton V. Kline (1956), one of the most distinguished

---

*Called by a Texas book dealer "the hottest thing since Norman Vincent Peale," the book caused the suicide of a teen-ager, a publicity stunt by Liberace, popular recordings with titles "Do You Believe in Reincarnation," "The Love of Bridey Murphy," and "The Bridey Murphy Rock and Roll," as well as numerous "Come As You Were" costume parties and booming sales of anything and everything having to do with reincarnation. Many people who ought to have known better made public statements which they later regretted to the effect that Bernstein had proved with scientific rigor the fact of survival after death!

experts on "hypnosis" at the time. In his book Kline and the other contributors showed how readily such past-life material can be obtained and how easily human subjects will role-play extreme regressions on demand. One of the contributors, F. L. Marcuse, reflected sadly:

> The popularity of Morey Bernstein's book, *The Search For Bridey Murphy,* seems to reflect the fact that, even in our modern and presumably enlightened times, the veneer of scientific thought is still very thin. The book also seems to indicate that it pays (financially) to practice mysticism, not to expose it, to utilize sensationalism, not to contradict it, and to ridicule scientific thought, not to advocate it.
>
> (p. 59)

Marcuse then proceeded in the rest of the article to demolish every claim and argument Bernstein made with regard to reincarnation, hypnosis, and Bridey's authenticity. Tighe, Simmons, or Bridey—take your pick—made so many factual errors with regard to Irish behavior, customs, traditions, and matters of historical fact that W. B. Ready, the purchase librarian at Stanford University, took her to task in a brilliant and funny article titled "Bridey Murphy: An Irishman's View," in which he proved her guilty of culpable ignorance on matters Irish (Ready 1956).

While one would have assumed that these critiques and exposés of the Bridey Murphy matter would have disposed of reincarnation claims once and for all, the gullible and the true believers are not so easily quieted. Not only have new editions of Bernstein's book been issued—along with claims that his critics were in error—but many other volumes making similar claims have also appeared, e.g., Edith Fiore's *You Have Been Here Before* (1978), J. Iverson and A. Bloxham's *More Lives Than One* (1977), C. E. Jay's *Gretchen, I Am* (1979), R. Macready's *The Reincarnation Of Robert Macready* (1980), Morris Netherton and N. Shiffrin's *Past Lives Therapy* (1978), Helen Wambach's *Life Before Life* (1979), and A. Weisman's *We, Immortals* (1979). All of these books either accept reincarnation as a fact, or maintain in a pseudoneutral manner that a belief in reincarnation is lent additional credence by the material uncovered by way of hypnotic regression.

Despite all such efforts of "the true-believers," the experimental evidence contradicts their endeavors. Edwin Zolik (1962), in a fascinating experiment, age-regressed a male subject and elicited a past-life personality for him called Brian O'Malley. The subject was then given a post-hypnotic suggestion of complete amnesia for all that had occurred. Four days later, just before the second hypnotic session, the subject was tested for the memory of Brian and the prior session and was found to be amnestic. Then a deep hypnotic state was induced, and the fantasy was investigated without age regression. Under questioning, the subject said he did not know anyone named Brian, but soon afterwards he remembered that he knew about him because when he was eight years old, his grandfather, who had been an important figure in the subject's childhood and early adolescence, told him about Brian. Brian was a man who had a relationship with his grandfather, and whom his grandfather admired. Unfortunately, the subject felt that his grandfather had rejected him, and to minimize this rejection he created another life for himself as Brian, whom his grandfather would admire. In this case the previous existence fantasy was obviously related to a major emotional conflict that the subject had repressed. (Zolik 1958)

In another study, Zolik age-regressed a subject who created a past life based upon a character he had seen in a film. This character was born in 1850 and died in 1876, after living a solitary life following the annihilation of his family by Indians when he was a child. This fantasy creation, Zolik notes, revealed the psychological conflict the subject had as a result of his feelings of isolation, concerns about his loneliness, his inability to relate to others, and self-blame (Zolik 1962). Despite Zolik's clear demonstration that past-life memories are nothing but a mixture of remembered tales and strong, symbolically colored emotions, the misuse of hypnotic regression has continued unabated by many amateur hypnotists and reincarnationists.

The English hypnotist J. Rodney, in his book *Explorations of a Hypnotist* (1959), has reported that he was never able to confirm any of the facts reported in his past-life regressions, and emphasized that elaborate and complex fantasies could be built on a few suggestions supplied by the hypnotist.

The ability of some individuals to store information cognitively, and then to forget it until some time later when every single item and every single detail can be accurately recalled has been noted and recorded on numerous occasions. One of the most dramatic instances of this involved a Cardiff hypnotherapist named Arnall Bloxham, who, because of his life-long interest in reincarnation, used past-life regression on well over 400 people. Of all of his cases, two were outstanding. One was the story of Graham Huxtable, a Swansea man, who under regression recalled a former life as a British seaman who participated in a war against the French two hundred years before.

The second, and by far the most impressive, was the case of a Welsh housewife named Jane Evans, who described six past lives that were remarkable for the tremendous amount of accurate historical detail they contained. In one of the lives she was a maid in the house of a wealthy and powerful merchant in fifteenth-century France. Mrs. Evans described accurately the house and all of its furnishings in great detail, as well as the members of the merchant's family. She made one very significant error in her account, however. She said the merchant was unmarried and had no children. In truth he was married and had five children, circumstances no maid would be unaware of. This same failure to mention wife and children turned up in a novel that had been written about the merchant, titled *The Moneyman* by Thomas B. Costain (1948). According to Melvin Harris, who investigated the case, the evidence is overwhelming that this book was the source of all of Mrs. Evans's "memories" of her life in fifteenth-century France (Harris 1986).

In another life that she reported, Mrs. Evans was a woman named Livonia, who lived during the Roman occupation of Britain. Her account of the historical facts of this period was so accurate that authorities on Roman Britain were astounded. Again, however, there were a few factual errors. Her knowledge of the period was traced to the 1947 best-selling novel *The Living Wood* by Louis De Wohl. Every single piece of information given by Mrs. Evans could be traced to De Wohl's book, and Mrs. Evans used his fictional sequences in exactly the same order as he had, and even spoke of De Wohl's fictional characters, Curio and Valerius, as if they had been real. The historical errors in Mrs. Evan's account were also found in the book. As Harris clearly demonstrated, Mrs. Evans had the ability to store vivid stories in her subconscious and then creatively combine and edit them to the point that she herself became a character in the story.

All such examples of recall are remarkable but not unknown or even rare. They are more good examples of the phenomenon known as "cryptomnesia," or hidden memories. Our minds are libraries of years and years of accumulated information, and fortunately for our sanity, most of it is not ordinarily available to us and subject to recall. On occasions, however, these hidden memories can be revived. Sometimes they occur spontaneously. And in situations wherein we are encouraged to be creative or to fantasize, they not only can be recalled, they can be recalled in minute detail and with uncanny accuracy in some aspects, but quite erroneously in others. Like most of our memories, these hidden memories also are confabulated. If the origin of such memories is also forgotten, we have a classic case of cryptomnesia. And unless a concerted attempt is made to ferret out the origin of the memories, it is easy to delude ourselves into believing they are proof of reincarnation and that we have lived before.

Another aspect of cryptomnesia is the willingness of the individuals involved to assume, because they cannot remember ever having acquired the knowledge, it must be due to their "psychic" powers. This unfortunate tendency is fairly common. If anything unusual occurs that defies an ordinary explanation, rather than seeking the natural cause, it is much easier to attribute it to psychic abilities. Again, our memories quite often play tricks on us. And because we forgot where the information came from, it is easy for us to mistake it for something newly created. A classic example of this is the story that Helen Keller wrote in 1892 titled "The Frost King." Shortly after it was published, it was discovered that it was a slightly modified version of a story by Margaret Canby that was published twenty-nine years earlier that Helen had heard and forgotten. Many cases of automatic writing that have been attributed to discarnate spirits turn out to have been taken directly from earlier publications. Often the individual is unaware of the fact that the material that appears seemingly "out of the blue" was perceived and stored years earlier.

In his introduction to Kline's 1956 follow-up on the Bridey Murphy matter, Harold Rosen tells of one of his patients who, when hypnotized, suddenly began speaking a language current in the third century B.C. in Italy, called Oscan. Since Rosen could not understand what the patient was saying, he asked him to write it out. Rosen took the written words to a language expert, who identified it as a magical curse in Oscan. Since the patient was unfamiliar with Oscan and was completely unaware of the meaning of what he had said and written, everybody was baffled, until it was discovered that a few days before the hypnotic session he had gone to the university library to study for an economics exam. Seated at the library table, instead of studying his textbook, he began daydreaming about his girlfriend while looking at a 1904 book called *Grammar Of Oscan And Umbrian* that was opened at a page displaying on a medallion below the name "Vibia," which looked like his girlfriend's nickname, the magical curse. Without being aware of it, he photographically imprinted in his memory the Oscan curse that emerged during the hypnotic session.

Similar sorts of occurrences have even happened in the laboratory. The Finnish psychiatrist Dr. Reima Kampman has studied cryptomnesia and cryptomnesiac origins of past-life accounts for many years. One of his most interesting cases was of a girl who created eight different past lives. Her life as a young girl in thirteenth-century England proved to be particularly interesting because she suddenly began to sing a song no one was familiar with, a song that she called "the summer song." A language student identified the words as old-style English, probably Middle English. The girl had no memory of ever having heard either the words or the music. The solution came some time later when she was regressed to the age of thirteen and remembered taking a book from the shelf in the library. Although it was a casual choice and she merely flipped through the pages, she remembered this was where her song came from and where she had seen it. It was the very famous "Summer Is Icumen In" with the words given in simplified medieval English. The recording of a song from a book briefly examined more than twenty years before is a clear example of how detailed information can be stored without any conscious knowledge that this had been done.

Christie-Murray (1981) reports a number of other cases of cryptomnesia which are all good examples of unconscious incorporation and incubation of fictional material that is forgotten until a much later date, when the individual concentrates upon recalling the past and does so. So-called hypnosis is not necessary for this to occur, though it is usually used.

After having read *The Search For Bridey Murphy* shortly after its publication, I developed a serious interest in the past-life regression phenomenon and began to "play around" with it. I soon became aware of the fact that in order to regress many individuals to a so-called "past-life," all that was necessary was (1) to discuss the phenomenon with them ahead of time, (2) maintain a friendly or neutral attitude toward the concept, and (3) have the subject relax, close his or her eyes, and suggest travel into the past. For 90 to 95 percent of individuals willing to play this game, this simple procedure is all that is required to bring about the recall of material that one could construe as related to a previous existence.

One might assume that only a few highly imaginative or fantasy prone individuals would produce cryptomnesiac material. Instead, over the years I have found that just about everyone—men, women, and children of all ages—not only has the imaginative capability of producing this sort of past-life material, but actually does so. This statement is much more than mere opinion, since it is based upon ten years of regressing university students, friends, and neighbors who have shown an interest in the phenomenon. It is important to note that my subjects were not all highly "select" volunteers, since many of the students were "forced" into serving as subjects because of class requirements for research participation.

There are, as you might assume, significant individual differences in both the ease with which this past-life material is resurrected and in the type and amount of material revealed. Highly imaginative and fantasy-prone individuals not only produce multiple lives but also provide hundreds of details about people, places, and things in the past, whereas more prosaic and mundane individuals find it very difficult to produce much more than names, places, and dates.

Out of an estimated five to seven hundred individuals regressed into the past and conducted into the future via age progression, I have encountered four or five individuals whose imaginative productions have approached the creativity of Bernstein's Virginia Tighe, Bloxham's Jane Evans and Graham Huxtable, and some of the cases reported by Edith Fiore and

Helen Wambach. One of my most fascinating clients was a middle-aged businessman, whom I will call Mr. R., who sought me out because of his confidence in the healing power of hypnosis. According to Mr. R., he had been plagued with migraines all of his life until a few years earlier when he had encountered a psychic who had hypnotized him, regressed him into the past, and had revealed that in another life Mr. R. had been an Indian sacrificial maiden who had been killed by a blow to the head by a priest. This blow, of course, was the source of the headaches. Once this knowledge and insight was obtained, the migraine disappeared, never to return. This convinced Mr. R. that past-life regression was a magical process. At his request and with no attempts to disillusion him, I agreed to hypnotize and regress him into the past in the hope that he could discover if, in one of his prior existences, he had been his maternal grandmother, who died before his birth.

Working with Mr. R. weekly for more than a year was a fascinating experience with regard to role-playing fantasies. With only a modicum of suggestions for relaxation—either upright or lying down—Mr. R. traveled into the past and became on successive weeks an Indian brave during the French and Indian Wars, a high priest in Atlantis, an impregnated pickaninny on a Southern planation during the Civil War, a cockney prostitute in London during the eighteenth century, a Spanish conquistador during the conquest of Mexico, an American airman during World War II, and others. Unfortunately, we were never able to place him in the body of his grandmother. During each of these incarnations, Mr. R. also ran the gamut of human emotions: living and dying and suffering all of the slings and arrows that flesh is heir to in the process. At times, fearing for his physical health, I moved him forward or backward in time to escape the terrors of one of his imaginative involvements. Each of Mr. R.'s excursions was taped and later reviewed carefully in an attempt to determine if any of the hundreds of specific details that emerged could be historically grounded in fact. Despite hours in every library in the area, and discussions with historical authorities at the university, none of the material could be historically confirmed.

On the other hand, most of the historical material produced by the less fantasy-prone could easily be traced back to its original source in events they had somehow encountered earlier. In general, most of the material produced by most of the regressees was easily recognized and identified by them. For example, a middle-aged school teacher when regressed reported that he was a singer in a nightclub in Cincinnati during the 1920s. On being asked to sing the lyrics to songs popular at the time he crooned "Always," "Alexander's Ragtime Band," "What'll I Do?" and so on. Queried after the session was over, he reported that in his younger days he had, indeed, been a singer of popular songs and had worked in a nightclub in Cincinnati for several years before becoming a schoolteacher.

Similarly, a student produced a tale about being a riverboat gambler on a steamboat plying the Mississippi during the late 1800s. The riverboat had the highly unusual name "The Wapsipinicon Queen." Queried later, it turned out the student was from Central City, Iowa, located on the Wapsipinicon River, and all during high school he had patronized a nightclub built around an abandoned steamboat where gambling sometimes occurred. Although some of the material uncovered was untraceable, nearly all of the major figures, places, and events could be connected to things in this lifetime that he had read, seen, or discussed, rendering unnecessary any excursions into previous existences for explanations.

The beauty of the human imagination and the power of suggestion in combination can create wondrous and enthralling tales. In 1987, to illustrate the effect of suggestion on this phenomena, I divided sixty compliant students into three groups. The first group heard a tape recording about "a new and exciting kind of therapy known as past-life therapy," and the students were also told: "You will be able to take a fascinating journey back in time." Following hypnosis, eighty-five percent of this group reported having had at least one other life. A second group of twenty students heard a neutral description of past-life therapy and were told: "You may or may not drift back in time to another lifetime." Under hypnosis, sixty percent of this group claimed they had lived another life. The third group was told that past-life therapy was a crazy ridiculous sort of game developed by a "bunch of far-out therapists on the West Coast." These students were also warned that under hypnosis they might accidentally drift back and imagine they were living in another lifetime. However, most normal people hadn't been able to see anything, they were also informed. During their hypnosis sessions only ten percent of the students in this group reported having had another life. Clearly, the study offers additional evidence that past-life regression phenomena, rather than being examples of the "reality" of reincarnation, are the results of suggestions made by the hypnotist, expectations held by the subject, and the demand characteristics of the hypnoidal relationship. Whether reincarnation is or is not a possibility cannot be determined on the basis of past-life regressions.

Spanos and his co-workers also have recently carried out studies of past-life regressions which agree with this conclusion (Spanos 1987–88). In one study involving 110 subjects, thirty-five reported past lives and provided numerous details about occupations, families, interests, etc. All of these subjects scored higher on hypnotizability than those who did not report past lives. In addition, individual differences in the vividness of these experiences and the credibility subjects assigned to them was predicted by the subject's propensity for imaginative involvement. The frequency with which subjects reported vivid daydreaming, and the frequency with which they reported becoming absorbed in everyday imaginative activities, correlated positively with the vividness of their past lives.

The best predictor of how much credibility subjects assigned to these past-life experiences was a composite of their attitudes and beliefs about reincarnation. People who believed in reincarnation, those who thought the idea plausible and who expected to experience past lives, found them more credible than those who questioned the concept of reincarnation. Despite the contention by Wambach (1979) that the historical information obtained from hypnotically regressed past-life responders was almost always accurate, when Spanos and his coworkers asked their subjects questions that could be checked on, they found them more often incorrect than correct. Moreover, the errors were of the type that people from the relevant historical epochs would have been unlikely to make. For example, the claimant who said he was a Japanese fighter pilot was unable to name the emperor of Japan, and incorrectly said Japan was at peace in 1940. Another subject claimed he was Julius Caesar, emperor of Rome in A.D. 50. Caesar was never crowned emperor, and he died in 44 B.C. Moreover, the custom of dating events in terms of B.C. or A.D. did not develop until centuries later.

Further experimental support for the fantasy construction hypothesis has been furnished by Kampman and Hirvonoja (1976) when they had their past-life regressees connect various elements of their past-life descriptions with events in their current lives. In this way they were able to uncover the source of the information used by the subjects to build their fantasies.

If one were so minded, one could claim hypnotic age regression also provides proof of evolution. Kline (1952) regressed a subject beyond birth and down the evolutionary ladder to an ape-like state. In similar fashion, hypnotic age progression can be considered as offering proof of "time travel," or as a form of a "time machine." John Gribbin, in his book *Time Warps* (1980), takes hypnosis researchers to task for their failure to investigate future lives. In his words:

> Blinkered by the established concept of reincarnation and the unspoken view that the future is yet to come and so has no form, Bloxham (like essentially all his colleagues involved in regression studies) has made no effort to investigate future lives. Yet, if there is anything in my hypothesis at all, the future should be accessible as the past to the unconscious mind in the trance state. Will some hypnotist now take up the challenge and investigate —what? Pre-incarnation? Progression?
>
> (p. 153)

Gribbin was obviously unaware that such hypnotic age progression has been a well-established procedure for some time. Kline (1951) studied a twenty-two-year-old woman and progressed her to age 65. In a more extensive study, Rubenstein and Newman (1954) progressed medical students to later stages of their careers as practicing physicians. Rather than demonstrations of "time travel," they are interesting demonstrations of the power of suggestion and the phenomenon of unconscious role enactment.

In a study I carried out in the early 1980s using fifty-three undergraduate students and building up strong expectations of both past and future lives, over ninety percent of the subjects were able to produce both past and future lives. Producing fantasy material about past lives was considerably easier for the students than producing future life material. This may have been simply due to the fact that memories of the past, material read, etc., provide the fantasizer with an already existing cognitive structure, whereas the future fantasy requires starting from scratch and creating something entirely new. In other words, it is easier to remember than it is to create. Though the students were equally cooperative with suggestions about living in the future and the past, the details of their future lives appeared to be considerably dimmer or more clouded than the details of lives they had previously led. It also may be that it is easier to see where you have been, than it is to see where you are going.

With regard to its therapeutic implications, the use of hypnosis, unconscious productions, and fantasy material are standard clinical procedures that are far from new. It is highly doubtful that any material obtained as a result of the past-life regression technique would defy explanation in more orthodox psychodynamic terms. Very little if any of the unconscious material coming out of past-life regressions requires the use of mystical or esoteric concepts like reincarnation or metempsychosis to support its use for therapeutic purposes. In fact, the use of such metaphysical terms may in the long run do much more harm than good.

Dr. Bruce Goldberg, a dentist who practices both past- and future-life therapy, and who has written a book about it called *Past Lives, Future Lives* (1982), also reports that progressing a person is much more difficult than regressing him. He explains this as due to the fact that all of us have been "programmed to believe that the future hasn't occurred yet." As Paul Edwards remarked in his excellent series of critical articles "The Case Against Reincarnation" (1986-87), Goldberg sees this as a serious error, and despite the widespread prejudice against the future, Goldberg progresses some of his subjects into distant centuries and these subjects provide us with lovely science-fiction accounts of marvels to come. Unfortunately, as Edwards notes, although hundreds of years ahead is a snap, information about next year, next week, or even the next two days seems beyond both Goldberg and his subjects. Edwards also observes that:

> Dr. Goldberg in his modesty has not realized that he himself constitutes the best evidence for reincarnation. His comic gifts are quite in the same league as those of Fatty Arbuckle and Ben Turpin. I do not for a moment believe that such a stupendous talent can be explained by ordinary genetics. The only adequate explanation would be in terms of one or more previous lives of assiduous labor or else the hand of God.
>
> (Fall 1986, p. 32)

In conclusion, there is little if any differences between subjects age-regressed to childhood and past-life reporters who construct elaborate fantasies by intermixing information taken from things they have read, seen, and heard, and imagining that these things had actually happened. More-over, because of the demand characteristic of the hypnotic situation, plus expectations and suggestions provided by the hypnotist, these subjects will act out and role-play other lives and personalities in such a convincing and elaborate fashion that even experienced and competent observers have been deceived into believing their recreations are something more than mere fantasy. Finally, these past-life reports can be obtained from nearly everyone—not just the fantasy-prone—provided the proper kinds of suggestions and expectations are provided in advance.

Hypnotic Progression

Because of my interest in hypnosis, for many years I have been intrigued by the fact that many people are so compliant and suggestible that hardly any effort at all is required to get them imaginatively involved in the hypnosis game. Others, even though very cooperative, show unmistakable signs of high muscular tension and resistance to any and all forms of suggestion. These more literal-minded souls require a great deal of persuasion and wheedling before they are ever able to relax and begin to use their imaginative powers. A few years ago I carried out a small demonstration (I hesitate to call it an experiment since the outcome was obvious) in hypnotic age progression (not regression). Two groups of ten volunteers each were taken one hundred years into the future. One of the groups—the experimental group—consisted of avid science fiction fans. These subjects scored in the upper quartile of a modified version of Tellegen's absorption scale (a measure of ability to immerse oneself in nonordinary reality). The second group—the control group—was made up of economics and business school majors. These subjects scored in the lower quartile of the absorption scale.

The experimental procedure consisted of relaxing each subject, putting each of them on a time machine which moved them 100 years into the future, and then requiring them to describe what they had seen and experienced. As expected, the science-fiction fans—without exception—described fantastic cities, unusual vehicles, planet colonization, trips to distant stars, exotic creatures, magical human powers, etc. On the other hand, it was like pulling eyeteeth to obtain any information at all from members of the control group. Many reported they were unable to see anything at all, while those who did envision a future reported one pretty much like our present world, except more crowded, more polluted, and with faster means of transportation. Three members of the control group focused on their grandchildren, jobs, sports figures, and records, in a world pretty much like the one we inhabit today. Four members of the control group had tremendous difficultly seeing anything at all, and only after much coaxing reported things like people in park-like settings wearing tunic-like clothing—men, women, and children clothed alike, as in "Star Trek"—and people living in domed cities with climate control, working in robot-controlled plants and offices. In terms of fantasy, the control of the visions of the two groups was dramatically different and reflected expected personality, concerns, and interests of the group members.

My efforts, however, were feeble indeed when compared with those of Dr. Helen Wambach and her successor, Dr. Chet B. Snow. Wambach, a deep and sincere believer in the reality of past lives as well as the reality of reincarnation, published two books on the subject, *Recalling Past Lives* (1978) and *Life Before Life* (1979). After having demonstrated to her satisfaction that her group process of hypnotic regression successfully enabled most people to dig up past lives, she wondered how it would work when applied to the future. In 1980 Wambach began to stage "future-lives" workshops in which participants were mentally "progressed" ahead in time to potential future life times in the periods between A.D. 2100 and 2200 and A.D. 2300 to 2500. She was assisted in these early efforts by a friend and by Dr. R. Leo Sprinkle, another psychologist and another believer in ESP, reincarnation, alien abductions, and also, interestingly enough, a UFOlogist and himself an alien abductee. Before Wambach was able to gather all the data she needed to publish her results, she fell ill and died. Fortunately, however, she was able to train Chet B. Snow in her methods and techniques and to turn over her files to him before her demise.

Snow, it seems, was the ideal person to take up Wambach's crusade. For Snow was not only a dedicated and devoted student, he was also in possession of "psychic" abilities himself, and was an excellent cryptomnesiac in that he was "able to relax and 'let go' of the conscious mind's control, thereby allowing hidden memories to surface quickly and easily." Moreover, Snow, who got his doctorate in psychology at UCLA under Wambach's supervision, was an avid reader of the older occult literature and a dedicated devotee of every aspect and nuance of "The New Age."

Snow not only continued Wambach's work, but he proved to be one of her best "progressees" when he underwent three hypnotic future progressions himself during his tutelage. His visions of the late 1990s form the first chapter of a truly "awesome" book entitled *Mass Dreams of the Future* (1989). For well over 300 pages we are regaled with some of the most outlandish and bizarre fantasies ever assembled between two covers. But the most outlandish and bizarre fact of all is that Snow not only takes seriously every occult idea he has encountered in the past, but he also sincerely believes that all of the imaginative material elicited from the several hundred hypnotized future-lives progressees—as well as his own fantasies—is not only true and accurate, but this is the way the future will be! Though Snow tempers these statements by confessing that "in no way would either Dr. Wambach or I present the following previews of the future, as seen personally or by our subjects as incontrovertible or irreversible. They are, nonetheless, part of the 'mass dream' of the future that we here on Earth are projecting, through our subconscious minds, today. As such they are important harbingers of what we may consciously be living through tomorrow." (pg. xix) In other words, though the future isn't set in cement, the way we say it will be is the way it's gonna be!

Moreover, we are living today in the midst of an "apocalyptic spirit," and whether or not one believes in the message of the Great Pyramid, astrology, biblical warnings about Armageddon, or the channelings of contemporary seers such as the psychic Edgar Cayce, all of these pronouncements of impending drastic change form part of it, i.e., today's apocalyptic spirit!

Snow's own trips into the future, surprisingly, are also apocalyptic. In December 1998, Snow prophesies, California has already sunk into the ocean and water stretches as far inland as parts of Nevada and Arizona. Both the world's weather and economy are in a tailspin. Food is hard to come by. Climactic changes have made the nation colder and the United States is all but cut in two parts. Snow also sees in 1998 that the Soviets have taken over West Berlin! In his words:

> Instead of moving with immediate humanitarian relief, the Soviets had taken advantage of our temporary helplessness to take over West Berlin and most of West Germany. Yugoslavia was being undermined by a vicious civil war

into which Soviet-led troops from Hungary and Czechoslovakia had intervened.

(p. 15)

Such are the perils of prophesy. Since Snow wrote his book in 1988 or early 1989, even he with his prophecies isn't fast enough to keep up with events in Eastern Europe which, interestingly enough, he failed entirely to foresee.

As for poor Japan: "Japan as a country doesn't exist any longer. A lot of it's fallen into the sea." Well, I guess we'll just have to wait and see how accurate he is on this one.

Even more preposterous is his prediction that by 1998 people will be communicating via "telepathic nets." Wambach also gives Snow a "near death," or "out of the body" experience complete with floating, seeing his body on the bed, white-light, and all. Moreover, Snow is surrounded by a host of nonphysical entities. According to the entities in the future, there would be only two categories of humanity: the "garbage" and the "garbagemen," and one would be able to discriminate the two by their smell. Just how this smell indicator works Snow doesn't say.

Wambach, according to Snow, also believed that once her subjects were in the "dreaming mind" state as she called it—high theta brain wave state on the EEG—they also activated latent telepathic abilities. The idea then occurred to her that this ability could be tapped to get answers about the future. She saw herself as a "Gallup pollster of the subconscious mind." According to Wambach-Snow:

The interference between what the mind reveals through the subconscious and what gets "remembered" and put into words is especially great when we deal with the future. Why is that so? Well. . . . the conscious levels of our mind are deeply involved in our individual futures as are our emotions. Together they are constantly planning and plotting what we say and do from day to day in order to bring us the most pleasure and least pain from any given situation. . . . Consequently, throughout history human beings have been fascinated with the idea of predicting the future. Moreover, due in part to the dual hemispheres of our brains, we have two fundamentally different ways of consciously expressing what our minds know, including future predictions. Thus, we either develop "right brain" imaginational and prophetic systems to tell us what tomorrow will bring or we set up rational "left brain" ways of collecting, organizing and comparing as much past and present sensory information as possible and try to predict from correlations among the data. Today we call the first kind of predicting "psychic" and the second "forecasting." They've had other names in the past, but it boils down to the basic difference of which part of the brain we're primarily relying on for answers.

(pp. 33-34)

If this bit of spurious psychological misinformation isn't bad enough, Wambach-Snow add insult to injury by comparing the future forecasts of the think tank organizations such as the Hudson Institute, Rand Corporation, and World Futurists with the predictions of the modern psychic channels and LO! we are informed that:

> Although both groups failed more often than they succeeded in predicting near-term trends, the psychics' "batting average" was as high, if not slightly higher, than that of the forecasters! This seemed to be especially true when the psychics' predictions had little immediate personal relevance or impact. It appears as if the conscious mind or ego interferes more with what we predict when it feels we may be personally affected.
>
> Rationalist left-brain future forecasting is less accurate than psychic predicting because it is performed solely by the mind's conscious level, where personal involvement with the future is greatest. Consequently, the forecaster's social needs, surroundings and shared expectations act to "contaminate" this kind of future predicting.
>
> (p. 34)

This was the reasoning that lay behind the Wambach-Snow decision to use reports

> ... from the subconscious minds of a large number of ordinary individuals in a light hypnotic state. Obviously, obtaining information about the future via hypnosis, where direct mental images are received through the subconscious, is closer to psychic prediction than to think-tank forecasting.

Nevertheless, Wambach combined the two methods. Wambach also confessed to Snow that a lifetime of clinical work taught her that "words are a smoke screen," and that real communication always takes place telepathically beneath the words. In Snow's words, "Helen felt that in the evidence she had amassed during her workshops that at least half of her hypnotized subjects could pick up thoughts and feelings telepathically was one of the greatest discoveries of her research." When she asked her subjects whether they found themselves getting answers in the form of images and impressions slightly before they had heard her questions, 50 to 60 percent consistently replied in the affirmative. This, for Wambach, clinched it. Her subjects are psychic at the unconscious level and though our conscious minds reject the idea that predicting the future is possible, the unconscious mind knows better—it knows that it can be done! We also learn from Snow that Wambach believed in "the general principle that one should not do anything to harm a patient. The same holds true for research subjects, naturally." This is most comforting since

Wambach-Snow with the help of Dr. Sprinkle managed to progress over 2,500 volunteers into the late 1990s and the period A.D. 2100 to 2300-2400. Before the progressions began, however, Wambach confessed to Snow that she had a profound near-death experience while undergoing heart valve bypass surgery, and she clinically "died" twice on the operating table. While in these out-of-body states, she had a psychic revelation of the Earth moving in vast cycles lasting from 25 to 26,000 years each. During these cycles the Earth enters a sector in which cosmic ray impingement significantly increases. These increases heat up the Earth's magnetic core, and cause increased geophysical upheavals such as volcanoes and earthquakes, i.e., global disasters which reduce the Earth's population and cause a planet-wide energy shift Wambach calls "beyond the ultraviolet." This energy shift affects all living organisms, including humanity, and favors the spread of psychic powers such as telepathy. Only those organisms that manage to adapt to these "higher vibratory rates" will survive.

Wambach admits that she had no hard scientific evidence to back up her scenario, but she was sure the change was already underway. Snow then takes us on an historical excursion back through Plato, Heraclitus, the Biblical prophets and their prophecies, the Roman diviners, Stonehenge, the Phoenicians, Choldeaus, Egyptians, Chinese, and American Indian Astrology, the Hopi, Aztecs, and Mayans, up to the present and the modern Biblical scholar Zecharia Sitchin. All of these prognosticators—even including Charles Berlitz and his book *Doomsday 1999 A.D.*—foresee cataclysms ahead.

Snow then leaps into the present with another bang: the ageless wisdom of Edgar Cayce, Shirley MacLaine, J. Z. Knight, and Jack Pursel. These modern seers owe a large debt to Alice D. Bailey, who channeled the "Ageless Wisdom" from 1919 to 1949. Snow then takes us on a visit to the *Akashic Record,* Jane Roberts Seth, Helen Schuchman's *Course In Miracles, The Law of Karma,* Dr. M. Scott Peck, *The Starseed Transmissions,* Rupert Sheldrake, and other gurus and channelers since time immemorial.

These are exactly the type of publications that should bear a warning label on their covers like those found on bottles of hard liquor and packages of cigarettes. WARNING: Reading and heeding this sort of material can cause severe constipation of the intellect, chronic irrationality, and eventual loss of contact with consensual reality.

The Mass Dreams

First of all it seems that humanity will encounter some sort of apocalyptic disaster in the twenty-first century but will be making its way back by A.D. 2300. Even though Snow is often shocked by the findings from the 2,500 progressees, e.g., "Why would third sex or androgynous reports be found only in future life data and never among past lives?" As for the content of the progressees fantasies for A.D. 2100-2200, we find many of them wearing a one-piece uniform or jumpsuit or loose-fitting tunics or robes, eating synthetic foodstuffs and pills, living in spaceships or space colonies or in an orbiting space station. Also prevalent were reports of extraterrestrials and flying saucers. Many reported a polluted or poisonous environment as well as intelligent machines and robots, and most reported significant declines in the standard of living. For the period A.D. 2300 and beyond most of the reports followed the typical science-fiction "earth colonizes other worlds" scenario with visits to the near planets, the colonization of Mars, and the Martian moons playing significant roles. Then movements to distant star systems and other planets were also reported. Despite these stellar sojourns more than half of the progressees in the 2300 to 2500 time frame returned to future lifetimes here on Earth. Most lived in cities and towns pretty much like those of today except they had improved transportation, food, clothing, and shelter facilities.

Most interesting and significant of all is that none of the feedback from any of the progressees involves anything startlingly new or dramatic, anything wholly new or evolutionary—anything, in a word, that is not already contained in our present-day visions of what tomorrow holds. Rather than being prognostications or prophecies they are merely projections and extrapolations from what the progressees have already read, seen, and imagined in their pasts. It is also quite clear that the content of these "mass dreams" has also been significantly influenced by the suggestions and queries fed to the subjects by Wambach, Snow, and Sprinkle. The only findings of any interest or significance whatsoever are two: (1) only a few of the hypnotized subjects reported being physically alive in either the twenty-second or the twenty-fourth centuries—only 4 to 5 percent for A.D. 2100-2200 and only 11 and 12 percent saw themselves in the A.D. 2300-2500 period. This indicates that most of the progressees were fully in touch with the fact they were "just playing a game" with one foot solidly on the floor in "here and now" reality. Despite Snow's claim that "only a few of the future-life data sheets reveal obvious 'fantasy' characteristics or clear-cut signs of ego wish-fulfillment needs," how could they possibly? Remember, most of them are dead! Snow also argues that the reports could not possibly be pure fantasy because "pure fantasy would have led to a much wider range of possibilities." This is highly unlikely. What possible "wider range" would he expect? Moreover, the setting, the questions, the time periods, and the demand characteristics are all quite limiting and constrain the subjects to a fairly limited range of responses. Within the set limits the range of the progressees' replies is certainly as wide as can be expected.

In the final chapters Snow dips into: quantum theory and how it makes precognition, future predictions, and prophecy possible; how we are being watched over by extraterrestrials; reports from UFO abductees and those who have had psychic contact with the aliens; and Dr. Snow's own personal religious encounter with a Christ-like figure. Finally, as Snow sees it, humanity has a choice between a violent apocalypse of conflict and destruction, or, if we are willing to evolve spiritually (via the New Age gurus one supposes), we "may awaken to our true multidimensional identity as immortal spirits." It is clear that Dr. Snow has read just about everything written by adherents of The New Age and believers in the occult tradition. And most incredible of all is that Snow, who supposedly has a Ph.D. in Psychology, shows not even a glimmer of either skepticism or scientific training on any of the book's 307 fantasy-filled pages. Apparently Snow believes, unquestioningly, everything he is told, everything he sees, and everything he reads related to the already passé New Age and its phantasmagoric belief system.

Snow's excursion into quantum theory brings to mind John Wheeler's 1979 remarks at the annual AAAS meeting in Houston. Speaking against the inclusion of parapsychology in AAAS, Wheeler argued:

> Surely when so much is written about spoon-bending, parapsychology, telepathy, the Bermuda Triangle, dowsing, and when others write on "quantified etherics," bioactochronics, levitation, and occult chemistry, there must be *some* reality behind these words? Surely where there's smoke there's fire? No, where there's so much smoke there's smoke.
>
> Every science that is a science has hundreds of hard results; but search fails to turn up a single one in "parapsychology." Would it not be fair, and for the credit of science, for "parapsychology" to be required to supply one or two or three battle-tested findings as a condition for membership in the AAAS? . . . .
>
> For every phenomenon that is proven to be the result of self-delusion or fraud or misunderstanding of perfectly natural everyday physics and biology, three new phenomena of "pathological science" spring up in its place. The confidence man is able to trick person after person because so often the victim is too ashamed of his gullibility or too mouselike in his "stop, thief" to warn others. . . .
>
> There's nothing that one can't research the hell out of. Research guided by bad judgment is a black hole for good money. No one can forbear speaking up who has seen $10,000 cozened out of a good friend, $100,000 milked out of a distinguished not-for-profit research organization, and $1,000,000 syphoned away from American taxpayers—all in the cause of "research" in pathological science.
>
> Where there is meat there are flies. No subject more attracts the devotees

of the "paranormal" than the quantum theory of measurement. To sort out what it takes to define an observation, to classify what it means to say "no elementary phenomenon is a phenomenon until it is an observed phenomenon" is difficult enough without being surrounded by the buzz of "telekinesis," "signals propagated faster than light," and "parapsychology."

(Wheeler 1979, pps. 12–13)

Before leaving the topic it is important that two particularly irksome misunderstandings about the human nervous system be corrected. The first is the widespread and fallacious assumption that the two halves of the human brain are specialized; the second is the absurd piece of folklore that at any given time we use only ten percent of our brainpower.

The Left (Rational), Right (Creative) Brain Myth

As mentioned by Snow earlier, almost everyone now knows: the left hemisphere of the human brain is rational, logical, and Western, while the right hemisphere is creative, intuitive, and Eastern. It seems that everyone is sure of this except those who did the research on which this fallacy is based. Unfortunately, this misconception arising out of Roger Sperry's split-brain research was aided and abetted by the work of a group of psychologists who assumed that right and left dominant thinkers could be spotted and identified by watching the direction in which they glanced when asked to perform a simple mental calculation. Left lookers were right-brain dominant and right lookers were left-brain dominant. This simplistic nonsense helped all of those looking for quick-and-dirty solutions to complex issues to assume that right-brain people are artistic and all that, whereas left-brain people are mathematically inclined.

Jerry Levy, a neurophysiologist at the University of Chicago, states unequivocally, "No complex function—music, art, or whatever—can be assigned to one hemisphere or the other. Any high level thinking in a normal person involves constant communication between the two sides of the brain." (Levy 1988, p. 5). This has been true since the beginning of time and it will continue to be true as long as man is the human being we know today. It is an error of the first magnitude to generalize from Sperry's split-brain operations on people suffering from intractable epilepsy who were, quite literally, radically different following their surgery from normal people. When the corpus callosum—the largest bridge of nerve filters in the brain—was severed by surgery the patients were almost literally of two minds. Sperry also discovered these two minds had different specializations, at different times, and with different activities.

Although the patients seemed normal after surgery things were far from simple. For example, if an object was placed in the left hand of a blindfolded, split-brain patient he or she would deny that the object existed. If the patients were asked to search through a collection of items for one that resembled the object they were told was in their left hand, they would invariably make the correct decision even though they insisted they were only guessing. Sperry diagnosed that the tactile information coming from the patients' left hands was transmitted to the brain's right hemisphere which is incapable of verbal expression. The right brain did, however, process the information nonverbally. There was thus no problem with the easy recognition by the left hemisphere when shown a similar item.

Sperry also noted that the left hemisphere was superior in the sort of logic used to solve geometry problems, but he also discovered that if the problem calls for the integration of information in order to draw a conclusion, the right hemisphere is crucial. In almost every human activity there is a constant interchange between the two halves of the brain. As for our verbal behavior, while the left hemisphere understands grammar and syntax, the right hemisphere is better at interpreting emotion and understanding intonation. In most of our verbal activities such as carrying on a conversation, or reading a story, *both* halves of the brain are involved in processing and assimilating the information.

The same thing holds true for music, art, and most other creative activities. In music, the right hemisphere is superior in the recognition of chords, but in discriminating which of two sounds came first the left hemisphere is necessary. To either play or create music these skills are not only necessary, but they must be integrated by both halves of the brain.

As for the corpus callosum, not only is it well known that only the mammals and more intelligent creatures have it, but also neuroscientists have found that the smarter the creature is, the bigger and better its connections. Not only *do* we use both halves of our brain all the time, but we *need* to do so if we hope to use "the brain" effectively for anything at all.

Some while ago Barry Beyerstein pointed to another logical fallacy invariably brought up by defenders of the paranormal. This one is called "the argument from ignorance." Defendants of the paranormal argue that if it cannot be proved that something is not the case, this somehow or other counts as evidence that it is true. According to Beyerstein (1989, pps. 12–14), the ploy he most frequently encountered is the assertion that normal people only use 10 percent of their brains. If we don't know what the rest of the brain is there for, then it must be there for our paranormal powers, i.e., for bending spoons, precognition, levitation, psychic healing, telepathy, clairvoyance, and other such supernormal abilities. Even if the 10 percent myth were true—which it is not—this in no way supports the existence of psychic powers.

Despite its frequent mention, nowhere in the neurological, physiological, psychological, or anatomical literature can one find any factual statements saying that we use any specific percent of our brains whenever we put it to use. The 10 percent statement, on the contrary, is at variance with much of what is known about brain functions. Not only is the brain costly to run, consuming approximately one fourth of the metabolic resources of the resting body, it is highly unlikely in the face of natural selections that scarce resources would be wasted to produce and support such an underutilized organ. Moreover, Beyerstein notes, although the brain has evolved a certain amount of redundancy in its circuitry as a safety precaution, little if any of this circuitry goes unemployed. EEGs, CAT, MRI, and PET scans, magneto-encephalography, and regional cerebral blood flow measures all show that even during sleep there are no idle areas in the brain. "Such tranquility would be a sign of gross pathology." "Logic alone," Beyerstein adds, "should give pause to the 10-percenters . . . . How well do you think you'd function if 90 percent of your brain were suddenly incapacitated?. . . . We all know stroke victims who have lost considerably less brain tissue and are severely debilitated." (p. 12)

We also know that the brain is not just one undifferentiated mass. Instead, distinct functions are distributed throughout the brain, and if the 10 percent argument was correct, 90 percent of each functional area would have to be unused in order not to lose certain functions totally in a 90 percent dormant brain. This is, of course, implausible. Beyerstein's research and that of others has shown that brain circuits atrophy from disease, and if 90 percent of our brains were idle, one would expect massive degeneration which does not occur in normal people. Beyerstein also notes that the myth might have been fueled by the remarkable ability of developing brains to reorganize and recover from brain damage. Children can recover a surprisingly normal level of function after loss of an entire hemisphere to injury or disease. While this is far less than 90 percent, even here dead nerve cells are not replaced and serious deficits still remain. Popular accounts of such recoveries could have led to the misconception they never needed the extra brain tissue in the first place.

Misinterpretation of early brain research could well have been another reason. Lashley's studies showed that rats with large portions of their cortex removed were still able to learn and behave. Serious deficits were nevertheless present, and misinterpretation of the findings added to the fallacy. What is referred to as the "silent cortex" is anything but silent. These areas of the brain are responsible for our language skills and our ability to engage in abstract thought.

Areas of maximal activity shift in the brain as we change tasks and vary attention and arousal *but* there are normally no dormant regions awaiting new assignments. . . . As a metaphor for the fact that few of us fully exploit our talents, who could deny it?. . . . As a refuge for occultists seeking the neural basis of the miraculous, the probability is considerably less than ten percent.

(p. 14)

In this Beyerstein is most certainly correct!

Hypnosis and the Epilepsies

Before leaving the topic of hypnosis, it is imperative that we look briefly at another commonly overlooked source of "trance-like" behavior: epilepsy. Epilepsy is, of course, not one but a number of different disorders having in common that there is a discharging lesion of some region of the cerebral cortex. Psychomotor or temporal lobe epilepsy often goes undiagnosed since the psychomotor attacks are local fits and the discharging lesion is restricted to one of the brain's temporal lobes. In these attacks the discharge does not spread to the rest of the hemisphere and thus consciousness is retained. Since the motor areas are not involved, there are no convulsions, although there may be slight twitchings around the mouth and eyes. Otherwise, there are few symptoms that indicate the patient is having a seizure. Mostly the patient appears to be in a light trance. Usually he or she is capable of speech, and can talk and carry on a halting conversation. The eyes may appear glazed and be staring, and for a few moments movement may be automatic and repetitive, and there may be a loss of memory, total or partial, for any events occurring during the attack. If it spreads to the adjoining parietal lobes, there will be an insensibility to pain. If the discharge reaches the limbic system, there may be gasping, swallowing, or chewing movements, and an excess of salivation. In many ways the patients appear to be, for a moment or so, hypnotized or in a trance.

Not recognizing these things for what they are, many people describe themselves as being in or under a spell or being bewitched. Others report hearing "voices without any sound" or as issuing from within, and others report seeing visions—visions of spectral faces, ghosts, phantoms, and other weird beings. People experiencing these things for the first time, of course, fear for their sanity and are reluctant to tell even their spouses, trusted friends, or their physician about the bizarre events. Better silence, they reason, than confinement in a mental institution and being thought crazy or insane. As far back as 1879 Hughlings Jackson described some of his patients reporting feelings of depersonalization and *déjà vu* that usually ushered in the attacks, which were often followed by trance-like episodes and elaborate visions.

Years later Wilder Penfield, in his work at the Montreal Neurological Institute, was able to evoke memories by stimulating the hippocampus in the temporal lobe. When Penfield stimulated the amygdala, another important nerve center in the temporal lobe, he produced the identical automatisms seen in the psychomotor seizure. What is most fascinating is that the chief phenomena in both so-called hypnotic behavior and the psychomotor seizure—automatisms, hallucinations, sensory disturbance, and amnesia—are identical. Of further interest is the fact that the same conditions, i.e., the induction processes used to instill "hypnosis" are the same as those known to produce reflex epilepsy. Thus, if the hypnotic trance is genuine, the individual is actually undergoing a psychomotor seizure. It is also more than a mere coincidence that the same auditory and visual stimuli used to invoke "hypnosis" can, in susceptible epileptoids, precipitate a psychomotor attack. Flickering stroboscopic lights, driving along a tree-lined street with the sun low in the sky, staring at changing patterns of light and shade or a flickering candle, gazing at bright lights and passing the hands back and forth to interrupt the beams (Mesmeric passes for example) are also known to precipitate epileptic attacks. Thornton has shown most convincingly that what Mesmer produced in his patients was, in fact, reflex epilepsy. Since he treated only patients with neurological disorders, a large number would have been suffering from epilepsy, and in these his so-called "Mesmeric fluid" would have been most effective.

The same auditory stimuli—drums, chanting, music, bells, hissing, natural repetitive sounds like surf and rain, as well as tactile stimuli such as repetitive stroking or patting—all have been used to induce the hypnotic trance, and all can also act upon an unstable area of the cortex to generate an abnormal electrical discharge. It should be strongly emphasized at this point, however, that a normal EEG does not exclude a diagnosis of epilepsy when there is a clear description of an epileptic event from the observer. Of course in most instances of clinical and laboratory "hypnosis" with non-epileptoid clients we have no reason whatsoever to suspect, nor do we find, any EEG differences between people who are wide awake and those who are reputed to be "hypnotized." (See Baker 1990)

Dangers of Regressive Hypnosis

Also discussed at length in Baker's 1990 book, *They Call It Hypnosis,* is evidence supporting the fact that regressive hypnosis is a dangerous, unreliable, and deceptive procedure (see also Baker 1988). Its acceptance both as a standard clinical technique and as a tool used by amateur psychotherapists outside the clinic, has grown by leaps and bounds. Both amateurs and professionals have managed to ignore scientific research cautioning the unwary, with the result that over the past twenty years regressive hypnotists have created a wide range of fictions, mistruths, and mythologies that not only mislead and misinform but also have caused a considerable amount of social pain and suffering. Four contemporary legends directly due to the misuse of regressive hypnosis are: UFOs and alien abductions, false memories of childhood sexual molestation, the myth of satanic ritual abuse, and iatrogenic multiple personality disorders. Each of these social myths has been successfully popularized by a number of best-selling books.

Although disagreement still exists as to whether hypnosis is or is not a separate "state of consciousness," there is considerable agreement among all major theorists that hypnosis is a situation in which people set aside critical judgment (without abandoning it entirely) and engage in make-believe and fantasy; i.e., they use their imagination (Sarbin and Andersen 1967; Barber 1969; Hilgard 1977; and Spanos and Chaves 1989). Though great differences in the ability to fantasize exist, most everyone has an imagination and uses it extensively. In recent years many authorities have made imagination a requirement for any successful hypnotic performance. Josephine Hilgard (1979) refers to hypnosis as "imaginative involvement," Sarbin and Coe (1972) term it "believed in imaginings," and Sutcliffe (1961) characterizes the hypnotizable individual as one who is "deluded in a descriptive, nonperjorative sense." Sutcliffe also sees hypnosis as an arena where people who are skilled at make-believe and fantasy are provided with the opportunity and the means to do what they enjoy doing and what they are able to do especially well. In sum, hypnosis is mostly and primarily a turning on of the imagination and a royal road to illusion, delusion, and fantasy land.

When regressive hypnosis is used on individuals, i.e., they are asked to imagine some past period of their lives, and this suggestion is followed up with additional social demands and psychological pressures to comply with the hypnotist's biases and convictions, the hypnotist will elicit anything and everything *but* the truth. Reports of being raped, of eating a baby's heart and eyeballs, reports of torture, murder, orgies and sexual molestation, or incest, and anything else that is feared or fearful are common. The clinician/hypnotist can readily produce "Twilight Zone" or "X-Files" tales and nightmares and anything his client has ever read or imagined or feared may emerge as an actual event or occurrence. Over eight years in the laboratory looking at hypnosis and memory, past-lives regression, future-lives *progression,* and other relaxation effects with over 500 students and community volunteers clearly showed that is is quite easy to persuade people that occurrences that never happened really *did* happen. Moreover, if the regressive and progressive patients take the time and trouble to make a sincere effort to account for the sources of their dreams, visions, and imagined scenarios they usually have little difficulty in doing so.

Hypnotizing people is also extremely easy. Anyone and everyone can learn to relax people and then use suggestion to create internal images. However, what you do after the client is relaxed and hanging on your every word is critical. Precisely *how* the hypnotherapist uses suggestion and exactly *what* he suggests determines whether he elicits fact or fiction. People who produce fictional stories are not deliberately lying; they try to remember and cannot. They encounter blank spaces in their memory and then they fill in these spaces with possibilities, not truths. If certain therapists believe in Satan and satanic ritual abuse, or that all behavioral disorders are due to childhood sexual molestation or that aliens lurk outside our windows every night in UFOs, then they will find what they are seeking, i.e., another sensational headline, a book, appearances on television talk shows, and money and attention for themselves and their victims. Many people are so starved for love, attention, and affection that they will even fake diseases and illnesses or they will physically wound themselves just to get medical attention. Known as "hospital hobos" or as those suffering from "the Munchausen Syndrome" (known technically as *factitious disorders*), such people literally drive physicians up the wall. Psychiatrists Marc Feldman and Charles Ford recently published a fascinating book, *Patient Or Pretender: Inside the Strange World of Factitious Disorders* (1994) detailing and describing such behavior.

By far the most serious errors made by therapists treating such patients are (1) buying into the patient's odd belief system; (2) assuming that some horrible trauma in the client's past is responsible for his or her complaint; (3) using regressive hypnosis as a tool for getting "the facts" as well as using it as a method of treatment; (4) believing in the Freudian concept of "repression" when Holmes (1990) and Pope and Hudson (1994) have convincingly shown that sixty years of experimental research has failed to support its existence; (5) assuming the client's problem will be solved once the repressed material is uncovered and recalled; and (6) believing that expressed emotional intensity is an indicator of the validity and truthfulness of the client's memories—perhaps the most serious mistake of all! Too many sympathetic and empathetic clinicians make the fatal mistake of confusing sobs, tears, moans, and confabulations with the gospel truth. "How could anyone carry on like that if what they're remembering were not true?" Personally, I have had many individuals put on an Academy Award performance with tears, groans, moans, screams, and hair-tearing from imagined scenarios in a *future* progression. Such emotional outbursts are also fairly common with people who relive past lives and experience personal tragedies, such as the death of a loved one and other sad events. When conscious and confronted with the tapes of their emotional outbursts, most will sheepishly admit that they broke down because it all seemed "so very real and terribly sad." It is amazingly easy to take people too young for World War II back to 1944 and have them relive D-Day and the channel crossing. If they're particularly imaginative and they have seen the movies and read the stories of the conflict, vicariously, then they will suffer deeply.

Many people claiming highly unusual paranormal experiences are not "crazy" or psychotic. However, they are "deluded," i.e., they do experience false beliefs. While they may have one or two fixed or truly strange ideas, their behavior is ordinary and normal in every other way. Nevertheless, they do make up an ever-growing group of disaffected and alienated people referred to in the past as "eccentric personalities" or people with a "schizotypal personality disorder." While they may be "odd," "spacey," or "strange," they are not schizophrenic. They seldom have any loss of affect, or repeated hallucinations. They manage to get along fine at home, on the job, and in familiar surroundings. Other than having some unusual habits or beliefs or becoming involved with fringe groups and causes, they appear normal. Typically, they will claim to have received messages from, or made contact with, religious entities such as angels, demons, Satan, Christ, or God himself. They also will claim to have had visions of ghosts or spirits and they may insist that they have supernatural abilities or magical powers, i.e., ESP, clairvoyance, or prophetic accuracy. Many will insist they have a secret mission here on Earth or that they have been sent here from another world to save our planet. They may also report odd perceptions, for example, sensing things that are not present, hearing and seeing things no one else can detect, and communicating with unseen forces or entities. They are often "loners" and "different" because of their fixed beliefs and strange ideas. Few of these people respond well to psychodynamic therapy and their greatest need is the acquisition of social skills. Behavioral treatment by therapists is often quite effective in helping them to deal with day-to-day problems. Therapists should offer comfort and advice without ridiculing their beliefs. Although it is usually the first step too many medical personnel take, neither medication nor hospitalization is recommended. Reassurance and relief from their paranoid fears is the best way to help them stabilize and become socially adjusted. *Increasing their anxieties by supporting their paranoid ideas and beliefs is definitely contraindicated! Regressive hypnosis definitely will not help!* If the therapist uses this approach, everything he gets will be colored, twisted, and confabulated. Explaining to the client how their imagination and dreams work, overcoming their anxieties and fears, and providing comfort and reassurance is the kind of therapy best suited for their social readjustment and eventual recovery.

The major problem with regressive hypnosis is that it switches on the client's imagination and with the unavoidable demands characteristic of the hypnotic situation, combined with the suggestions and biases of the therapist as he or she digs into the client's past, anything and everything the therapist unearths will be so distorted and fabricated that it will be impossible for either the therapist or the client to know what is fact and what is fiction. However, when the client's story is out, his or her "memories" (false as they are) seem to the client the only possible truths. This is why so many therapists sincerely believe that their clients were sexually molested, satanically abused, or abducted by aliens.

5

Calling All Corpses or Dial "D" for Dead

Communication with the dead is something I would urge you to avoid—
I mean even the idea of it, the possibility of it. . . . Trying to communicate
with the dead has been the downfall of many individuals, as my story amply
and tragically reveals.

—M. Lamar Keene, *The Psychic Mafia*, 1976

In 1959 a Swedish film producer, Friedrick Jurgenson, discovered some
strange, unaccountable voices on his tape recorder while he was attempting to record some bird songs. These "electronic voices" as they came to
be known presented a puzzle to electronic experts since they should not
have been on the tape. Not only were the voices impossible to explain scientifically, but the speech contents, the voice patterns, and the intelligent
thoughts expressed presented additional problems. Jurgenson, a devout
Catholic, having exhausted all other explanations, suggested the voices
could be, and in fact were, the voices of the dead. Jurgenson, who had
produced a documentary film about Pope Paul VI and was rewarded with
a Knight Commandership of the Order of St. Gregory the Great, took as
one of his pupils Dr. Konstantin Raudive, a Latvian psychologist. Raudive
also was convinced they were listening to the dead. Raudive, however,
soon became jealous of Jurgenson and began to work alone, publishing a
book in German in 1968 titled *The Inaudible Becomes Audible.* The book
attracted little attention until a revised edition titled *Breakthrough* was
published in English in 1970 with a preface by Professor Peter Bander.
Bander, who was quite skeptical about the whole thing at first, changed
his mind about Raudive's work after listening to one of the tapes. He

181

became convinced that one of the voices was the voice of his mother who had died three years earlier.

Over the next decade literally thousands of tapes were made, and hundreds of voices of men, women, and children in many different languages showed up on the tapes. Raudive's procedure for obtaining the voices was quite simple. He was most successful in trapping the voices on tape with the use of a *diode*. This, quite simply, was no more than what was called the "cat's whisker" in the old crystal set radios. It had a turned wire coil and a three-inch aerial highly useful for picking up anything. Nevertheless, when the noise thus generated was amplified and recorded, "voices" showed up.

A second technique consisted of simply connecting a microphone to a tape recorder. Sound waves are picked up, converted into electronic impulses, amplified in the tape recorder, and passed through the recording head onto the magnetic tape. When played back at an audible volume, if any voices are there anyone listening should be able to hear them.

Raudive's third procedure was to use a short wave or medium wave radio, which he tuned to some *inter-frequency* band not being used by a radio station. This is very difficult because there are so many stations in existence that broadcast twenty-four hours a day. If, however, one is successful, what you hear is static, or white-noise, i.e., noises of many different frequencies. This static is then amplified and fed into the tape recorder through the recorder head onto a tape. The result of this, in psychologist Peter Bander's book *Voices From The Tapes* is: "The resulting signals when they are obtained *are very faint and the experimenter has to listen to them for a considerable time in order to discover the meaning of the words.*" (p. 11) The difficulty in the listening is made quite clear since Bander follows with the suggestion:

> I have found it very helpful to cut the length of the tape on which the signal has manifested itself and form a loop by joining the two ends together. This enables the listener to concentrate on one particular section of the tape without having to move it forwards and backwards in the tape recorder. Alternatively, a recording can be transferred onto another tape several times over; although this enables the experimenter to amplify the voice, it should be borne in mind that the background noise and hissing will also be amplified and therefore the problem of identifying the sentence may have increased rather than diminished.
>
> (pp. 11–12)

When these electronic voices were first made known the first reaction was to explain them as freak pick-ups of random radio waves. Then they were explained as being of paranormal origin, but this was very hard for many scientifically-minded people to accept and other explanations were offered. Maybe the voices were coming from another planet, or some extraterrestrial intelligent source somewhere in the universe. Maybe our subconscious minds were sending out electronic impulses which are registered as human speech on the tape. Maybe the voices aren't there at all; maybe they're just imagined. This can't be because, on occasion, the voice recordings have shown up on a visible speech printer, and they can also be seen on oscilloscopes where they register as visible impulses. This is one explanation we will return to later.

Maybe they are the voices of people who have died and are trying to retain communication with those people who are still alive! This is the explanation preferred by Jurgenson, Raudive, and the other true believers. On a number of occasions, especially when pressed too hard by observers, Raudive has "been known to interpret radio pick up as genuine Voice Phenomena." In Bander's words, "Konstantin Raudive is capable of making mistakes which could be used as evidence against him." (p. 21) Of course, on many other occasions recordings were made which excluded the possibility of freak pick-up from outside transmitters. Bander, however, is not too happy with either Raudive or his theories and says quite frankly,

In my opinion, Raudive's theories are not the kind which are likely to convince an objective observor that the facts on which they are based are correct or that a breakthrough into another dimension has been achieved. . . . The voices of the famous or infamous which Raudive purports to have recorded have presented me with more difficulties during the discussions. I cannot help feeling that name-dropping, a very human weakness, has either entered the celestial realms or is being projected into them by Raudive.

(p. 29)

Of even greater interest is Bander's following statement:

The vast majority of the voices I have heard during the many tests and experiments carried out in my presence, seemed to come from persons who had a strong link with one or more of the experimenters. . . . I have come to the conclusion that the stronger the affinity has been between two people during their lifetime, the greater the chance of a voice manifesting itself after one of them has died. . . . I cannot prove it with hard scientific facts.

(p. 30)

Bander, finding Raudive almost impossible to work with, set up his own recording equipment and tried to get voices using the diode and microphone methods, but in his own words, "Our own experiments were not particularly successful." (p. 44) He also reported the problem of interpreting the voices turned out to be one of the most difficult handicaps he encountered. Moreover, the messages which were clearly understood by the experimenters were meaningful in content as well. Such messages, however, were few and far between.

One of the listeners to the tapes who seemed most intrigued was Bander's four-year-old Great Dane, Rufus, who listened intently to the tapes until he detected being watched; then he lost interest. Other canines, for example, one of the experimenter's black Labradors, ignored the tapes completely.

Things progressed nicely with the vocals from the void—Professor Hans Bender of Freiburg hailing the discovery as just as important, if not more so, than the discovery of nuclear physics—until the proponents began to contact electronic experts of the skeptical variety who told the listeners they could think of twelve different ways in which the voices could have shown up on the tapes. Another critic regarded the entire EVP as banal, and compared the information content of the voices to "the level of people playing about at a party with a ouija board ("Yes" in French and German) where you push it around and get messages." (p. 75) Other critics pointed out that some tape recorders are liable to outside interference. One person reported the case of a woman who had a "talking vacuum cleaner" that was picking up radio signals. Tape recorders, on occasion, have picked up fragments of radio and TV broadcasts. Wishful thinking and a little imagination is sufficient to convince many believers they are, indeed, eavesdropping on the dead.

The most telling and damning of the critics, however, was the careful, objective investigative work of David Ellis. After eighteen months of studying the voices, Ellis was convinced that the phenomenon is not as easily reproducible as Raudive claimed and that the voices—if they are of paranormal or supernatural origin—are not as frequent as Raudive believed. Of the voices Ellis listened to during his three visits with Raudive, a proportion, he was sure, came from normal radio sources. Ellis launched his investigation by studying Raudive and his tapes, rather than trying to duplicate Raudive's work. As one would expect, he found many flaws in Raudive's work. Some of the voices were definitely not genuine, and others were recordings of normal radio transmissions, while many of Raudive's interpretations were simply erroneous. When Ellis played one of Raudive's recordings of voices for some of his friends at Cambridge, the friends burst out laughing. They told Ellis that he had Radio Luxembourg on tape. They knew because they were sponsors of, and regular listeners of, the show that Raudive had captured on tape. Raudive, however, had misunderstood the words.

In Ellis's view, the crux of the matter lay in interpreting what the voices were saying. The matter of interpretation is such that one believer insists that his large collection of voice recordings are mostly from aliens circling the Earth in Unidentified Flying Objects. It is also significant that not everyone who listens to the tapes hears anything at all. Moreover, why some people can record voices on tape and others cannot is also difficult to explain. To true believers, however, the difficulties only serve to reinforce their belief in unearthly sources.

Bander adds the significant observation that

> There is little doubt that voices purporting to come from those with whom we have had a strong affinity during their lifetime make up by far the largest proportion of all recorded voices. . . . After more than two years of active involvement in the Voice Phenomenon, I have yet to come across any experimenter who has at will tuned into a particular voice if there was no link of affinity.
>
> (p. 145)

Another of the experimenters concerned herself with the voice content and emphasized the fact that all of those hearing the voices engaged in "frantic attempts on the part of the interpreters to make voices 'fit' the purported originators." (p. 145)

Bander concludes his book with the observation that the primary problem with the voices is getting the voices separated from the background noise, the hissing of the tape, and the frequent interferences.

> I suppose that every researcher has in time developed his own method of achieving a listening capacity. To me the noise resembles the sound of a waterfall between the speaker and myself. I, therefore, attempt to hear the voices above the noise. The real problem lies in the interpretation of recorded voices. Most of the experts have commented on the difficulties, and David Ellis considers interpretation an insurmountable obstacle.
>
> (p. 152)

Apparently, in having people listen to the tapes, Bander works with two or three people at a time. Each of the listeners has his own set of earphones which are connected by means of a junction box to the output of the tape recorder. Everybody writes down what he hears and it is important that they do not tell each other about their interpretations. Bander says he hears vowel sounds first, but others hear consonants, or even whole words. Sometimes the voice interpretation presents little difficulty. Half of the voices can be identified after six to ten playbacks; a quarter may take twenty playbacks or even thirty, the rest may take half an hour or longer, and usually there is disagreement on one or two of the words.

What is not mentioned is the tightness of the controls of both the *tape* and the *listeners.*

Readers who have followed the account thus far have probably, some while ago, solved the problem of the voices. Rather than being the voices of the dead, the voices are voices from within, i.e., projections of their own internal messages reinforced by mutual suggestions from members of the listening group. Suggestion also plays a major role in the content and the interpretation of the white noise for those tapes upon which no actual radio transmissions appear. On many of the tapes, of course, the voices are real, and are pick ups of actual transmissions—not from the dead— but from very live transmitters right here on Earth. Group suggestion and reinforcement can easily produce a "narrowing" effect in the group moving toward a common agreement on the nature of the voices, the speaker, and the contents. It is highly unlikely that a fresh, naive observer entering the group after the interpretations have been made would hear anything in common with the group's interpretation.

There is little doubt that the "hearing of voices" is nothing more than the common psychological experience of *projection,* exaggerated and amplified by *suggestions* from the experimenters presenting the stimuli and demanding that they listen for *voices,* specifically "voices from the dead." Highly suggestible individuals, as well as those with good or strong imaginative powers, will be those who hear the most, and hear them most clearly. If the reader doubts this, he can experience the phenomenon himself with any handy AM or FM radio. Take a pen and pad and find a point on the radio dial where no station is coming in and you will hear only static (white noise); turn up the volume; concentrate your attention on the noise for at least five to ten minutes; listen intently for any random voices or sounds; write down any words, voices, music, or anything else that you hear. Don't be discouraged if at first you don't hear anything, just relax and continue to listen. If nothing comes through after thirty to forty minutes, then quit and be happy in the knowledge that you are one of those few individuals who are highly resistant to suggestion. Elvis Presley fans who try this frequently report hearing a number of their favorite Elvis songs. If you don't have a radio handy, but do have a TV, tune the set to an inoperative channel, turn up the volume, and stare at the screen. Again, if you have a good imagination you will soon not only hear voices, but may well see the faint images of people and faces in the "snow" storms on the face of the tube. This is known in esoteric circles as Electrovisual Phenomena.

Do not be upset if you can see forms and hear voices that no one else can. By no means are you either "psychic" or "crazy"—you are merely experiencing the quite normal perception of internally psychologically generated stimuli.

One of the most dramatic experimental confirmations of this sort of psychological projection was carried out a few years ago by two Canadian psychologists, John R. Vokey and J. D. Read of the University of Lethbridge (November 1985). Vokey and Read specifically set out to experimentally answer a question about the use of subliminal messages in advertising and popular music. In the early 1980s a number of ministers, as well as a few politicians, charged that a number of Satanic messages were being recorded backward into popular rock music. When these recordings were then played in the normal forward fashion the messages, though not consciously perceived, would be unconsciously perceived. Upon hearing these messages the listeners would then be stimulated to engage in immoral behavior such as drug use or sexual licentiousness. This phenomenon, known as "back masking," stirred the legislatures of a number of states, including Texas, California, and Arkansas, to propose enacting legislation to control and prevent this sort of activity.

Investigating these claims, Vokey and Read found first that there was no evidence of any sort to support the claim that messages spoken backward were comprehensible, conscious or otherwise. Further, there was no evidence to support the claim that even if subliminal messages were there, and even if they were apprehended consciously or unconsciously, they had any influence at all on human behavior. If it could be shown that yes, indeed, such messages were present, this still offered no proof that the messages were effective. Despite the claims of individuals such as Bryan Wilson Key, a writer, and Reverend Gary Greenwald, a minister, that not only are such messages commonly found in advertisements and rock music, Vokey and Read were unable to find any empirical evidence to support their claims.

To test Key's claim that the advertisers use of the word "sex" embedded in the advertising copy and in their products enhanced memorability, Vokey and Read took a set of vacation photographs and embedded the word "sex" three or four times on each slide. In the control group of the same slide photographs nonsense syllables were embedded in the same locations as the word "sex." A third group of the same photographs had nothing embedded. Subjects then studied an equal number of each slide type in preparation for a test of retention. None of the subjects reported having seen the word "sex" on any of the slides, although they all saw it when it was pointed out to them. On the retention test, half of the subjects were tested immediately after the presentation and the remainder two days later because Key has frequently claimed an incubation period may be necessary for some of the subliminal effects to appear.

Despite Key's claims and concerns there were no differences in retention between any of the three conditions. Clearly, the embedding of the word "sex" had no effect.

Vokey and Read next tested two of the Reverend Greenwald's claims. First, they studied whether the content of backward messages exerted any influence on the listener—consciously or otherwise. Next, they studied whether messages purported to be recorded backward within rock music could reasonably be attributed to active construction on the part of the listener, rather than to the content of the recording itself.

Using as messages passages from Lewis Carroll's *Jabberwocky* and the *23rd Psalm,* these were recorded in the forward direction and then recorded in the backward direction; the only noise on the tape was that of the messages themselves. Next, sixty-five students were asked to listen to the tapes and to rate their degree of agreement with the statement: "It is possible to understand messages played backward." The results clearly indicated that, on the average, the students *did not agree* with the statement. The students were able, however, to discriminate between messages spoken by males and females, messages spoken by the same or different individuals, and they were able to discriminate between messages spoken in French, English, or German.

The experimenters then carried out studies to determine both conscious and unconscious comprehension.

> If the meaning of backward messages is gained at a subconscious level, placement of these statements into the five categories should proceed in some nonrandom fashion. It would be a devious unconscious mechanism indeed that allowed Christian messages to be labeled as pornographic or satanic and vice versa. But that was the result we obtained.
>
> (p. 1235)

Chance alone governed the subjects' assignments of the Christian messages to the various categories. On an overall basis, the meaning of the statements were not understood at any level conscious or otherwise.

Vokey and Read conclude their study by pointing out that people's perceptions of ambiguous auditory material is most likely a function of active construction on the part of the listener. They also stress that in his public demonstrations Greenwald does not merely ask his audience to listen and "hear" what they can. He prefaces the presentation of each passage with a statement of *what* the listener is to "hear." Under these suggestive circumstances it is little wonder that most listeners "hear" the messages for which Greenwald has prepared them. In similar fashion it is little wonder that Raudive's fellow experimenters "hear" what Raudive "hears" in his presence, while others out of his presence have such difficulty in hearing anything at all—unless, of course, Raudive has picked up Radio Luxembourg or Radio Free Europe. Voices of the dead? Hardly. The role of and the power of suggestion, expectation, and projection in all such interpretations of ambiguous stimuli can never be discounted. The importance of these factors has also been emphasized by the work of Thorne and Humelstein (1984) who also demonstrated their critical role in the perception of so-called Satanic messages in rock-and-roll recordings.

Nowadays, however, experimenters are also placing telephone calls to other dimensions. According to the late Mercedes Shepanek, who spent the last twelve years of her life working with EVP although she has recorded "thousands of excellent quality voices" on her tape recorder, using the telephone technique is much less satisfactory. In her words, "I have been working with the telephone technique and have had some results, mostly whispers. Two of the transmissions were 'We will call you' and 'We will ring you.' " According to Ms. Shepanek, the telephone procedure also requires:

> A telephone recording control (available from Radio Shack) and a telephone jack adaptor. To convert your existing telephone jack to a "two holer," you jack the device into the telephone wall jack along with your telephone and also into the mike and remote input of a cassette recorder. The method is as follows: Put the recorder into RECORD mode (it will not be activated until you lift the telephone receiver), lift the phone receiver, and dial any single digit. Make a brief announcement as you would in any tape session. You will have thirty-four seconds of clear line before the taped offer of assistance breaks in. Hang up and repeat the procedure. The obvious shortcoming is the brevity of the clear line time. An alternative is to arrange with a friend (preferably one acquainted with your strange life style) to call at a pre-set time and leave his/her telephone off the hook for whatever period is agreed upon.
>
> (Estep 1988, p. 161)

Believe it or not there is an American association—Electronic Voice Phenomena—founded in 1982 by Sarah Wilson Estep who has also written a book about the phenomena titled *Voices of Eternity* (1988). The EVP Association currently has over 200 members who live in forty different states, the District of Columbia, and twelve foreign countries. In Germany alone it is rumored there are already over a thousand EVP members. Not only has Ms. Estep talked with the dead via radio, telephone, and TV, she has also made contact with other EVP investigators all over the world and extraterrestrials who call themselves our Space Brothers. It may also be of interest to learn that the spirits communicate with us by using *ectoplasm*. This was startling even to Ms. Estep. Nevertheless, little else appears to faze her. Not only is she a believer in reincarnation, precognition, and clairvoyance, but she knows where UFOs come from: Alpha Centauri!

At least this is where the Space Brothers tell her they are from. The aliens also once showed up on channel 47 of her TV set. Her book contains detailed instructions on how to communicate with the voices including the type and kinds of hardware needed. The software is in your head.

According to John G. Fuller, not only can one pick up the voices of the dead, it is also possible nowadays to carry on a dialogue with them using an electronic system devised by Dr. George Meek, a research engineer, and William O'Neill, a technical genius and medium. In his book, *The Ghost of 29 Megacycles,* the indefatigable John G. Fuller (1981) is the first to admit the work in EVP leaves much to be desired. In his words, "Some of the results are weak. Some are sloppy. The sound is muddy. Some results are highly questionable because of their fragmentary nature. But the solid residue is clear and unambiguous. It is not hallucinatory." (p. 217)

Fuller is correct, it is not hallucinatory, but it is more than likely purely psychological, and due more than anything else to suggestions and projections.

While it is difficult to determine exactly where the EVP began, one of the first in modern times to report strange voices on tape was George Hunt Williamson who, in the early 1950s, argued the voices were coming from somewhere out in space and, therefore, must be messages from extraterrestrials. At the other extreme we have reports from many Indian tribes that the dead can be heard talking if one merely stands in a forest and listens to the wind moving through the trees. Others have noted that if one takes a tape recorder to the cemetery and records on a blank tape at maximum volume, when you play it back—if you listen carefully, you can hear the voices of the dead. Although they're usually faint and not very clear, if you listen long enough and hard enough, you can soon begin to hear the voices. As Terence Hines remarks:

> The tape recorder, while it is recording is picking up stray sounds from the environment and, especially, the sound of the breeze or wind passing over the microphone. When played back, these noises do sound strange and, at least to me, rather peaceful. If one expects to hear voices, constructive perception will produce voices. The voices, not surprisingly, are usually described as speaking in hoarse whispers.
>
> (Hines 1988, p. 76)

Strange as the electronic voice phenomenon may be, stranger still is what Jules and Maggie Harsh-Fischbach of Luxembourg call the Electronic *Visual* Phenomenon. Over the last few years these investigators have succeeded in getting visions of the dead—visual images—on TV sets when tuned between channels. Even more remarkable, they have also obtained meaningful messages on computer printouts in response to questions. Similar messages have even shown up on their telephone answering machines. Most interesting of all perhaps is that only a few months ago Konstantin Raudive—the late famous EVP researcher—appeared for 137 seconds on the TV screen accompanied by sound. According to Sarah Estep, who visited the Fischbachs and listened to some of Raudive's communiques, not only Raudive but Jurgenson also has spoken through the Fischbach equipment several times. Uncommitted observers who have witnessed the Fischbachs' Electronic Visual presentations reported seeing only a few vague, ill-deformed shadows on the TV screen snow as if the set was tuned to a station whose signal was much too weak for a clear and definite picture. None of the uncommitted observers were very impressed with either the Fischbachs' demonstrations, or their claims. In the skeptical observer's opinions any voices or visions that may have been present were not on the screen, but in the minds of the believers instead.

Since we have now entered the computer age, almost any day we should expect to see the dead showing up on the small screen monitors as well. Sure enough, according to Jeff Rovin in his book of ghost stories, *The Spirits of America* (1990), one Mart Abernathy of Minneapolis recently bought a used Apple III computer for his kids. For several nights in a row, even though the computer was OFF, and even disconnected, the monitor still continued to glow. Abernathy took it back to Dave, a computer expert who could not find anything amiss. Dave insisted that Mart call if it acted up again. The following night the computer and monitor again switched themselves on, and even when the plug was pulled, the machine continued to clatter. Dave showed up, and with Mart and Carole (Mart's wife), hooked up the Apple writer, inserted a formatted blank disk, and typed in: "Who Are You?"

The machine replied: "What are you doing at my keyboard?"

When Dave typed in: "The keyboard belongs to Mart Abernathy," the machine replied: "It does not. It belongs to me."

"Who are you?" Dave replied.

"Daniel Cohen."

Dave turned to Mart and asked if he had bought the computer second hand. Mart replied he had. Dave said whoever programmed it with a program he couldn't even find is damn clever. Dave then disconnected everything, and as the three adults watched in amazement the entire computer was surrounded with a whitish foggy glow and the words "What are you doing here?" appeared on the screen. Next, Carole typed in: "Mr. Cohen, are you alive?" the computer said: "Where am I?" Carole replied: "In our home." The machine responded: "No, it's dark." Checking up on Cohen the following day, they discovered that Cohen, an architect, had died of a heart attack in his office at the keyboard of this computer four months earlier.

Rovin also informs us that the ghost of a chess expert also has the ability to activate a dead computer and haunt a computerized chess game—only, however, when his plaster death-mask is placed nearby.

Any and all readers who believe this please contact the author immediately since I have a number of gold mine and oil well investments, as well as a few bridges that I can let you have at a bargain price. Send for details immediately. These are one-of-a-kind, once-in-a-century buys that no astute, clever, shrewd, or intelligent investor would dare to miss! Hurry! Hurry! While they last!

It will come as no surprise to learn that many clever schemers have figured out ways to capitalize on this "will to believe." One of the most inventive was one William O'Neill, a Pittsburgh native, electronics expert, and medium who, with his promoter George W. Meek of Franklin, North Carolina, established the Metascience Foundation whose purpose was to communicate with the dead. Calling their invention *Spiricom*—from the two words *spirit* and *communication,* O'Neill and Meek recorded a number of spirit voices on tape and tried to convince the world that the voices were those of people who had died many years earlier. Particularly impressive was the voice of one Dr. George Jeffries Mueller who had died fourteen years earlier. Upon hearing Mueller on one of the Spiricom tapes, Terrence Peterson, a writer, felt there was something very familiar about the voice but he couldn't place exactly what it was. Then, after Peterson read *The Ghost of 29 Megacycles* by John G. Fuller, his interest in the Spiricom tapes revived, and he began to examine them more closely. Since the spirit voices had a mechanical, robotlike tone to them, and the sound was also strangely familiar, Peterson finally remembered where he had heard these sounds before and the mystery was solved! Peterson remembered that when a person's voice box is removed by surgery (usually because of cancer of the larynx) the patient sometimes elects to use an artificial larynx. "The Spiricom voices, I suddenly realized, sounded as if they were coming through just such a device." Meek still insisted that the voiceprint of the spirit voice of Dr. Mueller and the natural voice of William O'Neill were entirely different. However, when Peterson sent the voice tapes to Dr. David Rivers, a speech and language expert at Baylor University, Rivers produced the essential wording of the Spiricom tape using his voice and an artificial larynx. Rivers used a Servox unit manufactured by Siemens. It is a hand-held, battery-driven, electromechanical oscillator. Peterson was unable to tell the difference between the artificial larynx voice and the spirit voice of Dr. Mueller. According to Peterson in his article "Spiricom or Spiricon?" (1987), while no one can say precisely how the Spiricom recordings were made, the simplest explanation is that they were made by a *living* agent using an audio frequency oscillator. This, however, proved to be one spirit "con" that didn't work.

Phone Calls from the Dead

There can be little doubt that both suggestion and projection also play an important—if not the *most* important—role in the odd phenomenon known as "phone calls from the dead." Given the considerable publicity by the late D. Scott Rogo and Ray Bayless (*Phone Calls From The Dead,* 1979), on certain occasions the dead apparently try to communicate via telephone with friends and loved ones they have left behind. For the most part such calls are initiated by the dead, particularly soon after the caller's demise.

Even though Rogo and Bayless are convinced only a paranormal theory can explain these strange voices from beyond, they do offer a few interesting normal psychological explanations for some of the calls. In some cases some of the people being called temporarily forgot that the person on the other end was dead. This kind of selective amnesia is most interesting in that it seems an excellent way to deal with very traumatic and shocking information. By blocking it out and forgetting it, i.e., forcefully rejecting the horrible news, reality is changed. This sort of *selective amnesia,* i.e., remembering everything else except a horror that cannot be accepted, can be handled in two ways. First, if one is used to talking with the loved one on the phone, receiving such a call is the way to prove conclusively the loved one is still alive. Or, second, no matter who is on the other end of the line one can always *pretend* it is the voice of the beloved. Of course another possibility is that the desire to hear the beloved is so powerful that the mourner not only hears a phone ring when it did not (far from being an uncommon occurrence), but also hears the voice of the beloved at the other end. Strength and support for this explanation is provided by the fact the phone company never bills for such calls, nor have any records shown such calls occurred. Moreover, as the research of Rees and Lutkins (1976), Kastenbaum (1969), and other students of bereavement behavior (Parkes 1972) have shown, approximately 50 to 65 percent of widows and widowers report experiences which involve them seeing or contacting people or other minds since they were deceased. Most people take great comfort from these events. As even the authors admit: wish fulfillment and psychological need can, indeed, do strange things to the mind. The authors are also candid enough to admit that:

> Phone contacts can occur only when many delicate conditions—psychic and otherwise—are met, most likely, the person receiving the call must be in just the right frame of mind before contact can be made at all. . . . otherwise these phone calls would be occurring all the time. . . . At the moment contact was made, all seemed to have been in a rather "receptive" frame of mind.
> (Rogo and Bayless 1979, p. 59)

This lends further support to a purely psychological and cryptomnesian explanation of the odd behavior.

Students of this phenomenon should also look at William Addams Welch's *Talks With The Dead* (1975), Susy Smith's *Voices of The Dead* (1977), as well as D. Scott Rogo's article "Paranormal Tape-Recorded Voices" in John White and Stanley Krippner's *Future Science* (1977). And by all means one must not miss a companion piece in the White and Krippner volume titled "Apparatus Communication With Discarnate Persons" by Julius Weinberger. According to Weinberger, who spent forty-one years in the RCA Laboratories and held over forty patents for electronic devices, after more than twenty-five years of studying the post-mortem survival of the human personality by conventional means, i.e., sitting with mediums, he took a new approach and proceeded to develop a system over which signals can be transmitted without the need for a "sensitive" intermediary, that is, a medium. His new system, according to Weinberger, is "more sensitive and reliable than previous attempts," and uses a sensitive plant, *Dionea muscipala* (the Venus Flytrap), as a device which Weinberger states "is able to respond to signals produced by discarnate persons." In other words, the Venus Flytrap displaces the medium.

According to Weinberger, he used his apparatus daily for well over four years to make literally thousands of observations. Weinberger devised his apparatus consisting of (1) a shielded flytrap, (2) electrodes attached to the plant's midrib, (3) a two-stage low frequency amplifier, (4) a recorder amplifier circuit, and (5) a stripchart graphic recorder. Weinberger developed his plant device to overcome the difficulty of trying to determine how much of the information comes from the medium's mind and how much from the dead person. Weinberger used the Venus Flytrap because it is sensitive to touch, it is easy to attach electrodes to, it is readily available, it quickly responds to stimuli, and it has been studied extensively. Most important of all, he believed it would respond to energy from discarnate sources because Grad's work showed plant growth could be stimulated by energy coming from a healer's hands.

To make contact with the discarnate sources a brief prayer is recited, followed by prayers of a personal nature, and a request for such cooperation for any discarnate persons who might be present. According to Weinberger, this apparatus and this procedure produces graphics pulses from the discarnate that are synchronized with and responsive to his verbal requests. For example, after the transmissions start coming in regularly by asking the entities, "Will you please stop transmitting for the next five minutes?," regular five-minute gaps will appear in the pulses being recorded. If your mind boggles at the thought of a serious scientist sitting beside a Venus Flytrap communicating via the plant with discarnate entities, join the crowd. Oh what fools we believing mortals be!

Spirit Possession or Delirium Tremors?

Related to the issue of postmortem communication is the primitive belief in *spirit possession,* i.e., the take-over of the body of a living individual by the spirit of a dead person. Since the beginning of time, literally thousands of gods, spirits, demons, or devils have been believed to enter into and seize control of human personalities. In the Bible, chapter 5 of Mark, Jesus encountered a madman and drove out his demon into a herd of swine. Just about every culture contains similar tales of demon possession and exorcism. For thousands of years any and all forms of physical and mental disorders were explained in terms of spirit possession. Although the spirits could be good or morally neutral, most often they were evil or impure. In the fourth century A.D. Zeno of Verona spoke of the wild emotional excitement of those who were possessed: "His face is suddenly deprived of color, his body rises up of itself, the eyes in madness roll in their sockets and squint horribly, the teeth, covered with a horrible foam, grind between blue-white lips, the limbs twisted in all directions are given over to trembling; he sighs, he weeps. . . ."

In the first three decades of the seventeenth century, in the French town of Loudon, a group of Ursuline nuns succumbed to an epidemic of hysteria (most likely due to ingesting ergot from mouldy bread and produced and fostered by the very physicians who were supposed to be restoring the patients to "health"), which was commonly known to afflict ill-regulated convents. The exorcists encouraged the Sisters to believe they were possessed by devils, and Urbain Grandier, the Vicar of Loudon, was eventually accused of having caused the Devils to assail them. Cardinal Richelieu disliked Grandier and made the case an affair of state. Subsequently Grandier was tried, condemned as a sorcerer, and burned alive. This did not stop the possessions, however. New exorcists were called in, and among these was the celebrated Jesuit mystic, Jean-Joseph Surin, and it was he who finally succeeded in driving the demons from the Prioress —who was the first and principal victim. Surin, too, unfortunately, fell victim to the psychological infection. This truly fascinating account of madness, superstition, and primitive belief was described in great and entertaining detail by Aldous Huxley in his classic *The Devils of Loudon* (1952).

A 1714 case reported by a German clergyman also described an emotional crisis with subsequent collapse and recovery. When he first visited a woman in a workhouse, according to the clergyman, "Satan hurled an invective at me by her mouth: 'Silly fool what are you doing in this workhouse? You'll get lice here' and so on." Taking the woman to church the clergyman read her two accounts of demonic possession from the New Testament, and ordered Satan to emerge and leave the woman's body. "Satan tortured the poor creature horribly, howled through her mouth in a frightful manner and threw her to the ground so rigid, so insensible that she became as cold as ice and lay as dead, at which time we could not perceive the slightest breath until at last with God's help she came to herself. . . . "

Demon Possession

Demons, according to the Medieval Church, were able to enter the body of a person and take over its functioning, and they were often more intelligent than the human beings they possessed. Although there were important local variations in their behavior, by the sixteenth century the victim's behavior had become fairly stereotyped. Among the most consistently occurring behaviors were convulsions, increased intelligence accompanied by clairvoyance, spontaneous amnesia, transcendent "feats," and the experience of the demonic behavior as occurring involuntarily. Other seemingly abnormal behavior included a general insensitivity to pain, unusual strength, and temporary and selective sensory-motor deficits such as temporary deafness or blindness.

According to the psychiatric historians, demonic possession was an idea held by superstitious people of more credulous eras to explain behavior disorders that we now know were hysteria, schizophrenia, or something similar. After the seventeenth century the demonic superstitions were gradually discarded, and mental illness was properly diagnosed, i.e., given the most common diagnostic label of *hysteria*. This was the famous Charcot's erroneous conclusion, a diagnosis that Slater (1966) stated was ridiculous. In his words, "The only thing 'hysterical' patients can be shown to have in common is that they are all patients. . . . The diagnosis of 'hysteria' is a disguise for ignorance and a fertile source of clinical error." (pp. 1395-1399)

From the fifteenth through the seventeenth centuries the idea of demonic possession and belief in witches were kept distinct and served different social functions. Nevertheless, a number of psychiatric historians have confused the two since the early nineteenth century. The reason for the confusion was that both witches and the demoniacs were often described as having similar symptoms. The demoniac was frequently—but not always—considered to be an individual smitten by a witch, and he or she was then encouraged to name the witch who caused the possession. Thus the person or persons accused were frequently defined as witches and, on the basis of such accusations, were often subjected to legal torture and execution. The demoniac, on the other hand, was not accused of being a witch and, though sometimes harshly treated, was never subjected to torture or execution. Instead, demonic possession was defined by common law as a species of insanity, and therefore involuntary. It was usually treated by means of exorcism, prayer, and fasting as opposed to legal punishment. On the other hand, the witch was seen as one who had voluntarily renounced God and taken up with Satan, and thereby deserved both torture and execution.

In a brilliant essay on demonic possession a few years ago, Spanos (1983) showed that looking at possession from the psychiatric point of view, and considering all such behavior as pathology or illness, is to fail totally to either comprehend or understand it. In other words, stating that demoniacs are hysterics, schizophrenics, or whatever does little more than restate the fact that these individuals behaved in ways that, to us, appear unusual. These sorts of diagnoses tell us nothing about the variables that produced or maintained the unusual behavior in the first place. Moreover, Spanos argues, in diagnosing these behaviors we have a strong tendency to wrench them from their historical context and interpret them within our own contemporary frame of reference. Reports, therefore, by demoniacs of seeing witches' specters—events that make a great deal of sense with the world view of seventeenth-century Puritans—are diagnosed as hallucinations because they call up in us "specters" of mental patients. Witches' specters, previously not understandable, now make sense. They become the products of diseased minds and, therefore, can be understood in terms of our "mentally ill" conceptual framework. This, unfortunately, leads us to believe we have explained phenomena that we have not yet begun to understand.

Rejecting the mental illness interpretation of possession totally, Spanos, in brilliant fashion, shows in step-by-step detail how the demoniac role is learned, played, rewarded, and how it serves to satisfy a number of important social and political functions for those claiming possession. The demoniac role, like other culturally prescribed roles, had to be learned. Among Catholics, for example, the single most extensive source of information concerning demonic role expectations was the exorcism procedure itself. In carrying out the exorcism, the priest never spoke to the possessed individual. Instead he addressed *only* the demon, and expected *only* the demon to answer. When the priest asked, "What is your name?", and the possessed woman replied "Ester," the priest would scream at her "Not you—the demon!" The priest would even threaten to strike the woman if she didn't answer. Accordingly, she would answer in a voice not her own, and give the name of the possessing spirit. Exactly how the possessed was supposed to act would also come from outside the exorcism situation in the form of coaching by people with a vested interest in insuring the demoniac gave a good performance, talking about the symptoms in the demoniac's presence, and watching the performance of other more practiced demoniacs.

Once a person was labeled a demoniac by the authorities there was no way to escape the role. Attempts to do so were seen only as the efforts of a wily demon to escape divine punishment at the hands of the exorcist. If the individual refused to appropriately act out the role, he or she could be bound and beaten into submission. Usually the only way the demoniac role could be escaped was by successfully playing it. And the social pressures on them were tremendous. First, they shared the same cultural frame of reference as the community that labeled them and were likely to see their own behavioral problem in the same light as their neighbors. Second, they were under continual social pressure from those on whom they depended most—family, friends, the parish priest—to accept the situation as demoniac possession. Finally, there were many social advantages to playing the role successfully. In France, for example, during the sixteenth and seventeenth centuries the most celebrated possession cases occurred among the nuns. Becoming a nun wasn't usually highly desired, and families would place their adolescent daughters in convents to avoid the financial burden involved in providing a dowry. Unless one was truly devout, being a nun left a lot to be desired. The life was hard, dull, filled with chores, frequent prayer, rigid rules, loneliness, no men, boredom, and monotony. The unwilling nun had no means of protesting against her predicament. If she adopted the demoniac role—and the script for this role was well known by all of the nuns—this was a relatively safe way to protest. The nun could take out her frustrations on her family, her superiors, and the Church, and act out her sexual frustrations on the exorcist and other males and blame it all on the nasty, possessing demon! Other advantages of being possessed included escape from unpleasant duties and responsibilities, being the center of attention, flaunting constrictive rules and regulations, as well as getting sympathetic attention from the higher ups, priests, physicians, and others. Moreover, the possessed nun instantly became a seer who possessed strange, magical powers—one who was due awe and respect. Once a nun was possessed, and her advantages were made apparent to other nuns—epidemics of possession would often sweep across the convents. Adoption of the possession role frequently led to a dramatic rise in social status. Moreover, the demonically possessed, despite their invective against God and Church, were more the unwitting servants of the clerical establishment than they were rebels against it.

The exorcist held enough social power to control and define what was or was not demonic possession. Any alternatives to his opinions were denied. The potential demoniacs were separated and isolated from anyone who might support an alternative definition of their behavior. If the demoniac tried to deny possession, the very denial was seen as a sure sign of possession. If the potential demoniac acted like a possessee, these role enactments were praised and admired. No praise, money, or rewards were given because any of these would have allowed the demoniacs to attribute their behavior to an external inducement rather than an indwelling demon. Punishment, similarly for inadequate role performance, was also always defined as punishing the demon in order to help the person possessed.

As for the exorcist, the successful exorcism of demoniacs was a powerful tool for converting unbelievers and redoubling the faith of believers. Truly, a successful exorcism served to illustrate the power of the Church, the triumph of God over the devil, and an affirmation of the Church's values and authority. To summarize, Spanos shows that exorcism was not simply a primitive or misguided sort of psychotherapy aimed solely at treating certain social deviates. It was, instead,

> . . . an ideological tool used to affirm a set of particular values and to win conversions while denigrating the values of religious competitors. Similarly, to classify demonic enactments in cases such as these as psychotic or hysterical manifestations is to miss their political import. These enactments were strategic. They were orchestrated (probably with varying degrees of conscious intent) by those who held power over the demoniacs for the purpose of affecting the attitudes and beliefs of potential converts. To view such enactments in terms of individual psychopathology is to seriously distort their meaning.
>
> (p. 180)

Spanos's position is that the application of modern psychiatric diagnosis has been of little or no value in understanding the manifestations of demoniac possession. All such manifestations can be better understood when seen in terms of the social setting, and the socially shared understanding of the participants. Citing the mass suicides at Jonestown, Guyana in November, 1978, rather than being seen as "mentally unstable" and "brainwashed," a social–psychological perspective suggests instead that this behavior is easily understood as the natural result of Jonestown's social organization, its members' beliefs with regard to salvation, forces in the "hostile" outside world, and their roles as religious martyrs. Socialization practices of the People's Temple were such that total satisfaction of all physical and emotional needs could be obtained only through the Jonestown community. This perspective was reinforced by "horror" stories circulated through the community about the consequences of capture or defeat by the various outside "enemy" groups. They even practiced suicide drills ahead of time. Thus, the mass suicides that did occur were fully consistent with the community's apocalyptic world view.

According to William Sargant, what is particularly interesting about all such accounts is their marked similarity to modern psychiatric case-histories and methods of treatment. During World War II, one of the techniques used to treat men suffering from combat neuroses was to induce the drugged patient to recreate mentally the stressful situation which caused his breakdown so that by reliving the situation he could deal with it better. By the end of the war it was discovered that it wasn't the reliving of the stress that was effective, but rather the release of the intense emotional excitement. This remained true even when the excitement was focused on some comparatively trivial occurrence, or even on an incident which was entirely imaginary. The essential emotions which need arousing are intense anger and aggressiveness, or intense anxiety and fear. In a nutshell, the patient's state of excitement would rise to a crescendo, which usually was followed by a temporary collapse, after which the patient felt that the abnormal fears and worries by which, in the ancient terminology, he had been "possessed" were now gone. Various kinds of shock treatment, including electroconvulsive shock (ECT) were based on the same premise.

According to Sargant, John Wesley's hell-and-brimstone revival meetings produced the same reactions he and his colleagues saw in their patients. Wesley filled his audiences with the fear of the horrors of hell which awaited them if they failed to repent. Some of them reacted like they were possessed—groaning, shrieking, shaking, covered with sweat, writhing on the ground, feeling pierced internally, and finally collapsing. Upon recovery they frequently felt mentally changed and spiritually reborn, at peace with themselves and the world—just as Sargant's patients reported when the old terrors had lost their hold.

Similar behavior was reported by some of Mesmer's patients in the later eighteenth century. It was also noted that women were more likely to experience this hysterical crisis than men were. Moreover, it was also noted that the patients became highly suggestible, and this suggestibility played a significant role in both the onset of the crisis and the subsequent cure, and that in many cases the behavior closely resembled that of female orgasm. This behavior was identical with that of the demonic possession cases in the French convents, e.g., at Loudon in the sixteenth and seventeenth centuries. Here again the possessed were mostly women, the contagion spread from one nun to another, the behavior of the victims was orgasmic, and they were also highly suggestible, spitting out torrents of filthy language and abuse in response to the suggestions of their exorcists that they were witches.

Janet reported the case of a thirty-three-year-old man who was consumed by guilt over a marital indiscretion who fell into a forty-eight-hour lethargy that was followed by convulsive fits broken by shrieks of Satanic laughter, shrieks of agony, and screams that he was being tortured by demons. In the patient's mind, he was condemned to hell for his sin. He clearly showed all the signs of demonic possession.

In more primitive societies like Ethiopia people are often believed to be possessed by spirits called "zars." Treatment must be carried out by a shaman who is also zar-possessed, but who works with his zar to help others. The shaman's zar talks to the patient's zar and negotiates a cure, i.e., a change in the patient's zar from an evil and unfriendly spirit to a kindly and helpful one. In India possession by a god or by the ghosts of the dead is common. Spirit possession, like so-called hysteria, is supposed to have two aspects: a basic condition due to the individual's psychological tension state, and the precipitating condition due to an event or situation involving unusual stress or emotion. In one case near Delhi a young woman who was possessed by a ghost first shivered and complained of feeling cold. Next she began to shake violently. The ghost which had taken over began to speak through her mouth to the woman's relatives. The relatives attempted to determine the ghost's identity and the name of the possessing spirit. This was so they could gain power over it and exorcise it.

In the Caribbean, particularly in Haiti where Voodoo is practiced, the main purpose of the religious rites is for one or more of the worshippers to be possessed by the *loa,* i.e., a god or spirit. Drumming and dancing help to bring on the possession. Whenever the *loa* enters the person, the person's voice and personality change, and the possessed person also begins to speak in the garbled incoherent words of the *loa.*

Another common belief related to possession is the idea that *madness* is a sign of holiness. If, for example, the witch doctor or shaman becomes possessed by a god or spirit, he can then serve as a conduit or channel for the god's words. Since the medicine man has now become the god with all of the god's powers, he can also heal the sick, cast spells, and bring good or bad fortune to the holy or the damned. Many of these "spells" prove to be very effective because of the worshippers' heightened suggestibility. For this reason also the medicine man's curses, or the idea of voodoo death, are not without factual foundation. If the accursed sincerely believes in the shaman's powers, the victim can be, literally, frightened to death.

Drugs, sex, and elaborate rituals and ceremonies have also been used to induce the experience of possession as well as to experience and contact the gods and higher powers. In many Indian tribes the taking of ceremonial psychedelics by the tribal members brings on common group visions of the tribal deities and demons. Symonds, the nineteenth-century art critic, reported that under the influence of chloroform, he thought he was dying when "suddenly my soul became aware of God, who was manifestly dealing with me, handling me, so to speak in an intensely personal present reality. I felt him streaming in like light upon me. . . . I cannot describe the ecstasy I felt." The magician and occultist Ahister Crowley experimented liberally with both drugs and sex, using them to bring on spiritual possessions.

Today not only do many primitive tribes still believe in spirit possession as the root cause of all mental derangements and afflictions, and ritual, magic, and spells as the cures for these disorders, but, unfortunately, so do a sizeable number of psychotherapists—including both psychiatrists and psychologists. Despite the evidence that has accumulated over the years that the bizarre behavior has nothing to do with spirits of any kind but is due instead to aberrations in the brain and nervous system, or to social role enactments for various rewards, many therapists prefer to ignore the science and embrace the supernatural.

Typical of these alienists was the early spiritualist psychiatrist, Dr. Carl Wickland, who in 1924 published a truly remarkable work titled *Thirty Years Among The Dead* (1974). For over thirty years the good doctor worked with mentally disturbed patients that he believed were possessed by spirits of the dead. Wickland's wife, Anna, was a trance medium and the possessing spirits spoke to her through her vocal apparatus. In this way the good doctor carried on a two-way dialogue with them and after assuring the spirits that they were dead and should go to the afterlife where they belonged, eventually he would persuade them to leave and lo, the patient was cured. For those spirits unwilling to leave Wickland would use a type of electroshock therapy to drive them out. Wickland was also convinced that he was assisted by a group of helpful spirits he referred to as *The Mercy Band* who not only helped him remove the possessors, but also helped the possessors become adjusted to conditions in the afterworld. Wickland was not only convinced that mental illness was due to spirit possession, but he was able to convince a number of other prominent and intelligent individuals as well. One of these was Sir Arthur Conan Doyle who admired Wickland greatly and praised his work. "I have never met anyone who has such a wide experience of invisibles. No one interested in obsession or the curing of insanity by psychic means should miss this book" (1926). This is the same Conan Doyle, you should remember, who also believed in fairies.

Apparently a number of psychotherapists took Doyle at his word and did read the book. One of these was the British psychiatrist Arthur Guirdham who, in 1982, published his book *The Psychic Dimensions of Mental Health.* After more than forty years of practice, Guirdham is convinced that every form of severe mental illness can be caused by spirit interference. Using techniques quite similar to those of Wickland, he talks out the easy spirits, and uses electroshock on the tough and stubborn ones.

Not to be outdone, another psychiatrist, Adam Crabtree, also believes in spirit possession and sees it as the best possible explanation for the multiple personality disorder (MPD). In his 1985 book *Multiple Man: Explorations in Possession and Multiple Personality* (1985) Crabtree describes a number of cases which he believes exemplify spirit possession, and he describes his patients' conditions in terms of possession by earthbound spirits, as well as various dissociative reactions and splittings of the individual's own personality. Fortunately, Crabtree forgoes electroshock therapy in favor of persuasion, drugs, and the talking cure.

Another MPD specialist, the psychiatrist Ralph B. Allison, is another believer in spirit possession. Not only does Allison believe that disembodied minds can exist, but he also thinks that embodied minds are capable of much more than was once thought. In Allison's view—a fairly common one—the mind and the brain are not one and the same thing. The brain is a biophysical structure, whereas the mind is the energy patterns that inhabit that structure. Allison perceives the out-of-body experiences as proof-positive that the mind can come and go independent of the brain. Allison talks to the alleged spirits of his clients and doesn't care where the information he needs to help them comes from. He's very pragmatic. Nevertheless, his experience has convinced him that contrary to the closed model of the human being, i.e., all of the alter personalities arise from within the mind, some of the alter personalities are actually coming from outside the multiple's psyche—as in the case of unwanted spirit possession. Allison's notions and philosophy are set forth in his 1980 book *Minds in Many Pieces.* From his practice Allison has identified five separate types of possession: *Grade I* he sees as identical with the obsessive-compulsive neurosis in which the patient is controlled by an idea, obsession, compulsion, involuntary act, or addiction to alcohol or drugs; *Grade II* is the result of the influence of a negative alter personality developed by a person with a hysterical personality structure—an example would be a man who creates an imaginary friend who hates all women and eventually rapes and kills several victims, or a Dr. Jekyll and Mr. Hyde; *Grade III* occurs when the controlling influence seems to be the mind of another living human being, i.e., witchcraft; *Grade IV* possession is control by the spirit of another deceased human being, e.g., a patient controlled by the spirit of a woman who had drowned herself; and *Grade V* possession is control by a spirit that has never lived before, and identifies itself as an agent of evil or Satan.

Grade V possessions can be cured by priests who follow the rules of exorcism laid down in 1614 in the Catholic *Rituale Romanum.* "Only the power of God and his angels," Allison believes, "can conquer such entities." Allison is the consummate physician doing whatever is necessary to benefit his patients the most. In his words, regarding spirit possession, he says:

> My own sense of ease with these concepts is probably a result of my religious training and beliefs. Furthermore, I simply cannot dismiss the experiences of my patients—the entities I discovered in many of these cases simply do not reflect the classic, accepted pattern of multiple personality.
>
> (p. 200)

Allison goes on to say that he is not the only psychiatrist to reach the same conclusion. While this statement is true, it should also be noted that many other less religious psychiatrists specializing in MPDs do not agree with such a conclusion (e.g., George Ganaway), and feel that any and all notions of spirit possession are medieval if not atavistic.

Nevertheless, another well-known psychiatrist, Dr. M. Scott Peck, author of the two best-sellers *The Road Less Travelled* (1978) and *People of the Lie* (1983), is also a firm believer in demonic possession, and he is also convinced that some cases of multiple personality are the direct result of Satanic possession. As far as Peck is concerned, the question is not "Is the patient possessed or is he or she mentally ill?" but, "Is the patient just mentally ill, or is he or she mentally ill *and* possessed?" In his book *People of the Lie,* Peck describes, in detail, his carrying out of two exorcisms using, in the first case, a team of seven trained professionals working four days for twelve-sixteen hours a day and in the second case, a team of nine men and women working for twelve-twenty hours a day for three days. According to Peck, both these cases were unusual in that they involved Satanic possession. Peck makes it quite clear that he is a deeply religious man, and one who believes deeply in Satan and, in a word, *Evil* with a capital E. Peck, though calling himself a hard-headed scientist, makes it very clear that his religious beliefs come first and take precedence in his thinking. Not only does he discount the role of the exorcist in exorcism, but he attributes any successes to heavenly powers. In his words:

The critical moment of the exorcism is what Martin calls the "expulsion." It cannot be rushed. In both the exorcisms I witnessed, it was initially attempted prematurely. I cannot fully explain what happens at this moment, but I can state that the role of the exorcist in this moment is the least important. The desperate prayers of the team are more important. The prayers are for God or Christ to come to the rescue, and each time I had a sense that God did just that. As I said earlier, it is God that does the exorcising.

(Peck 1984, p. 93)

Peck does add that even God cannot heal someone who does not want to be healed, and ultimately it is the patient herself or himself who is the exorcist. Peck also emphasizes that on occasions even the exorcist is not sure whether or not the exorcism worked. What does come through loud and clear is, at least for Peck, religion and mysticism are the powerful forces at work in many cases of multiple personality disorders. In his words,

Mystically again, I have an inchoate sense that these exorcisms were not just isolated events but almost cosmic happenings. Still it is the patients who served as the very center and focal point of these happenings. . . . Through the torment and courage of their struggle with Satan they won a great victory not only for themselves but for many people.

(Peck 1984, p. 96)

It is most important to note here that Dr. Peck's two cases of demonic possession grew directly out of a charismatic Christian religious practice called "deliverance"—a form of confrontal prayer challenge in which the participants (usually a minister and a prayer group), exhort a possibly possessed person to bring forth his demons. If the patient is, or believes he is, possessed, the entities controlling his body usually will emerge and reveal their identities by speaking through the victims. Most often they will call themselves by the particular evil or vice they believe themselves guilty of. In terms of charismatic Christianity this could be the demon of lust, the demon of greed, or even the demon of epilepsy. In Peck's two cases the evil spirits showed up only after he and his colleagues engaged in prolonged and intensive sessions and countless exhortations with the patients. Clearly, here is another good example of therapist–created disorders, demons inspired, engendered, and aided by strong social pressure and powerful suggestions to create in highly imaginative and deeply religious individuals powerful feelings of sin and guilt that can only be expiated through the release of the internal demons who are, of course, the cause of his or her feelings of guilt and distress. While Peck is not a religious fanatic, he certainly failed to see the social psychological forces obviously at work in these two cases.* It is to the credit of D. Scott Rogo, an avowed paranormalist, who in his work *The Infinite Boundary,* a study of spirit possession and multiple personality, also calls attention to the role of suggestion in Peck's cases. In Rogo's words:

> It is certainly interesting that exorcism seemed to work with these cases, which points to their spiritistic nature. But there is also a phenomenon seen in clinical hypnotherapy that closely resembles the deliverance ministry but which is produced solely through psychological suggestion. Could this phenomenon be the clue to cases seen by Dr. Peck . . . ?
>
> (p. 249)

Yes, indeed, Mr. Rogo, it could be.

In primitive cultures whenever individuals suddenly undergo radical personality changes and behave in radically uncharacteristic ways the reason for it is also attributed to possession by spirits or demons. In Western Europe displays of demonic possession were relatively common occurrences from the sixteenth through the eighteenth centuries, but other than the aforementioned believers in demonic possessson are relatively uncommon today. On the other hand, these altered personality states have been relabeled and instead of demonic possession they are now called multiple personality disorder (MPD). Moreover, within the last fifteen years, there has been a dramatic increase in the frequency with which these disorders have appeared and have been diagnosed. According to Spanos (1989), the hypnotic procedures used, *first,* to uncover the "other resident personalities" and, *later,* to banish them have served primarily as secularized exorcisms. As far back as 1959, Dr. Rawcliffe argued most persuasively that not only are true cases of multiple personality quite rare, but that in nearly every so-called case of MPD, the therapists' own treatments and experiments have been mainly responsible for the emergence of the subsidiary personalities (1959). In other words, multiple personalities are iatrogenic, i.e., caused by the hypnotist himself! Since the hysterical neurotic is normally highly suggestible, and hypnosis is the standard method of treat-

---

*Peck's treatment of these clients with exorcism could well have been the worst thing he could have done. Even he admitted that in one case he wasn't sure that the patient had a relapse. By reinforcing the suggestion of demonic possession he could well have exacerbated the initial condition. We will, of course, never know whether or not a different approach using medication would not have broken the delusion sooner. Can we ever be sure Peck's approach did not aggravate the condition by validating the patient's conviction he was evil and therefore possessed? In the hands of a therapist less religious and less sure of the reality of demons the patient might well have recovered much sooner and with considerably less trauma. We'll never know, of course. We have only Peck's anecdotal analysis and his appeal to all believers in religious mysticism.

ment, it is easy to see why many cases of MPD could be due simply to suggestion, i.e., they are artificially therapist-hypnotist created personalities. Until recently, no experimental evidence supporting this contention was available.

In 1985, and again in 1986, however, Spanos and his co-workers measured the role that the situational context played in MPD production by exposing simulators to an interview under hypnosis that had been used to produce an altered personality in an accused murderer. As is common in suspected cases of MPD, the hypnotic interview provided numerous cues calling forth the altered personality. In both studies the simulators exposed to the interview frequently displayed the cardinal symptoms of MPD, i.e., a secondary personality with a name different from that of their primary personality. While these results implied that the "acting out of a secondary personality by nonsimulators is also elicited and maintained by the situation and the cues supplied by the hypnotist hypnotic interview the exclusive use of simulators prevented a direct test." (Spanos 1986)

Therefore, in a series of four separate studies carried out in 1990, Spanos and his co-workers administered past-life hypnotic suggestions to various groups of subjects who were asked to regress back beyond birth to a previous life. In the first study the development of a past-life identity was unrelated to any sort of psychopathology, but those who were most deeply involved showed the greatest ability to fantasize and engage in imaginative role-playing in everyday life. In the second and third studies the subjects developed past-life identities that reflected the expectations transmitted to them by the hypnotist. In the fourth study the credibility which the subjects assigned to the past-life experiences was determined by whether the hypnotist defined such experiences as either "real" or "imagined." The ease or difficulty with which the subjects were "hypnotized" predicted the subjective intensity of the past-life experiences but not their credibility. Alternatively, the subjects beliefs, attitudes, and expectations with regard to reincarnation did predict the degree of credibility assigned to the experience. These results clearly support the view that hypnotically induced past-life identities are contextually generated, rule-governed, and goal-directed fantasies—fantasies which the subjects construct in order to meet the demands of a hypnotic regression situation. Since the suggestions used in these situations require that the subjects' fantasies be framed as autobiographical historical minidramas narrated in the first person singular by an alter or secondary personality, the subjects tend to choose historical times and places with which they are relatively familiar or in which they have a special interest. Within such constraints they construct a life story weaving together plot lines, details, and characters taken from a wide range of sources such as personal experience, TV shows, novels, etc., and presented as a first person narrative.

Spanos sees the past-lives creations as interpersonal products geared to the expectations of the hypnotist. Both the present study as well as the findings reported by Wilson (1982) showed that the regressees construct their past-life fantasies to correspond to the hypnotists' expectations.

While many theorists believe that hypnotizability reflects a capacity for *dissociation,* and that *dissociation* is the common element in past-life responding, MPD, and hidden observor responding (Bliss 1986; and Hilgard 1977), a better and more parsimonious hypothesis argues that hypnotizability correlates highly with the alternate personality creations found in past-life regression, MPD, and hidden observor contexts because in each of these contexts an alternate identity responding is explicitly tied to hypnosis. Consequently, each situational context is likely to call forth the same attitudes, expectations, and interpretational sets as the hypnotizability test situation. Seen from this perspective, it should not be particularly surprising that people having the personality traits, attitudes, skills, expectancies, etc., needed to successfully respond to the hypnotic suggestions making up the hypnotizability tests also tend to respond successfully to hypnotic suggestions for alternate personality creations when these are delivered in past-life regression, hidden observor, or MPD diagnostic situations. Relevant, in this connection, is the work of M. K. Johnson (1981, 1988) and her associates who found that fantasies were increasingly likely to be defined as real events rather than imaginings as the fantasies became richer in perceptual detail and more embedded in supporting systems of knowledge and belief.

Ganaway (1989), a saner and more sober psychiatric expert in the treatment of MPD, points out that MPD patients should be considered as high risk for contamination by pseudomemories in the hands of therapists who, unwittingly or not, verbally or otherwise, cue them to respond to the therapists' expectations or needs. There are, of course, sources of contamination other than the therapist. Other exogenous sources—books, movies, special childhood and adult relationships—also provide material that is assimilated in a dissociated state, and later under "hypnosis" is recalled by the subject and believed by the subject to be personal experience. Such cryptomnesias are most frequently seen in the reincarnation stories elicited during hypnotic age regressions. Ganaway notes that in the MPD patient created alternate personalities (Alters) may take the form of children, adolescents, or adults of either sex, or not be human at all. Ganaway has encountered demons, angels, sages, lobsters, chickens, tigers, a gorilla, a unicorn, and "God," to name only a few, among the alters of MPD patients he has interviewed. Moreover, the landscapes in which these alters have existed have ranged from labyrinthine tunnels and mazes to castles in enchanted forests, to high-rise office buildings, and even a separate galaxy.

As Ganaway observes:

The degree to which fantasy is incorporated into the development of dissociative defenses may vary from patient to patient, but can be expected to be present to some degree in every multiple, since it represents one of the basic ingredients necessary to construct the often elaborate inscape, or internal world of alters living by the laws of trance logic. In this regard it is no coincidence to discover that multiplicity appears to have its developmental origins in the preoperational, somewhat primary process cognitions of early childhood. Fantasy and magical thinking not only are normal and acceptable at this time, but often are a preferable alternative to an external environment that by comparison may be perceived as dull, unstimulating, and unproviding of narcissistic need gratification. . . . Or conversely perceived as so pervasively traumatic as to be massively overwhelming to the psyche in a life-threatening sense (situations of severe recurrent physical, sexual and/or emotional abuse with recurrent boundary violations).

(pp. 209–210)

Among the reported traumatic memories Ganaway has encountered which he considers to be fantasy and/or illusion include: abuse experiences reported by alters claiming to represent pre-incarnations, i.e., past lives; malevolent demon possessions by alters claiming to be invading spirits from outside the body; pre-birth traumata creating intrauterine dissociative splits (N.B.: There is no anatomical or physiological basis for any sentience whatsoever prior to twenty weeks gestation and no meaningful EEG pattern or electrical activity until at lease thirty weeks); and childhood ritual abuse memories of having one's heart removed and replaced with an animal heart while the living victim was fully conscious. The range of the human imagination is, indeed, awe inspiring!

Curiously enough, the feeling of having one's body being taken over by another "personality" could easily mislead one into believing they are being possessed by some external spirit or agency. Possession experience is psychologically important, and this is shown by the fact that such experiences are fostered by a wide variety of cultures in many diverse formal and informal settings. While usually perceived as illness, or the result of sin, it can have a positive side besides those noted earlier—a way to engage in otherwise taboo behavior. For example, possession by the Holy Spirit also allows the discharge of inhibitions and repressed and suppressed feelings. When possessed by the "holy spirit," many believers not only shout and dance around like the Holy Roller sect, but others also engage in a sort of strange verbal behavior called "speaking in tongues," or *glossolalia*. The emotional release that comes from these enraptured possessions can not only be ecstatic but also therapeutic.

This "speaking in tongues" is an interesting form of spirit possession in that it is not only fairly common in the southern part of the nation, but many Christians regard glossolalia as a sign of "possession by the Holy Spirit." Many Christian charismatics and the Pentecostals believe this verbal babbling is unique to Christians and that it represents an ancient, foreign, or spiritual tongue with a unique spiritual meaning that can be discerned by another believer.

In no way, however, is glossolalia peculiar to Christianity; it exists in many different cultures and in many different religions. When linguists attempt to analyze and study the utterances, they find that the so-called "language" is nothing other than strings of nonsense syllables made up of random patterns of sounds put together haphazardly but emerging in word groupings like sentences. If the speaker is at all clever and uses smiles, head nods, and the appropriate gestures, anyone watching would swear the person is speaking in a legitimate strange and esoteric language. After a few weeks of practice, I have become very adept at "speaking in tongues," and do it frequently to baffle and tease my friends and grandchildren. Despite the claims of those who attempt to (or state that they do) fully understand what is being said, it has been shown that their interpretations are unrelated to the utterances, i.e., when two such texts are compared—one of a glossolaliac, and the other of its interpretation, no related patterns of any sort are found.

Rather than being a supernatural or paranormal phenomena, it turns out to be more or less an act or a role that anyone can learn to play with a little practice, effort, or the proper motivation. Spanos (1986) has shown how easy it is to train college students to become glossolaliacs. The ease with which so many individuals are able to channel spirit guides, discarnate entities, etc., and the ease with which they are able to alter the pitch, timbre, and sound of their voice, as well as their facial expression and manner of speaking, also attests to how readily and well these "roles" can be enacted.

Christie-Murray has devoted an entire book to the subject (1978) and argues that a great deal of such behavior—if not most—is also a form of cryptomnesia. Rather than automatic writing, much of this verbal behavior can truly be characterized as *automatic talking.*

It is well known—and if it isn't it should be—that the human brain of the central nervous system is the most complex thing in the universe. It is certainly understandable that with something this complex there are many, many ways in which something can go awry. There is, in fact, a version of Murphy's Law for psychology: If anything *can* go wrong with the human mind, it *will* go wrong with the human mind. With the vast range of mental disorders and aberrations, as well as the large number of chemical substances that can have mind-altering effects, plus the hundreds of psychological sources of social and sensory stimulation that affect our perceptions, memories and emotions, it is little wonder that things occasionally go awry.

For these reasons alone there is no need to venture outside the confines of the human nervous system whenever we encounter something bizarre or unusual in the area of human behavior. In fact, there is very little—if anything at all—with regard to human behavior that has not, or will not yield to careful and persistent scientific analysis. Certainly to resort to a supernatural, occult, or extraterrestrial explanation of behavior is no explanation at all. It is, rather, a cop-out, a literal throwing in of the proverbial towel, and an admission of defeat. Whenever we encounter something odd about human behavior, we do what our ancestors did: we attribute the bizarre goings-on to witches, spirits, or demons. This proclivity for resorting to the supernatural for all explanations Paul Kurtz refers to as "the transcendental temptation," a most apt description.

As we approach the twenty-first century, what is particularly distressing to students of human behavior is the antiscientific biases and metascientific attitudes being promulgated and promoted by a few members of the professional community. For example, nothing is more typical of this mind set than the overworked, much abused rationalization that "no one knows what we mean by real." This is nonsense. It can be said, with no equivocation whatsoever, that most of us who live in the everyday world of job, home, family, friends, newspapers, magazines, TV, and operate in the three-dimensional scientific world, definitely do know what is real, and what is not. Except for the few and rare occasions in which some of us have a hallucination, or false perception or two, we manage to maintain our contact with consensual reality with little or no difficulty. Thank God that we do. We could not live a civilized existence in a civilized society unless we shared a "real" world in common, a world with reliable and dependable laws that we all respect and obey in order to survive. Nevertheless, not all "alleged" members of the scientific establishment share these views. Felicitas Goodman, an anthropologist, for example states quite frankly, "That what is accepted as being real in a particular situation is decided not by the individual but by the culture into which the situation is embedded." True to a point, but she goes on to say, "If we maintain that in our world people are real and spirits are not that is in the final analysis merely an opinion. It presupposes that we know what we mean by 'real'. . . ." (p. 81)

Goodman not only sees all cases of multiple personality as examples of demonic possession, she also sees exorcism as the treatment of choice. In her view, "While Western-type psychiatric and biomedical treatment of the condition often remains ineffective, it seems at least in some cases exorcism works promptly and well." (p. 84)

Although Goodman is well aware of the position of skeptics like her fellow anthropologist Weston La Barre and his quip, "Nothing down here but us people," this is a view she disdains in favor of religious faith—no matter what flavor it is, or how bizarre, or how far removed from worldly concerns. She states:

> The attacks directed at the Pentecostals are well known usually taking the form of allegations that the speaking in tongues is faked. But the worst situation in the West is the one involving demonic possession. Those afflicted by it need help. Exorcism works, other strategies do not, yet their diagnosis and treatment are determined not by what works but by the prevailing attitudes, the paradigm concerning the nature of reality.
>
> (p. 125)

Goodman's charge may well have been true in certain rare instances with one or two isolated cases, but her assumptions that other strategies do not work and that the prevailing view of reality keeps the afflicted from receiving the exorcism they need and, consequently, a "cure" is grossly in error. For religious believers, both psychiatrists and psychologists have used and have recommended exorcism when all else has failed. As for other strategies not being effective, this is simply untrue. Both psychoactive drugs and psychotherapy have been effective in many so-called cases of "possession."

Whether many of these alleged cases of hers are "true" cases of possession, or represent other forms of human behavior or pseudo-possessions, is also a possibility that cannot be ignored.

Goodman is convinced in the reality of spiritual beings and she argues,

> What can we say about the reality of spiritual beings? We can at least point out that the experience of their presence during possession is accompanied by observable physical changes. We should remember that whether these changes are internally generated or created by external agencies is not discoverable. No one can either prove or disprove that the obvious changes in the brain map in possession or in a patient with a multiple personality disorder, for that matter, are produced by psychological processes or by an invading alien being.
>
> (p. 126)

Once again she is in error since in many cases of MPD it has been shown that the physical changes observed were internally produced, and that identifiable psychological and physiological processes do, indeed, underlie MPD phenomena. Spiegel (1985), Braun (1983), and Ludwig (1972) have argued that specific and unique EEG changes accompany the personality shifts in MPD patients, and suggest that secondary personalities comprising cases of multiple personality tend to be biologically independent of each other as well as psychologically independent. These studies must be kept in perspective, however, since no EEG differences could be found between the three personalities in *The Three Faces of Eve* (1957) case. Of even greater interest is the curious fact that EEG changes can be produced by people simulating multiple personality (Coons, Milstein, and Marley 1982), which again suggests the social cognitive role-playing nature of the MPD disorder as suggested by Spanos.

With regard to the nature of reality and cultural relativity, a bit of illuminating insight was supplied a few years ago by the psychiatrist Dr. Alexander Leighton, who was interviewing a Nigerian shaman. Through an interpreter the shaman said, "This man came here three months ago full of delusions and hallucinations; now he is free of them." Leighton, thinking about the practice of witchcraft and such things that in the West would be considered delusional, asked, "What do these words 'hallucination' and 'delusion' mean, I don't understand?" The native healer looked puzzled, scratched his head, and replied, "Well, when this man came here, he was standing right where you see him now and he thought he was in Abeokuta (a place about 30 miles away). He also thought I was his uncle and he thought God was speaking to him from the clouds. Now I don't know what you call that in the United States, but here we consider that these are hallucinations and delusions." I think that despite cultural differences, most human beings have a pretty fair concept of what is "real" and what is not.

Without a doubt, however, the *pièce de résistance* of possession literature is the psychologist Dr. Edith Fiore's 1987 book, *The Unquiet Dead*. Despite an early disclaimer that "I am not attempting to prove that spirits exist nor that my patients are possessed," Fiore proceeds in the rest of the book to prove otherwise, stating openly:

> My patients and I use the working hypothesis that personality *does* survive the death of the body. . . . Helping these possessing spirits to leave resulted in eliminating their devastating effects, often dramatically changing lives. Because depossession works, I felt a need to write this book.
>
> (p. XI)

Early in her career as a supernaturalist, Fiore published a book on the wonders of past lives regression titled *You Have Been Here Before* (1977). Stating that she originally did not believe in reincarnation and life after death, she now confessed, "Through the years, I have evolved from a disbelief of—but fascination with—'the supernatural' to intellectually accepting the concepts of reincarnation and the continuation of personality." (p. 11) Moreover, she admits that "I view the possessing entities as the true patients. They are suffering greatly, perhaps without even realizing it. Virtual prisoners, they are trapped on the earth plane feeling exactly as they did moments before their deaths, which may have occurred decades before." How does Fiore know this? By talking with them of course!

Fiore not only explains what happens when we die (we're just as alive as before), why spirits remain among us (ignorance, confusion, fear, obsessive attachments, and unfinished business), effects of possession (earthbound entities are "freeze-framed," i.e., they stay just as they were moments before their death), what can be done to prevent being possessed (where our auras are vibrating at high frequencies they can't be entered by spirits vibrating at lower ones—our aura strength protects us from possession), how to detect spirit possession, and how to do depossessions. In short, Fiore gives us a complete system. Perhaps the most interesting chapter of her work is the one on the detection of spirit possession. According to Fiore, the one characteristic that every possessed person experiences is a persistent lowered energy level. The second most important aspect is character shifts, or mood swings. The third indicator is inner voices speaking to the person which, of course, is a classic indicator of something being amiss. The fourth, Fiore insists, is substance abuse. In her words, "If you abuse drugs or alcohol, you can be sure you are possessed." If this is true, we can then assume that somewhere between four to six million U.S. citizens are possessed. A fifth index is impulsive behavior. A sixth is memory problems which are linked to poor concentration. Experiencing sudden anxiety or depression for no discernible reason is another characteristic, as is the sudden onset of physical problems which have no obvious cause. If you found Fiore's book hard to read, or if certain sections were anxiety-arousing, then you are probably resonating to possessing spirits. Of course, if you haven't read it, or don't read it, then you have defeated at least one of the symptoms! Fiore is a lover of checklists and recommends that it is "the overall picture" that is important. For each of the above ten items, if you find yourself with one of these conditions sometimes, then score yourself one point. If you find that you have this condition always or most of the time, score yourself two points. An overall score of 10 or more suggests possession. Moreover, a score of two on items 2, 3, 4, or 10 *strongly suggests possession.*

This checklist was so appealing I felt that it would be interesting to submit these ten most common signs to a group of experienced professional psychotherapists and ask them for their diagnosis of someone having these symptoms. Presented to them as a problem in clinical diagnosis, and recognizing the difficulty in making a blind diagnosis, they were asked to make a best guess as to what might be wrong with such a client. Below is the checklist I sent to them. It lists eleven typical clinical disorders with a twelfth left blank—an additional category was provided. Included in the list as item number seven was spirit possession. A total of thirty therapists responded to my request—twenty licensed clinical psychologists and ten licensed psychiatrists. Each of these professionals had a minimum of four years of either teaching or practical experience, and a total of more than over 400 years experience as a group.

What was most interesting about the results was that none—*not one single therapist*—checked item number seven, spirit possession, as one of the possible diagnoses or as a source of difficulty. Nor did any of the thirty professionals mention this in their brief description of possible problems.

While my sample was, admittedly, a restricted one, and limited to therapists here in the state of Kentucky, I feel quite confident in predicting that if it were extended to cover the other forty-nine states, similar results would be obtained.

Although there was considerable disagreement among the therapists as to specifics, in general most of the therapists mentioned anxiety neurosis, depressive reactions, and schizoid behavior. These were the most common themes reported. With regard to spirit possession as the cause of the symptoms, or as the symptoms being clear indicators of spirit possession, in the opinion of the Kentucky professionals either (1) they are unfamiliar with spirit possession as a clinical entity, (2) they are professionally incompetent, or (3) they do not agree with Dr. Fiore's conclusions and interpretations of clinical symptomatology. Of the three options, I am inclined to accept the last one.

Finally, with regard to depossession one must consider the poor possessing spirits. In Fiore's words, "Rather than thinking of this procedure as 'getting rid of' or 'kicking out' the entities, think of it as a method of helping them in the greatest possible way." (p. 124) According to Fiore, if she just forcibly ejected them, she would not only be creating a horrendous problem for the entities (they'd be out in the cold with no place to go), but also for other people whom they would later latch onto. The essential exercise for depossession is prayer and talk—convincing the possessing spirit he or she will be better off elsewhere than in the body of the possessed. After forming a defensive spiritual barrier by surrounding yourself with dazzling white light—imagine you have a miniature sun in your solar plexus—you address the spirit in a kindly and loving manner and assure him spirits never die, and he should rejoin those other loving discarnate spirits of which he is one. Then bless him or her and send them off with love, after perhaps making the sign of the cross. Non-Christians may say any prayer that is apropos.

A PROBLEM IN CLINICAL DIAGNOSIS

Suppose one of your clients came to you and presented the following symptoms:

1. Low energy level.
2. Frequent mood swings and character shifts.
3. Inner voices speaking to them.
4. Frequent abuse of alcohol and/or drugs.
5. Impulsive behavior.
6. Memory problems.
7. Poor concentration.
8. Sudden onset of anxiety or depression.
9. Sudden onset of physical problems with no obvious cause.

Recognizing the difficulty of making a blind diagnosis, but just on the basis of the above symptoms, what in your opinion would be the best diagnosis you could or would make? What would be your best guess as to what is wrong with this client? Please write your opinion in the space below:

(Now please turn the page and answer the questions there)

Using the symptoms checklist on page #1, look at the categories of human mental difficulties listed below and check one or more of the things that, in your opinion, could be wrong with the individual having the symptoms listed on the previous page.

1. Neurasthenia   _____
2. Schizophrenia or schizoid behavior   _____
3. Anxiety neurosis   _____
4. Depressive reaction   _____
5. Possible brain tumor   _____
6. Chronic stress reaction   _____
7. Spirit possession   _____
8. Senile psychosis   _____
9. Conversion reaction   _____
10. Paranoid reaction   _____
11. Epilepsy or some form of epileptic reaction   _____
12. Something not listed above—Fill in your diagnosis _____
   _____
   _____
   _____
   _____

Name: _____ Degree: _____
(MD, MSW, PhD, PsyD, etc.)

Please return to Bob Baker when finished.

If you can picture a therapist sitting in his or her air-conditioned office praying to a ghost, the anachronism ought to be apparent. In this situation, it should also be clear that the wrong person is receiving the therapy.

When we study Fiore's five case histories of spirit possession, there is also strong reason for believing that most—if not all—of these cases are iatrogenic. After showing up in her office with a cluster of neurotic symptoms, Fiore, with her suggestions and hypnotic regressions, takes them into a full blown case of spiritual invasion. In every case it was Fiore who suggested the use of hypnosis to determine if her clients were suffering from spirit possession. Many of Fiore's clients were very superstitious, and believed in ghosts and spirits before meeting her.

To protect our homes from spirits, Dr. Fiore advises us not to invite spirits into our homes, not to arrange séances, not to use the Ouija board or do automatic writing, and not to use drugs. Surround your home with white light. Ask Jesus for protection. Keep your home happy and filled with love.

Certainly no one could quarrel with this advice. One of the ukases that is repeated continually is Dr. Fiore's proscription against alcohol and drug abuse. One cannot help but conclude that maybe the spirits she is referring to are of the alcoholic variety, and that yes, indeed, when one overindulges one is indeed possessed by spirits. Persistent overindulgence, a common daily occurrence not only in the United States but all over the globe, leads to a pattern of mental and physical disorders much more serious than discarnate spirit possession, a relatively minor neurosis at worst! Annual public health estimates tell us that in the United States three to four hundred thousand deaths annually are attributable to alcoholism, i.e., excessive alcohol use, as compared to few if any deaths attributable to discarnate spirit possession! On the continent of Europe there is now one retailer of alcohol to approximately every hundred inhabitants. The number of alcoholics in the United States is estimated to be well over 10 million, with a recent estimate of another 2.2 million Americans addicted to cocaine. In the past—through medieval and early modern times—the individual intake of alcohol was probably even greater than it is today. Nowadays, where we drink tea, coffee, or Coke, our ancestors drank wine, beer, mead, and later gin, vodka, or brandy. Failure to drink an intoxicant was once considered to be socially deviant. Alcohol is but one of the many drugs used to escape from the daily rigors of reality. According to a recently released Senate Judiciary Committee report, 2.2 million Americans in 1990 were found to be "hard-core" cocaine addicts, meaning that they use the drug once a week or more. Every day millions upon millions of civilized men and women consume mind-altering substances such as alcohol, hashish, opium and its derivatives, barbiturates, cocaine and its derivatives, amphetamines, tranquilizers, and literally hundreds of other chemical agents. Despite the current so-called "war on drugs" here in the United States, and the fact that in most civilized communities public opinion is opposed to debauchery and drug addiction as being ethically wrong, there is no indication that the use of these substances is or will ever diminish.

There can also be no doubt whatsoever that all of these chemicals when ingested have some effects, pronounced or mild, upon the human nervous system. Otherwise they would not be ingested in the first place. Since human beings are subject to misperceptions, illusions, delusions, and hallucinations without any chemical assistance of any sort, what happens when the body is loaded down with agents having direct Central Nervous System effects? The natural tendencies are, of course, amplified.

In the case of the alcoholics, research has shown they are both psychologically and physiologically vulnerable. Psychologically it seems that there is a prealcoholic personality pattern that predisposes certain individuals to drink to excess. It is made up of the following traits: a low capacity for handling tension, egocentricity, hostility, dependency as well as strong feelings of inadequacy, inferiority, and insecurity. Not all people who possess these predisposing traits drink to excess, and of those who do not all can be considered alcoholics. To explain why certain individuals and not others eventually lose all control over their drinking along with psychological vulnerability, we have to add physiological vulnerability as well. It requires additional internal factors—either inborn or acquired through heavy alcohol intake—to produce actual addiction. Nutritional deficiencies—enzyme and vitamins in particular, brain damage as a result of heavy alcohol consumption, endocrinological disfunction (particularly adrenal exhaustion), and pituitary dysfunction also seem to be involved. The end result is physical dependence and pathological desire, i.e., excessive drinking. As daily prolonged consumption increases, a number of pathological changes occur in the individual. The most common form of disorder in the stomach is alcoholic gastritis, an inflammation characterized by loss of appetite, frequent periods of nausea, and occasional vomiting after a drinking episode. Irritation of the lower intestinal tract is also common. Among the physical changes associated with excessive drinking is alcoholic tremor, or "the shakes," which may persist long after the patient has stopped drinking. In fact, the tremors may be aggravated when the patient attempts to stop drinking, and they reach their peak of intensity immediately after complete alcohol withdrawal.

While the exact causes of the specific cerebral metabolic disturbances produced by alcohol withdrawal are unclear, the effects are hyperactivity in a number of cerebral structures, either in the form of abnormal functional stimulation, or as a release phenomenon caused by the exhaustion of a governing mechanism. At the end of a prolonged bout of drinking the behavior is, in any case, characterized by acute tremulousness, or "the shakes" that are caused by motor hyperactivity. The patient also suffers from severe anxiety, insomnia, disturbing feelings of unreality, and a marked inability to concentrate. He or she also shows evidence of acute dehydration as a result of the diuretic action of the alcohol, and also of starvation as a result of reduced food intake, nausea, vomiting, and diarrhea. Withdrawal from alcohol is serious business similar to that of withdrawal from barbiturates and other depressants. In fact, withdrawal from alcohol is more dangerous than withdrawal from heroin since heroin withdrawal is rarely fatal, while alcohol withdrawal can be.

For about one quarter of tremulous patients hallucinations may develop within twenty-four hours after alcohol withdrawal, though the patients can often communicate coherently and even describe their hallucinations. Known as the DTs, or delirium tremors, the DTs are difficult to control and reverse. The tremors appear to be a combination of both tremulousness and hallucinosis in their severest form. Grand mal seizures, or "rum fits," may trigger the syndrome, which usually occurs after the first, and before the fifth, day of abstinence. Tremor is coarse and severe, and the patient is almost impossible to divert to reality. The patient mutters constantly, or speaks incoherently, and is disoriented as to time, place, and person. His hallucinations are vivid, and they often assume the form of bizarre, usually large, moving animals—the proverbial pink elephants— or animal-human combinations. Auditory delusions or hallucinations are less common, and when they do occur they usually take the form of threatening human voices. Along with these symptoms there are autonomic system disturbances in the form of increased blood pressure, tachycardia, pupil dilation, and excessive perspiration. Despite the absence of infection, elevated temperature may also occur.

Many individuals who have been drinking excessive amounts of alcohol over a long period of time suffer from a syndrome known as Korsakoff's Psychosis. While the exact cause of this disorder is unclear, more than likely damage to the myelin sheathe surrounding some nerve fibers and lesions to the brainstem and limbic system in the midbrain due to the alcohol, as well as avitaminosis play a major role. For our purposes, there are two classic behavioral signs of Korsakoff's psychosis: *anterograde amnesia* and *confabulation*. Anterograde amnesia is the loss of memory for immediately preceding events; the patient usually has no recollection of something that occurred immediately before being asked about it. Confabulation, as we discussed earlier, is the tendency to fill in our memory gaps with false or fantasized material. The patient will report things that never happened without a qualm, and will talk about the wildest, most bizarre, and impossible events as if they were normal everyday occurrences. If the patient is asked why he is in the hospital, he is likely to deny it is a hospital, and even if he admits that it is, he will have an incredible reason for his being there. Usually these patients are lucid and friendly, but they see nothing amiss with their wild and improbable stories. At other times apathy, confusion, and disorientation predominate their thinking. The onset of Korsakoff's Psychosis is gradual, and people unfamiliar with it may assume the victims' wild, confabulated accounts of aliens, monsters, UFOs, demons, and apparitions may well contain elements of truth since early in the game the patient is affable, friendly, and superficially, at least, seems in possession of his facilities rather than possessed by alcoholic spirits.

Mention should also be made of the fact that long term regular use of barbiturates may also lead to paranoid delusions, increased hostility, and violence. Even the regular use of tranquilizers, which also act upon the limbic system of the brain while their effects are generally less extreme than those of barbiturates, can also produce hallucinations as a side effect in some users. And, of course, the hallucinogenic drugs like PCP, psilocybin, LSD, and datura can also take their users into never–never land with ease, and convince them that they are talking with the dead, are possessed by spirits, or are levitating to UFOs that will fly them to the stars.

According to Antero Alli (1989/90), one rather banal reason why some of us are drawn to communicating with the dead is that we don't have any real living friends to talk to. Moreover, establishing a link with the "guides" in channeling is merely a way of compensating for a lack of love, good sex, and genuine human interaction. Spooks, like our childhood imaginary playmates, might just offer the security, status, and "strokes" missing from a broken home life. Yet, Alli asks, if ghosts do exist, why do we assume they are any wiser than the living? Based upon the inane and vapid material dredged up by channelers, most of the entities seem to be suffering from terminal cases of stupidity. Death, it seems, did nothing but make them dumber than they were when alive. Before turning to other topics, we could not, of course, omit one of the greatest authorities of all on possession—the one and only Ruth Montgomery, America's greatest psychic. In her truly amazing book of 1981, *Strangers Among Us,* Montgomery asks us to believe that enlightened spirit beings and extraterrestrials are taking over human bodies with full permission of their original owners. The reason? Well, they have a mission and it is to guide us through our upcoming crisis. Believe it or not, for some reason that is unstated, the Earth is going to shift on its axis any day now since it is supposed to happen, according to Montgomery's sources, near the end of the century. So, these secret and anonymous other-worldly souls called "Walk-Ins" will be our guides and mentors in the "perilous days ahead."

According to Montgomery, the number of "walk-ins" is increasing every day. In fact, *you may be one and not even know it!* How about that? When I finished Ruth Montgomery's book, it suddenly dawned on me that I myself was a "walk-in," and I, too, had a mission: my mission is to warn all potential readers about the blithering idiocy that is found in the pages of books such as *Strangers Among Us* by Ruth Montgomery. Avoid it while there is still time! If you hurry away, you can escape from drowning in the flood of such nonsense now pouring daily from the presses. All the best of luck!

6

Mediums, Channels, and Out of Body Experiences

In this new age, the channelers are off on a new kick. Instead of getting in touch with relatives who have "passed over" they now contact ancient entities that inhabited this earth thousands of years ago. These prehistoric sages dispense advice to the anxiety-ridden people who eagerly pad the bank accounts of the channelers. So what we have now are dinosauric Dear Abbys dishing out deceptive and devious divinations to the duped.

—Henry Gordon, *Channeling into the New Age*

Mediums: Remembrances of Channels Past

I attended numerous spiritualist gatherings, formed acquaintances with famous mediums and watched them during their work. But I did not experience even once anything interesting, anything that would have deserved serious thought or anything that passed beyond the frontiers of the mind . . . . Remember, how unimportant and commonplace the alleged utterances of the most famous "spirits" are!

—Anatole France, cited by Paul Tabori in *Pioneers of the Unseen*

Channeling, despite its modern trappings, is but a revival of the mediumistic phenomena of the last half of the nineteenth century. The phenomena was as spurious and deceitful then as the pronouncements of our contemporary trance channelers are now—if not more so.

During the heyday of spiritualism, "One may lay it down as a principle," wrote Flammarion in his *Mysterious Psychic Forces*, "that all professional mediums cheat. But they do not always cheat." This statement typified the attitude of most members of the intellectual community at this time.

The desire to believe in the reality of spiritualistic phenomena was so strong and so pervasive that even after the investigators had exposed the medium—caught him or her red-handed in an out and out fraud— the investigator rationalized it away with statements like Flammarion's. More revealing still was a statement by Frank Podmore who suggested that in a trance the medium may undertake to apport flowers in the next séance and then, in the waking state, he may buy and secret them about his person without conscious knowledge. In other words, the medium didn't mean to cheat, he did it unaware, automatically, while in a state of "dissociated consciousness." Fodor in his *Encyclopedia* (1966) rationalizes their behavior even further by quoting Edison to the effect that:

> There are more frauds in modern science than anywhere else. . . . They have time and again set down experiments as done by them, curious, out-of-the-way experiments that they never did, and upon which they have founded so-called scientific truths. I have been thrown off my track often by them and for months at a time. Try the experiment yourself and you will find the result altogether different.
>
> (p. 150)

From this we are to conclude that because there are cheats in science, and then just because there are a few cheats in spiritualism, the validity of the latter is as high as, and on the same plane as, the former!

In Fodor's section on "Fraud" in his *Encyclopedia of Psychic Science* (1966), a veritable gold mine of mind-boggling examples of human credulity, the author admits that many mediums did resort to fakery and deceit but then he states, "In the past charges of fraud often resulted from a lack of sufficient knowledge or unsuspected possibilities." Mumler, the first spirit photographer, was promptly accused of trickery when, instead of the spirit of the dead, the negative of the living appeared on his plate. Richet *admits* (obviously he did not wish to do so) that:

> There is a quasi-identity between the medium and ectoplasm, so that when an attempt is made to seize the latter a limb of the medium may be grasped, though I make a definite and formal protest against this frequent defense of doubtful phenomena by the spiritualists. More frequently the ectoplasm is independent of the medium, indeed, perhaps it is always so.
>
> (p. 149)

The will to believe, the desire to see spiritualistic phenomena as valid is so powerful that nothing can change it. The urge to defend as true the spirit-tricks of Eusapia Paladino was so powerful that scientific observers, when they caught Eusapia cheating, blamed it not on her but on the scientists who were observing her. Since many mediums are hysterics, the reasoning went, whenever they felt their mediumistic powers ebbing, they could not resist the temptation to supplement it by artifice. In other words, they are so extremely suggestible that they often *will obey the secret urgings of the hostile audience.* Ochorowitz used this as a defense of Eusapia when she was caught cheating in Genoa.

> When it is understood that the medium is but a mirror for reflecting and directing the nervous energies of the sitters to an idea-plastic purpose, it will not be found surprising that suggestion should play an important part. With controllers imbued with the notion of fraud the medium will be dominated by the suggestion of fraud.
>
> (p. 149)

In other words, poor Eusapia suffered so much during her productions of physical, other worldly phenomena that if she were not carefully watched time and again, she would follow the line of least resistance and cheat. Geley, one of the investigators, went so far as to state "when a medium tricks, the experimenters are responsible." Even Heyward Carrington, one of the more "scientific" of the investigators of spiritualistic phenomena stated that when a "genuine" medium is caught resorting to trickery, the investigator should "say nothing but let the medium see by one's manner that one is displeased and the phenomena evidently not convincing. If she perceives that such attempts are useless, she will settle down, pass into a trance, and *genuine* (emphasis mine) phenomena will be obtained."

The attitude of these so-called unbiased scientific investigators is clear: "Don't worry—even if we catch you cheating, we'll forgive you and wait patiently until you *really* fool us. Don't worry, no matter what you do we still believe in you and your spirits." People with this attitude are enemies?

Even the distinguished William James and James H. Hyslop used the hypothesis of *unconscious fraud* in defense of the mediums. When Hyslop made flashlight photography of a medium's production of some physical phenomena, and showed them to a medium later, "she was shocked and dumfounded when the pictures were shown to her." Even she was unaware she was doing it—it was supposed to be the "dead," or her "control." Such examples are legion, and books could be filled with case after case in which the mediums were exposed or, in many cases such as the Fox sisters—Margaret and Kate—where they exposed themselves.

The readiness or will-to-believe on the part of so many investigators during "the heyday of spiritualism" was so strong that even among the more enlightened of the investigators any hypothesis, no matter how bizarre or far-fetched, was considered worthy, and was taken seriously by otherwise sane and level-headed scientists. For example, to explain a hallucination experienced by Sir John Heschel in which after watching a building demolished one day, on the following day he saw it still standing, Edmond Gurney—an acknowledged expert on hallucinations—believed that they were induced telepathically. In Heschel's case, Gurney suggested, in his *Phantasms of the Living* (1886), that:

> A person thinking of a given place which is at the time actually experienced in sense perception by some other persons, may obtain thereby to such a community of consciousness with the other persons as to be able, under some unknown circumstances, to impart into the consciousness of a second person, in the guise of hallucination, a thought existing in his own.
>
> (Fodor 1966, p. 157)

In sum, many hallucinations people believed in the past were due to telepathy. This tendency to explain one unknown behavioral phenomenon with another higher and more abstruse unknown was not confined to scientists of the past. In our own time the well-known parapsychologist, R. A. McConnell, has recently argued that all hypnosis is nothing but clear-cut examples of *Psychokinesis*—one mind directly controlling that of another. The failure of the scientific world to acknowledge the brilliance of this hypothesis set off a fascinating exchange of charges and counter charges between McConnell and the editors of a number of scientific journals. (McConnell 1983).

One cannot mention ESP without thinking about its defenders and their occasional bizarre logic.

One of the most incredible rationalizations in the history of ESP research, as well as one of the lowest of "lame excuses" in the history of paranormal thought, was stated by B. Inglis in 1983. Inglis sees in the "experimenter effect"—the experimenter's belief affects the outcome—the reason why parapsychology has been unable to come up with a repeatable experiment and may never be able to do so. Inglis believes that all of the efforts of parapsychologists to prove paranormal effects to the greater scientific community may be jeopardized by this factor. The "decline effect," a variation of experimenter bias, is another good example. The decline effect showed up in Neal Miller's early work with biofeedback in which he showed rats could learn to control their heartbeat, their blood pressure, urine formation, etc. Four years later, much to Miller's dismay, he was totally unable to repeat the initial results that were demonstrated by six different experiments. Albert Sabin, in his early work with the polio vaccine, experienced similar problems. The decline–effect also shows up in psychopharmacology research where new drugs show remarkable results initially, only to prove ineffective as their use is increased.

Inglis argues that *unconscious skepticism* on the part of the scientific community is the reason for this outcome. As soon as one begins to question whether the results are real or illusory, and whether one has been deceived, this affects the experimental results. This secret skepticism, Inglis believes, may account for this "decline effect." Inglis also argues for a "witness-effect" in which he argues that certain paranormal effects will not occur when a skeptical witness is present. Furthermore, Inglis also poses the existence of a "location effect," which is the total inability of psychics to perform in laboratories or under carefully controlled objective conditions.

Inglis forgot to add another effect—the "believer effect," which is the total inability of logic, reason, scientific proof, evidence, replicable experiments, or 120 mm. armor-piercing ammunition to make a dent—much less penetrate—the bone-deep convictions of believers in the occult and supernatural to whom paranormal phenomena are real and true, and who believe every claim ever made—no matter how improbable or far-fetched —must be true. Otherwise no one would have mentioned it.

The difficulties, therefore, are very great if we set out to prove that a certain message comes from a discarnate mind. It should not only be clear that the contents of the message were unknown to the medium, but also that they were unascertainable. And as we do not know the powers of the subconscious to acquire information, those instances in which the information may have been acquired from books should only be provisionally accepted, if at all. Many of the spiritualists believed that the discarnate controls could read books, therefore, an incarnate mind, in a trance, could do the same thing.

As for the mediums themselves, all of them without exception—especially those who gave many sittings over a period of several years—ran into difficulties of one sort or another. Charles Bailey, a famous Australian medium, was highly skilled with apports—various objects being produced supposedly from another world—and he did very well with his conjuring until he ran into disaster in Grenoble in 1910. Here he produced two small birds that were supposedly from out of nowhere. Unfortunately, a local dealer who was a member of the audience recognized Bailey as the man he sold the same birds to the day before. Colonel de Rochas and W. Reichel, his sponsors, also discovered Bailey had concealed the birds in his intestinal opening, the one place Bailey refused to allow the investigators to examine. Bailey's Hindu control claimed, of course, the birds came directly from India.

The Bangs sisters, Laesa and May, specialized in direct writing, drawing, and painting. In sealed envelopes, which were brought by the sitters and were enclosed between two slates, messages in ink were produced in broad daylight. The sitter would place the envelopes between a pair of slates and hold them under his hand while either of the mediums, Laesa or May, sat on the opposite side of the table. Following a trance lasting anywhere from a few minutes to an hour, raps on the table would announce that the message was ready. In Chicago in 1909 Hereward Carrington investigated and caught the sisters in a fraud. Carrington addressed a letter in a sealed envelope to "Dearest Mother Jane Thompson" (who never existed), and he received a reply addressed to "Dearly Loved Son Harold," signed by his devoted mother, Jane. Moreover, Carrington had the magician David P. Abbott duplicate the Bangs sisters' work exactly. Over the years a number of charges of fraud were brought against them, and fraud in their slate writing and their masquerades as materialized spirits were convincingly established.

Even the famous Helen Blavatsky failed to pull off her charades and fool her audiences. One of her strongest supporters, A. P. Sinnett, who wrote a number of books about Helen Blavatsky and Theosophy, painfully admitted:

> That she sometimes employed the Coulombs, husband and wife, as confederates in trickery is the painful though hardly intelligible state of the facts. Even with me she has done this. For example, on my return to India, after having published *The Occult World*—after she knew that I was rooted in a personal conviction not only that she possessed magic powers, but that I was in touch with the Masters and devoted to the theosophical cause, she employed M. Coulomb to drop a letter from the Master intended for me through a crack in the rafters above, trying to make me believe that it had been dropped by the Master himself—materialized then and there after transmission by occult means from Tibet. M. Coulomb told Hodgson that he had been so employed on this occasion, and his statement fits in with the minor circumstances of the incident.
>
> (Fodor, p. 32)

The idea of the survival of mind, memory, and personality were considered by most spiritualists as proven facts. Typical of these beliefs were those of Frederick B. Bond, the author of *The Gate of Remembrance,* published in 1918. Bond's work both jelled and crystallized into one spiritualistic system a number of major tenets of the spiritism belief system. In this work Bond put forward a tentative explanation of the recall of the olden-time memories by suggesting something in the nature of a cosmic reservoir of human memory and experience in which the element of personality was preserved and welded into a collective association extending through all time. This, Bond argued, not only would tend to perpetuate individual character, but actually emphasize the force and clarity of its expression by enriching it with added elements of a sympathetic nature. Individual personality is, in Bond's view, progressively developed and perfected through the multiplying of its sympathetic contacts. Bond's conception of immortality has a significant bearing on mediumship, for he pictured subliminal consciousness as a magnet which is constantly attracting other elements of personality sympathetically linked with the physical being of their host. Therefore, we are, alike, sharers in the great life of the subliminal world and are an integral part of it, the only barriers being our own intellectual and emotional limitations. The communications are based upon sympathetic spiritual association. Where this exists there will always be the probability of a recall of the veridical memories of old, and of their right translation into language. If, however, there is no such spiritual link present, you will have only the reflection of the personal subconscious mind of the medium, and there will be no sure indication of the entry of a really independent personality. Bond's theory thus brings the extreme psychological and spiritualistic views into a well thought-out harmony.

It is of some interest that Robert Browning (1812–1889), the poet, attended one of D. D. Home's sittings and caught him in a fraudulent act. Browning then wrote a poem about this titled "Mr. Sludge The Medium." The essence of the poem was:

> . . . Now don't, sir! Don't expose me! Just this once!
> This was the first and only time, I'll swear,
> Look at me—see, I kneel—the only time,
> I swear I ever cheated. . . .
> Well, Sir, since you press—
> (how do you tease the whole thing out of me!)
> Now for it, then!. . . .
> I cheated where I could.
> Rapped with my toe joints, set sham hands at work,
> Wrote down names weak in sympathetic ink,
> Rubbed odic lights with ends of phosphor-match,
> And all the rest—
>
> (Fodor 1966, p. 39)

The poem did great harm to Home's reputation and was widely quoted in the press, even in America.

Although the number of credulous and eccentric ideas they entertained were countless even in those days, a number of so-called scientists embraced some very non-materialistic and highly unscientific notions as well. One salient example was Dr. J. Rhodes Buchanan (1814-1899), dean of the faculty and Professor in the Eclectic Medical Institute of Covington, Kentucky. Buchanan, one of the pioneers in psychometric research, discovered phrenomesmerism, the combination of phrenology and mesmerism. In 1843 Buchanan published a new neurological map of the brain and the phrenological organs. He also discovered the "region of sensibility" and found that if this area was well developed, it contained an unknown psychic faculty which he named "psychometry," or the measure of the soul. He also discovered that certain people were very sensitive to atmospheric, electrical, and other physical conditions. One individual, for example, told Buchanan that if he touched brass in the dark, he would know it immediately because of an offensive metallic taste in his mouth. Acting on this, Buchanan carried out a number of experiments and found that students from a Cincinnati medical school received distinct sensory impressions from medicines they held in their hands. To eliminate thought transference the substances had to be encased in heavy paper and mixed. Buchanan gradually became convinced that some sort of an emanation is given off by all substances—even the human body. People who are sensitive or "psychic" can feel and interpret these emanations Buchanan called "nerve auras." Not only was he overwhelmed with this discovery, but Buchanan also boldly proclaimed:

> The past is entombed in the present, the world is its own enduring monument; and that which is true of its physical is likewise true of its mental career. The discoveries of Psychometry will enable us to explore the history of man, as those of Geology enable us to explore the history of the Earth. There are mental fossils for psychologists as well as mineral fossils for the geologists; and I believe that hereafter the psychologist and the geologist will go hand in hand, the one portraying the earth, its animals and its vegetation, while the other portrays the human beings who have roamed over its surface in the shadows, and the darkness of primeval barbarism. Aye, the mental telescope is now discovered which may pierce the depths of the past and bring us in full view of the grand and tragic passages of ancient history.
>
> (Fodor 1966, p. 39)

Even though Buchanan was an avowed spiritualist, he believed psychometry was essentially a human faculty which had nothing to do with spirits. Buchanan believed the psychometer needed only an object belonging to the person to be read in order to give an accurate reading. Later Buchanan believed that not even the object was necessary. Anything that would lead the mind of the psychometer to the subject would suffice. On one occasion, Buchanan said he wrote the name of a friend on a piece of paper and put it in the hands of a skilled psychometer, and she gave a detailed and accurate reading of a person she had never seen.

Not only did Dr. Buchanan defend the spiritualists and mediums—including the Fox sisters—but working with his wife Cornelia, a skilled psychometer, he received a direct pencilled message signed by St. John. For a number of years afterward, messages and portraits were also received from spirits in contact with Jesus, Moses, Helen of Troy, John the Baptist, and Confucius. As for Cornelia, Buchanan stated: "The past was to her as open a book as the present, and during the years in which she portrayed historic characters of whom I knew nothing, I never found her deviating from the truth as far as I could discover." In 1897 these psychometric communications were published under the title *Primitive Christianity Containing the Lost Lives of Jesus Christ and the Apostles and the Authentic Gospel of St. John* (Fodor 1966, p. 40).

Another scientist with a noticeable weird streak was one Dr. Titus Bull, a New York physician and member of the AAAS (American Association for the Advancement of Science), who directed the James H. Hyslop Foundation For the Treatment of Obsession. The treatment was done by psychic methods using mediums. According to Dr. Bull, all cases of obsession are due to the presence of earthbound spirits. They do not necessarily mean any harm—all they want is to enjoy an earthly existence again. Some of them, however, may commit acts of revenge or other harm owing to their ignorance. If an evil personality gains control, the obsessed person may be driven to criminal or insane acts.

Following his twenty years of study of obsessions at the Hyslop Institute, Bull, in 1872, published his master work, *Analysis of Unusual Experience in Healing Relative to Diseased Minds and Results of Materialism Foreshadowed.* In this book he stated:

An obsessing personality is not composed of the soul, mind and will of one disembodied being, but is, in reality, a composite personality made up of many beings. The pivot obsessor, or the one who first impinges upon the sensorium of the mortal, is generally one with little resistance to the suggestions of others. He or she, therefore, becomes as easy prey to those who desire to approach a mortal in this way.

. . . Some people, moreover, may be born with tendencies which make it easier for them to become victims of mental alterations later in life. . . . There is an influence which can be exerted upon the minds of mortals by ideas embodied in thoughts from their departed ancestors. In other words, some departed ancestors, whenever possible, attempt to mould the lives of those incarnated who are akin. . . . There is a type of mortal whose mind is easily influenced by the stronger minds of the family group. . . . The more clannish the family group, the more likely is this to be true on both sides of the veil. It is, however, not to be considered as spirit obsession in the true sense. . . . The intervention of shock, however, or anything that could upset the nerve balance of a member of such family group, would place him in actual danger of becoming a victim of true spirit obsession. . . . The primary obsessor, in this case, would likely be one who claimed the right by ties of blood, who had no desire to do anything but to keep the mortal in line with family ideals.

According to Dr. Bull obsessors "have three major points of impingement; namely, the base of the brain, the region of the solar plexus, and at the center governing the reproductive organs. As there are three major points of impingement, it may be assumed that there can be three composite groups, each starting with a pivot entity. What satisfaction is to be gained this way includes the whole gamut of human emotions."

The pivot entities "upon which the mound of entity obsession is built" act as automatic channels for the others. Many of them were victims of obsession before their passing. Others may become obsessors "through the machinations or wiles of others." Not understanding what has happened to them they may be readily influenced to turn to obsession.

Another important point is "the possibility of obsessions passing on the body of mortal pangs which were part of their own physical life." They retained in their memory the possibility of producing pain and as often they are unable to inhibit the production of it in the obsessed body, it must be beyond their control. "Therefore," states Dr. Bull, "it is a fair assumption to say that often the migratory pains of the living are caused by the memory pangs of the dead." The prime reason of why the production of pain should be beyond control is "the domination of another and more crafty entity who is using the pain-producer for his own purpose. . . . "

(Fodor 1966, p. 267)

Next, we come to Dr. Robert Hare (1781–1858), professor of Chemistry at the University of Pennsylvania, discoverer of the oxyhydrogen blowpipe, author of more than 150 scientific papers, and one of the first scientists to publicly denounce American Spiritualism. In his words, he was duty bound "to bring whatever influence he possessed to the attempt to stem the tide of popular madness which, in defiance of reason and science, was fast setting in favor of the gross delusion called spiritualism." He was soon, however, to significantly alter this stance.

In 1853 at the age of seventy-two, Hare designed a number of instruments and began a series of experiments designed to prove that spiritualism was bunk.

So in 1853, at the age of seventy-two, he began his investigations and devised a number of instruments which, contrary to his expectations, conclusively proved that a power and intelligence, not that of those present, was at work.

His first apparatus was a wooden board about four feet long, supported on a fulcrum about a foot from one end, and at the other end attached by a hook to a spring balance. A glass vessel filled with water was placed on the board near the fulcrum, a wire gauze cage attached to an independent support, and not touching the glass at any point, was placed in the water and the medium had to effect the balance by simply placing his hand into the wire cage. The medium was Henry Gordon. The balance showed variations of weight amounting to eighteen pounds.

The other apparatus consisted of a revolving disc attached to a table in a manner that the movements of the table actuated the pointer which ran around the letters of the alphabet printed on the circumference of the disc and spelt out messages. The disc was so arranged that the medium could not see the letters.

His book, *Experimental Investigation of the Spirit Manifestation,* published in 1855, summed up the results as follows: "The evidence may be contemplated under various phases; first, those in which rappings or other noises have been made which could not be traced to any mortal agency; secondly, those in which sounds were so made as to indicate letters forming grammatical, well-spelt sentences, affording proof that they were under the guidance of some rational being; thirdly, those in which the nature of the communication has been such as to prove that the being causing them must, agreeably to accompanying allegations, be some known acquaintance, friend, or relative of the inquirer.

Again, cases in which movements have been made of ponderable bodies of a nature to produce intellectual communications resembling those obtained, as above-mentioned, by sounds.

Although the apparatus by which these various proofs were attained with the greatest possible precaution and precision, modified them as to the manner, essentially all the evidence which I have obtained tending to the conclusions above mentioned, has likewise been substantially obtained by a great number of observers. Many who never sought any spiritual communications and have not been induced to enrol themselves as Spiritualists, will nevertheless not only affirm the existence of the sounds and movements, but also admit their inscrutability."

The book, the second part of which described afterlife as depicted by the communicators, passed through five editions. Reaction was quick to set in against its influence. The professors of Harvard University passed a resolution denouncing him and his "insane adherence to a gigantic humbug." He was howled down by the American Association for the Advancement of Science when in Washington, in 1854, he tried to address them on the subject of Spiritualism. Finally he paid for his convictions by resigning from his chair.

A. D. Ruggles, a professional medium who often wrote in languages unknown to him, was one of the subjects with whom Professor Hare experimented. Later he himself became a medium. This is known from a letter of his to Judge Edmonds which contains this paragraph: "Having latterly acquired the powers of a medium in sufficient degree to interchange ideas with my spirit friends, I am no longer under the necessity of defending media from the charge of falsehood and deception. It is now my own character only that can be in question."

In the revelations from the other world the communications are taken at their face value. There is no careful sifting or criticism and the fact that they came from spirits appears to have attested their credibility for Dr. Hare.

(Fodor 1966, p. 158)

Finally, we come to the case of Dr. Johann Zollner, professor of Physics and Astronomy at the University of Leipzig, who wrote an excellent scientific text about comets. Unfortunately, Zollner became enraptured by the antics of the medium Dr. Henry Slade. Slade, a master prestidigitator and slate writer, was exposed by Professor Lankester as well as by Henry Sidgwick, Edmund Gurney, and W. B. Carpenter. Even the famous Alfred Russel Wallace, however, defended Slade and believed his slate writings were, indeed, produced by spirits of the dead. Slade, however, was caught using trickery on several occasions and was finally exposed by the Seybert Commission in 1885. Zollner was so enthralled by Slade that he wrote a long book titled *Transcendental Physics,* in which he argued that Slade used the fourth dimension to carry out his spiritual wonders. Zollner's theory argued that mediumistic phenomena would soon lose their mystic or mystifying character and would then pass into the domain of ordinary physics and physiology. This, in turn, would extend to all of the sciences and boost Zollner into the company of great scientists like Galileo and Newton. The work was not well received, and brought Zollner persecution, contempt, and ridicule from the scientific community. The Seybert Commission report stated that Zollner, at the time of his experiments, was of unsound mind. Those close to him, however, denied it. Zollner also investigated several other mediums and also found them to be authentic. Before he could publicize their achievements, however, he died suddenly of a brain hemorrhage in 1882. The curiosity, *Transcendental Physics,* was translated into English and published in 1880 in London.

It is also sad to note that even after Eusapia Paladino, one of the most famous of all mediums, and all of her many medium tricks were exposed, both her champion, Hereward Carrington, and the other European investigators who studied her were not influenced at all by the exposure. In fact, they argued that had Eusapia been studied long enough and carefully enough, genuine phenomena would have been observed as well as the fraudulent ones to which she resorted when genuine manifestations failed to appear. Despite the exposure, and a full explanation of every trick in her repertoire—incredible as it seems—her reputation grew even stronger after her death! Once a believer, always a believer, the facts be damned.

Unless one is a true believer in the paranormal, the world of spiritualism, and mediumistic phenomena, it is taken for granted that supernatural manifestations are fraudulent. The manifestations did, of course, vary dramatically in quality from the crude muslin-covered, ectoplasmic ghosts and fake and flimsy spirit photographs, to startling and baffling feats of mind-reading and apportments that were difficult indeed to understand and explain. It is obviously impossible to investigate and uncover the clever ruses and techniques employed in each and every case of mental magic. Moreover, since many of the eye-witness first or second hand reports were erroneous and exaggerated, their authenticity or lack of it is also beyond doubt. It is possible, nevertheless, to let one allegedly impregnable and well-documented case of true mediumship worthy of the best productions of Mrs. Piper represent all of the rest of the claimed cases of "true extrasensory or spiritual perception." This is the case that Bernard O'Donnell refers to as "The Masked Medium Spoof," or the one case in which it appeared absolutely impossible to question its authenticity.

One day O'Donnell, a professional writer in London, ran into his old friend P. T. Selbit, a professional magician. Selbit reported that he intended to stage a séance and win the 500 pound award offered by the editor of *The Sunday Express* to any medium who could produce a spirit under strict test conditions imposed by its own appointed committee. Selbit chose the date of 21 March 1919 and the place—his own flat in Bloomsbury—for the performance.

The elite committee appointed by the editors included Sir Arthur Conan Doyle, Lady Glenconner, Sir Henry Lunn, Dr. Wynn Westcott (the well-known coroner and occult expert), Dr. Edwin Smith, authority on forensic medicine, Superintendent Thomas of Scotland Yard, Stuart Cumberland (an authority on thought transference), David Gow (editor of a spiritualist journal), Ralph Shirley (editor of the *Occult Review*), and Sydney A. Moseley, a well-known author.

The flat was a long, wide, third-floor room with four windows looking out on Shaftesbury Avenue. One end of the room was heavily draped with black curtains. Before the medium was introduced, the committee members made an exhaustive search of the room, lifting up the carpets to see that there were no trapdoors or any other form of trick apparatus. They examined the walls and windows, looked for electrical wires, and made sure the lighting arrangements were not rigged in any way. Selbit then produced a small black cigar-box to which a lock was attached. He handed this to the committee members to examine carefully. Next, he produced a small silk bag which they also inspected. The committee was then invited to place any articles they wished—connected either with the living or the dead—into the bag which was then placed in the box. Selbit reminded the committee to observe closely that the locked black box was never out of their sight.

Next, he brought in the medium—a slender young woman in a white evening dress, a stark contrast to the black hair and dark eyes gazing out at the group over a veil. She was shown to a seat at the curtained end of the room where Selbit placed the box on her knees. The lights were dimmed, and at the committee's request Selbit took a seat at the opposite end of the room as far away from the medium as possible.

After a few minutes, a cough and a sigh, the medium began to speak. Slowly, and after a few pauses in which she seemed to be groping for the right words, the woman mentioned first a surname, then the name of a member of the staff of the newspaper who had been sent along with a sealed letter which was the special test devised by the editor of the paper. The medium said, "I see machinery—cotton mills—mills in the north—Yorkshire. They are at Halifax—now I see words—German words—but not real German—I see the word *Ober-intellect.* . . ." It's important to note the amount of specific detail in the medium's revelations about a letter which she has never seen—a letter enclosed first in a thick blue cover, which was then placed in an envelope sealed with wax, and then stamped with a private device. Perhaps her most remarkable performance (that's what it was) was her deciphering of the cryptic message in the letter which read "Liebe Ober-intellect, Ich habe until January 10 ein extension gewangled!" This was a faithful and accurate rendering of the exact words in the letter and a most convincing proof of mediumistic phenomena.

Once the committee's confidence was gained, the Masked Medium—as she was known—went on from one success to another. She described next a medal which had belonged to the dead son of Sir Arthur Conan Doyle. Cumberland agreed with her description of the broken stud he had put into the bag. Dr. Westcott had deposited a medallion of the occult society he presided over. It had his initials W. W. W. interlaced with the society's letters Q. S. N. The medium described it with uncanny accuracy and detail. She did have difficulty with one item, but her failure to give a complete description was more convincing than if she had been completely successful. "I see a swan. . . ." she said hesitantly, "I see something black. . . . eyes a swan. . . . it is something to do with correspondence. I'm sorry I cannot tell you any more."

What she described was, in fact, a *black swan fountain pen.* Its owner was, of course, absolutely convinced of her psychic powers. She, of course, had none whatsoever. But just how was it done?

Well, just before Selbit introduced the medium, he called attention to the fact that *the box never left their sight.* He then opened the door and the medium—wearing a mask—entered the room. Every eye was naturally focused on her. In that precise moment Selbit switched the box, which he held, to an assistant behind the door, receiving in its place a duplicate box which the medium subsequently held in her lap. It was done so quickly and with such dexterity that no one noticed the exchange.

The real box was taken to another room where it was unlocked with a duplicate key, and where a radio transmitter had been set up. The medium's mask concealed two tiny ear pieces which served as radio receivers. While the medium was sitting before the committee, the assistants were counting and observing the articles in the box and unsealing the test letter by means of a hot knife they used to melt the wax, and copying the contents word for word. Then they fed the information to the medium, literally telling her what to say. While she was reeling off the information about the articles in the box, the assistants were resealing the letter and returning the articles to the box.

When the medium said she felt tired and would like to rest for a few minutes, Selbit suggested Lady Glenconner should retire with the medium and carry out a search of the medium's person in accordance with terms of the test. Just across the passage was a small room. Here a maid held the door open and the medium, with a polite "After your ladyship," ushered Lady Glenconner into the room. The maid used this moment to change the box carried by the medium for the original box containing the objects she had just described. Immediately the medium handed the box to Lady Glenconner, asking her to hold on to it so she could assure the committee it hadn't been changed. Then, throwing aside her mask and thus also discarding the radio receivers, she submitted to the search.

The séance, however, was not over yet. There had to be the materialization test. Once more the medium—minus the radio receivers—took her seat. The committee, to encourage favorable conditions, sang a few hymns. Then in the shadowy darkness there appeared to come from the side of the medium a sort of vaporous figure in human form. It grew larger, took on a human shape, and then suddenly disappeared.

This phenomenon was also cleverly produced by Selbit. First, Selbit lured an acrobat who, when the room was sufficiently dark, slipped out a window in the flat next door and crept along a narrow ledge to one of the windows at the curtained end of the séance room where the medium was sitting. Clad from head to foot in black tights and under the cover of the hymn singing, he raised the window, slipped in behind the black curtains, and made his way to the medium's side. Once there, from his pocket he pulled some phosphorescent muslin which he gradually formed into a human-like shape. After forming the ghost, he returned the muslin to his pocket and made his way back the way he came.

This séance was so convincing that Sydney Moseler, the author, wrote a book about it, and Lady Glenconner later wrote, "The medium possesses remarkable powers, and deserves, and has, our gratitude for placing them before our circle of investigators in so generous a manner." Although Conan Doyle was skeptical of the ghostly apparition, he firmly believed in the clairvoyant manifestations.

Selbit, interestingly enough, refused to accept the five hundred pounds, realizing that if he did so, it would constitute obtaining money under false pretenses. He did, however, show how easy it was for a skillful illusionist to fool even the wisest of men. (O'Donnell 1955)

Channeling, Channelers, and Entities

Ninety-five percent are not conscious frauds. Some are split personalities. Everyone has the potential. People have enough information to act out hundreds of personalities with details. Creative artists and writers have learned to tap this. Most of us haven't. It comes out under severe conditions when hypnotized, when sick or deprived, or in some mystical ritual.
   —Quoted in Lynn Smith, "The New, Chic Metaphysical Fad of Channeling," *Los Angeles Times,* 5 December 1986

Accompanying the so-called "New Age" movement in America has been the phenomenon of "channeling." Perhaps the best definition of this behavior is the one given by Jon Klimo in his book *Channeling: Investigations on Receiving Information from Paranormal Sources* (1987). According to Klimo:

Channeling is the communication of information to or through a physically embodied human being from a source that is said to exist on some other level or dimension of reality than the physical as we know it, and that is not from the normal mind (or self) of the channel.

(p. 2)

Klimo is careful to rule out communication from one's own normal mind as a source, as well as communication from other physically embodied minds. In other words, the information has to come from beings who inhabit a higher dimension of reality than our own. Over the years these mysterious contacts have been known by a number of names including "discarnate entities," "spirits," "spirit guides," "soul partners," etc. Around the beginning of the twentieth century, during the age of Spiritualism, individuals who gained contact with such beings were referred to as "mediums." Today they are called "channels," and they operate in the same manner as their earlier counterparts, just as they are said to serve as a conduit for information and teachings from the spiritual dimension or other higher planes of being and reality.

Although much, if not most, of the material channeled is of a religious or spiritual nature and seems to be emanating from transcendent sources, little if any of it is of an orthodox religious nature. Little wonder that most members of the clergy find the channeling phenomenon disturbing, and most scientists or skeptics find it ridiculous or outright fraudulent. The psychologist Ray Hyman does not see the channels as conscious frauds, but rather as split personalities or fantasy-prone types (Hyman 1986). He notes that everyone has the potential to be a channel, since we all have enough psychic information that we can act out hundreds of personalities quite convincingly.

While many, like Hyman, see the phenomenon as harmless, others believe it is potentially dangerous. Louis J. West, director of UCLA's Neuropsychiatric Institute, sees it as "a New Age confidence game that can aggravate psychiatric illness . . . and a force drawing [the psychiatric patient] further away from his already poorly grasped relationship with reality."

Other critics have called attention to the shallowness and vapidity of the messages that supposedly emanate from the channeled entities, as well as the lack of personal enlightenment and achievement among the channelers and their followers.

Klimo (1987) notes that:

> . . . a disturbing lack of agreement can often be found among the channels and their material, giving rise to mutually contradictory claims. Intellectual limitations, grammatical incompetence, and historical and scientific inaccuracies also appear in the expressions of the channels and their purported sources. All of this makes it much more difficult—if not impossible—for the logical mind to accept channeling outright, or to believe that authentic channeling is actually taking place on all the fronts where it is reported. . . . Trickery and lies have clearly been exposed in many who claimed the channel's skills.
>
> (p. 14)

Most of the material that is channeled from worlds beyond or the higher planes by such master channelers as J. Z. Knight and her Ramtha, Kevin Ryerson and his John, and Jach Pursel and his Lazaris, harp on the same basic themes:

> Everything is one, the universe is a unity. The universe is basically spiritual and each of us is in tune with it. We are all spiritual and immortal beings within. We are all like gods or we are God, part of him, yet unconscious of this identity. We must all work to overcome our debilitating negative self-image and we must love one another because love is the most powerful

force in the universe. We must contact and align ourselves with our higher self.

(Klimo 1987, p. 70)

This is essentially the same message of Helen C. Schucman's *A Course In Miracles* (1976), a three-volume set that has now sold hundreds of thousands of copies. Readers are impressed with its sincerity and simplicity of language, and most readers feel that the words they read are meant for them personally, and that the message is the truest words they have ever heard. This message is that our vision of ourselves is false, and that our ordinary, day-to-day ego is not our true self. Each of us is part of a larger spiritual reality within which our true identity resides, and within which the ego is only an artificial and transient presence. Heaven is the awareness of the perfect oneness of which you are a part. The course also provides a series of exercises, one for each day of the year, to help the student get over all of the past negative programming. Even though Schucman professed to be an atheist, the material in the course quite clearly seems to have come from the Holy Spirit, and most readers are convinced that the true author of the words is Christ himself. In her later years Helen Schucman apparently shared this belief.

Anyone experienced with hypnosis and self-hypnosis could argue very convincingly that all of these so-called trance channels are not one whit different from their medium precursors, and that, without exception, they are playing a role and behaving exactly in the manner that they think channels in a trance should behave. Some skeptics, willing to give these gamesters the benefit of the doubt, argue that some of them are sincere and not consciously aware that they are being deceptive. In a few rare cases this may well be true since many cryptomnesiacs do, most sincerely, believe that the voices they hear from within, are not from their own subconscious, but from "the great beyond," or "out of the blue."

Relaxation and suggestion can easily trigger the release of hundreds of buried memories that are connected in complex associative chains, and that once revived appear to come from "out of the blue" since the original stimulus and storage has long since been forgotten. Once these subconscious or unconscious sources have been tapped, and the creative wellsprings have released the flood of fantasy material that is organized and made semi-logical by the conscious cognitive processes, even the individual undergoing the experience is astounded. To onlookers and bystanders, the channel does appear to speak with the tongues of angels and to bring messages from the gods.

Anyone who has read the works of some of the New Age channels, or who has attended any of their costly channeling sessions would agree with James Randi's assessment of channeling as "the latest supernatural fad" and of channels as a group of:

> wild-eyed persons who ranted about entities who said they were "speaking through channels into this world." . . . I could extract not one bit of sense from them about evidence for the reality of these "entities" other than one lady's enthusiastic observation that "if it happens in my head, then it's *real!*" That was a statement I could hardly accept.
>
> (Randi 1986, p. 13)

We should be very suspicious of many things that happen inside our heads, particularly of those entities or godlings of the depth of the psyche, whether we call them Seth, or Ramtha, or Lazaris, or John, or even Christ. It is much too easy to shift the responsibility for our own lives and our own decisions onto one or more of such discarnate entities, abdicating responsibility for improving the material world we live in. One lesson all channels need to learn and remember is: Gods help those who help themselves! On second thought, some of the channels seem to have learned this very well. J. Z. Knight, for example, has become a millionairess from channeling her Ramtha. Many others have reaped—and are currently reaping—similar profits. Seems that P. T. Barnum was right.

The subtitle of Klimo's comprehensive study of *Channeling* is: *Investigations on Receiving Information from Paranormal Sources,* and it should come as no surprise that Klimo's sympathies lie with believers in the paranormal and supernatural, although he does make a valiant attempt to tie these beliefs into the fabric of modern physics. In the final summary chapters of his treatise Klimo states:

> Much of the channeling literature is predicated upon an extradimensional universe, one that allows messages to be sent from other levels of reality to ours. The recent multidimensional unification theories of physics seem to lend at least some credence to such a possibility. . . . While physics has ample empirical evidence to support most of its theories about the physical universe, it has little or none with regard to such highly speculative areas as: (1) whether mind or spirit has anything to do with the physical or could be contained within any kind of grand unified theory; (2) the existence of information-carrying frequency domains beyond the known electromagnetic spectrum; (3) anything like a mental domain involving thought waves; (4) signal propagation operating beyond the speed of light; (5) the existence of nonphysical dimensions beyond the three of space and the one of time; (6) whether there could be any such thing as disembodied intelligence living in and communicating from such dimensions, either completely nonphysical life forms or life forms whose bodies are of a higher physical or subtle-energy sort compared to ours.

All six of these areas are largely speculative at this point. First, mainstream physics does give us *some* grounds, at least, from which to make these speculations. Second, there appears to be a strong consensus within the channeled literature, especially in the past thirty-five years, for an explanation of channeling very much along the physics lines suggested. . . .

(pp. 292–293)

Klimo sums up his position in what he calls a concluding metaphor. The metaphor is presented in two stages. In the first stage Klimo sees "each of us is an individuation out of the one universal physical energy ground of Being (physicalizing the mental), or out of the one Universal Mind or spirit (mentalizing the physical) depending on your perspective." According to the second phase or stage of the metaphor,

Consider, now, that *we are* all *sub-* or alter personalities within one Universal Mind, or Godhead. . . . Continuing this metaphor, we subpersonalities of the one Universal Mind maintain our dissociated states, relatively unconscious of our deeper identity, and in a kind of involuntary or autonomic state with regard to the possibilities of access and interplay with the parent ground. Channeling, then, as well as normal interpersonal communication is the activity of different kinds of subpersonalities communicating with one another. . . . Within our metaphor, then, what many of us tend to call the Supreme Being or God is the omniscient apex of the Universal Brain/Mind. Only *it* can fully understand and coordinate all of its own brain-children, its own subpersonalities. As these subpersonalities, we are shards of its own mind living out our existences—and living out *its* existence—with varying degrees of dissociation and forgetfulness with regard to our true identity and possible integration and expansion.

(pp. 292–295)

This transcendental interpretation of the channeling phenomena places it beyond the reach of either science or psychology. It is, in Klimo's view, something divine, or at least related to the divine and only to be fully understood in the religious dimension.

Earlier in the book Klimo does, however, review the psychological explanations for the channeling phenomena but finds them wanting, and concludes the section with a discussion of the existence of a "psi receptor" and the existence of "disembodied intelligences."

As for psychological explanations, they are of two types: closed models and open models. Closed models can account for the phenomena of channeling within the framework of unconscious mental forces—perception memories and representation dreams not readily available to conscious awareness which give rise to our dreams, imagination, visions, and other creative mental acts—cryptomnesia, for example. Nothing outside the conscious and unconscious aspects of the human mind is needed to account for channeling. On the other hand, open models assume that channeling is the result of external forces impinging upon or acting through the mind of the channeler. The open models are all, of course, paranormal explanations dependent upon extrasensory perception, i.e., telepathy, spiritual communication, clairvoyance, psychokinesis, etc.

Among the closed system explanations, Klimo presents the "conditioning and learning" model, but gives it only cursory treatment. This model views channeling behavior as the result of learning, i.e., learned behavior resting upon networks of unconscious associations in the mind from environmental stimuli and various internal representations. Since we are largely unaware of the basis of much of our own behavior (unconscious conditioning), when an individual hears a voice that seems to come neither from himself nor from the known environment, or the individual experiences someone other than himself using his hand to write or his vocal cords to speak—it is easy to believe such experiences are due to external sources rather than as functions of certain patterns of association formed unconsciously by memories, mental representations, and the confusing play of creativity. When ideational planning and motor execution programs are also involved, along with many other subtle programs for making meaning, there is no need to raise mythical notions about nonphysical or spiritual beings to account for the channeling phenomena. Most of the material dredged up and presented by the channelers is either: (1) creative imaginings; (2) cryptomnesiac—memories of which they were unaware; or (3) fraudulent.

The fact that this material is produced by the channelers when they are—or appear to be—in some sort of a trance-like, hypnotic, or altered consciousness-state in no way substantiates or authenticates the validity of the verbal outpourings.

It is also curious that in a rather lengthy survey of opinions about what various theoretical and clinical psychologists think about the channeling phenomena there is no mention or reference at all to cryptomnesia, nor to the fact that most or all of this verbal diarrhea was the result of material read and encountered earlier, filed away and forgotten until the time and circumstance made its recall in the channeling setting appropriate.

There can also be little doubt that for many—if not most or even all—of the so-called channels, their entire performance is a deliberate hoax, i.e., an admittedly very clever bit of dramatizing similar to that of a skilled preacher or evangelist, concocted to hoodwink and convince the spiritually deprived and existentially needy that there is, indeed, life beyond the grave, and wise and ancient spiritual entities concerned enough about the pain and suffering of the living in the here and now to offer wisdom and comfort through the body and mind of the charismatic mediumistic "channeler" at $300 to $400 dollars a throw.

What is of particular interest is the fact that in the case of channeling, even some of the staunchest supporters of the supernatural and the occult have expressed outrage and disgust with the shallowness and superficiality of many channelers in general, and several of the most famous names in the channeling business in particular. Hans Holzer, authority on ghosts, psychics, and most other supernatural topics, as well as the author of hundreds of popular books and articles on occult topics, in the June 1990 issue of *Fate* magazine sticks quite a number of pins into the channeler's balloons (pp. 74–86). Comparing the modern channelers with the turn-of-the-century trance mediums, Holzer points out that the channelers look like trance mediums when they close their eyes or roll them dramatically before going into their so-called "trance state." Shortly thereafter they will speak in a voice claiming to be someone other than the channeler. The difference between the channeler and the medium is not in technique, but in what comes out of the channeler's or medium's mouth. In Holzer's words:

> With a trance medium, any good researcher will demand identification of the alleged communicator and usually gets it quickly, if only in bolting sentences. The researcher will then proceed to have a dialogue with the spirit entity—using the trance mediums as a kind of telephone—and elicit as much detailed and personal information as he is able to, in order to verify it later on. *This is not so with the channelers. Attempts at questioning these "entities" for personal background or real names leads to platitudes about the high level of their mission or fantasy names and circumstances that cannot be verified. When it sounds as if they might be capable of scientific verification and this is attempted, it invariably turns out that it cannot be traced in any known records.* (Italics mine)

It is *most* curious indeed that most of the entities are so ancient, so little known, or so obscure that they are buried forever in timeless mud and sand, safely beyond any possibility of historical resuscitation and denial. J. Z. Knight's "Ramtha" allegedly lived 35,000 years ago. That's a "purty fur piece back." Jach Pursel's Lazaris claims that he is not now and never has been physical or human. He is rather a group being living in another dimension. Now you can hardly get any more secure or safer from being checked up on than this. "John," one of Kevin Ryerson's chief entities, is supposedly a member of the Essene Hebrew sect who was last incarnate at the time of Christ. Again, that's pretty safe from prying investigator types. Helen Schuchman's inner voice that dictated the 1,200 pages of *A Course in Miracles* is the voice of Christ, she claims. Jessica

Lansing's "Michael" is made up of over a thousand "old soul" fragments, none of whom are identified or identifiable. Of course, channelers who talk to the "Space Brothers" and other extraterrestrials and "the Archangel Raphael" (Ken Carey) make it particularly difficult to do anything in the way of follow-up. One of the newest star channelers, Penny Torres, channels "Mafu," last seen on earth as a first-century Greek. Alan Vaughan has come up with "Li-Sung," last incarnated as a small-town philosopher in eighth-century northern China.

Holzer sees two causes for the fake channeler. "First, an eager audience of followers supplies energy that feeds the channeler's ego (and often money as well). Second, an otherwise ordinary personality uses deeper levels of the consciousness to act out fantasies satisfying a craving within that personality." Holzer points out that channeling has indeed become a big business. It includes not only the channels who conduct seminars where the faithful gather, and at a stiff price (as much as $400 to $500 per session) are allowed to partake of the "questionable pearls of wisdom" dropping from the lips of their channeler. Audio and videotapes, books, magazines, follow-up books, more seminars, and question and answer sessions where people can get personal help from the entity add to the channeler's take. J. Z. Knight, one of the most famous and financially successful of channelers, has become a multimillionairess as the result of being given national attention by Shirley MacLaine in her 1985 book, *Dancing in the Light,* and by her channeling "Ramtha" for thousands of adherents at $400 a piece. Though Knight characterizes "Ramtha" as a native of India who "lived 35,000 years ago," anyone familiar with Indo-Germanic language roots will know that the name Ramtha (also known as Ramatha) could not have existed 35,000 years ago, as the people whose language may have used that name were still unborn in what some 15,000 to 20,000 years later became known as the Pamir plateau, north of India. Moreover, Holzer points out much of Knight's style used in her portrayal of "Ramtha" is borrowed from Edgar Cayce—the inspiration for hundreds of would-be mediums. One of Knight's disillusioned followers stated a few years ago that Knight would often impersonate "Ramtha" without going into a trance. "We thought she did a better job of doing Ramatha than Ramatha," she said. "In fact we couldn't tell the difference." (Pamela McNeeley quoted by George Hackett and Pamela Abramson in *Newsweek,* 15 December, 1986)

As for the wonderful material itself—the pearls of wisdom—that is channeled: does it offer brilliant, mind-boggling answers to all of life's questions and troubles? Does it provide enlightenment and wisdom of the ages? No, it does not. Most of the material is inane, simple-minded, and asinine. In Holzer's words, "Any fairly intelligent person, with a smattering of psychology and religious orientation, could come up with similar advice. You don't have to be 35,000 years old to do it." One must hear it, read it, or experience it to truly appreciate how vapid and innocent of intellectual content and substance the drivel really is. A typical excerpt from a two-hour session of a local channel, Lea Schultz, who channels a thirteenth-century Scotsman named Samuel, is given verbatim on the following page.

QUESTION: How does one have the mental and spiritual union?

SAMUEL: May I ask how does one not? I will say this: Your being is often run by your physical self. Do you recognize this? Your physical needs of hunger, for instance, determine how your day works. When you are not eating properly, your chemistry goes awry, and you tend to get headaches. You find yourself susceptible, sometimes, to illness of one sort or another. That is often because you are once again prey to the physical element. You also have certain hormonal responses that bring about the desire for sexual union. Often you have known that to be very powerful an experience! Very easy to say that the purpose of sexuality, sexual meeting, is simply to increase population. That is not so. The purpose of sex, of physical union, is to increase the whole being. Everything has a double side. Lessons in physicality, on its lower levels, often show up when not taking care of the body—illness, being the slave to appetite of whatever variety. But on a spiritual level—spiritualized, working in your highest way possible to bring forth that which is good, your highest levels—your physical level is a doorway to greater, stronger spiritual union. Unfortunately for many, this doorway is totally misunderstood and misused. Instead of it becoming an offshoot of spiritual growth, spiritual growth never comes about, because the lower physical self takes over. And the being never gets beyond physical growth and initiation into the mental and the spiritual because they become so enamored with what the physical is able to offer. What a tease the physical be, eh? As you grow, physical appetites start showing themselves, and to concentrate on them becomes a detour. Granted, my darlings, it's not to say that you're not going to reach the end of your path. Simply that in detouring, you've chosen a slower route. I do not say that it is not correct to have physical desire, but that the desire does not control you, but you control it.

There is an actual chemical change that happens within the chemical body, your etheric self, upon the act of sexual union. This connection brings about a stronger being. It is addictive. And as the runner chooses to go for the "runner's high," even to the detriment and breakdown of the body, so it is that that beautifully wrought spiritual union through sexual intercourse becomes addictive, and it is desired to have the "thing" instead of the whole picture, and therefore sight is lost.

How to overcome? You overcome. There is reason that many great teachings seem to be oriented around celibacy. When you purposefully turn your mind away from a thing, that new awareness brings about a change. The energy that is brought up by your hormones can be redirected, and I encourage you to do it, and usually the awareness of the purposefully redirected thought processes, the awareness alone will affect your mental level, and the results of that effect work in your spiritual. To immediately go beyond the physical, without the experience of conflict, does not bring great growth. Harmony through conflict, my dears. Your experience on this Earth is meant to be a constant balancing and learning to control, to act and react. So do not fret that you have this beautiful sexual nature, but wait to use it until you have a stronger understanding of what your total being is about. How much there is to learn. Do you know everything there is to know? Are you satisfied with how much you've grown in your mental states? Are you controlled emotionally? Well, if not, perhaps you need to work on these things, on harmonizing these things, rather than the physical levels. Start at the top instead of at the bottom; start with the spiritual inclinations instead of the physical ones. Oh, but doesn't that make for many a lonely winter? What is it that you said at the meeting last night, Stuart dear? For the Board you said, "You know, there comes a times that it's not quantity, it's quality." And that be true in all things. If you allow yourself to wait, my dears, to come to a place where you love and understand yourself, that love will naturally spread out to others, and relationships grow naturally on their own from there—without manipulation, fretting and thinking of self, but a positive outgrowth. Then you will have that quality, and you will likely be with one who works very well with you, and with whom you can spend many years of growth, and therefore not have problems with the breakdown in the moral fiber of these states. Start from the spiritual aspect. Your power is in your spirit. Your conflict is in your mind. And more often than not your downfall is in your body. So start from the top.

Did that sufficiently answer your question, and still get in what I've been just delighted to talk about?!

(Schultz 1988, pp. 13 and 20)

Schultz delivers her "pearls" in a heavy Scottish brogue most of the time as she channels Samuel. We say most of the time because Schultz frequently forgets in the excitement of the delivery of her message, and lapses back into her own natural voice on many occasions. This "slip of the channel" is by no means unique. Dr. Sarah Thomason, a linguistics professor at the University of Pittsburgh, has studied a number of channelers in order to see if their accents were true to life—since they claimed to have led real lives in the past. What she found instead was pseudodialects, the kind of behavior characteristic of someone who is faking his or her speech. Moreover, her analyses showed that the "entities" speaking through the channelers also used pronunciations that do not occur and have never existed in their native languages. She also observed other channelers losing their dialect during the channeling, pronouncing the same word in different ways, and mispronouncing words they should have been intimately familiar with. In the case of Mrs. Schultz and Samuel, Dr. Thomason's conclusions were provided in a personal letter to the author after Dr. Thomason and a colleague listened to an hour-long tape recording.

You asked for a judgment about the authenticity of Samuel's speech—that is, about the suggestion that Samuel's speech is that of a 17th-century or a 13th-century Scotsman. Our answer is that Samuel's speech patterns are definitely not those of a Scotsman of any century. In fact, since he displays a hodgepodge of linguistic features from several different American and British Isles dialects, Samuel is not a believable speaker of English, period. And his accent cannot be attributed to Scots Gaelic (the other likely native language for a Scotsman), because his speech displays no traits of the sorts that one would expect Scots Gaelic to leave in a speaker's English.

First, it should be noted that if Samuel were a 13th-century Scotsman we would not be able to understand his speech at all. The sound systems of all dialects of English have changed so much since the 13th century that the Middle English of that period would be unintelligible to modern ears— just as Chaucer's 14th-century Middle English is unintelligible to modern readers.

In any case, Samuel's speech contains sounds that have never existed in Scots English, and it lacks sounds that have always been present in Scots English. In addition, his vocabulary contains an enormous number of words that were borrowed into English only after the 13th century—mostly from French or Latin, such as *label, actually, assure, connect, communicate, recognize, relax, convince,* and *specific,* but also from other languages, notably *potato* (a 16th-century borrowing from Spanish) and *yin* and *yang* (20th-century borrowings from Chinese). Of course, he could have learned such words while hovering in the ether waiting for Lea Schultz to come along and act as his channel; similarly, he could have replaced such characteristic Scots words as *ken* with American English *know.* But no such explanation will account for his un-Scots phonetics.

If, as I gather from your letter, Lea Schultz's own dialect is an ordinary American English variety, then the only rational way to account for Samuel's many non-American dialect features, given that they do not represent Scots or any other specific English dialect, is to assume that Lea Schultz has invented his odd accent by grafting onto her own speech bits and pieces of Irish English, Cockney, and other British Isles dialects. (It is interesting to note, in light of your comment that Ms. Schultz lived in Scotland for a year, that the only discernible Scots English feature in Samuel's English is the highly salient *r* sound. A person with even a moderately acute ear would surely have managed to pick up a few more features of Scots in a whole year.)

In sum, Samuel's speech patterns do not resemble any archaic dialect of English, Scots or otherwise. All of his pronunciations are modern. However, his accent does not represent any one dialect of modern English, and particularly not Scots English. We could add many more examples in which Samuel's pronunciations do not match those of a real Scotsman, present or past. So the non-American features in Samuel's speech can't be attributed to a Scottish origin, but—unless they are identical to Lea Schultz's natural dialect—they also can't be attributed to the influence of the channeler's own speech. We conclude, therefore, that the accent is faked by someone who doesn't know enough about Scots English to do it well.

Since Samuel was supposedly speaking from the Isle of Arran, Daniel J. Phelps, another local skeptic, wrote to the Isle of Arran Museum Association and sent along a tape recording of one of Mrs. Schultz's Samuel channeling sessions. A key paragraph from the Association's reply is given below.

> To answer your various points; with regard to the tape, we did not consider the accent Scottish at all. In fact it seemed to keep changing from almost Irish, to Northern English, to even at times South African (Africaans). Also the English used in the tape was modern with many modern words which would certainly not have been used by an English speaker in the 13th Century.
>
> In the 13th Century, the language spoken in Arran would have been Gaelic with a considerable amount of Norse. The Norse withdrew from Arran, Kintyre and South West Scotland after being defeated at the Battle of Largs in 1263.

Dr. Thomason's analysis of the speech of a number of the channeled entities including Pat Rodagast's "Emmanuel," Azana Ramanda's "St. Germain," Ken Carey's "Jesus Christ," Julie Winter's "Mika," J. Z. Knight's "Ramatha," Penny Torres's "Mafu," and Marjorie Turcott's "Matthew" all revealed that the entities could not possibly be who they claimed to be since their language gives them away. In Dr. Thomason's words:

> When channeled entities speak in accents that are not native to their channelers, the authenticity of the manifestations can be checked by linguistic analysis. Analysis of the speech of several such entities shows that the accents are fake. . . . if the funny accents help attract customers for the channelers' lucrative workshops, the channelers needn't be too concerned about the possibility that professional linguists will confront them somewhere. In any case, most channelers, like most other people, are naive about language, and probably they don't realize how much information their entities provide when they speak in odd accents.

Another failing of the channelers mentioned by Holzer is the failure of the entity to provide us with details about his or her time and place. In Holzer's words:

If we can't find his name listed in a directory, couldn't he enlighten us with definite, specific, and truly detailed knowledge of his time and place? Then we would have a certain feeling of authenticity that is the next best thing to actual proof. Assuming, for the moment, that some very illustrious historical figures chose to manifest through a channeler, wouldn't it be likely that their personality, character, and style would somehow come through even if it is in English?

(Holzer 1990, p. 78)

Instead, Holzer says, we get the example of the psychic who claimed to be the channel for St. Thomas Aquinas. Instead of theology, deep thoughts, or history we get

. . . pretty much the same platitudes you get from most UFO contactees about the dear old space brothers who want to save the world from itself. . . . This St. Thomas was strictly unreal. "But I channel his essence," she intoned. Essence? Impersonating a Saint? Anyone with a gift of turning a clever phrase can claim to be channeling some exotic long-ago personality or "Master."

Nothing in scientific research is an absolute, and not every "ascended master" is a figment of the imagination, but some kind of evidence should be required before accepting the communication as genuine and as something external to the channeler or medium. And later, Holzer also insists that the "alleged communicator from the Great Beyond should identify himself in some manner subject to verification, if not by individual name then at least by authentic knowledge of the period and place claimed by the communicators." Obviously they do not. Holzer rightly insists that those people participating in group sessions, those plunking down their money to do this, have the right to question the communicating entity directly, and the nature of the material coming through "the channel" itself should be examined critically. In addition, those channelers claiming only some vague long-dead Master as their source should be questioned when they are themselves and not channeling, and the differences, if any, in style, knowledge, background, and delivery of phrases between the channeler and the entity should be examined. If the claimed source is someone very well known, it's even easier. "Only a very naive and little educated person," Holzer says, "should be taken in by such pretenses."

If Holzer, an avowed occultist, is particularly harsh with the channelers, what, pray tell, do some of the skeptics have to say? One of the most articulate of this group is the Australian, Harry Edwards. In a brilliant and amusing essay titled "Calling All Spirits," Edwards notes that the inestimable quantity and quality of knowledge that could be attained from past Earth dwellers, never-incarnated spirits, and those purporting to come to us from the future, "is unfortunately not forthcoming because the spirits exhibit a singular reticence when it comes to parting with anything more edifying than convoluted pop philosophy, apocalyptic forecasts, homilies, and more often than not, sheer unadulterated nonsense." Edwards also takes all of the channels to task, pointing out that if the entities possessed any reality at all, the fortunes amassed by J. Z. Knight and Jack Pursel would be small potatoes indeed. As Edwards says:

> Both their fortunes would seem like petty cash, however, when one considers the potential value of invisibility to the various Defense departments, the secret of anti-gravity to NASA, instant transportation facilitating inter galactic exploration, and the overcoming of language barriers just to mention a few, all of which are seemingly second nature once we are freed from our earthly constraints.
>
> (Edwards 1989)

Edwards notes that in this phenomenal resurgence of spiritualism, where reliance is now placed on the charisma of the medium, the entities' voices, and the audiences' credulity, is that unlike the spiritualists of the past whose "controls" were generally contemporary, many of today's channelers have moved into the space age. For example, the channel Daryl Anka channels "Bashar" from the Essassain civilization—a civilization Anka says is "three hundred light years in the future." Light years are, of course, a measure of distance, not time—a fact which seems to have escaped the wisdom of "Bashar." Pamela Newstreet channels "Soncha" from Sirius and Jannie Sims visits with "Leah" from Venus. What is most irritating to Edwards, however, is the fact that none of these ET visitors deems it necessary to explain how they spanned the enormous distances, or why the beings from advanced technological civilizations that one would associate with such voyages are content merely to "hang around" at the beck and call of a bunch of earthling nonentities.

According to Edwards, the problem with all of this nonsense is that if these so-called spirits and entities are "real" they would, of necessity, have to live in an invisible material world in proximity to our own—so close in fact, if the evidence is to be believed, as to be within the range of a human whisper, or even a thought. This is so implausible that, according to Edwards, "In view of the billions who have passed on since man first evolved, and the incredible pulsating celestial congestion such a concentration of spiritual and material matter would create just above our heads, one would have thought that this would have been an implausible concept even to the most credulous of minds." Moreover, instead of being the wise, all-knowing, spiritually enlightened, and superior intellectual beings worthy of emulation and adoration, their activities are generally "confined to simple party tricks and comments incompatible with that which one would expect of the all-seeing, all-knowing." The fact that they are presented as something very like commercial freaks at a side show is also demeaning. What is most puzzling perhaps is the fact that the entities refuse to answer questions about their origin, pompously answer intelligent and pertinent questions with replies that lack "even a modicum of intellect, expertise or common-sense," and, if pressed, they will "explain away, rationalize, or invent any excuse no matter how inane or infantile" to stymie any attempt at rational communication. And, Edwards asks, if they are truly "spirits of the dead," why should they be so evasive? Why would dead spirits bother to get in touch with the living when they have nothing to say? If It were possible to come back from the dead, wouldn't the spirits return to those who love, cherish, and need them rather than to strangers who exploit them? Finally, considering the millions of people who die prematurely and accidentally, those who didn't want to die—why the reticence on their part to not come back either singly or en masse? Edwards's biting and telling conclusion is that:

> The evidence to date, for the existence of spirits from our own and other worlds, can be seen by the critical analyst as being a travesty of serious research, and in the absence of somewhat more substantive and tangible proof, to suggest that communication with the dead is possible is simply wishful thinking by the deluded, whose vulnerability makes them delectable pickings for the carrion crow.
>
> (Edwards 1989, p. 59)

If there are sincere and honest channelers—cryptomnesiacs, i.e., people so deluded that they are convinced they do, indeed, hear internal voices, voices that claim to be those of dead or alien entities that persistently and consistently supply them with messages that are of socially redeeming moral, religious, or therapeutic value—and such value can be independently established by rational and intelligent living human beings, then such channeling might be worthy of society's time and attention. Until such channelers appear—and so far they have not—we can dismiss the efforts of the rest of them as nothing more than fraudulent hoaxes or the cryptomnesiacal delusions of people in need of correction, counseling, or psychotherapy.

How To Channel. Never one to overlook a good thing, many of the channels are desirous of passing their skills on—for a price of course—in private sessions while some channelers, of a more generous nature, have provided instruction in written form. One of the less offensive of these efforts is Dr. Kathryn Ridall's *Channeling: How to Reach Out to Your Spirit Guides* (1988). Ridall, a practicing counselor, is a New Age devotee and an admirer of Edgar Cayce and Jane Roberts as well as a practicing psychic. In her introduction Ridall confesses that her channeling of the entity Diya—an otherworldly entity she picked up from a friend, Richard Ryal—may well be nothing but an aspect of her own consciousness. But, she states:

> I ultimately concluded that it didn't matter where the information came from as long as the experience was valuable for me. I realized that it didn't matter if it was just my imagination, for even that explanation would mean that my mind was a far richer and far more complex instrument than I had previously imagined.
>
> (p. 7)

A number of channels are profiled including Sanaya Roman who channels Orin—a discarnate entity she found with a Ouija board after reading Jane Roberts's books, and Joanna Bougiovanni, a "radio receiver"-channel who channels a number of entities including a group of extraterrestrials. Joanna considers channeling to be an art form. "I really enjoy it, because I'm also an actress." As for Diya, he has informed Dr. Ridall that "we are all multidimensional beings who have many simultaneous experiences, some of which we call past lives. We create simultaneous lives with beings who are compatible with us in intention and in basic energy frequency. And we create these realities with the same beings, who all belong to our soul group, again and again. In saying that many channeling relationships involve members of the same soul group, Diya means that communication still continues even though not all members of the soul group have taken physical form in the same time-space reality."

Congratulations if you can understand this! Not only are there a number of different types of channeling relationships, but they also come from the spirit world to us because we make agreements to work with them before we're born, when we're in our pre-incarnational phase. Although what the guides teach differs widely, they do have a number of common messages, several recurring ideas they all seem to share: (1) the universe is evolving toward higher levels of compassion and love; (2) more highly developed beings can help us; (3) the earth is at a critical point in its development; (4) the people on earth need to change their values and lifestyles; (5) the new energies coming from the spirit guides will cause psychological and social unrest; (6) we are all God; (7) we create our own experience on all levels of reality; (8) our beliefs create and shape our physical reality; and (9) though we seem diverse, we are all one.

Even though people desiring to channel have their doubts, all they have to do is learn to relax and meditate and soon the spirit guides will come to them. Ridall recommends a seven step process developed by Dr. Margo Chandley. Step one, *conceptualization,* consists of remembering an experience of nonphysical reality. This could involve hearing voices, seeing apparitions, having an out-of-body experience, or having unusual flows of energy. Phase two involves deep relaxation, meditation, and visualization. In the third step, the channels begin to feel the physical and nonphysical energies within themselves. At the fourth stage, the channel works out a relationship with the entity, and usually gives it a name. At the fifth stage, the channels become verbal and transmit the wisdom and information they receive in verbal form. The sixth stage involves the development of trust between the physical and nonphysical systems, and the seventh and final stage involves a merging of the physical and nonphysical systems into a single integrated entity.

This is all there is to it and this is how it's done! But this is the hard way to do it. The author has a much simpler and quicker technique that guarantees success on your first attempt. Get a Bible, the *Urantia* book, or some other massive tome such as the works of Helen Blavatsky, and read the material carefully, selecting those passages that have something in the way of majestic alliteration, resonance, and spiritual profundity (if you can find any such passages), and tape them onto a microcassette tape recorder. An excellent recorder for this purpose is Radio Shack's Micro-26, Model No. 14-1043. With the microcassette tape you can record ninety minutes on each side of the tape, and the recorder itself is so small— a little thicker than a credit card—you can stick it into any pocket anywhere. With a small ear-button mike and putting the wire inside your shirt, it is easy to hide the wire in your hair and appear to casual observers as innocent of any audio assistance. Next go on stage, turn on the tape recorder, and recite, i.e., repeat at the top of your disguised voice every word of wisdom you recorded earlier. If you throw back your head, gaze at the ceiling, and shout that the words are coming to you from the spirit guide "Nagon," an Egyptian oracle of the first century, you've got it made. If you can find a cooperative child, you can have him or her do this for you and really blow your audience's mind. It must be the spirit—no child would know these words of wisdom! This idea was central to the plot of an excellent mystery novel, *The Four Last Things* by Timothy Hallinan (1989). If such delicious deceit is foreign to your makeup, you can take comfort in the fact that the channeling phenomenon seems to be on the wane. Writing in a recent issue of *Critique* (October–January 1989–1990), Antero Alli notes:

One serious side-effect of disembodied spirituality can be seen in the now-fading Channeling Epidemic, wherein scores of otherwise normal people learned how to throw their power away to the homogenized axioms of disembodied entities. One rather banal reason why some of us are drawn to communicating with the dead is that we don't have any real living friends to talk to. Establishing a link with "guides" may attempt to compensate for the lack of love, good sex and genuine human interaction in our lives. Spooks, like our childhood "imaginary" playmates, might just offer the security, status and strokes missing from a broken home life. Yet, if ghosts do exist, are they any wiser than the living? Is death a Ph.D.?!

(p. 58)

Most likely, many simple and deluded people answer the last question affirmatively because they have made many efforts to get in touch with, and learn from, those who have passed on.

Glossolalia. Another interesting phenomenon related to channeling is what was earlier called "speaking in tongues," but what is now known in psychological circles as *glossolalia,* i.e., a stream of unintelligible sounds or pseudolanguage supposedly spoken in an altered state of consciousness or a state of religious exaltation. The practice has a long history. The religious rites of many primitive tribes include glossolalia. Early Hebrew prophets were given to wild dancing and glossolalia. Glossolalia appeared again among the faithful after the death of Jesus. In Mark 16:17–18 Christ told his disciples,

And these signs shall follow them that believe: In my name shall they cast out devils; they shall speak with new tongues; they shall take up serpents; and if they drink any deadly thing, it shall not hurt them; they shall lay hands on the sick, and they shall recover.

Many fundamentalists believe that on the feast day of Pentecost, the Holy Spirit entered the disciples and "they were all filled with the Holy Ghost, and began to speak with other tongues." This specifically refers to the disciples preaching in languages they were not familiar with. This is known as xenoglossy. Many fundamentalists also refer to the Unknown Tongue, a supernatural language understood only by God and the angels, which is first mentioned in Paul's First Corinthians. Later, Paul cautions that while glossolalia does the speaker good, it is of little help or use to others. Although first-century Christians engaged in the practice regularly, it gradually disappeared to appear only sporadically over the centuries. Glossolalia was revived by the Methodists in the eighteenth century, and after 1900 a number of churches sprang up in the rural south that grew into the denominations now called Pentecostal. There are approximately thirty-five such groups today, the largest of which is the Assemblies of God.

Glossolalia invaded mainline middle-class Catholic and Protestant churches in the 1960s, and gave rise to groups calling themselves neo-Pentecostals to distinguish themselves from the poorer, unlettered "classical" groups. Both neo-Pentecostals and classical Pentecostals are called charismatics. It is estimated there are approximately five million charismatics in the United States today. There is considerable tension between the orthodox Protestants and the Catholics and charismatics. Orthodox believers are appalled at the "speakers," and particularly at TV evangelists such as Jim and Tammy Bakker—members of the Assembly of God who believe that speaking in tongues is essential to all Christians. On the other hand, many would agree with Jerry Falwell, the Baptist fundamentalist who once compared speaking in tongues to "the belly rumblings of someone who had eaten too much pizza." The Vatican is inclined to agree with Falwell and sees glossolalia as an "uncouth manifestation of demon possession."

While charismatics do not regard speaking in tongues as essential for salvation—only conversion is—they do believe that every Christian should seek a second baptism by the Holy Spirit. Accompanying this baptism, they believe, is the ability to glossolate. Readers interested in the religious and historical origins of glossolalia should consult David Christie-Murray's authoritative *Voices From the Gods: Speaking With Tongues* (1978) or William Samarin's earlier work, *Tongues of Men and Angels* (1972). For a shorter, amusing overview of the entire phenomenon, Martin Gardner's 1989 article "Glossolalia" in *Free Inquiry* (Spring 1989) is heartily recommended.

For those who have never heard it spoken, glossolalia is difficult to describe, primarily because the sound will vary according to who is speaking and the circumstances under which the voices are elicited. Some individuals in the throes of religious ecstasy will babble excitedly, emitting screams, yells, moans, and groans that are punctuated at random by streams of meaningless babble. Others of a more staid and disciplined disposition will jabber quietly in a foreign-sounding language that, linguistically, makes no sense whatsoever and, though it may resemble and sound like a known foreign language, is not like any language on earth. However, these false or pseudolanguages must be carefully discriminated from the behavior of many glossolaliacs who can, on certain occasions, start speaking languages they knew years ago but thought they had forgotten. These examples of cryptomnesia are widely reported in the medical literature. A typical case, reported by Christie-Murray, concerned Murray's wife.

Born in Assam, and bilingual in English and Bengali until she moved to England at seven, she forgot the Bengali entirely except for a few odd words and a line or two of a lullaby. When she was in her forties and working as a British Council guide, she was showing two Eastern Pakistanis the sights of London when they started to step in front of an oncoming bus. She shouted "Look out!" in Bengali—a phrase she did not know that she knew or had ever known. Until her guests told her, she thought she had shouted the warning in English.

Christie-Murray also reported the case of an English officer who, while under hypnosis, spoke Welsh, which he had spoken as a child but had long forgotten. This experience was shared by a hospital patient who, following a severe head injury, started speaking Welsh again after a thirty-year absence. When he recovered from the head injury, he again lost all knowledge of Welsh. A German woman who was married to an Englishman was accustomed to speaking English, but as a result of an illness she lost her English completely and could talk to her attendants only through a German interpreter. There are many similar cases in which bilingual patients have lost one language (often their native tongue), and could converse only in the other.

A more complicated case of recovery of past languages was that of a woman in a delirious state from the thirteenth to the sixteenth of March in 1902. On the thirteenth and fourteenth of that month she spoke Hindustani which she had not spoken for sixty-six years. Then on the fourteenth she began to mix English with Hindustani. On the fifteenth she spoke English, French, and German. Knowing her history explains the strange event. Born in India where she was cared for by Indian servants until she was three, she had spoken only Hindustani. At age four she was sent to England where she learned English. Then later, as a student and traveler on the continent, she learned French and German to a high degree of fluency. Her doctor said that her case was remarkable for its perfection, completeness, and good authentication, and noted further:

> It seems as if structural memories were laid down in the nervous system in strata, the memory of each successive experience overlying the memories of previous experiences; and as if, in senile loss of memory, the removal of the upper layers allowed of an over-activity of those that remain.
>
> (Freeborn and Mercier 1902, pp. 279–83)

Not only is this another excellent example of cryptomnesia, but it is a remarkably prescient view of the nature of the memory process as well.

Samuel Coleridge, in his *Biographia Literaria,* tells the story of a young Gottingen woman who, when she was in a fever, spoke Latin, Greek, and Hebrew. Their source was traced to an old Protestant pastor who had taken her in as a child, and whose custom it was to read aloud to her from his favorite books in those languages. (*Everyman Library,* pp. 58–60)

In another case, a young lady suffering from epilepsy had spent six months in France five years before her seizures began. During her stay, she learned only a little of the language. During her seizures, however, she would enter a state of ecstasy, recite poetry in French, and deliver orations about virtue and godliness in correct and fluent French. Her doctor considered her to be an excellent example of a trance-medium and gleefully reported:

> The materialistic influence of bromide of potassium, however, cured her catalepsy and epilepsy, destroyed her knowledge of the French tongue and made her corporeal structure so gross that the spirits refused to make further use of it for their manifestation.
>
> (Hammond 1876, pp. 292–293)

Schizophrenics, on occasions when they are delusionary, will also engage in babblings and mutterings, and will rattle on for minutes at a time speaking what is known as "word salad." Anyone listening carefully, however, can clearly detect words and phrases in plain, discernible English, as well as meaningless words and syllables mixed together in a clearly psychotic jumble.

Cases of multiple personality and believers in reincarnation have also used glossolalia in attempts to validate the reality of their fantasies. In one reported case, a woman reported alternating dual personalities in which "A" was the normal, primary personality with "B" the secondary personality believing she was the reincarnation of a Spanish woman of the previous century. At times this patient spoke automatically in a tongue consisting of fragmented Spanish with a few traces of Italian—totally untranslatable into English. Inquiries determined that while the patient was attending convent school she did, periodically, overhear three Mexican girls talking Spanish to each other. Unconsciously, she assimilated their speech. The death of the patient's father came as a severe emotional blow and precipitated the personality split. This situation was aggravated by her infatuation with a man of half-Spanish blood and full Spanish appearance who was the emotional source that precipitated her secondary personality. While she may have learned some Spanish words from her lover, her sample of Spanish contained references suggesting that she heard the three Mexicans orally repeating lessons in Spanish history. There were also a number of words which sounded like Spanish but were not.

Such cases as these show again how cryptomnesia works. Language known or even subconsciously heard is absorbed and becomes a part of the CNS. If the motivation is sufficient at a later date, this material can emerge automatically.

Christie-Murray states that there is no evidence in existence of any recognizable language spoken by a glossolalic which cannot be accounted for by cryptomnesia or some other such psychological explanation.

Yet for most cases of glossolalia we are apt to encounter outside of a clinic or mental ward, we will seldom encounter any of the 2,800 languages and dialects spoken in the world today, in addition to all of the languages spoken in the past (see Sherrill, J. L., *They Speak With Other Tongues,* 1965, chapter 9). This is particularly true in the case of the charismatics, or televangelists like Oral Roberts, Jim Bakker, Jimmy Swaggart, and Pat Robertson. Their glossolalia has no discernible grammatical structure and semantically, syntactically, and in every other linguistic way defies the logic of any human language spoken anywhere on earth. Their utterings are merely a flowing cadence of made-up nonsense words, often multisyllabic, that when strung together and punctuated with hand gestures, facial expressions, and variations in tone and volume can convince even the most skeptical that one is, indeed, talking in an obscure esoteric language that bears, at times, faint resemblance to American Indian dialect, Russian, Swahili, or something else strange but at moments vaguely familiar.

Studies of charismatics and tongue speakers show they are psychologically no different from anyone else with the single exception of their strong belief in the supernatural, and the religious importance of speaking in tongues, and their decided lack of emotional inhibition. Most such people are great weepers and wailers, and are prone to talk directly with God and see visions. As Martin Gardner reports:

> The autobiographies of [Oral] Roberts, the Bakkers, Swaggart, and Robertson drip with episodes of weeping. Tammy sobs on almost every page of her book, and her husband, someone recently said, cries if the breakfast toast burns. Swaggart constantly works up crocodile tears while he sings, waves the Good Book, begs for money or asks forgiveness for his sins. . . . Oral has described several visions of Jesus and angels and in 1986 revealed that Satan had invaded his bedroom and tried to strangle him. When Robertson bought his first television station his devout mother had a vision of large bank notes floating down from heaven into her son's hands. Tammy's visions are marvelous. In one of them Jesus wore a helmet and brandished a sword.
> (Gardner 1989, p. 48)

William Samarin reports that more than half of the glossolalists he studied said it was easier to speak the unknown tongue than to speak ordinary language. "You don't have to think—just let the words flow. One minister said he could 'go on forever: it's just like drumming.' " (Samarin 1972, p. 70)

He is correct because it is very easy to do, and it in no way requires an altered state of consciousness or some strange, transcendental religious trance. While some glossolalists may go into or simulate a trance-like state, most tongue speakers are wide awake and very much in touch with consensual reality. It is, quite simply, a bit of learned verbal behavior that anyone and everyone can master with only a few minutes of practice. Martin Gardner reported, "I, myself, while researching this article, began to practice tongues speaking and now can babble it fluently. 'Drawk cabda erfi esnes nonton.' " (Gardner 1989, p. 48) A few years earlier, the psychologist Nicholas Spanos demonstrated that after only two brief training sessions that included practice at glossolalia, encouragement, and modeling, seventy percent of a group of sixty college students spoke fluent glossolalia throughout a 30-second segment of continuous pseudolanguage post-test. All of the students spoke recognizable glossolalia throughout most of the post-test period. (Spanos, Cross, Lepage, and Christine 1986, pp. 21–23) Spanos's results are consistent with reports that in religious groups some individuals begin speaking glossolalia on their first try and after only brief exposure to other glossolalics. (Samarin 1972)

How to Become a Glossolalic. Of course, it is much more difficult to teach such a verbal skill by written word than orally. Nevertheless, it is an easy skill to acquire. If you find it difficult to make up or compose strange new words out of consonants and vowels and syllables of ordinary English, there is a very simple way to begin.

Take each letter of the alphabet and make up a word using each letter. For example:

Aruss	Benonen	Cadnus	Doga	Ejah
Fornistan	Gomen	Hoganah	Ingah	Jurak
Kenos	Lomin	Maynug	Nagra	Ospinow
Panis	Quareno	Rigna	Sentuh	Tavarish
Ulogno	Vanis	Wizzack	Xanith	Yenuss
Zabney				

Next, read each word aloud rapidly, running the words together in pairs, i.e., Arussbenonen, Cadnusdoga, Ejahfornistan, Gomenhoganah, Ingahjurak, Kenoslomin, Maynugnagra, Ospinowpanis, Quarenorigna, Sentuhtavarish, Ulognovanis, Wizzackxanith, and Yenusszabney.

Now go back to the original list and repeat at random some of the made-up words and insert a number of guttural syllables such as ig, mog, hin, rin, sig, caw, pak, kig, lob, bog, and faz between the alphabetical pairs. For example: Arussbenonen ig Cadnusdoga nee Ejahfornistan gah

Gomenhoganah, etc.

If while you are doing this you use hand and arm gestures, smile in a friendly and open manner, and point to people and things in the environment, you have already won the battle of convincing your listeners you are indeed speaking an unknown tongue.

With a little practice at making up words and mixing sounds and syllables as you speak, you will soon find it very easy to create new words while you are pronouncing the old ones. It will very quickly become automatic and as easy as drumming, requiring no thought or hesitation whatsoever.

Credibility can also be enhanced by interspersing a number of well known legitimate place or personage names in the midst of your babbling. For example:

> *Noguss paragouid nee begova. Aknaw befunden gan pegonia Presidente Bush nigana zid mouova. Assain Hussein nigidova pid loskanova igneetis a bon Baghdad. Vestino agonia Washington pooh reno anah senitizz a gen befunden. Muh Nations Uniss parano le gunden muhvalina litt a noranto espahdeeh conogga.*

With a little more practice, you can learn to make up nonsense words to sing along with well-known and familiar melodies. Here, for example, is a glossolaliac's "Star Spangled Banner":

> *Agha Naw sayno gree, vow lib grebe's marna pron*
> *Rosta Lind Wagnah puz la vow reenah's nag zeering*
> *Mara's poladun pin aganosto bun no fah*
> *   zeeno conda maysetta*
> *Niska coudo maygah rota leemuh pegah molo pah segah nale*
> *Loho nomee cndaro la peenoggia cantaro*
> *Oskano anna drine eh now sovahira breve!*

Again, practice makes perfect, and if at first you don't succeed, try, try again. If all your efforts fail, try talking as rapidly as you can without using your tongue! If this doesn't do the trick, give up.

My Mind Has Eyes

One of the most startling and profoundly impressive delusions that a person can have is to fall asleep one evening and later in the night awaken to find oneself floating near the ceiling while one's body is still in the bed below. With a little experimenting, we also discover that one can walk through walls and doors or shoot across the landscape by merely willing it.

Of all such travelers, however, there is one individual who has made a career of promoting such out-of-body trips and is, beyond all doubt, the premier proponent—the Eugene Fodor—of this form of travel. We are referring, of course, to Robert Monroe, a former vice-president of programming for the Mutual Broadcasting System. In 1958 Mr. Monroe had his first out-of-body experience and he thought he was dying. After talking with a psychologist friend about the experience, he realized that what was called "astral projection," or the separation of the "astral" or "subtle" body during sleep, trauma, or at death, was well and commonly known in the metaphysical literature. Believers in the paranormal believe this "second body" is also capable of traveling not only in the real space-time world, but also in the spirit world, or on the "astral plane," a region well known in occult circles. Monroe believes deeply in this level of reality. According to him, it is infinitely vast, includes both heaven and hell, and is a place where the conventional laws of time, space, and motion do not apply. It is a place we visit occasionally when we're asleep; it is also a place where the newly dead are welcomed and indoctrinated to their afterlives ahead. Moreover, it is where the souls of the drugged and insane live and roam aimlessly. It is a place where raw emotions—rage, fear, and sexual desire—run wild. There are, however, a number of "helpers" or spiritual guides here. Fortunately or unfortunately, this astral plane Monroe calls *Locale II* is not detectable to us people here in *Locale I*— the ordinary world. There is also, according to Monroe, a *Level III,* a sort of "antimatter duplicate" of our physical world, but Monroe is, as far as he knows, the only one to have ever been there. According to Monroe, our physical reality is only one of a vast spectrum of realities in the universal energy system.

Monroe's first book, *Journeys Out of the Body,* was published in 1971 and became an immediate favorite of the occult establishment. In 1985 he published his second book, *Far Journeys,* in which he reports on his discovery of a way to make out-of-body experiences (OBE) accessible to anyone and everyone. The technique uses sound waves to synchronize both hemispheres of the brain, and Monroe has patented the process, calling it "Hemi-Sync." Proponents of Hemi-Sync claim it not only gives them an OBE, but also better in-body experience as well, including relief from pain, stress, insomnia, etc. Recently, it has also received a great deal of acclaim from believers of The New Age.

In 1971 Monroe opened the Monroe Institute For Applied Sciences in central Virginia to explore "expanded states of consciousness," and ever since its opening the MIAS has attracted a large number of believers and New Age searchers. Most of the visitors sign up for the Gateway Voyage, a week-long workshop using the Hemi-Sync as the principal exploratory tool. It is, of course, most attractive to the paranormalists and fringe scientists. Among the 6,000 Voyage graduates are Rupert Sheldrake, Joseph Chilton Pearce, Elizabeth Kubler-Ross, and Whitley Strieber. Another estimated 200,000 people have experienced Hemi-Sync through the audio tapes the Monroe Institute sells.

Monroe, like many other people, believes that all of us survive physical death, and the Gateway program, he believes, enables you to know this through direct experience. By means of chanting, rhythmic breathing, relaxation, and suggestions from Monroe—plus the more powerful suggestions from the entire social environment—many highly suggestible souls are led to believe that they are indeed "out of their bodies." What is particularly fascinating is that many people finishing the Voyage, even though they had no out-of-body experience, were still strongly affected by the experience. The writer Jean-Noel Bassoir, for example, wrote following his week at the Institute, "While many people (including myself) did not claim to have an out-of-body experience, it became apparent to most of us that it didn't matter. The state of consciousness we explored seemed genuine." ("Astral Travel," *New Age Journal,* Nov./Dec. 1988, p. 84) There is no doubt that listening to such sounds and suggestions in a state of profound relaxation can have powerful effects upon one's psyche. Certainly such subjective experiences can be very powerful emotionally, and the Hemi-Sync sounds could very well promote hallucinatory experiences in certain sensitive individuals. Although Monroe has both the laboratory and equipment for a truly scientific exploration of the OBE experience, he has yet to carry out any carefully controlled or double-blind experimental studies with the appropriate controls. According to Monroe, however, such things don't interest him anyway.

Monroe, however, represents only one of the many points of view—a minority view in fact—surrounding the OBE experience. On the physical side, it is well known that drugs and neurological disorders such as epilepsy, migraine, temporal lobe disorders, and many of the dissociative disorders also generate out-of-body experiences. In fact, there is good reason to believe that almost any individual, highly sensitive to stimuli that would affect certain parts of the brain, would be among the first to react with this sort of dissociation. As an explanation of the phenomenon this alone should suffice. There is, however, much more known, and the experience is, to put it bluntly, well understood.

According to Andrew Neher (1980), there are two psychological mechanisms important in producing the out-of-body experience. The first is the loss of the proprioceptive sense, i.e., the sense that tells us where our body is. This comes after we are very quiet and still for a while. It is also interesting that out-of-body experiences rarely occur while people are active. In an experiment carried out by Lydiard Horton (1981), out of thirty subjects who were completely relaxed, twenty were able to retain consciousness as well, i.e., they didn't fall asleep. Of the twenty who stayed awake, eight reported an illusion of floating, or levitation, and they felt the sensation was very real. Another study by John Palmer (1978) found that relaxation coupled with suggestive imagery produced out-of-body feelings in almost fifty percent of his subjects. On some occasions a sinking or falling sensation is reported, but the feeling of floating or rising is much more common and is, of course, in line with our conditioned associations. Related here is the almost universal experience people have when, after retiring and relaxing all of their muscles, there is a sudden sensation of falling and we will suddenly be jerked awake. This is due to the massive reduction in proprioceptive impulses flowing into the spinal cord and up to the brain. This sudden massive reduction in stimulation provides the illusion of falling and we then try to "catch" ourselves.

The second mechanism is suggestive imagery. When powerful suggestions of being detached from one's body are provided, along with deep relaxation, some people can easily feel that they *really* are detached, and that they can see their body from outside. Of course, when we are dreaming, we see ourselves from a point outside of our sleeping body, and in those with strong imaginations, it is easy to see them envisioning detachment in waking fantasies and visions.

When these two mechanisms are linked with strong personal needs, the OBE is even better understood. A few years ago one of my clients was in a motorcycle accident and suffered from chronic pain in his anal-genitourinary region due to hours of sitting in his wheelchair. Although he used analgesics for some while after, the accident left him a paraplegic, and they were not totally effective in killing the pain, nor were they without unpleasant side-effects, e.g., drowsiness and apathy. Following one of my hypnosis lectures, he asked if hypnosis could be of help in his case. Using deep relaxation and repetitive suggestive imagery, after a period of two weeks of daily intensive practice he was able to reduce his proprioceptive input to the point that he could no longer feel his lower body. Nor his upper body either for that matter. Not only did the floating sensations occur early in the practice stages, but out-of-body experience was a constant and continuing condition throughout the latter stages of his therapy. As a result, he was able to give up the drugs and he now uses relaxation and imagery to maintain himself in an almost pain-free condition. If the need or motivation is strong enough, the OBE can certainly be attained.

Ehrenwald (1974) and Palmer (1978), among others, have also pointed out that out-of-body feeling, when it does occur seems to be related to our religious upbringing and the human need to believe that consciousness survives death. Additionally, the strong feeling of release and freedom that comes with deep bodily relaxation is something that many people seldom—if ever—experience, and the accompanying emotional pleasure along with the reduction in tension can also be a powerful, almost overwhelming experience in its own right. Little wonder then that many religions and quasi-religious systems such as Scientology, the Rosicrucians, Eckankar, and other New Age cults stress the wonders of soul travel or astral projection. Rumors of or arguments that the OBEs do represent real and true visits by the discarnate mind to distant locales are merely that—unfounded claims. The few studies that claim to have shown such things have never been replicated, and all of the original studies had serious flaws (Rogo 1978). On the other hand, experimental studies have shown that the vast majority of subjects cannot perceive distant events during an OBE even though they strongly feel that they did (Osis 1974).

Two psychoanalytically trained psychiatrists, Glen O. Gabbard and Stuart W. Twemlow, have also looked closely at the out-of-body experience. In their 1984 book, *With the Eyes of the Mind: An Empirical Analysis of Out-Of-Body States,* they define the OBE as "an altered state of consciousness in which the subject feels that his mind or self-awareness is separated from his physical body and that his sense of self-awareness is more vivid and more real than a dream." (p. 5) They also prefer to define the experience phenomenologically, i.e., in terms of the subject's personal experience. This is done with the rationale that "the subject is in a better position than the investigator to decide whether or not he or she has had an out-of-body experience." The authors also provide a rudimentary classification of a number of different types of the OB experience. First is the sense of a complete functioning self located outside the brain that sees the physical body from an "outside" location. Second is an experience analogous to the religious or mystical sort described by William James in his *Varieties of Religious Experience.* This form is often reported as a "near-death experience" and might also be called the ecstatic type—the Greek word ecstasy means, literally, "to stand outside one's self."

A third category is known as the esoteric type of OBE. These are generally described as travels in the netherworld of "astral planes" where precognitive and mystical information is gained. Subjects of these experiences also consider their travels to be "real," and the information received of "real" value. Finally, there is a rare but frightening and nightmarish variety of experience which may or may not be a true OBE.

As far as the incidence of the out-of-body experience is concerned, a variety of surveys indicate that 14 to 25 percent of the general population has reported one or more of the above types of experiences. Phenome-nologically, consciousness is not clouded in the vast majority of cases, and the perception of the subjects is that the OBE is far more real than a dream is very clear. Subjects who are fearful during the OBE tend to have a more negative reaction. The typical experience occurs when one is in a state of physical relaxation and mental calmness, emotional stress is usu-ally absent, the experience is quite pleasant, and the subject typically feels sensations of calm, peace, and even joy. Unpleasant affects are much less common, and feelings of going crazy are rare. The subject usually finds himself in the same environment as his or her physical body, and feels he or she has a "new body." The experience is vivid in quality and clearly more real than a dream state. The OBE typically has a profound influ-ence on the individual's subsequent life—providing a feeling that his or her life has significantly changed. The subject may also see it as a spiritual experience and is likely to believe in life after death as a result of the OBE. Most people are fascinated with it and have no objections to experi-encing it again.

There is little or no psychopathology present, and most people hav-ing the experience seem to be quite normal—both mentally and physically. They are also equally likely to be male or female, and there are few indi-cations of either alcohol or drug abuse.

It is also clear that OBEs are distinctly different from depersonaliza-tion, which is usually experienced as unpleasant, pathological, and strange, whereas OBEs are perceived as religious, spiritual, and poetic or akin to a religious conversion experience.

OBEs are also clearly distinct from *autoscopy* and autoscopic hal-lucinations, i.e., literally "seeing one's self," or the "doppelganger or dou-ble" experience discussed earlier. Lukianowicz (1958) has described and defined the autoscopic phenomena in some detail, giving us the following characteristics:

> From this case and the six others, Lukianowicz derives the following char-acteristics of autoscopic phenomena: 1) the phantom double ordinarily ap-pears suddenly to the subject, without advance warning; 2) certain patients with seizure disorders or migraine headaches may have an autoscopic ex-perience before, instead of, or after an attack; 3) normally, the autoscopic double appears only as the face or a face and torso—it is uncommon for the entire body to be well visualized; 4) the image is usually seen clearly and with all the details of a mirror image; 5) the double is ordinarily color-less and transparent; 6) in most cases the phantom imitates all the move-ments, and particularly the facial expressions, of the "original"; 7) it is com-mon for the subject to perceive the double with more than just the visual senses—kinesthetic, intellectual, emotional, and auditory perception are pos-

sible accompaniments of the visual perception; 8) the most frequent emotional reaction associated with seeing the autoscopic image is sadness, although bewilderment may also be present; 9) a peculiar form of detached insight into the unreality of the experience is present in most cases; 10) the double is most frequently localized in the visual space directly in front of the subject, about a yard away; 11) the experience generally lasts a few seconds at a time and may occur with a frequency of once in a lifetime to a continual presence; 12) dusk is the most common time of appearance of the phantoms; 13) demographic factors such as sex, intelligence, education, and age seem to play no role in subjects who experience autoscopy; and 14) there does not seem to be a causal relationship between autoscopy and psychosis.

(p. 67)

A fair number of autoscopic cases are directly linked to specific brain pathologies: most often irritative lesions in the temporo-parieto-occipital areas. Other neurologists have linked it to epileptoid seizure disorders or migraine headaches, labyrinthine disorders, alcohol and drug intoxication, hypophyseal tumors, encephalitis, posttraumatic cerebral lesions, terminal cancer, and postelectroconvulsive confusion. Autoscopy has also shown up in normal individuals subjected to physiological stress states such as anxiety, fatigue, or exhaustion. Other authorities have argued for the existence of idiopathic autoscopy, i.e., experiences that occur in states without any known brain pathology and which seem to be caused by psychological causes due to alterations in normal mind/body perception, although, technically, the autoscopic phenomena may not be a true form of altered mind/body perception since the mind remains identified with the body. Subjects know they are not seeing their true bodies; rather they know they are seeing a phantom of themselves. Perhaps the most significant difference between the autoscopic experience and an OBE is that in the OBE the mind and point of perception are experienced as *outside the body*; whereas in the autoscopic experience the mind remains identified with the body, and the perceptual point of view is unchanged.

Because of poorly established body boundaries, the schizophrenic patient often feels "out of the body" and his or her subjective reports may be confused with the OBE of a psychologically healthy individual. Since skeptics are so frequently inclined to dismiss an OBE as merely a delusion or the hallucination of a psychotic, it is important to separate the two. Body boundary disturbances of schizophrenics show the following symptoms: fusion phenomena—being in another person's body and vice versa —over and under estimation of body size, omission of the hands and feet as part of the body, and feeling that one's body is unreal or a machine— all of these are part of broader and general false perceptions of the entire environment. The experiences of the schizophrenic and the person having an OBE are quite different, although a schizophrenic's loss of body boundaries can and may be confused with an OBE. In the psychosis, there is a loss of reality testing; in the OBE, reality testing is intact. Similarly, in the psychosis, body location is often uncertain; in the OBE, the body location is clear. Further, in the schizophrenic where there is a profound personality regression, no such regression is seen in the OBE.

There are also distinct differences between rapid eye movement (REM) dreams and OBEs. In the OBE, the consciousness is clear, the physical body is usually seen, recall of the experience is easy, the experience is usually very pleasant, and the reality of the experience is emphasized. In REM, dreams consciousness is hazy and confused, a physical body is usually not seen, recall is difficult, the experience is only occasionally pleasant, and the unreality of the dream is accepted after awakening. Similarly, for lucid dreams the differences are also many and marked. The OBE usually occurs when awake, the OBE-er is a passive and objective observer, the OBE-er perceives himself as separated from his physical body, consciousness is ordinary and like being awake, and the physical body is usually visible. The lucid dream occurs only during sleep, the dreamer is able to consciously program the dream, the dreamer and his body are still integrated, consciousness is vivid with mystical qualities, and the physical body is not visible.

The OBE is also categorically different from daydreams and from hypnogogic and hypnopompic imagery. Daydreams are common, occur in everyone, are manifestly wish fulfilling, are known to be imagined, are future-oriented, and are like primary-process thinking. OBEs, on the contrary, are unusual, occur in only 15-25 percent of the population, are not clearly wish fulfilling, seem to be very real, are usually present-oriented, and are more like secondary-process thinking. In the hypnogogic states, the imagery is usually visual or auditory, variations in the shape and size of images is common, disturbances of body image are also common, and are commonly experienced by the general population.

In the OBEs, the imagery is usually spatial, the imagery is unvaried, body image disturbances are unusual, and they are very uncommon in the general population. An OBE is, of course, one of the experiences commonly reported in the "near death experience" or NDE. Gabbard and Twemlow conclude that the NDEs are characterized by exclusive features that are not present in other forms of OBE. They also are convinced that the NDE cannot be written off as simply a typical OBE that is totally unrelated to the threat of survival.

The authors also conclude that there is a very close and intimate relationship between the phantom limb phenomena and the out-of-body experience, i.e.,

What we witness in the phantom limb phenomenon is what we witness in the out-of-body experience, namely, a body scheme fully cathected with bodily ego feeling without a physical body component . . . a full ego feeling and an intact ego boundary are both present in an out-of-body state. Thus, percepts experienced in this state are viewed as real because they impinge on an intact ego boundary. Whether or not they contradict reality as we know it, they are nevertheless perceived as real because of the operation of the ego boundary, just as a dream image may strike us as real despite its contradictory reality. When the external ego boundary loses its cathexis, as in depersonalization, external objects, however distinctly they may be perceived, are sensed as strange, unfamiliar, or even unreal. This mechanism underlies derealization and depersonalization. In the schizophrenic patient, loss of reality consists of losing both mental and bodily ego boundary cathexes. Ordinarily, whatever is sensed as mere thought is a mental process that lies inside these boundaries, while whatever is sensed as being real lies outside the boundaries. With no ego boundary what-soever, there is no means of differentiating what is real from what is thought, which is one of the central features of the schizophrenic process.

(p. 182)

In summary, Gabbard and Twemlow have developed as an explanation what they call the "ego-uncoupling model." In their view, all OBEs occur in an altered state of consciousness in which there is both mental calmness and physical relaxation, and in which both the sensory input from external sources and the proprioceptive input from internal sources diminish in importance and receive less attention and emotional energy. The out-of-body experience begins when the charge of psychic energy is withdrawn from the bodily ego and a dissociation, or uncoupling, occurs between the bodily ego and the mental ego.

Whenever the individual has the sensation that his or her mind is separated from his or her body, there is an immediate "perceptual restitution" effect which tries to make internal psychological sense of what is happening. The body image is then reinvested with psychic energy so that the individual feels "whole" again, and internal images of what would ordinarily be seen if one were looking at the world from some point "outside the body" are generated. These internal images, which are only approximations of the actual or real environment, are viewed or experienced as real. The spontaneous and unexpected appearance of these images also contributes to the feeling that they are strange and somewhat meaningless, as well as giving them a quasi-perceptual quality. Moreover, while these internal images are being experienced, there are few external sensory experiences coming in with the result that unreal fabrications and fantasies are accepted as real, which helps to make internal sense of the unusual experience. This internal sense is, of course, that one's mind has separated from one's body.

Interestingly enough, there seems to be an electroencephalographic pattern indicating a particular neurophysiological state accompanying the uncoupling of the bodily ego and the mental ego. Whether this state causes the OBE, or is the result of the OBE, is unclear. What is clear is that this uncoupling is the final common pathway of many, many different causative factors. Many different kinds of stimuli may work alone or in concert to bring about such an uncoupling. The mere reduction in a number of proprioceptive signals alone may be sufficient to cause an uncoupling. Cardiac arrest may serve as another stimulus. So may temporal lobe seizures. So may migraine auras. Drugs such as the hallucinogens, alpha-methyldopa, or haloperidol have also been reported to cause uncouplings characteristic of the OBE. To sum up the 272 pages of their investigation of the so-called out-of-body experience, it is only necessary to quote those sentences found on page 232 of their book:

> The "reality" of the out-of-body state is not real in any "objective" sense that will ever likely be demonstrated in a laboratory. It is real to the OBE subject in a powerful and persuasive subjective sense. This fact is most interesting to us and serves to explain partially why we are more interested in the psychology of the phenomena rather than in the objective demonstration of separation of mind from body.

Of course! One can be done; the other is impossible!

Gabbard and Twemlow also argue that OBEs should not be regarded as "hallucinations of a diseased mind." The evidence simply does not support such a conclusion. Again, it is important that we stress the fact that many, many people without pathology or any mental illness whatsoever still have unusual or anomalous experiences. Spontaneous OBEs share few if any characteristics of mental illness or loss of contact with the everyday world. Gabbard and Twemlow seem to be in full agreement with the contention of our thesis that just because a psychological experience is unusual is no indication that it is, therefore, pathological.

With regard to the Near Death Experience and the accompanying OBEs, there are a number of psychological explanations that are more satisfactory than those theories arguing for a physiological one. Citing Reed's *The Psychology of Anomalous Experience* (1988), Alcock argues that OBEs are most likely a psychological reaction to stress or conflict, and this reaction is known as "ego-splitting," a condition in which the subject feels as if he is actually outside of his body at some vantage point from whence one can calmly observe and hear oneself in the third person. Being close to death certainly causes stress and conflict. Phenomenologically the OBE is a mental state, like a dream or any other altered state of consciousness, and hypnogogic or hypnopompic dreams account for most of them. OBEs are due to hallucinations and imagination, and their elements are products of one's own memory and imagination. The evidence seems clear that the experience does not in any way involve an actual mind-body split. The psychoneural identity theory holds that mind and brain are one and the same: no brain, no mind and no mind, no brain.

While the psychoneural identity theory, i.e., mind and brain are one, cannot be *proved* empirically, there is a massive array of data supporting the view that thinking, perceiving, remembering, and feeling are functions of the human brain. Most psychologists, neurologists, psychiatrists, and other brain scientists accept as unquestioned the fact that "mind" is due to the fact we have a brain. Even most parapsychologists agree with this although they hope and believe, along with Sir John Eccles, that the mind and consciousness are much more than the mere material brain.

As for the scientific view, perhaps no one has expressed it better than James and Jean Goodwin:

> Science admonishes us not to give up too soon, not to call something unknowable merely because we have not yet figured it out. On the other hand refusal to acknowledge the impossibility of understanding the brain contributes to one of the greatest conceptual anachronisms of the modern era—that of mind-body dualism. While it is easy to trace the concept of mind-body dualism, it is somewhat more difficult to understand why the last century of brain research has not led to the demise of that concept. . . . Brain research has shown with increasing clarity that mind-body dualism is an artificial and fundamentally incorrect construct. There is no "mind" apart from the "body." The "mind" of the consciousness of self is a product of a functioning central nervous system, which is part of the body. All thought can be potentially reduced to organic events, changes in ion channels in nerve axons, release of neurotransmitters at nerve endings, release of neurohormones, triggering of feedback circuits and so forth. Thus were we to start anew today to develop a philosophy of selfhood we would not need to call up a mind separate from the body. We cannot totally explain how the electro-chemical reactions in the brain result in a concept of self, because the brain is too complicated; it is impossible to understand. But we no longer need to go beyond the brain in order to explain selfhood. Mind-body dualism, a major part of western thought over the past several centuries has become scientifically obsolete. This concept is not so easy to get rid of however. . . .
>
> (pp. 52–53)

If it were true that the mind could journey out of the body and operate separately and completely independent of the brain, the psychoneural identity theory would be in trouble. Fortunately for the theory this is not the case. Beyerstein (*The Skeptical Inquiry,* pp. 153–173) has noted that out-of-body experiences can be accounted for in terms of present neural and psychological knowledge. It has been well known for some time that many disorders of the temporal lobes of the brain can produce floating, disembodied sensations including the viewing of one's body from a distance. Electrical stimulation of these areas during surgery has also produced OBEs. A variety of drugs, epileptic seizures, hypoglycemic and migraine episodes as well as neurochemical changes near death can also bring on an OBE. It should also be noted that the brain generates similar sorts of "detachment or floating" imagery during dreams, and even in visual memories and daydreams.

Melvin Morse, in his book *Closer to the Light* (1990, Villard Books) speculates that NDEs have a biological origin in the Sylvian fissure, a small section of the hippocampus that produces OBEs when stimulated with electrodes.

The release of endorphins at the point of death has long been argued as being partly responsible for the NDE phenomena. Psychologically, Russell Noyes has a good point with his suggestion that the same sensation of detachment—transient depersonalization—reported by people experiencing falls, drowning, and other such near fatal events is also involved.

In fact, a number of factors can temporarily disable the higher brain mechanisms that confirm the reality status of percepts. It should come as no surprise, therefore, that the out-of-body experience is "all in the mind."

Simon Tabin, in a superb review of what is currently known about the OBE experience reports (*The Skeptic,* Spring 1988, pp. 23–27) that not only is the OBE experience poorly defined, but large discrepancies about the content and incidence of the experience exist. Some hold that a dream in which they see their own body constitutes an OBE experience, while others who merely imagine their body from a different perspective report an OBE. A consistent and agreed upon definition is needed. As for the experimental evidence, what little there is, is methodologically poor, lacking adequate controls, and the conclusions drawn are based upon inadequate data. Finally, the psychological explanations set forth by Alcock (*Skeptical Inquiries,* 1983, pp. 75–77), Blackmore (*New Scientist,* 1988, pp. 45–46), and Beyerstein (1988) are much more satisfactory and revealing than theories requiring a physical separation of the consciousness from the body.

It is particularly ironic that one of the occult's most vigorous and intelligent defenders, D. Scott Rogo ("Is Religion in the Brain?", *Fate,* Nov. 1990, pp. 80–92) has suggested that not only OBEs and NDEs may be due to physical changes in the brain, but also that many so-called "religious experiences" are also due to changes in brain physiology. Looking at temporal lobe disorders, Rogo notes that it has long been known that stimulation of the temporal cortex can cause vivid hallucinations, and the person having these will create fantastic interpretations of them. Since many temporal lobe epileptics (TLE) rarely exhibit convulsions, TLE is frequently mistaken for schizophrenia. But strange behaviors, e.g., sudden religious conversions, and strange beliefs that change frequently and suddenly are primary symptoms and take the place of convulsions. Anti-convulsants, instead of helping, usually acerbate the problem. Citing Frazer's *Golden Bough* with its suggestion that early man's failure to understand the natural world, animism, and belief in ghosts, gave birth to religion—Rogo goes on to suggest that religious conversion is a typical symptom of the TLE, and that epilepsy is often complicated by "spiritual" insanity. Rogo cites several classic conversion cases to support his claim that sudden religious conversion and epilepsy are linked. His best evidence refers to the work of Stephen Waxman and Norman Geschwind (*Neurology,* July 1974) and David M. Bear and Paul Fedio (*Archives of Neurology,* 1977) in which hyperreligiosity, hypergraphia, unusual sexual behaviors, as well as a number of other personality characteristics were all precursors to religious conversion. Conversion is not, however, the direct result of the neural discharge. Changes of consciousness result from the neural firings, which excite more primitive and emotional levels of the brain. In order to find "meaning" in these sudden changes in consciousness and perception, the epileptic draws upon his or her early religious background. Thus the epileptic erroneously interprets the strange experiences as the result of some external force—God, Jesus, or Satan—not as events produced within his or her own body. Geschwind doesn't think the religious syndrome is solely produced by epilepsy. He sees it as psychologically intrinsic to the patient and due, most likely, to some sort of disinhibition in the limbic system—the system regulating our emotional reactions—causing extreme emotional responsiveness to ordinary events. Along with electrical stimulation of the temporal cortex, the resulting hallucinations are also incorporated along with the emotional reaction into a religious belief system. Rogo prefers a different interpretation, however, and sees that stimulation of the temporal lobe in epileptics causes "spiritual or religious" insanity, but in normal people the temporal lobe may regulate a deep connection between the brain and its capacity to establish contact with the spiritual world. Rogo also suggests that man may be neurologically and genetically programmed for religious belief.

Rogo, however, was far from being the first to suggest that religious experiences—trances, divine union, divine missions, ineffability, illumination, etc.—are all due to "the lawful workings of our psychophysiological organism." In 1925 James H. Leuba in his *The Psychology of Religious Mysticism* (1925) came to the same conclusion. According to Leuba, when we carefully examine the experiences regarded by uncivilized man as revelation of, or union with, the Divine, we find that everyone of these impressions and beliefs can be satisfactorily explained as the result of psychophysiological forces set in motion or inhibited by drugs, disease, or some kind of physical or psychological disorder. In Leuba's words:

> In all these ecstasies, the same fundamental characteristics were discovered, and we came to the conclusion that there need be no differences between religious and non-religious ecstasies other than those due to a different interpretation—the interpretation itself being the cause of important affective and volitional phenomena.

(p. 315)

Leuba also noted the specific effect of epilepsy, drugs, hysteria, and neurasthenia on the production of mystical religious states. In his words:

> Particular attention was given to the impressions of ineffability and of illumination or revelation; for they, perhaps more than any other feature, are responsible for the persistency of the belief in the divineness of ecstasy. Both these traits are frequent in trance—whether it be produced spontaneously or by drugs such as ether and nitrous oxide. They occur also in near-sleep conditions arising naturally. [Note: He refers to hypnogogic and hypnopompic dreams here.] Any narrowing of consciousness or any dissociation of mental connexions, whatever the cause, may be accompanied by these strange impressions. We have offered a psychological explanation of the impression of illumination which to us appears sufficient.

(p. 315)

Readers of Leuba's work will, I am sure, be inclined to agree.

Regarding the NDE, like most skeptics Dr. Ronald K. Siegel, a psychopharmacologist at UCLA, argues that visions of the hereafter are really hallucinations. Siegel has noted (Siegel 1991, p. 73) that when research subjects are given the anesthetic drug ketamine, they too report typical near-death experiences complete with the out-of-body experience, the tunnel, the white light, and heavenly visions. At the hospital where Siegel worked, a middle-aged woman suffered complications during major surgery and stopped breathing for several minutes. Not only did she have an NDE, but after she left her body she was abducted by an alien spaceship. Her account was so unusual Siegel reported it to his friend, the late D. Scott Rogo, who arranged an interview. During the interview Rogo found her story strangely familiar. Not only did the woman have a large collection of Rogo's books, but passages describing NDEs and UFO abductions were underlined. Confronting her, the woman confessed to Rogo that she had made up her story in order to gain attention. Shortly before his death,

Rogo also expressed the point of view that many—if not most—NDEs could be explained in terms of hallucinations or fantasy. Since the NDE evidence is, of necessity, anecdotal, it is doubly interesting when NDE reports come from skeptical and/or scientifically trained experients. Not long ago the California psychiatrist John J. Preisinger, Jr. fell off the roof of his home, fractured seven ribs, and caved in his chest. Conscious, but unable to breathe, Preisinger believed he was going to die and underwent the typical NDE. In his words:

> Succumbing to the lack of oxygen, I began to feel progressively more euphoric. Time seemed to be suspended; I felt that I was floating through a long, dark grey tunnel, the end of which was illuminated by a brilliant white light. I had wispy flashes of events from my life. I saw many vague, shadowy people along the length of the tunnel, but could not identify any name. I knew this was the end and did not even think in terms of regret since I felt such a sublime great pleasure.
>
> (Preisinger 1990/91, p. 52)

When Preisinger's wife discovered him and lifted him, his ribs popped back in place, his breathing resumed, and he recovered, regretting the need to "come back." Analyzing his experience, Preisinger notes that when oxygen to the brain is reduced, as happens during the administration of anesthesia, drowning, and in altitude sickness, a great euphoria results along with confusion and disorientation. People suffering from decreased and insufficient oxygen have the feeling that they have little or no concern as to the consequences of the deprivation. Similarly, body shock from injuries produces the same results with pain sensations absent or dulled. As noted earlier, the brain's temporal lobe—where visual hallucinations, light and tunnel visions occur—is also affected. The oxygen deficit also serves to reduce the sensations of pain, thus accounting for the euphoria.

Preisinger also reported that he told his experiences to Dr. Raymond Moody, author of several NDE works. Moody refuses to accept Preisinger's "scientific" explanation, preferring instead to see the NDEs as proof of an afterlife. The fact that Dr. Moody is also a deeply religious man makes his resistance understandable.

In all considerations of the NDE, two facts must be kept in mind: (1) the majority of people who come near to death do not have an NDE; and (2) there is little difference in the content or sequence of NDEs occurring in the dying compared with those who only believe themselves about to die (Greyson 1983). Moreover, none of the NDE components are unique to near-death situations. OBEs are found in psychogenic crises, trances, coma, and anesthetic use. Some practiced individuals can induce it voluntarily. Meeting with hallucinated entities occurs in circumstances of extreme stress. Panoramic memory occurs in temporal lobe epilepsy and direct stimulation of the temporal lobe. Complex experiences with many NDE elements are reported when the dissociative anesthetic Ketamine is used. Parallels between the NDE and LSD intoxication—time distortion and hallucinations—also exist. No one reporting an NDE can properly be considered to have died, all the NDE separate elements can occur in non-life-threatening situations, and typical NDEs can be chemically induced (Roberts and Owen 1988).

We are also indebted to Drab (1981) for another persuasive psychophysiological explanation of the NDE. Using Gregory's perceptual model (Gregory 1966), Drab is most convincing. Perception, he notes, is a continuing process of information-gathering and processing and decision-making. Therefore, it is highly dependent upon the reliability of incoming stimuli and the brain's discriminating and organizing capacities. Our brain is built in such a way that it must make sense of whatever information it is given. Perception, thus, is the brain's best guess as to what the incoming stimuli mean. If the incoming information is distorted by drugs, disease, fever, anesthetics, injuries, accidents, or strong emotions such as fear, or if the information is incomplete or ambiguous, then the brain's perceptual process does the best it can but still makes mistakes, which are the perceptual errors we call delusions or hallucinations. Such perceptual breakdowns and disorganizations are, by no means, rare or uncommon. They show up frequently when we ingest drugs or alcohol, subject the body to excessive stress—either physical or psychological and particularly—in one of the most stressful situations of all—the near-death experience. The specific NDE imagery will, or course, depend upon the individual's stored memories, the sociocultural setting, and his or her emotional state. Nevertheless, the resulting preoccupation with internal imagery, i.e., the complex hallucinatory state, plus the perceptual disorganization does serve an adaptive purpose: it provides the person who believes he or she is dying with comfort, security, and a sense of wholeness or integration in the face of impending destruction and total disintegration. What more can any dying brain do for a helpless human being?

Finally, in her recent work *Dying To Live* Susan Blackmore (1993) carefully explains NDE delusions and illusions. She emphasizes the fact that people will fight and die for the ideas they like the best, but death is definitely an idea that they do not like. On the other hand, the "self" is an idea that they do like, and the idea of an everlasting eternal self is even more attractive. Science began tackling the nature of human origins more than 130 years ago, and Blackmore says that it is now time that it tackles the nature of human death. For the past twenty years there has been great progress in the study of NDEs and what happens to us physiologically and psychologically when we begin to die. Blackmore's review of the psychology, biology, and neurology of the dying brain and its illusions and delusions is simply summarized without the usual medical or mystical jargon. Her book should be widely read.

Blackmore's coverage of the issues surrounding the issues of death and dying is thorough and comprehensive as well as highly critical of other attempts to account for the subjective phenomena in earlier religious, philosophical, and pseudoscientific terms. She is at her most brilliant when she takes on the particular subjective phenomena reported by those who have experienced an NDE and those who support a religious, mystical, or otherworldly interpretation, for example, Raymond Moody, Melvin Morse, Jeffrey Iverson, and Kenneth Ring.

Blackmore neatly demolishes Ring's psychological and "holographic theory" in her chapter "Realer Than Real." Ring, in *The Omega Project* (1992), assumes that consciousness is a "field effect, an all-pervading element in the universe, perhaps associated with space-time in ways not currently apparent to us." In other words, an "alternative reality" accounts for the experience being "realer than real." Ring assumes consciousness can function in this other reality without the brain. This, according to Blackmore, is nonsense. Does this hypothesis account for other NDE features? No. Does it have to invent a new world, ad hoc? Yes. Does this hypothesis make any testable predictions? No.

Blackmore's arguments are clear and effective:

1. The *consistency* argument—the joy and peace, the tunnel, the light, and the noises are consistent because of the natural way the cells are laid out in the visual system. The OBE is consistent because it is the brain's way of dealing with the body image and its image of reality. The feeling of peace and the life review are consistent because of the release of endorphins or natural opiates that cause random activation and seizures in the temporal lobe and limbic system where memories are organized. The same effect leads to the time breakdown, dissolution of self, and the consequent mystical experiences and their aftereffects. No afterlife hypothesis is necessary; the dying-brain hypothesis is better.

2. The *reality* argument, i.e., the NDEs feel so "real" that they, therefore, *must be* real. Not true. In the brain's normal process of model building some models seem very real and some do not. There is no one, no person, self, or ego, to travel out of the body, nor is there any next world to go to!

3. The *paranormal* argument, i.e., that the experience cannot be explained by science and, since science can't solve it, this proves it is real. Hardly, Blackmore says. Psychology, physics, and biology say otherwise. The dying-brain hypothesis accounts for the experiences of familiarity, insight, déjà vu, and the psychic aspects.

To appreciate fully Blackmore's philosophical stance and her psychology we need to look at what modern cognitive psychology tells us. Human decisions are the consequence of large amounts of parallel intellectual processes coming together to produce a willful action, a word, or a remembered event. The brain is a very complex system doing lots of things in parallel and making lots of decisions at once. There is no one *person or self* inside the brain doing it all. Neither is there an "I" separate from this system to make a decision. This "I" is a delusion. The brain creates a vast set of mental models about reality, and the "I" is one of those mental models. Our brains build us. My brain builds "me" and your brain builds "you." My consciousness and your consciousness and my awareness and your awareness are products of the way this brain system builds its model of reality.

During its normal day-to-day operations the brain builds many models of possible as well as impossible things, but only what we take to be the world "out there," Blackmore explains, seems real. The brain's major problem is deciding which of the things it has to confront are real and which are imaginary. This is not always an easy task, and mistakes are often made. It not only has to model an external world with a "self" in it, but it also has to try out possible actions in the imagination, manipulate ideas in dreams and fantasies, separate the real from the imaginary, and predict its own future actions and those of others as well. To succeed, it must have a very clear idea of which of the models are the "experimental ones" and which represent the "real world."

Isn't the brain smart enough to know which came in from the world outside and which were created out of memory and imagination? Not really. From the beginning, the processing of information from the eyes and ears gets mixed up with information from memory. When the mental memory models or the imagination's models are compared with visual input, the brain is not certain that just because it came from the eyes it must be real. It has to check up on the model to see what it does next. If it changes from moment to moment it must be imaginary. In Blackmore's words, "Our reality at any time is the brain's collection of stable mental models built largely out of present sensory input and memory, integrated to form a model of the self in the world." In other words, all of our beliefs are merely mental models.

It is difficult for many people to grasp the idea that hallucinatory experiences are very much like reality, so much so that we cannot always tell the difference. These false perceptions are much more common than most people realize, and they lead us very easily into false beliefs or delusions. The psychological process of remembering and imagining is the same; it's identical.

Blackmore makes all of this crystal clear by bringing us back to the marvelous but fallible human brain. Wonderful though the brain may be, it is far from perfect. What reports of satanic ritual abuse, alien abductions, OBEs, false memories, NDEs, and hypnopompic and hypnagogic hallucinations have in common is a deluded brain.

As John Lilly (1978) noted years ago, just a small dose of the anesthetic Ketamine can also bring on the typical NDE experience. On the "Oprah Winfrey" show of January 3, 1994, which was devoted to NDEs, a female former drug addict who had overdosed underwent a typical sleep paralysis with hypnagogic and hypnopompic hallucinations in which she was subjectively paralyzed with heavy suffocating pressure on her chest and surrounded by satanic demons. This she interpreted as an NDE visit to hell. During this show Oprah introduced a group of women who reported NDEs during childbirth. Apparently, whenever it is subjected to unusual mental or physical stresses and strains, the human brain responds appropriately and typically, that is, it responds neurochemically with hallucinatory defensive reactions, i.e., misperceptions. These we color with our religious beliefs, our folklore, and our hopes and fears. This is the source of all those guardian angels we create to protect our threatened egos and to fend off terror.

Like the Buddhists, Blackmore believes that all we are is "a collection of mental models," and that all we can ever experience *are* our mental models. In her words, "This idea can be just too horrible to accept and we will go to enormous lengths to invent something more substantial to hang on to." When she talked with ex-psychologist Richard Alpert (Baba Ram Dass) about this human problem of having to live with these insights and difficulties, Blackmore reports, "He said simply, 'Aha, and you know it's much worse even than that.³ Oddly enough this was the most comforting thing he could have said" (p. 163).

7

The Little Coed Who Wasn't There: Hallucinations, Delusions, and Such

One of the sanest, most rational, and well-adjusted people I know told me recently of a strange experience she had during her freshman year in college. Coming back to her college dorm one evening after a physically exhausting athletic trip, she went into the dorm's bathroom, took a shower, washed her hair, and proceeded to carry on a conversation with one of the residents. After a few minutes of this her roommate came and queried, "Who were you talking to?" Raising her head and looking around, my friend was amazed to discover there was no one in the showers but her and the roommate who had just walked in. She could not believe that for the last five minutes she had been talking to a phantom coed who had never been there in the first place!

Such experiences, baffling and startling as they are, are not uncommon. In fact, they happen quite frequently to many people who are free of drugs and intoxicants, people who are perfectly normal and in full possession of all their faculties. They are, moreover, psychologically fascinating because they provide considerable insight into how our minds work and the important roles that habit, expectations, and suggestion play in our everyday perceptions and behavior.

My female friend, for example, was so used to the communal bathroom usually being filled with her fellow floor mates, and rarely ever being alone in the facility, that she *expected* to see friends in the room since she *habitually* did see and talk to them there. It never occurred to her fatigued vision and hearing that the place would be empty. Some slight noise, or a shadow or reflection in the mirror of a passing student was a sufficient trigger in a steam-filled room to delude my friend into imagining someone was there asking questions and providing answers. Vocal noises from the hall or neighboring rooms provided sufficient suggestion to place the speaker in the bathroom—especially since my friend's major concerns and activities consisted of washing and grooming herself, and the major portion of her attention was devoted to these tasks. If you doubt this explanation or find it hard to accept, then you are perhaps a believer in ghosts and phantoms.

Mental and physical fatigue along with exhaustion also contribute to our perceptual errors. In past centuries when most people believed in and accepted the prevalence of spirits and spirit possession, of ghosts and goblins, of demons, of witches and warlocks, and other such nonentities, such misperceptions were much more common and frequent than they are today. Anything that went amiss was due, of course, to actions on the part of some unseen force which was seldom benign. In those days demons, ghosts, and witches were everywhere and were not only accepted but were as "real" as trees, houses, and living beings. In such a psychological atmosphere dominated by ingrained belief in the supernatural and otherworldly phenomena it is little wonder that strange religious beliefs, witchcraft, and spiritualism thrived. In modern times with the advance of science and a broader, deeper, and better understanding of nature's laws and natural phenomena, such primitive beliefs have, of course, diminished and have become the exception rather than the rule. In enlightened and educated circles, in fact, when gross errors and anomalies of perception are encountered, the affected, rather than assuming spirit possession or the presence of demons, usually attribute the phenomena to a mental aberration or something they ingested, i.e., to *some rational* cause.

Of course, they are correct. In fact, there are so many ways in which our minds can go awry that there is a Murphy's Law to cover it: If anything *can* go wrong with the human mind, it *will* go wrong with the human mind. Because of the enormous chemical complexity of the central nervous system, and the many, many things in the environment that can affect its normal or ideal operation adversely, it certainly should come as no surprise when individuals behave in strange or unusual ways.

It is simply because of this sensitivity and complexity that so many things can and do go wrong with our minds—even when our behavior is not specifically aimed at altering or changing reality through fantasies, self-delusions, drugs, or chemicals of various kinds. We deliberately alter reality so often and in so many different ways it may be very difficult for many people to determine when and if a "normal" or "unaltered state" even exists. Nevertheless, for the vast majority of human beings who share in the very large world of everyday reality—i.e., materialistic, three-dimensional, consensual, unaltered, historical, physical reality—misperceptions, delusions, and hallucinations are still fairly rare and infrequent. Yet, even here, they do occur and happen more often than most people realize. The fact that many perfectly normal, mentally healthy, intelligent, and clear-headed individuals occasionally hallucinate—even though they are neither drinking nor on drugs—is not commonly known.

Hallucinations

Surprisingly, the literature on hallucinations is quite small considering the fact that perceptual inaccuracy or sensory deception is far from rare, and in some cases is just as common as accurate perception. In earlier times when a person saw visions and heard voices, they were often assumed to be of either heavenly or Satanic origin. In the fifteenth and sixteenth centuries, they had to be defended against. Torturing and burning were accepted ways of dealing with those people who were possessed by demons or suspected of witchcraft. Today such people would be regarded by most of us as mentally ill or psychotic. It wasn't until the eighteenth century, however, that the medical viewpoint dominated the view of the church.

According to Slade and Bentall (1988), the word *hallucination,* taken from the Latin and meaning "wandering of the mind or idle talk," was introduced into English in 1572, but no distinction was made between *hallucinations* and *illusions* until Esquirol in 1832 explicitly separated the two.

> In hallucinations everything happens in the brain (mind). . . . The activity of the brain is so energetic that the visionary, the person hallucinating, ascribes a body and an activity to images that the memory recalls without the intervention of senses.
>
> In illusion on the other hand, the sensibility of the nervous extremities is excited, the senses are active, the present impressions call into action the reactions of the brain.
>
> (Esquirol 1832, p. 6)

Although Galton argued for a continuity between all forms of visualization, from almost a complete absence of it to a complete hallucination, the medical view that hallucinations are almost always pathological and distinct from other mental events became the dominant point of view.

There are, of course, some conceptual difficulties in dealing with hallucinations. First of all, they are objectively unverifiable—we have to accept the hallucinator's report and such first-person reports may be erroneous. Because hallucinations share some qualities of other forms of sensory deception even with normal mental imagery, the question of whether or not a particular happening is hallucinatory may be difficult to ascertain —even when the reporter gives a good account of the experience. Cultural values and context also play a role. Ghosts, from a materialistic point of view, are hallucinations, yet we seldom regard the seeing of a ghost as a sign of mental illness, especially if the culture believes in ghosts. Hallucinations can also be actively sought, e.g., deliberately ingesting LSD, mescaline, psilocybin, hashish, etc., or they can be passively received. They also differ in complexity and they are essentially private and subjective. Also, they have been distinguished from illusions and pseudo-hallucinations, i.e., recognized by the percipient as nonveridical. Moreover, like various other forms of vivid mental experience, the hallucinations seem "very real" and are like "actual perceptions."

Perhaps the best definition we have is the one provided by Slade and Bentall who define a hallucination as: "Any precept-like experience which (a) occurs in the absence of an appropriate stimulus, (b) has the full force or impact of the corresponding actual (real) perception, and (c) is not amenable to direct and voluntary control by the experiencer." (p. 23)

Hallucinations In Normal Individuals

A major issue, however, is in finding a dividing line between those forms of sensory deception which are considered normal and those which are considered to be pathological. Since hallucinations have been found to occur in association with a wide range of organic and emotional states, they are currently seen as predominantly examples of abnormal or pathological perceptual experience. While hallucinations are common in progressive deafness, high fevers, food and water deprivation, reduced respiration rates, sensory deprivation, etc., various medical conditions and nervous system disorders such as brain lesions, acute organic brain syndromes, alcoholic states, and functional psychiatric disorders—they do not *always* appear with these disorders. With regard to the common psychiatric disorders, auditory hallucinations are more than twice as common as visual hallucinations in schizophrenics. For those suffering from organic or affective disorders, visual hallucinations seem to be more common.

Although it is commonly assumed that all hallucinatory experiences are strictly pathological in nature, and that they occur only in mentally or physically ill individuals and are, therefore, qualitatively distinct from normal mental events, such assumptions are unfounded. On the contrary, we have found that hallucinations share much in common with dreams, vivid imagery, and other mental events. Many vivid nonpathological experiences and hallucinations are psychologically related. In part, the evidence for the existence of hallucinations in people who do not consider themselves to be in any way odd or deranged is very high.

Over the years there have been a number of attempts to measure the prevalence of hallucinations in the general population. Most of these attempts were motivated by an interest in religious or parapsychological phenomena. While the sampling procedures were far from optimal, the results, nevertheless, show that hallucinations are not exclusively pathological. One of the earliest studies was carried out by Sidgewick in 1894 by the Society for Psychical Research. A total of 7,717 men and 7,599 women were interviewed and all people who suffered from mental or physical illness were excluded. Of this group 7.8 percent of the men and 12 percent of the women reported at least one hallucinatory experience in their lifetime. Hallucinations were most frequent in the 20- to 29-year group, and visual hallucinations were more common than auditory —the opposite of schizophrenics. The most common type of experience was that of seeing living persons absent at the time of the experience as we noted earlier. Visions with a religious or supernatural content made a small but significant minority.

Edmund Parish, in 1894, following up work undertaken earlier by Edmund Gurney, published a study called *Nature and Frequency of the Occurrence of Hallucinations in the Sane,* which was part of a larger study called *The International Census of Waking Hallucinations* (Parish 1897). Data for this census was gathered in America by no less an investigator than the notable philosopher and psychologist William James. In France the data was collected by Louis Marillier, in England by the Society For Psychical Research, and in Germany by Parish and Von Schrenck-Notzing. One of the questions put to all persons included in the study was:

> Have you ever, when believing yourself to be completely awake, had a vivid impression of seeing or being touched by a living being or inanimate object, or of hearing a voice; which impression, so far as you could discover, was not due to any external physical cause?

In response to this question, 27,329 answers in all were received, of which 24,058 were negative and 3,271 (or 11.96 percent) were affirmative; that is to say, 3,271 persons stated that they had experienced hallucinations.

Although a certain proportion of these might be explained away, as due to mistaken identity, for instance, or in the example of auditory phenomena to the real banging of a door or the creaking of furniture and such, when we consider the high percentage of results and the careful investigation of a number of the individual cases—especially among the English group—it is impossible to doubt that the frequent occurrence of so-called "waking hallucinations" is proved. It is also reasonable to assume that some of the reports from the population of alien abductees might also fall into this category. If so, the abductees would not be in bad company. Among the great and distinguished people who have reported waking hallucinations we find Socrates, Thomas Hobbes, Savonarola, Luther, St. Ignatius Loyola, Oliver Cromwell, Theodoric the Great, Raphael, Montagna, Benvenuto Cellini, Sir Walter Scott, Tasso, and Schumann. These notables discussed their waking visions at length in their work. That such waking dreams are not reported more frequently today is perhaps due to the fact that in a psychological and psychiatric age to report seeing things that are not there too often is the quickest possible way to get tossed into a loony bin. Among the luminaries listed above, the most frequently reported waking dream was that of hearing the voices of the people the recipient knew were not there, or seeing a vision or the bodies of dead friends or of friends who were far away in another country. It is quite reasonable, of course, that true UFO believers would say they heard alien spacemen and saw alien spaceships in lieu of the dead or distant.

In 1948 D. J. West (1948, pp. 187–196) thought that in our more sophisticated time hallucinations would be less common and, covering the same topics as Sidgewick, West questioned 1,519 subjects. Of that group 217 or 14.3 percent reported having experienced hallucinations. As in the earlier survey, females reported more than males, and more experiences were visual than auditory. Multimodal hallucinations were fairly rare—11.6 percent in 1894 and 8.4 percent in 1948. Interestingly, in contrast to Sidgewick, West found that none of the reported hallucinations were convincingly veridical.

McKellar carried out the first modern census on the subject in 1968. Questioning a group of 500 "normal" people, he found that 125 reported at least one hallucinatory experience and they were, for the most part, genuine. Many of them were religious experiences, e.g., seeing God, angels, the Devil. Others were of hearing voices, the sound of a dog known to have died, feelings of being touched, the smell of food cooking, and so on. Similar findings were reported by Posey and Losch (1983, pp. 99–113) who questioned 375 college students and found that 71 percent reported some brief hallucinated voices during periods of wakefulness. The Schneiderian symptom of hearing thoughts spoken aloud was reported by 39 percent, and 5 percent reported carrying on a conversation with their hallucinations. Slade and Bentall, using the Launay-Slade Hallucination Scale, which measures hallucinatory tendencies, carried out several studies on normal individuals and found that a large proportion of normal individuals marked some of the "most pathological" items on the scale as applying to themselves. For example, for one of the items, "I often hear a voice speaking my thoughts aloud," 17.7 and 13.7 percent of the "normals" answered affirmatively. Other results were in line with the findings of Sidgewick and West.

Added evidence that hallucinations are not strictly pathological is provided by studies of hypnotic suggestion. While claims of auditory and visual hallucinations under hypnosis are suspect, Barber and his colleagues (1970) have, nevertheless, investigated the effects of suggestions to hallucinate in the absence of hypnosis. In 1964 Barber and Calverly (pp. 13–20) tested seventy-eight secretarial students suggesting, "I want you to close your eyes and hear a phonograph record with words and music playing 'White Christmas.' Keep listening to the phonograph record playing 'White Christmas' until I tell you to stop." After thirty seconds, the subjects were asked to check a rating scale: (a) they had not heard the record; (b) they had a vague impression of hearing the record; (c) they had clearly heard the record but they hadn't believed it was being played; and (d) they had clearly heard the record and they believed it was being played. Forty-nine percent reported that they had clearly heard the record and 5 percent stated, in addition, they believed the record was being played. On a similar visual task when subjects were asked to visualize a cat sitting in their lap, 31 percent reported seeing the cat and 2.5 percent reported believing that the cat existed. This surprising result was replicated by Bowers (1967) who used forty undergraduates as subjects and by Spanos and Barber (1968) who used ninety-eight female nurses. Subjects in these two studies scored higher on the average than Barber and Calverly's original group. While these results might be attributed to the particular social context of the experiment, it is nevertheless quite clear that a lot of normal people have the capacity to hallucinate—in fact, *many* more than the pathological medical model would indicate is the case.

In many cultures hallucinations, rather than being considered as evidence of derangement, are actively sought after and are considered as desirable—especially those involving communing with the spirits and the seeking of guidance. According to Kroll and Bachrach (1982), the particular folk theory of visions and voices that the culture adopts pretty much determines whether a hallucination is viewed as veridical or as evidence of insanity. Visions in the Middle Ages, though similar to the experiences of present day schizophrenics, were considered as true perceptions of heavenly or hellish events, not of madness. Moreover, during Victorian times apparitions, i.e., ghosts, were relatively common when compared to today. It is, therefore, clear that hallucinations occur to a limited extent in individuals who are not otherwise mentally ill. Moreover, as Slade and Bentall note, the social context in which the hallucinator is imbedded is also important both in determining the reporting of hallucinations and in attributing or not attributing mental pathology to the hallucinator.

It is also evident that hallucinators mistake their own internal mental or private events for external or publicly observable events. In other words, mistaking the "imaginary" for the "real" is the essence of hallucinating. What we need to understand is how people tell the difference between self-generated or imaginary events, and events in the external world. To do this the term "reality testing" is normally used. We know that people can and do make wrong inferences about their own mental events. Moreover, they will often infer the causes of what they do on the basis of observations of their own behavior and the context in which it occurs, with the result that their accounts of their own mental strategies may be seriously inaccurate when compared with their performance of actual tasks. Mislabeling one's own behavior or emotional state is far from uncommon. In other words, it seems that individuals base their judgments as to whether an event is real or imaginary on a range of available information, and judgments about the real and the imaginary will err when either the evidence is misleading or when the individual fails to get the relevant information.

Research has also shown that reality discrimination errors can be shown in normal individuals who misclassify either imaginary events as real, or, conversely, real events as imaginary. C. W. Perky demonstrated this in 1910 (*American Journal of Psychology*, pp. 422–452). Subjects were told to look at a blank screen and imagine seeing a banana. Unknown to them a picture of the banana was back-projected onto the screen, and its brightness was slowly increased until it could be clearly seen by anyone in the room. Amazingly, all of Perky's twenty-nine subjects failed to report seeing the picture and, instead, made statements to the effect that their imagery was unusually vivid, the object appeared at an abnormal angle, etc. The subjects really thought what they were seeing was a product of their imagination. Since Perky's subjects were "trained introspectionists," they might have let their skilled status delude them. To test this possibility, Segal carried out a number of studies of the Perky effect using undergraduate students (Segal 1968; Segal and Nathan 1964; Segal and Glicksman 1967). Though the Perky phenomenon occurred less readily than for the introspectionists, it was increased by giving them a placebo tranquilizer, or by having them lie down, or by making them thirsty. Segal also applied signal detection theory to the phenomenon, and on the basis of these studies concluded that the imagination task did actually reduce the subject's ability to discriminate the real from the imaginary.

More recent evidence of reality discrimination failures in normal individuals has come from a number of studies carried out by Johnson and

Raye and their colleagues. Using an entirely different approach to the tendency of subjects to classify some imaginary events as real, Johnson and Raye (1981, pp. 67–85) explored the way in which people sometimes confuse memories of real events with memories of thoughts. Though they called the skill of distinguishing between memories of real events and memories of imaginary events "reality monitoring," it is clearly closely related to reality discrimination.

In a number of studies, Johnson and her associates found that memories of events and memories of thoughts are usually sufficiently different to make discrimination between them comparatively easy when compared with the difficulty involved in distinguishing between events belonging to the same class. As in the Perky phenomenon, however, sensory information seems to be an important determinant of the accuracy with which reality monitoring can occur. It was also found that subjects were better able to discriminate between self-generated and externally generated items when the self-generated items were harder to generate. This result shows that one of the cues that people use to distinguish the real from the imaginary is "cognitive effort." Since thinking and imaging require effort, people tend to regard experiences associated with such effort as the product of their own minds.

In summary, the experimental evidence supports the idea that inferential processes are involved in the skill of distinguishing between real and imaginary events. Also, hallucinations result whenever defective reality judgments are made, i.e., from a dramatic failure of the skill of reality discrimination leading the hallucinator to repeatedly misattribute his or her self-generated private events to a source external to him or herself. Though it is entirely possible that the sensory properties of vivid private experiences might mislead one into describing the events as externally caused, it is not proof that this is a necessary or sufficient condition for a hallucination. Not only could other types of information be responsible for one being misled, but the mistake could be not in the information itself, but in the inferences the person makes on the basis of that information. As Slade and Bentall emphasize, their reality discrimination model accounts for the observed subvocal activity seen during auditory hallucinations, accounts for the observed effect of concurrent verbal tasks which inhibit normal inner speech and bring auditory hallucinations to a halt, explains why hallucinations are sometimes experienced by otherwise normal individuals, and lends support to the view that hallucinations exist on a continuum with nonhallucinatory mental states. Since hallucinators make over-rapid perceptual judgments and are more willing than nonhallucinators to believe that a perceived event is real, they do not have the problem of mistaking their own cognitive processes for events in the external world.

Among the factors affecting hallucinations we find ample evidence that *stress-induced arousal* increases the probability that a person will hallucinate. Moreover, any trait that leads a person to make overly rapid judgments about the sources of his or her perceptions, that deprives the person of relevant information, or that provides the person with misleading reality discrimination cues is likely to lead to hallucination. Also, when the environmental signal-to-noise ratio is poor, hallucinations are more likely. *Perceptual set* or expectancy also is known to lead a person to "see" an ambiguous stimulus as either one thing or another. Furthermore, I one's particular beliefs and expectations can lead the individual to experience ambiguous events as either real or imaginary. While we normally assume that delusions or false beliefs are subordinated to hallucinations, the role of expectancy in causing hallucinations implies that hallucinations may, on occasion, be secondary to strongly held beliefs.

While it is assumed that defective judgment is the root of hallucinations, it is not assumed that the process is a deliberate or conscious one. When one hallucinates, one doesn't consciously stop and consider whether the perception is real or imaginary. Neither does the nonhallucinator. In fact, hallucinators spend less time dwelling on the source of their perceptions. When we see an ambiguous stimulus, we normally expect and assume it's one thing or another and see it accordingly. It is also well known that complex perceptual judgments are made quickly and automatically.

Hypnagogic and Hypnopompic Hallucinations

As briefly noted on page 22, another common but not well-known experience is a sleep disorder known as "sleep paralysis with hypnagogic and hypnopompic hallucinations." Though well-documented in the medical literature, it has not received the attention it deserves. It is of particular interest now because of the remarkable similarity between the reports about people alleging alien abduction and the medical reports about people suffering from sleep paralysis with hallucinations. There is good reason to believe that many, if not most, of the people claiming to be abducted are also reporting this highly unusual and less known sleep disorder. In fact, the book *Hypnogogia* by Andreas Mavromatis published in 1987 covers this unique state of consciousness between wakefulness and sleep in great detail. Pulmonary specialist Dr. Stanley Rehm has also studied the phenomena at length (1991 and 1993). As far back as 1982 psychiatrist Otto Billig studied the case of three Kentucky women claiming an alien abduction. He convincingly showed how the hypnagogic experience combined with regressive hypnosis convinced them that their abduction dream was real (Billig 1982). Numerous reports from the clinic of hypnagogic and hypnopompic dreams and the reports from alleged victims of alien abduction are amazingly similar. The following excerpts from Dr. Ronald Siegel's 1992 book *Fire in the Brain,* which details his hypnopompic experience, shows clearly how powerful and convincing such experience can be:

Table 1a. Description of Hypnagogic and Hypnopompic Hallucinations

I. Hypnagogic Hallucinations: Unusually vivid dreams associated with REM sleep. These occur as the individual is falling asleep. Our thoughts change into dreams as we are falling asleep. Our disturbed perception makes it difficult to tell whether the perception is real or illusory.

Physiological Effects	*Psychological Effects*
Reduced proprioceptive impulses	Feeling of floating and falling; clonic spasms or "jerks."
Alpha waves (wakefulness) replaced with theta waves (sleep)	Out-of-body experiences may occur.
Relaxation and muscular paralysis	Loss of volitional control.
Increase in brain activity	*Ishakower Phenomena*: sparks, flashes or balls of light, faces, or animals—all rushing at sleeper; cloud-like masses overwhelming sleeper.
Organic vestibular disturbances	Gritty, salty, or milky sensations around the mouth.
	Dizziness, feeling of falling or sinking, and distortions of space perception.
	Feelings of being overwhelmed or of being engulfed or manipulated.
	Both *Sequences* (random images of people, objects, and things) and *Episodes* (clearly defined themes and schemes, i.e., stories) occur. Similar to hypnotic state, i.e., suggestibility heightened.

*II. Hypnopompic Hallucinations: These occur when the sleeper is waking up. Many characteristics of hypnagogic state also present.

Physiological Effects	*Psychological Effects*
Paralysis of all voluntary muscles including speech.	Inability to move or talk.
Rapid heart rate (tachycardia).	Vivid visual hallucinations.
Difficult or labored breathing (dyspnea) and restricted or reduced breathing.	Auditory hallucinations.
	Extreme fear and feelings of paralysis and helplessness.
Hyperventilation causes reduced oxygen flow to the brain.	Feelings of floating, rising, and being moved about.
Autoerotic asphyxia.	Feelings of being sexually stimulated or violated.
Hyperacusis, i.e., all sounds are amplified.	Feeling of being awake, aware, and conscious.
Eyes are open and visual senses are intact.	Dreamer hears, sees, smells, and feels things that are actually present in the environment.
Heavy perspiration flow.	Dreams seem very real and life-like.
Skin temperatures and skin resistance changes.	Tingling sensations and feelings of cold.
	Emotional responses of fear and panic are present.
Dilated pupils.	Shadows and distant objects are seen as monsters, ghosts, demons, or aliens.
	Extreme fright may cause PTSD in some victims.

*The most commonly reported hypnopompic hallucination is of ghosts—usually ghosts of friends and relatives who have recently died.

**Table 1b: Summary of Sleep Paralysis with
Hypnagogic and Hypnopompic Hallucinations**

A. Prevalence in general population: 4 percent to 5 percent.
B. Cause: Not well known or established but stress, high anxiety, unusual beliefs, e.g., ghosts, demons, elves, fairies, etc., erratic sleep-wake cycles, poor health, digestive disorders, and excessive drug and alcohol use can trigger these hallucinations. These are implicated in some instances but not all.
C. Predictability: Low; some individuals may have only one attack in a lifetime. Others may have three or more in a month. One experience also seems to trigger other attacks in the same individual.
D. History: Called "Old Hag" attacks in folklore. Known during the Middle Ages as *Incubus* (male demons attacking sleeping females) or *Succubus* (Female demons attacking sleeping males). There are many literary references.
E. Associated with: Cataplexy or partial paralysis and narcolepsy or inability to stay awake, as well as sleep apnea.
F. Hallucinatory content: Determined and influenced by media reports, science fiction stories, religious beliefs and themes, and UFO abduction stories, as well as current psychological motives, emotions, and needs.
G. Commonality of reports: All known medical, psychological, clinical, historical, and literary accounts of the phenomena are so similar as to be judged *identical* except for variations in hallucinatory content, i.e., ghosts, elves, demons, fairies, monsters, or extraterrestrial aliens. Particularly striking in terms of reported physiological and psychological effects are the similarities between the experiences of people claiming alien abduction and individuals *known* to have experienced sleep paralysis with hypnagogic or hypnopompic hallucinations.
H. Recommended reference: Andreas Mavromatis, *Hypnogogia.* London and New York: Routledge and Kegan Paul, 1987.

When a typical hypnopompic report is compared with the alien abduction reports by Strieber in *Communion* (1987), there can be no doubt of their overlap and similarity:

> I was awakened by the sound of my bedroom door opening. I was on my side and able to see the luminescent dial of the alarm clock. It was 4:20 A.M. I heard footsteps approaching my bed, then heavy breathing. There seemed to be a murky presence in the room. I tried to throw off the covers and get up but I was pinned to the bed. There was a weight on my chest. The more I struggled the more I was unable to move. My heart was pounding. I strained to breathe. . . . Suddenly a shadow fell on the clock. *Omigod! This is no joke.* Something touched my neck and arm. A voice whispered in my ear. . . . In my bedroom I could see only a shadow looming over my bed. I was terrified. . . . I signaled my muscles to move, but the presence immediately exerted all its weight on my chest. . . . *This is no dream! This is really happening!*
>
> A hand grasped my arm and held it tightly. The intruder was doing the reality testing on me! The hand felt cold and dead. . . .
>
> (Siegel 1992, pp. 83–85)

Sometime during the night I was awakened abruptly by a jab on my shoulder. I came to full consciousness instantly. There were three small people standing beside the bed, their outlines clearly visible in the glow of the burglar alarm panel. They were wearing blue coveralls and standing absolutely still. . . .

I thought to myself. *My God, I'm completely conscious and they're just standing there.* I thought that I could turn on the light, perhaps even get out of bed. Then I tried to move my hand, thinking to flip the switch on the bedside lamp and see the time.

I can only describe the sensation I felt when I tried to move as like pushing my arm through electrified tar. It took every ounce of attention I possessed to get any movement at all. . . . Simply moving my arm did not work. I had to order the movement, to labor at it. All the while they stood there. . . . I was overcome at this point by terror so fierce and physical that it seemed more biological than psychological. . . . I tried to wake up Anne but my mouth wouldn't open. . . . Again it took an absolute concentration of will . . . but I did manage to smile.

Instantly everything changed. They dashed away with a whoosh and I was plunged almost at once back into sleep.

(Strieber 1988, pp. 172–73)

The unusual and interesting phenomena with both their physiological and psychological effects are summarized in Tables 1a and 1b. It should be evident that anyone suffering from these physical effects could easily be persuaded that something incredible is happening. Such an experience, coupled with its psychological concomitants and any acquaintance with the alien abduction urban legend, would certainly suffice to convince anyone that the little grays are at work again.

Delusions

Although it is commonly assumed that delusions are also due to a pathology of cognition, many delusions are, in no way, pathological.

Delusions or *false beliefs* are not only very common but, unfortunately, not very well understood either. While experienced clinicians can describe delusional beliefs and distinguish between beliefs that are delusional and those that are not, a good definition is hard to come by. Delusions are not common to all psychiatric patients: delusions appear frequently in some disorders, e.g., schizophrenia, and not in others. Usually they are considered under the notion of *false ideas,* which gets one into trouble over the definition of "truth."

Some authors have suggested delusions should be seen as points on a continuous distribution from the normal to the pathological. Conviction, absence of cultural determinants, preoccupation, and implausibility are characteristics of delusions that also should be considered in any useful definition. Oltmanns (1988) considers a delusion as a belief in which: (a) the balance of evidence is such that other people consider it completely incredible; (b) the belief is not shared by others; (c) the belief is held with firm conviction; (d) the person is preoccupied with the belief and finds it difficult to avoid thinking or talking about it; (e) the belief involves personal reference rather than unconventional religious, scientific or political conviction; (f) the belief is a source of subjective distress and interferes with the person's functioning; (g) the person doesn't report subjective efforts to resist the belief.

It is also known that several personality traits predispose an individual to the development of delusions. Unconscious homosexual desires, fear of loss of control, and sensitivity to humiliation are believed to be involved. Faulty thinking or information processing, or cognitive defects such as failures of logical reasoning are involved as well. Maher (1988) argues that delusional beliefs are founded as the result of attempting to explain anomalous experiences. Other authorities emphasize that interpersonal incompetence and the resulting social isolation causes people to develop bizarre ideas because the person does not receive social validation for his beliefs and attributions. Once the delusionary belief is formed, the individual behaves in a manner that elicits from others further confirmation of the original misconception.

Since delusions are fundamentally private, we are forced to rely on self-report, and here we have to recognize that the individual's statements about the belief are manifestations of the delusion and are not, necessarily, synonymous with the delusion. We must also recognize that even if the individual stops talking about the belief, this does not mean the delusion has disappeared. In fact, eliminating the social feedback relevant to the belief system may cause it to harden and become further entrenched. Moreover, it is not always possible to say that a belief is delusional on the face of it since the great majority of false beliefs are not, on the surface, fantastic or incredible. We also have the "Martha Mitchell Effect," i.e., the situation in which what appears to be preposterous or bizarre turns out to be true. Martha's claims that illegal activity was taking place in the White House was, indeed, correct, and she was not suffering from a pathology. We need to determine hwether or not there is any logic in the delusional system since delusional thinking is not, in itself, aberrant. Delusions are, according to Maher, best thought of as theories that provide order and meaning for one's observations and provide explanations for puzzles and discrepancies in the world around us. Such delusional theories—like other theories—are not easily surrendered unless they can be replaced with theories that better explain one's experiences. In other words, delusional beliefs are developed in much the same way that normal beliefs are developed and they serve, essentially, the same purposes.

Clinically, delusions have been associated with over seventy pathological conditions from paranoid schizophrenia to twenty neurological syndromes, sixteen metabolic and endocrine disorders, and many syndromes associated with alcohol and drugs. All seem to involve some disturbance of bodily function. Reasoning ability in delusional patients—apart from the delusions themselves—appear to be unimpaired and, as with hallucinations, normal subjects under anomalous environmental conditions are easily provoked into irrational beliefs. Under conditions of sensory impairment, sensory deprivation, undiagnosed hearing loss, and hypnotic suggestion, delusional beliefs can be created fairly readily

Maher (1988) has argued for some time that all delusions can be understood as responses to anomalous experiences, i.e., ones that seem inexplicable in terms of normal principles of causation. Hearing voices when no source of the voice is evident, or having thoughts when one is not aware of thinking those thoughts, are common examples. Maher argues that delusions are rational and systematic explanations of such experiences and that, moreover, they are actually reasonable conclusions. Such explanations are also arrived at by the same process that scientists use and, furthermore, like the scientist, the delusional patient investigates alternative interpretations before settling on a delusional one.

In the Chapmans' study of delusions (*Delusional Beliefs,* 1988) and aberrant beliefs, college students high on scales showing a proneness to schizophrenia, and controls without such inclinations, were studied. For the perceptual aberration-magical ideation subjects, 63 percent reported psychotic or psychotic-like experiences, and almost all of these deviant experiences involved aberrant beliefs. For example, some subjects reported the experience and belief that other people put thoughts into their heads by action from a distance. Other subjects reported the experience that other people heard their thoughts. These aberrant beliefs seemed to be continuous with full-fledged delusions both in content and in degree of deviancy. Not only did the aberrant beliefs have themes similar to those of psychotic delusions, e.g., many subjects believed their thoughts were read while others thought their thoughts were being broadcast, but many of the non-psychotic aberrant beliefs were similar to the delusional beliefs seen in psychotic episodes. When the Chapmans examined the relationship of beliefs to experiences, they found their subjects responded to similar experiences with beliefs that ranged from the normal to the fully delusional. They found some cases in which a delusion was the clear result of an anomalous perceptual experience because acceptance of the veridicality of the experience:

> . . . demanded or almost demanded, a delusional belief. Other subjects reported delusions or aberrant beliefs that had no apparent relationship to

any unusual experiences. Still others reported delusions that had some relation to their unusual experiences, but yet were not necessary, or even reasonable, interpretations of those experiences.

(Chapman and Chapman 1988, p. 87)

The Chapmans reported that among those whose aberrant beliefs
clearly reflected anomalous experiences were subjects who actually felt
thoughts leaving their heads and going into the ears and minds of other
people. "The belief in thought transmission directly reflected their perceptual experience. Indeed, the belief was required if the subject accepted
the experience as veridical." (p. 89) Another subject observed bad thoughts
in her mind without believing she had anything to do with them. The
way she saw it, an evil spirit had seized control of her mind, which to
her was a reasonable interpretation.

Much more common among the subjects, however, were anomalous
experiences that did not require any particular interpretation and in response to which subjects differed widely in the deviancy of their beliefs
about the event. The subjects' interpretation of the experience determined
its deviancy. Voice experiences are a good example since they can be interpreted in a deviant or nondeviant manner. Many of the Chapmans' subjects described vivid inner voices that criticized their behavior. These
anomalous sensory events caused marked variations in belief. The most
common interpretation—even by those whom the voices tormented—was
that the voice was that of their own conscience. A few subjects, however,
believed the voices came from other people. One young woman heard the
voices of her dead father and grandmother arguing about what was best
for her. Other subjects attributed the voices to God, or the devil, or both,
depending on the subject's religious convictions. Some subjects had outer
voices, and some recognized them as products of their own minds, while
others developed delusional beliefs concerning their origins. One typical
subject who lacked delusional beliefs reported hearing the voice of his mother
or boss, but added, "I knew it couldn't really be true."

Therefore, the individual's interpretation of the anomalous experience
is what determines the presence or absence of a delusion. Moreover, the
processes by which subjects reach delusional or nondelusional interpretations of anomalous experiences are not equally reasonable. According to
the Chapmans, the nondelusional person takes the usual step of considering more information about the world than the anomalous experience
itself, while the delusional person reacts to the experience as if this is all
the information he'll ever have. Delusional interpretations can also be adopted
from other people as in the case of the subject who hallucinated an outer
voice but never knew where it came from until a cult group interpreted

it for him. This subject also claimed to have a spirit guide who accompanied him constantly while it whispered messages in his ear. Though he had heard the voice for many years, he didn't know what it was until he met members of a group that interpreted psychic experiences. They told him he was fortunate in having a spirit guide.

Even though some of the voices were intensely vivid, most of the subjects still believed they were responsible for them and did not consider the experiences to be veridical. The Chapmans also argue against Maher's position that an anomalous experience is required for forming a delusion by showing that some subjects develop delusional or aberrant beliefs based on experiences that would certainly not be considered anomalous to most people. For example, two subjects thought that night shadows indicated the actions of spirits. Other subjects seemed to be preoccupied with the idea someone was reading their minds. The Chapmans also reported that in some instances the deviant belief gave rise to the anomalous perceptual experience instead of vice versa. Some of their subjects reported they could see auras—a glow of light—around other people's heads and bodies. Those subjects not only believed in the existence of these auras, but they belonged to cults that encouraged such beliefs. Undoubtedly, the shared belief system sustains and promotes the perception of auras as well as the initial perceptual experience.

Many of the Chapmans' subjects also showed a number of formal thought disorders; and when some of the subjects were asked to explain their deviant experiences, they talked instead about their acceptance of other paranormal beliefs such as horoscopes, or UFOs, or the Bermuda triangle. One subject, in describing her inner voices which she accepted as veridical, said they were more "a revelation than a voice." She also said, "The voices are a sort of power that is transmitted between people." (p. 178)

In summary, it seems clear that the delusional individual limits the information he uses to reach a conclusion and either ignores or gives short shrift to data from his or her other life experiences which would, ordinarily, contradict the delusional belief. An individual, for example, who sees shadows as reflecting the actions of dead spirits is failing to incorporate the fact that shadows are commonplace and result from the play of light on material objects. People who think thoughts have been injected into their head with a hypodermic needle are failing to take into account all of their experience and knowledge which contradicts thought transmission by such means. This explains why people fail to reject delusional beliefs as unrealistic. Delusional people also ignore contradictory evidence in reaching their conclusions—far more obvious and clearly relevant information than scientists ignore—and they, also, deny well-established facts of physical reality that they and others have experienced all their lives.

Our major concern here, however, is to explain why so many people are unwilling to abandon their delusions, and to explain why they seek them out or prefer them to more naturalistic explanations in the first place. To comprehend this we must recognize that for many of the deluded the delusionary theory is much more satisfactory and does a better job of explaining the deluded's experiences than the factual, natural, or scientific theory does, i.e., particularly for the simple-minded or uneducated delusionary. As Maher notes, "To ask patients to abandon the delusion is, from this point of view, tantamount to asking them to trust the evidence of other people's senses in preference to their own—something that is not impossible to do, but something that is not readily done by most people." (p. 26)

Maher also argues that since there is a widespread need for the mystical and marvelous, and since this need is at odds with the cold unemotional logic of science and since the former far outnumber the latter, then it could be well-argued that it is the rational and skeptical scientist who is statistically aberrant—not the deluded patient with his beliefs about demons, UFOs, and waves from outer space. Many normal people readily offer implausible explanations for anomalous experience, and this is not in any way pathological. We also know that the psychological mechanisms that produce delusions are the same belief mechanisms in both the deluded and the nondeluded. We also know that delusional beliefs are perpetuated in part by the self-fulfilling prophecy mechanism, and the delusion of persecution gains validity as a direct result of the antisocial behavior of the patient. We also know that the failure of deluded patients to modify their delusions in spite of poor validation is due simply to the fact that no one changes his beliefs easily—no matter what the counter-evidence. That belief itself, we know, has a major selective effect upon determining what is, and what is not, perceived as evidence. In other words, the delusion is perpetuated and reinforced by exactly the same processes as those that maintain normal beliefs in spite of poor empirical support.

Some of the most intriguing questions regarding hallucinations and delusions have to do with our perceptions, and how we are able to discriminate between "what is *out there* in the real world" and "what is *in here* in our heads." Did it really happen out there in the world, or did we just imagine it? One way of looking at our lives is to consider them as a series of events or happenings. But how do we know for sure that all of these events really happened? Did we just invent or imagine some of them? How can we tell which of the events are those we invented and which ones *really* happened? Most of us have experienced false memories, and most of us have had erroneous beliefs at one time or another. Moreover, we sometimes use our imaginations to create events that are self-serving and then we proceed to forget they are imaginary since the self-deception now serves us so well. These "illusions" we will take up a little later.

We also often confuse things we imagine with things we perceive and even more often we have trouble with our memory. Quite often we find ourselves in the position of not being sure whether certain events in our past really happened, or whether we just imagined that they happened. Even if we were sure about the event when it happened, we may not be so sure years or even months and weeks later. Moreover, our dreams— what we wish had happened—and our memories of what actually *did* happen, quite often get confused. Then we also have trouble with the source of the information and give perception credit for things that were only imagined. As Johnson notes, our memory preserves both the results of perceptual processing and the results of more self-generated processing such as thought, imagination, and some types of inferential thinking, and because the system is veridical and preserves whatever it has processed, we sometimes accurately remember very specific details. Then again, we easily confuse what someone told us with something we saw, and vice versa. Johnson and Raye also contend (1981, pp. 67–85) memories that originate in perception have more perceptual information, e.g., color, sound, more time and place information, and more meaningful detail. Memories that originate in thought, however, have more information about the cognitive operation, e.g., reasoning, search processes, and decisional and organizational processes that took place when the memory was established. A memory with a great deal of cognitive operations information and little sensory data would be judged to have been internally generated. The memory of a conversation with someone might be attributed to a fantasy if you know you don't know the person.

In addition, our judgments will be affected by our assumptions about how our memory works. In some memory models imagined information and perceived information are assumed to have essentially the same underlying representation. In other models, however, they are separated simply by tags specifying the external or internal origin of the information. In the former case, there would be no basis in memory for separating externally derived and internally generated information. In the latter case, confusion is believed to result because the tags are lost and memory for the origin results from the retrieval of the correct tag. In contrast, and in Johnson's model, it is assumed that the representation of information in memory reflects its processing history and emphasizes the role of decision processes in both confusing and discriminating memories from these two sources. She emphasizes that memory for origin is actually the outcome of a judgment process that evaluates the characteristics of revived or activated information. This judgment process is sensitive to many factors (e.g., the amount of sensory detail expressed in a memory, whether it gives rise to supporting memories, how it fits with prior knowledge). The idea or notion of an all-or-none retrieval of a tag does not do justice to the importance of all these many factors.

Johnson has carried out a considerable number of experiments which support her "reality monitoring" model and show that (1) the class characteristics of memories from external and internal sources seem to differ, and discriminations within a class are more difficult than discriminations between classes; (2) confusion is increased by the sensory similarity between memories from the two sources; (3) confusion is reduced with increases in the information about cognitive operations associated with internally generated memories; (4) memories based in perception have better spatial, temporal, and sensory information, and people's tacit assumptions about these characteristic differences are reflected in metamemory assumptions that influence reality monitoring judgments; and (5) reality monitoring and recognition may draw on different characteristics of memories. This last point is important because it emphasizes the fact that information can be quite familiar (thus, memory for it is good), yet we can be mistaken about where it came from. This reality monitoring model also predicts that the more imaginations are like perceptions in sensory detail, the more subjects will confuse their imaginations with their perceptions, or, to put it another way, the more sensory overlap there is between memories derived from perception and memories generated via imagination, the greater will be the confusion between them.

Although delusions are usually classified in terms of their content, e.g., paranoia, or grandiosity, Johnson classifies them in terms of (1) whether they seem to involve false perceptions, or memories of specific episodes, or (2) whether they have more of the character of false beliefs or knowledge that is independent of memory for particular episodes. It is likely that delusions of the first type are a precursor of delusions of the second type and may signal the eventual development of a full-blown delusional system. With regard to delusional beliefs we know that people's conviction in them does fluctuate. One patient, for example, said "Forty-nine percent of me knows that what I am thinking is too weird to be real," and another patient had a staff member take him around the hospital grounds so he could see if it really was a political prison.

From a reality monitoring perspective, delusions are likely to involve imagined sensory information, such as another person's voice, that is difficult to separate from actual perceptual events. Delusional people also lose control over their thinking and often spend a lot of time thinking about and embellishing their delusions. This loss of control, even without any increase in frequency or vividness of imagined experiences, tends to make the thoughts seem external. Further, frequent rehearsals and embellishments of a delusion make it seem even more real, both because sensory aspects are preserved that normally would fade away, and because of the process of embedding, i.e., becoming more firmly entrenched in memory. If the rehearsal of the actual events focuses on their emotional as opposed to their perceptual aspects, this may decrease one's ability to discriminate between actual and imagined events. Social isolation may not only decrease opportunity for social verification, but it can also increase the rehearsals and the embedding. Moreover, delusions may be sustained by faulty reality monitoring criteria applied inappropriately. Together, loss of control, frequent rehearsals, embedding, and inappropriately applied criteria should all work together to produce experiences that almost everyone would regard as real.

Reality monitoring is a complex skill that some people are good at and that others fail to do well. While it is possible that people can learn to do a better job of detecting false memories, separating constructed from perceived events and even learning to become more aware of the biases that operate in the processing of incoming information, there is no doubt that without such educational efforts delusional beliefs are universal, common, and wear their own natural armor of conviction and reality. While it is possible there is some sort of fundamental difference between normal and delusional thinking, current research shows that those factors involved in normal memory and judgment also are involved in and contribute to the development and maintenance of delusions. It is highly unlikely there are any other additional or extraneous factors that cause delusions. Again, as we have seen with the case of hallucinations: false perceptions, delusions, and false beliefs are also matters of degree, and mere extensions of or aberrations of those psychological processes that underlie and are responsible for normal or ordinary human believing and the resulting beliefs. As Maher has noted (Oltmanns and Maher, p. 336), we have no evidence that abnormal cognitive processes are at the root of delusions. If delusions are due to a pathology of cognition, we have yet to find and identify either the abnormal process or processes or the specific pathology.

Illusions

> "What's so great about reality?"
>
> (clinical patient, 1988)

For a long while it was commonly assumed that in order to be mentally healthy one had to be firmly in touch with reality. In the last decade, however, psychologists have clearly established that rather than being firmly in touch with reality, the average or normal human mind distorts incoming information in a positive or optimistic direction, and it construes events in a manner that promotes benign fictions about the self, the world, and the future. The normal human mind is, with some significant exceptions, intrinsically adaptive and oriented toward overcoming—rather than succumbing to—the adverse events of life. (Taylor 1989) In other words, the healthy mind engages in self-deception and systematically distorts reality in order to successfully adjust and adapt. We are so constructed mentally that we find benefit in tragedy and manage to protect ourselves in such a way that we will not be overwhelmed by the pain and stress of life.

Rather than self-deception being seen as a mark of illness, it is now clear that it is exactly the opposite. Rather than perceiving themselves, the world, and the future accurately, most people regard themselves, their circumstances, and the future as considerably more positive than is objectively likely or that reality can sustain. These biased perceptions or *illusions,* according to Taylor, fall into three general categories: (1) *self enhancement,* or the perception of one's self, one's past behavior, and one's enduring attributes as more positive than is actually the case; (2) an exaggerated belief in one's *personal control,* involving the perception that one can bring about primarily positive but not negative outcomes; and (3) *unrealistic optimism,* namely a perception that the future holds an unrealistically bountiful array of opportunities and a singular absence of adverse or negative events. Normal human thought and perception, we now know, is marked not by accuracy, but by positive self-enhancing illusions that are, moreover, actually adaptive, and *promote,* rather than undermine, good mental health.

The research evidence also clearly indicates peoples'—both children's and adults'—assessments of their own capabilities are ego-enhancing rather than realistic. Such ego-enhancement also characterizes most of our perceptions most of the time. There is also a fundamental overpowering need for a sense of personal control, freedom, and will in everything that we do. These things are vital to all normal human functioning. We not only see these things clearly in children, but we also know that most adults believe the world to be inherently controllable. We also believe that people succeed through their own efforts even though evidence all around us points to the role of random and chaotic forces in many aspects of life we either play down or ignore. We also confuse what we want to happen with what we actually caused to happen, and if the desired event comes about, we conclude we caused it to happen. We are also superb at finding examples that confirm our prior beliefs, and even go so far as to believe that we can cure ourselves of serious illnesses through positive thinking. We often read about the positive examples of this, but never the negative; and we never see the statistics showing how many people tried to cure their illnesses through positive thinking and failed. Nor do we read about the number of people who did not try to cure their terminal illnesses and survived nevertheless, nor the number of people who didn't make the effort and died. As Taylor notes, "to establish that people can survive a serious illness if they have effectively tried to control it, one needs all four types of information." (p. 28) Sadly, the world of disease is full of people who have tried valiantly to cure themselves of their illnesses and have ultimately failed. This situation almost caused O. M. Simonton to abandon his efforts to help cancer patients and to leave the field of psychoneuroimmunology. The point is: we simply don't know if people can improve their health by maintaining a positive attitude. What we do see is our beliefs confirmed by incomplete evidence, and we jump prematurely to the desired conclusion, ignoring the evidence that is also highly relevant.

We also make the error of assuming we have much more control over events than we actually do. We fail to discriminate between controllable and uncontrollable events, i.e., between events involving chance only and those where skill is involved. In skill situations there is a causal link between one's behavior and the outcome. On tasks or events determined by chance, our behavior has no effect at all. In a fascinating series of studies, E. J. Langer (1975, pps. 311–328) showed that by introducing skill-related cues into a chance situation, people came to behave as if the situations were under their personal control and not a result of luck at all. No wonder addictive gambling is so difficult to control! Langer's research has implications far beyond that of gambling, however. What it shows is that any situation in which a person has options, develops strategies and plans, and devotes thought to the problem is vulnerable to an illusion of control. We know that people can endure extreme distress if they believe they have the ability to control the source of that distress. Control is important to us because it enables us to make sense out of things—it enables us to bring structure—order, logic, and process—to an otherwise chaotic and meaningless universe. We are characteristically hopeful and confident things will get better. When we are asked to predict the future, most people predict what they wish, or would like to see happen, rather than what is objectively likely or more probable. All of us believe we can accomplish more in a given period of time than is humanly possible. Check your "things to do" lists. One of the significant differences between *delusions* and *illusions* is that delusions are false beliefs that persist despite the facts, while illusions manage to accommodate the facts albeit with a considerable amount of unwillingness. Taylor points out that we all suffer from unrealistic optimism and the illusion of progress, as well as a number of other mental illusions that may be downright dangerous. We think, for example, that we can avoid health problems by giving up smoking, getting enough sleep, or eating well, forgetting that hereditary factors, chance meetings with viruses and bacteria, environmental threats, or drunken drivers can override all of our careful plans.

All such illusions are false mental images or conceptions—perceptions that represent what is perceived in a way different from the way it is in reality—that may be a misinterpretation of a real appearance, or may be something imagined. As Taylor reminds us, people hold mild and benignly positive illusions about themselves, the world, the future, and these illusions are common, widespread, and easily documented. They are, moreover, natural and an intrinsic part of our cognitive makeup, although they are not bizarre, unreal, and distorted as the delusions we see in mental patients. As we already noted, in most cases they are adaptive, and such positive distortions often increase rather than decrease as matters regarding the self become more important and consequential, i.e., when the outcome is important, self-enhancing casual attributions become more likely. It is important here not to be misunderstood. Certainly, most people do not distort reality to a substantial degree and, of course, there are some people who see themselves in a highly negative light, whereas most hold slightly positive self-perceptions. There are, of course, thankfully, only a few egomaniacs, but such cases never show up in our clinics since they seem to live quite successfully. Nevertheless, these common illusions contribute to our misinterpretation and misreading of the world we inhabit, and provide an attitude and mind-set as well as expectations that significantly influence our perceptions, thoughts, and beliefs. They create, quite literally, the world we live in day after day and night after night. It is these illusionary beliefs that make up our private world and determine our unique individual personalities. Some of the more culturally determined and common illusionary beliefs are, for example, the belief in a just world; the belief in a personal and benevolent deity; the belief in our own immortality; the belief in spirits, ghosts, and a spiritual world; the belief that our lives are significant; the belief in the desirability and efficacy of education; the belief in personal freedom, including free will; and the belief in the power of reason and the scientific method. For most of us these things are not considered *beliefs* at all—they are givens, fundamental tenets no one would dare question—especially the holder of such beliefs.

Entertaining certain kinds of illusory beliefs can, of course, be both dangerous and self-destructive. Steven Starker, in 1986, called attention to a particular kind of mindset with its accompanying group of beliefs that can be very destructive indeed. This mindset Starker calls "parathink," or the paranoia of everyday life. Although we usually tend to think of paranoia in terms of mental illness, and disturbed patients proclaiming they are Christ, the Devil, or Superman, this limited view blinds us to the fact that in many of our own quite normal thoughts, actions, feelings, and fantasies we engage in paranoid-like behavior ourselves. In fact, it happens so often that we begin to take it for granted. It shows up most often in a number of common everyday situations such as power struggles at work with our supervisors and co-workers; whenever we get involved in social, political, or religious issues; whenever we have problems with our parents or our children; routinely when we find ourselves as members of any closely knit group, club, or organization; as a result of any marital or romantic problems; at any attempt we make to establish new interpersonal relationships; whenever we have feelings of envy or jealousy; and in any situation where racial or sexual prejudice and stereotyping is possible. Each of these common experiences can elicit covert paranoid thought, or what Starker calls "parathink," and very few of us are able to resist its appeal. In no way, however, does this indicate or suggest that we are, or about to become, mentally ill. Although normal and healthy, our thinking can, temporarily, take on many of the characteristics of true paranoia. When this happens, certain distortions, deletions, and oversimplifications appear among our perceptions and ideas. Moreover, important errors of judgment are likely to occur. Then defensive and aggressive behaviors can be set in motion which, in the long run, are unnecessary, self-defeating, and otherwise harmful. Even if you do not become a practitioner of parathink, you are quite likely to find yourself on the receiving end of parathought on the part of your boss, spouse, or friend.

Normal people who engage in parathink usually have a set of assumptions and principles that they follow, and by holding to these beliefs they engage in behavior which is not in their best interests. The ten principles or assumptions most often defining parathink are:

1. The world is a dangerous place.
2. People cannot be trusted.
3. It is somebody else's fault.
4. The worst interpretation of any event is the correct one.
5. All those in authority are villains.
6. Simple explanations are the best ones.
7. Uncertainty is intolerable.
8. Some information is best ignored.
9. Others are inferior—but they are still dangerous.
10. Self-protection should always receive top priority.

Many people would argue that a few of these assumptions are "truths," not assumptions! The world *is* a dangerous place! Simple explanations *are* often the best ones. Uncertainty *is* painful. The important issue here is not whether or not any of the above assumptions can be defended as justifiable, but whether or not these assumptions can sneak up on us while we are unaware of them and influence our reactions and behavior. Since unconscious assumptions and expectations are known to have power over our perceptions, feelings, and behaviors, the principles of paranoid thought can be very powerful and very dangerous.

The motives underlying parathink are also quite ordinary, and its primary goal is security, supported by the desire for certainty, a need for power, and a desire to feel important. It is these motives that drive certain types of people to behave in certain ways, and to show personality traits representing a relatively stable style of living and thinking that we would label paranoid. Although they are able to remain outside of hospitals and clinics, and to hold jobs and support families, they nevertheless have paranoid attitudes and exhibit the following traits that define the paranoid personality. First of all, they are highly suspicious, never trustful, and are always in a guarded or defensive position. Second, they are never responsible for their own problems, always finding someone else to blame, and they never admit their own failings. Third, they have feelings of grandiosity, and they always insist on their superiority and rightness. Fourth, they are extremely rigid and unwilling to change their position, behavior, attitudes, or points of view. Fifth, they quickly and easily misinterpret, distort, or reinterpret all events so that they will corroborate their existing beliefs. Sixth, they maintain an attitude of aloofness and avoid all close interpersonal relationships, and show little or no interest in social activities. Finally, they are aggressive and pugnacious, concerned about their rights and beliefs, often taking legal actions against others, and also, on occasions, becoming physically violent.

Starker points out that a few paranoid personalities can be found in even the smallest community. These are the people who are always calling the police to complain about their noisy neighbors, kids playing on their property, or the suspicious actions of their neighbors. They will show up at every town meeting or gathering to question and challenge every proposal for change or improvement, or to express their outrage at some fancied injustice. They also show up in courtrooms, or at the county courthouse, complaining about some new inequity or appealing some one or more prior legal decisions. As Starker notes, "They are also the ones most often bringing charges of libel and slander at the least provocation and experience any criticism or disagreement as a personal attack." (p. 27)

Starker also states that it has been made uncomfortably clear to him through years of observation and research that examples of paranoid thinking are frequent, ranging in degree from minor paranoid-like behaviors and fantasies up through deranged paranoid psychoses. The paranoid adaptation style can also be found at all levels of personality development, and at all degrees of pathology from the minimally neurotic to the profoundly psychotic. Given adverse circumstances—such as overwork, physical illness, humiliation, rejection, and any other serious threat to our self-esteem—Starker observes, any normal person can change his attitude from that of an open, tolerant, and optimistic person, to that of a parathinking one who now sees the world as unjust, evil, and hostile. While brief flashes or intervals of paranoid fantasies are not likely to do much harm, there is the ever present-danger that such temporary ways of thinking, feeling, and acting could become habitual. The fact that they sometimes do means that we should be more vigilant than we usually are. We have to remember that parathought is illusory; it is neither reality nor the truth. It is another form of, and another example of, a systematized and dangerous illusionary belief.

The critical question here, perhaps, is *truth* and this, of course, varies from group to group, and the same belief can be seen as a delusion or the gospel-truth depending on the social situation of the believer. If the believers think the same way that others in their group think, then they are in no way aberrant or deluded as far as their group is concerned. Their subjective reality is accepted as the consensus reality. This subjective reality in other groups could be regarded as totally delusional, and the work of a deranged mind. For many people in our society who, to all appearances, are in no way delusional in that they can carry on ordinary *everyday* activities at work and play in socially accepted ways, still harbor beliefs that most of us—the majority of upper middle class—would consider, if not wholly delusional, certainly extremely odd or bizarre.

Some while ago the sociologist Sorokin (1957) argued that there was a basic split in Western epistemology, two separate mentalities that he tagged the Sensate and the Ideational. In his words:

At one extreme is a mentality for which reality is that which can be perceived by the organs of sense; it does not see anything beyond the sensate being of the milieu. . . . Those who possess this sort of mentality try to adapt themselves to those conditions which appear to the sense organs. . . . On the other extreme are persons who perceive and apprehend the same sensate phenomena in a very different way. For them they are mere appearance, a dream, or an illusion. True reality is not to be found here; it is something beyond, . . . different from this material and sensate veil which conceals it. . . . Whether [true reality] be styled God, Nirvana, Brahma, Om, Self, Tao, Eternal Spirit, *l'elan vital,* Unnamed, the City of God, Ultimate Reality, *Ding für und an sich,* or whatnot, is of little importance. What is important is that . . . true reality is usually considered supersensate, immaterial, spiritual.

(Sorokin 1957, pp. 25–26)

According to the sociologist Heise (1988), in our contemporary civilization the sensate subculture is, of course, dominant since science and materialism and their associated beliefs of individualism, progress, and utilitarianism are ascendant. The ideational elements of our civilization play a secondary role, even though large numbers of people are concerned with occult and supernatural phenomena. According to a 1978 Gallup Poll, 57 percent of the American public believe in UFOs (which is really saying they believe in extraterrestrial spaceships and aliens), while 54 percent believe in the existence of angels, 51 percent believe in ESP, 39 percent believe in devils, 29 percent believe in astrology, and 10 percent or more believe in ghosts and witches. As Heise shows, the ideational culture also has organized such concepts into a system of knowledge that often requires years to construct. It embraces the sacred writings of the Eastern religions, theosophy, Rosicrucianism, various metaphysical systems, ascended masters, psychic research, the Cabala, spiritualism, ESP, Edgar Cayce, psychic powers, lost continents, reincarnation, the Akashic Record, UFOs and extraterrestrials, the *I Ching,* Tarot cards, out-of-body experiences, etc. Believers safeguard the integrity of their knowledge by reinforcing their beliefs through organizing both large and small social groups; reading and discussing specialized books, journals, and newsletters; and carrying out organized attacks on unbelievers. Added to this is the fact that most members of such groups also strive to learn and grow spiritually and intellectually, and every new belief, no matter how bizarre, is taken as a sign of progress.

Determining whether a particular belief is delusional or not is not (to the ideationalists at least) as easy as it might, at first, appear. The very idea of "reality testing," Heise notes, presumes a sensate epistemology, and those with an ideational philosophy can always claim that an empirical test constitutes no proof at all. Moreover, all of our so-called objective tests are made selectively for their *confirmatory* value, not in order to disconfirm. Though we like to think of our scientific observations as predetermined and unbiased, Heise argues, they are, in fact, selected and interpreted within the very framework they are supposed to test. Possibly many delusions *are* supported by reality tests, although not the ones *we* think should apply. Heise uses the example of the Aztecs to show how this can occur. Because of the Aztecs' belief that human blood was food for the sun and the only thing that keeps the world going, as many as 20,000 human beings were sacrificed each year. By our standards of knowledge, this belief was outrageous, yet to the Aztecs it was confirmed by reality testing every day. Hearts were torn out on such and such a day and the next day the sun rose again. While we can say that they should have stopped killing and seen the sun rise anyway, we forget that this is our test, not *theirs.* Their fear was too great and their belief too strong for them to take such a risk.

Another important point in Heise's argument is that facts do not absolutely credit one belief or another, because facts themselves derive their validity from a system of knowledge, and facts are social constructions as much as a representation of nature, even in science. Thus, according to Heise, the judgment of delusion is intrinsically social, involving a comparison of minds in which one is treated as authoritative and the other as deficient. Each party is certain about the validity of his or her mental productions and is sure that the other person is wrong and, once alternative realities are admitted, there is no absolute basis for settling the dispute.

People in the ideational subculture abhor the sensate beliefs. Only by "turning off our rational conscious minds can we open up the subconscious, intuitive, alogical mind and make contact with the higher spiritual realities." (Heise 1988, p. 267) Heise's position is that ideas of reference and external control, of mystical power, of persecution, asceticism, and possession are common themes in the ideational subculture as they are in delusions, but that psychiatrists' diagnoses of delusion are not based upon favoring one system or knowledge over another. Eschewing truth and falsity as criteria— since truth and falsity cannot be determined without taking an epistemological stand—Heise argues that *social currency* alone is the only criterion of thought disorders, and the only basis for a psychiatric judgment that someone is deluded. Heise gives three examples of what he argues are nondelusional ways of thinking.

(1) A woman sits alone in her room writing messages from outer space all day, and the messages say she alone is to be saved in a coming world cataclysm.

According to Heise, she is not a candidate for psychiatric concern because (a) she bases her beliefs on an *accepted body of knowledge* (what this is Heise doesn't say. The UFO literature perhaps? Accepted by whom?) and (b) she is sharing her revelations and her fate with others. The social activity of creating a cult absolves her, according to Heise, from psychiatric concern.

(2) Clovis, a warlock, and a member of a witches' coven denounced a female novice. According to Clovis, he had learned "psychically" that he and the novice had been in a group together in a previous lifetime in the Middle Ages and that she had betrayed the group. Clovis also claimed the novice was from another planet. The high priestess and others considered the charges valid and the novice had little defense.

Clovis's story, according to Heise, is nondelusional since it was (a) believable to all the witches in the coven, (b) it was relevant to the group, and (c) it had important implications for others.

(3) A man is convinced that his continued existence depends on killing another person each day and tearing out their heart.

In psychiatric terms, he would, indeed, be considered dangerously deluded. These conclusions would not, however, be applied to the Aztecs. Instead, they have been regarded as "one of the most religious civilizations ever developed." (Fagan 1984) Because the Aztecs—all hundreds of thousands of them—had a shared and socially supported belief of a religious nature, it *must not* be considered delusional. Heise also argues that delusions are out of the psychiatric realm if the believer has a social commitment, and the belief has social significance. In other words, according to Heise, sociopolitical movements are of no direct concern to psychiatrists since one of the key missions of clinical psychologists and psychiatrists in contemporary society is to keep the population in a reasonable balance between social commitment and individuality. According to Heise:

> Psychiatrists are vested with authority to define the limits of individuality, the breakdown of social commitment, the development of excessive egocentricity. . . . A belief becomes a delusion when the psychiatrist judges that no one wants to hear it, and that the patient does not care to adjust the belief in the direction of social value. Factuality is not part of the diagnostic process; rather, a judgment of falsity is part of the control process—removing authenticity from the patient's reality.
>
> (p. 270)

Heise goes on to argue that delusions are mental constructions so egocentric that they have no social currency. The judgment of delusion occurs, he maintains, when someone is creating a reality no one else wants to share, and the believer is not responding to this social isolation. Ergo, if, however, others can be persuaded or coerced into sharing the belief, then it is no longer a delusion. In Heise's words:

Indeed, the objectivity of diagnosing the state associated with delusion probably would improve if the concern for factuality of belief were discarded and the focus on sociality sharpened. This approach would make extra interview information even more important than it is now—not to check the factuality of a client's beliefs but to check explicitly for a social circle that supports the believer's thinking.

(p. 270–271)

In other words, if a psychiatrist engages in a conversation with the Reverend Jim Jones, and Jones tells him the FBI is plotting against his church and is controlling the minds of his followers with laser beams, he should not call the FBI. Instead, he should look to see if Jones has a group of followers who also believe this. If such a group is found, then—bingo!—Jones is not delusional!

As clever as Heise's arguments are, and putting all casuistic reasoning aside, there is something gut-wrenchingly wrong with his logic and thinking. First of all, delusions are universally defined as *false* beliefs, and we cannot so cavalierly discard the issue of truth or falsity. Second, societies also (and especially small societies such as covens, satanic and other cults, etc.) are and can become and have in the past become delusional (i.e., embraced false beliefs wholesale), deranged, and sick. A number of psychiatrists, Erich Fromm in particular, have written at length about "sick" societies and have never questioned the concept of delusional or sick societies. As for psychiatrists being the final arbiters of what is or is not a delusion, and as for them bearing sole responsibility for social control—psychiatrists do not have (nor do they desire) either the prestige or the power to carry out such a role. Finally, defining delusions numerically, i.e., in terms of a single, as opposed to multiple, believers may make sociological sense, but it ignores the psychological actuality that in countless "social" situations it is the heretic—the lone individual—whose perceptions and beliefs are correct and the masses' perceptions and beliefs that are wrong, i.e., deluded.

Before the fifteenth century, most of the world believed the Earth was flat, and before Copernicus, "society" believed the Earth was the center of the universe. These are, indeed, delusions or false beliefs and they have had devastating social and intellectual consequences. Delusional beliefs—beliefs in witches, devils, demons, ghosts, and particularly religious beliefs—have plagued mankind since the beginning of time. If we look at the sensate-ideational split in the light of the history of human welfare and the future well being of the human race, there is little in the way of choice. Beyond question the ideational mind-set has caused more human horror and human misery in the name of religion than any other force in history. There is no ferocity or mania that comes close to matching that of religious zealots and sanctimonious ideologues acting in the name of their god or gods. Rape, wholesale murder and slaughter, massive torture of children and the aged, unspeakable acts of unimaginable horror have all been carried out in the name of delusionary religious beliefs. Endless wars have been and continue to be waged over which delusionary belief system is true and which is false and both are justified by the ideational mentality.

A catalog of the horrors perpetrated by individuals with such mindsets has been recently compiled by James A. Haught (*Holy Horrors,* 1990). Delusions have been, are, and can be dangerous, very dangerous, not only to the individuals who hold them, but to others who unwillingly become victims of those holding these bizarre and dangerous convictions. It is cold comfort, indeed, for the victims of the Aztec idiocies or the Nazi gas chambers to be told, "Don't worry, neither the Aztecs nor the Nazis were delusional." Clearly, delusional societies and groups led by fanatical overzealous delusionaries—small, medium, and large—are much more dangerous to the civilized world at large and to the future of humankind than the lonely isolated individual. To argue that one man's delusion is another man's truth is to argue that we either lack or eschew the power to discriminate, that there is no right or wrong, and that there is no way of distinguishing truth from fiction. Fortunately, such arguments are mostly academic and lack consensual validity. Most of us know right from wrong and can get through the day, week, month, year, and even decade without confusing the two. Most of us, while we may well harbor an illusion or two, engage in parathought at times, and on certain rare occasions even have a hallucination or two, but for 99 percent of the time or more we are able to tell the difference between reality and dreams, and fact and fiction.

Most of us know that we must obey the physical laws of the universe or suffer the consequences. We are not like the Russian psychic who, after stopping horses, bicycles, and cars, held the deluded (and unfortunately fatal) belief that he could stop a train. Most of us have moral and humane standards and principles that we live by and we do, for the most part, respect and honor the rights of others. We acknowledge and respect the power of science and scientific laws, and we do not allow our religious beliefs—if we have any—to dominate and control our behavior, or overrule our common sense. We are, for the most part, reality-oriented, and we know the difference between sane and insane thinking, and rational and irrational behavior. Although we may not be as intellectually astute and sophisticated as logicians and academic specialists, we are not fools either. Fortunately, education—primary, secondary, and higher—is not a total failure. Though we may carry and share many illusions of one sort or another, we still have only a few (and rarely so) delusions and hallucinations. We are, most of us that is, of the sensate mind-set, and look askance at those who find reality in some other world rather than this one that all of us—both ideational and sensate—inhabit and share. Is this a sensate bias? Yes, indeed, and thankfully so, since it leads to survival and the enhancement of human welfare. While it can be maintained that the ideational does also and emphasizes the "higher" aspects of human existence and leads humanity to higher and more exalted levels, the historical record tells us another, quite different story.

Of most importance is the fact that it is only in the ideational world that all beliefs are of equal validity. The only way the truth or falsity of an ideational belief can be determined is by entering the sensate world and using the tools and operations of science. This fact and the difference between the two mentalities is profound and of the utmost significance: it is the difference between science and superstition. Heise's arguments regarding the social relativity of what is truth and what is falsity hold water only so long as we stay ideational, e.g., "My God is more powerful than your God!" According to every rooster on Earth, the sun comes up every morning because he crows. To the Aztecs, it was because they ripped out a few human hearts the previous day. The truth or falsity of both claims can only be determined by empirical scientific tests in the sensate world. That's the beauty of science, and the fatal flaw in both superstition and Heise's arguments. The failure of both the roosters and the Aztecs to make an empirical test perpetuates the error and the stupidity of the ideational. Quite simply, the only way any ideational claim can be confirmed or denied is through sensate tests. Of course, if your aim is to protect and safeguard your delusion, the last thing on Earth you would want to do would be to expose its fragile bones to something as harsh, cruel, and uncompromising as a scientific test.

We discussed earlier the fact that many people have a strong need for fantasy and prefer magic, mystery, and the marvelous to the mundane or factual truth. Science is never, and never was, as much fun and as easy—or as intriguing—as the paranormal. Roszak (1981), some years ago, in an insightful article dealing with this issue argued persuasively that there is a deep-seated, perhaps universal need for transcendent experiences. In his words:

> Over the past several years, in the opportunities I have had to travel and speak, I have become acutely aware of this restless spiritual need in the audiences I meet. They wonder: Have I a vision, an epiphany, an uncanny tale to relate? A moment of illumination or unearthly dread, a close encounter with arcane powers . . . ? It is a need, I hasten to add, which I have never tried or been able to gratify. This hunger for wonders powerfully en-

gages my sympathetic concern, but utterly outruns my knowledge and skill. I have, however, seen it fasten upon others about me in ways that often leave me sad or fearful, because the appetite can be so indiscriminately eager, so mindlessly willing to be fed on banalities and poor improvisations on the extraordinary. . . . Beyond such formal, religious affiliations (evangelical and charismatic forms of Christianity), the hunger for wonders expresses itself in countless forms of pop psychiatry and lumpen occultism which thinly disguise the same impetuous quest for personal salvation. The most widely read newspapers in the United States—weekly gossip and scandal sheets like *The National Enquirer*—carry steady coverage of UFO cults and ESP, spiritualism, reincarnation, and faith cures! Esoteric forms of Oriental meditation have been opened to the public by university extensions and the YMCA; they have even been organized into successful franchise businesses that promise tranquility and enlightenment to anyone who can spare twenty minutes a day. At the other extreme from transcendental calm, there is the undiminished popular fascination with Gothic horror, which makes Satanism, demonic possession, supernatural thrills and chills one of the film industry's most reliable attractions.

(pp. 55-56)

Roszak also argues that while the bizarre has always appealed to the masses, only recently have the academic and professional worlds been touched by the same metaphysical fever. He gives a number of examples of professional people "deliberately and unabashedly dabbling in a sort of higher gullibility, an assertive readiness to give all things astonishing, mind-boggling, and outrageous the chance to prove themselves true. . . or true enough." One of his friends, a prominent psychotherapist, told him that people sleep and die only because they have been mistakenly "programmed" to believe they have to. The therapist also had a technique for therapeutically undoing the erroneous programming. A neurophysiologist told him that everyone could learn to exert mental control over pain, infection, and aging. A psychologist had himself operated on by Philippine psychic surgeons. Another psychologist told him about travelling out-of-his-body. A physicist friend believes in "imaginary energy" telepathic communication and precognition. Other academic friends were deeply involved with Edgar Cayce's trance explorations of past and future which they accept as valid. A historian friend believes that we can, by altering consciousness, plug ourselves into the power points of the Earth's etheric field, and by so doing move matter and control evolution. An engineer friend told Roszak that it was possible to influence the Earth's geomantic centers and telluric currents by mental manipulations. This is the technology, the engineer believes, that built Stonehenge and the pyramids. Roszak calls those notions *scientific superstitions,* i.e., the loose use of scientific or quasi-scientific ideas to appease an essentially religious appetite. The scientized mystics argue that the revolution in modern physics has abolished the objective reality of nature and sanctioned all forms of paranormal and mystical experience. The need for the miraculous is evident even among the professionals.

The crux of Roszak's argument, however, is that despite the three-century effort on the part of Western society to win the world over to "an exclusively science-based reality principle," the campaign is failing and even losing ground in the urban-industrial heartland. In his words, "In the deep allegiance of people, in the secret crises of decision and commitment, the scientific world view simply has not taken, though it continues to dominate our economic and political life." (p. 57) As for the majority of the people in our society, they are still "deeply entangled with piety, mystery, miracle, the search for personal salvation—as much today as were the pious many when the Cartesian chasm between mind and matter was first opened by the scientific revolution."

Roszak scolds the secular humanist establishment for ignoring humanity's spiritual and transcendent needs, for debunking their superstitions, and poking fun at their gullibility and naiveté. This behavior, Roszak says, "is like scolding starving people for eating out of garbage cans, while providing them with no more wholesome food. Of course, they will finally refuse to listen and become more rebellious." Roszak here has, indeed, touched a sensitive nerve. The scientific humanists, like their clerical counterparts, have, indeed, failed to enlighten, to inspire, and to meet these palpable human needs with a fully and deeply satisfying philosophical vision. These needs are urgent and must be met if either the clerics or the humanists ever expect to win the war for the mind and spirit of modern man.

8

No, Virginia, Those Lights
in the Sky Aren't Spaceships!

We might learn a whole lot more about the whys and wherefores of UFOs
if we first looked to inner space instead of outer space.

   —Gene Steinberg, "Time To Come Clean," *Caveat Emptor*

UFOlogy has always been ruled by the politics of unreason with misguided
egos serving as a substitute for intellect and misinterpretation standing in
for methodology. . . . If you want to learn all about UFOlogy you should
read any good study of religious fanaticism. . . . Such seemingly psychotic
behavior is, unfortunately, rather common among UFO hobbyists, many
of whom are pathological liars (thus their intense preoccupation with lying
among witnesses and their paranoid fears), and a psychological study of their
emotional problems would be a logical first step to understanding the whole
UFO field.

   —John A. Keel, "The Sorry State of UFO Research," *Caveat Emptor*

Of all the impossible things people believe in, perhaps the most absurd
is the widespread belief that the planet earth for the last forty-three years
has been invaded by extraterrestrials in saucer-shaped spaceships, and that
some of these alien visitors have recently been abducting earthlings, taking
them aboard their craft, examining them, studying them, and experimenting upon them in order to carry out some sort of intergalactic breeding
experiment. Moreover, the worst part of it is we earthlings are perfectly
helpless in the face of this invasion and there is nothing we have done
or can do to prevent it.

Before you become too alarmed, however, it is important to realize that in spite of the millions of words that have been published—hundreds of books, thousands more articles about UFOs—since Kenneth Arnold first spotted nine silver discs floating through the air near Mt. Rainier in Washington State in 1947, there is not now, nor has there ever been, any physical, i.e., solid material evidence of any shape, form, or fashion to prove that such extraterrestrial vehicles have ever existed or currently exist. Perhaps the most damning evidence of all is the fact that if such extraterrestrial vehicles perform in the manner described, they violate all the laws of physics as we know them (Markowitz 1967). Simply put, the reported UFOs cannot be under extraterrestrial control if the laws of physics are valid. There is, to put it bluntly, no evidence that any aliens of any sort have invaded our skies, landed on earth, or have established any kind of contact with *homo sapiens*. Photographs, drawings, eyewitness testimony, rings on the bare ground or in the grass, and scratches and scars on the human body—while of some interest—are each and every one subject to possible error, forgery, and distortion. Every one of such manifestations can be the result of human manipulation and intervention rather than being due exclusively to extraterrestrial action. *We simply do not have the reliable or valid—much less irrefutable—evidence necessary for scientific convictions or conclusions.*

Despite the hundreds of claims of alien contact and abduction, the thousands of unknown and unidentified things seen in our skies, to date no one on earth has either in hand or on hand any material artifact that unquestionably proves alien spaceships exist, or that alien forms of life—intelligent or otherwise—exist, or that any human beings (living or dead) have ever been aboard an alien spaceship. Until such completely irrefutable hard evidence is on hand, and until such evidence has been publicly presented and authenticated by reputable scientists, skeptics will remain unconvinced of any and all reports of aliens, alien spaceships, and alien abductions. But we are getting ahead of ourselves. What we should do first is present the reason why so many skeptics like Philip Klass, Robert Shaeffer, Hilary Evans, and others do not believe that the unidentified flying objects that have been reported on hundreds of occasions are spaceships from either outer space or some other dimension. Next, we need to look at the psychology of those people who do believe in spaceships powered by aliens and, specifically, those few individuals who also believe they have been abducted by aliens. Finally, we will look at the motives of those people who have championed the believers and the abductees, and who have aided and abetted the construction of a new "alien mythology."

The Reason for Skepticism

Reports of seeing strange things up in the sky are far from new. One night in April 1897, two farmers in Springfield, Illinois, encountered an airship, its pilot, and passengers. The pilot, a bearded man, stopped to ask directions. At the time no such airships existed. Their story appeared in the local newspapers, and it soon spread across the nation. Their story was by no means novel. From November 1896 until the middle of 1897, thousands of people across the United States reported seeing airships or the lights of airships in the sky. When Thomas Edison was consulted about the matter he predicted such things would soon come to pass, but that it was absolutely absurd to imagine someone could construct a successful airship and keep the matter secret. According to Nigel Watson, when the first few stories were collected from dusty old newspaper files it seemed clear that the airship reports:

> . . . represented sightings of a phenomenon—that with chameleon-like finesse adopted itself to the assumption of the people at the time. Thus, the mysterious force that made people see the airships was considered to be the same one that makes us see flying saucers today. However, increasing research has shown that what were at first thought to be the most convincing cases were nothing more than journalists' hoaxes designed to attract publicity and increase newspaper sales.
>
> (p. 50, 1989)

It is also of interest to note that America was not alone in "airship" sightings. Both England and the rest of Europe had similar experiences in 1909 and 1913. The fact that such sightings are common clearly indicates that we have to take all such sightings and all such reports with a grain of salt. Without exception, the more careful and intensive the investigation one makes into UFO reports and UFO encounters, the greater is the probability that we will discover human error in one form or another. We will find in all of these claims contradictions and absurdities, faulty investigative techniques, improbabilities and exaggerations, as well as hoaxes and outright lies. Hilary Evans recently stated the case for UFO skepticism as well as anyone. He argues that it is not enough for the skeptic merely to show the shortcomings of a UFO explanation; he should also be able to offer a better one. Using the example of an elderly woman and her daughter who saw a large, bright, yellow object in the sky that changed shape periodically and also, at times, emitted smoke, British UFO investigators were able to establish conclusively that the UFO was merely the moon obscured occasionally by clouds. Although we can explain the stimulus (the moon), this by no means explains the two witnesses' responses. Clearly there were psychological factors involved which predisposed the two women to turn a natural event into something unnatural. A truly skeptical approach, according to Evans, by establishing the fantastic nature of the event reveals what was *really* going on, i.e., some sort of psychological event in the minds of the two observers, and if we are to fully understand the event, then we need to look into the psychological makeup of the two observers as well. The same thing, of course, is true of the thousands of other cases involving misinterpretation. Evans suggests that since so many cases have shown a psychosocial rather than a material and physical basis, is it not possible that this is true in *every* case? Belief in UFOs is in many ways similar to a belief in witches. In the case of witches, the Church created a monstrous but plausible fantasy, which, because its raw materials were popular beliefs cunningly distorted, was accepted by the common people who responded to the fantasy in accordance with their conscious beliefs and their subconscious motivations. Could something of the same sort be happening in the case of UFOs?

As the reader has seen throughout this book, and as Evans also maintains: *there are scarcely any limits to the ability of the human mind to delude itself.* This is certainly the case in the matter of UFOs, aliens, and so-called alien abductors.

Let us look at a few recent examples of this fact:

On January 20, 1988, Faye Knowles, forty-eight, and her three sons were driving along a deserted highway in the southern Australian desert when they noticed a strange light in the sky. This brilliant light quickly turned into an egg-shaped object that terrorized the family for an hour and a half. It descended on their car, lifted it into the air, and then dropped it onto the road. The family dived into some roadside bushes and hid until the UFO departed. After changing a tire, they drove to the next town and reported the encounter to the police.

The story attracted a great deal of attention worldwide, and, for a time, was hailed as a major bit of evidence for UFO believers. However, when Keith Basterfield, a field investigator for UFO Research, Australia, was able to interrogate the Knowles family along with other investigators, the true story came to light.

Twenty-one-year-old Sean Knowles had been driving when a bright light approached the car. The family heard a thump on the roof and thought this light had landed there. No one remembered looking up and seeing anything on the car's roof nor did anyone remember looking out the window and seeing the road while the car was supposedly in the air. They did note that the luggage that had been strapped to the roof was gone. When the car was examined, it was concluded that the marks on the roof of the car were old and due to normal wear and tear. Basterfield believes the Knowleses told what they thought was the truth, but that they were badly misled. What really happened, Basterfield learned, was that the family had been driving nonstop for many hours and, shortly after seeing the light, a blowout occurred while Sean was driving. The family next heard a thump as the luggage jolted loose. Then, the right rear end of the car struck the ground and Sean hit the brakes hard. As he tried to pull the car off the road, it began to vibrate and the dogs started barking. The Knowleses rolled down their windows, and then they smelled the smoke from the strained front brakes. All these things made the family dive into the bushes and swear later they were attacked by a UFO. While Basterfield admits he has no explanation for the light, it was very clear that nothing attacked the Knowles car.

Basterfield also reported on a 1972 case investigated by Gary Little and Bill Stapleton of Melbourne, Australia. In early 1972 Maureen Puddy reported observing a disc-shaped object in the sky. Later she reported that her car stopped by itself as the same object hovered overhead. Several months later she reported that she was abducted by a UFO and taken into a room where she saw an alien entity. This latter event occurred, however, while two other persons were physically present with Mrs. Puddy. They reported that nothing happened except that Mrs. Puddy lapsed into unconsciousness. On a later occasion Mrs. Puddy claimed that the entity again appeared to her when she was driving her car down the highway. This is typical of many "mental abduction" cases, and has led many researchers to interpret all so-called alien abductions as merely psychological aberrations due to altered states of consciousness, i.e., hallucinations, delusions, or hypnopompic or hypnogogic dreams.

In 1949, Mrs. Marian Keech, a Chicago housewife, began to receive messages from extraterrestrials warning her that the destruction of the world was about to occur. Those who believed in extraterrestrials and UFOs, she added, would be saved. Mrs. Keech was able to persuade a number of other people, including a physician, Dr. Thomas Armstrong, of the validity of her vision. The two began to persuade others of the coming catastrophe and they soon had a sizeable following. The believers gave up their jobs, left their homes, sold their property, and joined Mrs. Keech to wait hopefully for the day of deliberation. Messages were received daily from beyond, and during the last few days before the predicted end, the messages became more and more bizarre and contradictory. When the flying saucers failed to arrive, the believers clung together hopefully before they gradually dispersed.

Incognito among the believers were sociologists who took the opportunity to study the cult from within. Their report on the life and death of such a cult and its believers was published as *When Prophecy Fails* by Festinger, Riecken, and Schacter (1956). The book shows clearly how people, driven by hope and fear, can easily mistake illusion for reality.

A similar case involved a man named Gordon who was told by a group of extraterrestrials to construct a giant flying saucer named "The Bluebird" which would be used to take them to a paradise in the stars. After seven years of effort, Gordon's Institute for Cosmic Research came apart at the seams.

Then in California in 1975 an organization known as HIM, or Human Individual Metamorphosis, was funded by a psychiatric nurse and one of her patients. Known as Bo and Peep by their followers, this incredible duo convinced a large number of believers that they should take up an ascetic, less earthly lifestyle and, by simplifying their lives, they would soon be ready to be taken to a better world by a fleet of UFOs. No one went anywhere except Bo and Peep, who made a great deal of money before flying the coop!

More recently an American evangelist, Elizabeth Clare Prophet, leader of the Church Universal and Triumphant, has been able to convince well over 200 of her followers that earthquakes, economic collapse, and nuclear war is coming soon, and that if they expect to be spared and taken up to heaven by a fleet of UFOs, they should get rid of all of their earthly possessions and move to Montana. According to Mrs. Prophet, Montana "is an ideal place to be because scripture says head for the mountains." As a result of this delusion, a large number of otherwise sensible middle-class citizens have sold their homes and businesses and have bought several acres of sagebrush and a quonset hut in Paradise Valley, Montana. They have also surrounded their huts with concrete and sandbags, and have stocked up on canned goods, gold coins, arms and ammunition, and bottled water—all in preparation for this coming holocaust and their trip to the stars.

Bizarre as this group may appear, they were upstaged and outdone early in the summer of 1990 by six U.S. soldiers—five men and one woman —who deserted their intelligence posts in Augsburg, West Germany, caught a plane to the United States, rented a Volkswagen, and headed for Gulf Breeze, Florida, where they were stopped and arrested. Army Specialist Kenneth G. Beason, the leader of the group, told the arresting officers that he was on his way to meet Jesus, who was in a spaceship. Believing that Jesus is an astronaut, that the world is about to end, and that the Rapture—the second coming of Christ in which he returns to earth to take the believers with him while the rest of the earth is destroyed—was about to occur. The five soldiers sincerely believed Jesus was an alien and was coming for them—the chosen—in a spaceship. They were heading for their rendezvous with Christ at Gulf Breeze because Gulf Breeze, of course, was the site of the recent claims by Ed and Frances Walters of a number of UFO sightings reported in their book, *The Gulf Breeze Sightings: The Most Astounding UFO Sightings in U.S. History* (1990).

According to friends, Beason believed he and the others had been called to form a welcoming committee to greet an alien spacecraft the next month on the Gulf Breeze beach. He believed Jesus was coming in the spaceship. Beason was raised as a Primitive Baptist, a very fundamentalistic system, so fundamentalist, in fact, that Beason thought that if he drank just one beer God would strike him dead. Beason also wrote a book about spaceships and religion a few years earlier and, on occasion, he would put himself into a trance and be convinced that dead spirits were talking to him. When Beason left his post in Germany, he told friends he had been given a mission by God. The mission required that he assemble other believers and hide with them in an underground dwelling for a period of three years. During this waiting period, wars initiated by Lebanon would bring the world to an end. At the end of the three years some of earth's people would remain undecided about God, but Beason and the other group members would steer them to God and then they, too, would be taken up to heaven!

This peculiar admixture of fundamentalist religion and science-fiction is far from novel, however. In his fascinating book, *In Advance of the Landing: Folk Concepts of Outer Space* (1985), Douglas Curran reports, "Every single flying-saucer group I encountered in my travels incorporated Jesus Christ into the hierarchy of its belief system." The book itself is a marvelous collection of strange beliefs associated with the UFO mythology.

Regarding the so-called Gulf Breeze sightings, most unbiased observers are now convinced that the entire sorry episode is another sad example of human greed and credulity. Early in the pro-UFO movement, one of the leading national organizations—the National Investigative Committee on Aerial Phenomena (NICAP), headed by Major Donald Keyhoe—decided to exclude from serious consideration any and all persons claiming multiple sightings, trips aboard saucers, communication with aliens, and hoax photos. The Walters book, unfortunately, violates all of the foregoing precepts in that it contains multiple sightings, trips, communications with aliens, as well as hoax photographs. The Walters UFO was described by one wag as "looking like a Victorian street lamp or perhaps one of those gag UFOs that used to be advertised in the back of comic books." According to Philip Klass, who has studied the photographs extensively, they are nothing more than double exposure using an old Polaroid camera—which, in addition to having no shutter lock, produces no negatives—the first shot taken of a model against a black background, the second a horizon view from the

Walters's backyard. It is also interesting that all the photos are taken at dusk. This is necessary because too much light would drown out the initial image of the model. More amusing is the fact that the fakery is obvious in some of the photographs. In some, the model is stationary but the background moves. When viewers criticized some of the earlier photos by pointing out that the windows on the UFO were not evenly spaced and were out of line, later views of supposedly the same craft had these deficiencies corrected. Blue beams allegedly coming from the UFO are brighter at the ground, indicating they are probably nothing but spotlights. This criticism resulted in later photos reversing the effect—now they were brighter from above. All of these flaws—including a NASA scientist's conclusion that the photos were faked—should have prevented the book from being published. The story line of the book is also equally absurd. According to Ed Walters, the aliens speak Spanish, they warn him of their arrival, and they project pornographic images into his brain. They "beam" him (like in "Star Trek") into their ship and then "beam" him back to earth where his faithful wife hands him a camera so he can get another good shot. As one wag put it, "Can you imagine that? You've just been kidnapped by a UFO and miraculously returned to earth. You see your wife. Do you tell her to flee? No, you ask her for a camera."

The topper to the whole tawdry affair, however, came when the *Pensacola News Journal* on June 10, 1990, reported that a UFO model was discovered under insulation in the attic of Walters' former home. On June 19, Gulf Breeze attorney Tom Smith, under oath, held a news conference in Pensacola to disclose that his son had been told by Ed Walters more than two years ago of his intention to profit from a UFO hoax. According to Smith, "We don't know what anyone else has seen, but we do know that what Ed disclosed early on was a fabrication." Walters refused to take a lie detector test, but he did sign a sworn statement denying any knowledge of the model UFO. Walters also pointed out that the model does not exactly match the object in his photos. Willy Smith, however, previously reported that at least two models were used by Walters, since after Smith published his early findings of asymmetries in the UFO's vertical axis and windows, Ed's later photographs show a more symmetrical object. Therefore, it probably *is* true that this recently discovered model is not the "Gulf Breeze UFO" that shows up in Ed Walters's book.

Additional Reasons for Skepticism

When we sift through all of the claims of UFO sightings and alien contact, we notice that most occurrences are solely visual, usually at a considerable distance, and under conditions that amplify uncertainty and ambiguity, such as waking up in the middle of the night, or driving alone on lonely highways in remote unsettled areas. Moreover, as we have just seen, many witnesses claim not only physical contact, but metaphysical contact as well. They are in contact with the aliens via telepathy, or on a spiritual plane. These emotional encounters are, however, no guarantee that the UFO exists. On numerous occasions such encounters have been claimed even when the UFO has been identified as a natural or a man-made object —an IFO. For these reasons we are hardly to be criticized for being very skeptical about eyewitness testimony—which is notoriously unreliable. As Spencer and Evans note, the way we evaluate a witness's claims may well depend on what it is he is claiming. If it is a distant light, then we try to determine just how odd its behavior was and whether it can be accounted for by a natural phenomena such as a star, planet, satellite, balloon, or aircraft. If the description is of an ambiguous object, it is not its existence we question so much as the interpretation the witness puts on the sighting. At this point, there is no need to question the witness's integrity or credibility since misperceptions and misinterpretations are fairly common. If a balloon is mistaken for an interstellar spaceship, this is an error anyone could make, and it does not imply either a delusion or a hallucination. If the witness, however, claims he was abducted and then spent an hour aboard an alien spaceship, the reality of this claim is almost impossible to determine. In Spencer and Evans' words:

> The fact that the witness can produce no supporting physical evidence, such as a souvenir of his encounter, or an unambiguous photo or physical tract, must make his story less probable: as does the fact that there is never any convincing supporting testimony from other, independent observers. But unless we can prove beyond doubt that his experience never occurred, there is no way we can prove it was nothing but illusion or fantasy.
>
> At the same time, we all know how many and how varied are the circumstances under which someone may see something that "isn't there." Sickness, or drugs, fatigue or lack of sleep, sensory deprivation or sensory overload, the wrong diet or not enough food, stress of many kinds—these and many other factors can lead to a condition in which a person will have experiences that, which they may be real enough to him, have no reality outside his own mind.
>
> Evaluating a contact claim, then, involves a process of escalating sophistication in the questions we ask, to match the escalating strangeness of the claims. It is not enough that we be familiar with the many natural phenomena and man-made artifacts that can cause misperceptions: we must also be alert to the infinite complexity of the human mind.
>
> (Spencer and Evans 1989, p. 81)

The Legend of the Crashed Saucers

According to Andy Roberts (1989), the very idea of *crashed UFOs* and their retrieval reads like science fiction. It should because it.is. Like UFOs themselves, the story of crashed airships is by no means new. An account of a downed UFO was reported in 1884. According to the published story, four Nebraska cowboys witnessed the crash of a large cylindrical object that destroyed everything except some red hot glowing shards of metal and a few cog wheels. On April 17, 1897, in Aurora, Texas, an airship passed over the town one evening, lost altitude, and crashed into a windmill, scattering its wreckage over a wide area. The citizens of Aurora reported the airship was built of an unknown metal resembling aluminum or silver. Undecipherable hieroglyphics were also found on scraps of paper in the wreckage. But most astounding was the fact that a pilot was found in the wreckage, and according to an Army officer, the pilot was an extraterrestrial—a Martian.

Shortly after these reports, both stories were proved to have been hoaxes conjured up—like the Amityville Horror hoax—by bored journalists. There is every reason to believe that the two most widely known modern crash/retrieval stories—The Roswell Incident and The Aztec Case—also fall into the same category. The general details are certainly well known due primarily to the book *The Roswell Incident,* by Charles Berlitz and William Moore (1980), and numerous magazine and journal articles. Though no physical evidence of any kind was produced, its proponents have argued that a flying saucer crashed, and both the saucer and its occupants were captured and hidden away by the Air Force and other governmental authorities. As the gist of the story goes, the remains of the saucer were discovered by a local ranch manager, Mac Brazel, and his son and daughter, who did not report it to the Roswell sheriff until several days later, when Brazel went into Roswell for supplies. The sheriff, in turn, reported it to officers at the Roswell Air Force Base. RAFB sent two intelligence officers to investigate and once they gathered up the wreckage it was flown to Wright Field, in Ohio. The official Air Force report was that the debris recovered was that of a crashed weather balloon. Unfortunately, however, the Roswell incident entered the UFO mythology as positive proof of a crashed UFO with occupants, and this caused the United States government to hide this evidence from the public and even to engage in a campaign of disinformation. According to lore, the United States hid this data because they did not want to start a "panic" like that which accompanied Orson Welles's famous broadcast of *The War of the Worlds.*

There is little doubt that something did indeed crash at Roswell. The argument is over *what it was* that crashed. From the evidence obtained at the site and the appearance of the wreckage discovered and handled, it seems more likely to be pieces of a balloon and a radar weather target than of a saucer-like disc. Cloth, threads, balsa-like struts, a foil-like substance are all in line with materials used in the construction of weather equipment rather than that of spaceships. Of course, we do not have any saucers to compare it with so we can't rule out the possibility that UFOs are made of balsa, foil, and cloth. Still, knowing the rigors of our earthly atmosphere, climate, and reported speeds and performances of UFOs, alien vehicles made of substantially tougher and sturdier materials seem far more likely. We also know from Air Force records that a number of secret balloon experiments were underway at this time. When we study the behavior of the Air Force team in clearing the area, interviewing the witnesses, etc., it seems clear that experimental testing of some sort of classified device affords the best and most plausible explanation. There is simply no need to invoke the presence of a UFO or space alien.

Although there is no way to conclusively establish the truth or falsity of the Roswell incident to the satisfaction of everyone concerned, this is not true of the report made by Frank Scully in his book *Behind the Flying Saucers*. In this 1950 publication Scully claimed that a flying saucer, complete with its crew of sixteen aliens, crashed on a remote desert plateau east of Aztec, New Mexico. According to Scully, a newspaper columnist, the saucer was ninety-nine feet in diameter and held the bodies of its crew. Scully didn't see the crash or the crash site in person, but he reported what was told him by two men, Silas Newton and Leo Ge Baur, also known as Dr. Gee. The book became a best seller primarily because of this report. In 1952, however, an investigative reporter named J. P. Cahn published an article in *True* magazine exposing Newton and Gee as skilled con artists and the story of the crash at Aztec a hoax. Their hope was to sell the story and script to Hollywood and make a fortune on an aroused public's interest. It is also apparent that even in 1949 when Scully first heard the story, there was a well-known set of details about "saucer crashes" making the rounds.

Other stories, of course, have appeared as the years wore on. Rumors of "pickled aliens, i.e., bodies on ice or in pickle jars stored at Wright Patterson [Air Force Base], collections of extraterrestrial debris, and an occasional photograph or two of dead aliens" have surfaced from time to time. One of the funniest of these appearances was the attempt on the part of a couple of New York journalists to pass off the dead body of a shaven monkey as an alien body dumped from a UFO. Another fake photograph appeared in a German newspaper on April Fools' day. Other reports involving a fire fight between aliens and a U.S. Army platoon, aliens who have died in captivity, and aliens who have died from diseases contracted here on Earth make the rounds among UFOlogists year after year.

What is significant by its absence, however, is anything in the way of convincing—even acceptable or even plausible—physical or material evidence that proves the existence of UFOs. Besides the accounts, i.e., the stories themselves, the evidence in support of any crash and a subsequent retrieval is slim indeed. Within the past few years William Moore, Stanton Friedman, Jamie Shandera, and a few other members of the UFOlogy believers have done their best to convince the world that the United States government is conducting a coverup, and there is a conspiracy afoot to keep the truth hidden from the public. Their efforts have not been successful, and within the past year two separate investigations carried out by Philip Klass and Joe Nickell (1990) into the alleged MJ-12, or *Operation Majestic,* a secret government project dealing with UFOs and aliens, have convincingly shown that documents, supposedly signed by then President Harry Truman and authenticating the existence of and contact with extraterrestrials, were blatant forgeries.

Roberts (1989), who is very skeptical of all such claims of governmental conspiracies and coverups, has made a number of very compelling points in this regard. First, if the conspiracy or coverup is to be effective, it must be restricted to a very small group of people. Yet if there have been a number of crashed discs and aliens, the number of people involved must have been sizable. When we add the number required to guard the vehicles and bodies over the years, plus the sizable number of scientists and professionals required to study the bodies and machines, we are talking about a *very large* number of people. It is almost inconceivable that of all of these people one would not have leaked this information to family members, friends, and relatives who in turn would inform others. Moreover, with all these various people involved, something in the way of material or physical evidence would have been exposed. Yet we have nothing at all—not one smidgen of evidence that we would take to, say, a grand jury. In spite of all the so-called books, articles, etc., screaming about the government's hiding the facts, we have seen nothing in the way of a sustained effort on the part of either the FBI or the CIA to "shut people up," or to prevent such stories as told, for example, in Howard Blum's *Out There* from being given the widest circulation and distribution. And as Roberts notes,

> Perhaps the greatest argument for the nonexistence of crash-retrievals is this: If any government on Earth really were in the long-term possession and knowledge of an alien technological device and alien biology, whichever government had access to this information would have by now managed

to use at least some of it in its defense. This has patently not occurred. No world government has displayed any aspect of technology which can be said to have come from the study of an alien craft or its occupants.

(pp. 105–106)

Recently claims have been made that alien technology showed up in the Stealth bomber project. If so, why then, according to believers, do UFOs show up on radar?

We must also take into serious consideration the fact that all of the nineteenth-century reports of crashes were shown to be hoaxes, and there is little or no difference in any aspect between those reports of this century and those of the last. If the United States government has been involved in the propagation of such stories, it is probably for the purpose of protecting and keeping secure a number of military secrets involving satellite launches, missiles, reconnaissance vehicles, and other Star Wars type defensive and offensive operations. It is well known that the Soviets deliberately fed such information to their own UFOlogists. Disinformation campaigns are an excellent way to divert and distract attention from other terrestrial events you wish to keep hidden.

Finally, as numerous investigators have hypothesized, all such tales are part and parcel of a new myth, a contemporary folk tale, another urban legend. Largely based on rumor and passed on verbally from person to person, the stories are amplified and distorted in the process of being passed along from person to person and finally to the media, where the final modifications are made prior to publication. Little wonder, as Roberts says, that:

> This type of folk tale is self-perpetuating, helped in its development by the beliefs of the UFO researchers, the sensationalism of the media and the false information fed by the intelligence services . . . As with so much of ufology, there remains an unresolvable dichotomy between the event as reported and the tangible evidence available, and this can and should lead researchers to be highly skeptical.

(p. 108)

Aliens and Abductees

One line of evidence that lends considerable credence to the "modern folk lore" interpretation of the UFO and alien encounter hypothesis is the almost total lack of agreement about the physical nature of the UFO occupants. In earlier times most airship occupants were described as ordinary human beings of various sizes, shapes, and colors. But in our time only rarely are the aliens described as human. Even the "Space Brothers" are described as extraordinarily fair, blonde, angelic supermen and women. For the most part the aliens are described as humanoid—*like* but definitely *not* human. They are seen as tall, short, fat, thin, hairless, covered in fur, large heads, small heads, one-eyed, three- and four-eyed, one-fingered, two-fingered, claws like a lobster, humanlike hands, extremely large ears, no ears, very large eyes, very small eyes, big mouths, small mouths, child-like, monstrous, dwarflike, grotesque, skeletal, handsome, and so on. While many are articulate and are able to communicate with humanlike voices, other gabble in unintelligible dialects or communicate silently using telepathic voices.

In fact, the tremendous variety of all these alien creatures suggests that the planet Earth must serve as the galactic museum—a gathering place for all the various life-forms in our galaxy. Interestingly enough, some of these alien life-forms are described as robots, or robot-like mechanical creatures, while others are described in animal-like terms. Not only does it appear that none of the aliens seem to be aware of, or communicate with each other but, in the past, where they seemed to come from Venus, Jupiter, Mars, or Saturn, nowadays they come from places much further away—even from alternate or parallel universes. There is little doubt that this change is due to our gain in astronomical knowledge about the physical conditions for life on Venus, Jupiter, Mars, and Saturn. In the past, in the period between 1880 and 1913, the airship occupants were ordinary, normal-looking men and women dressed in clothes compatible with the time. Today the aliens are creatures from TV movies, science-fiction films, science-fiction novels, and the farther reaches of human imagination. Today, like then, the occupants fit the temper and tastes of the time. Today, the aliens are synonymous with the prototypes seen in films like *Close Encounters of the Third Kind,* or *ET,* and those described in *Communion* and *Intruders,* and *Missing Time.* In the years ahead there is little doubt that the aliens our descendants will encounter will assume a completely different appearance. What our forefathers encountered as gods, angels, ghosts, spirits, fairies, and humanoids our descendants will probably encounter as intelligent balls of pure energy, thought forms, or something else appropriate to the times and cultural milieu.

Alien Abductions and Abductees

With regard to the abductees and their experiences, it should be made clear at the outset that, once again, we have nothing substantial in the way of either physical or confirmatory evidence that any abductions have occurred. What we have, again, are verbal reports, and, again, we should note that throughout history abductions of one sort or another have plagued mankind. These abductions were also carried out by small, unusual, and often grotesque creatures: fairies, dwarves, leprechauns, gnomes, and such. In these abductions time was reported as often standing still, as if the entire event seemed to take place in a dream. The abductee's body was bound, frozen, immobilized, and so forth, and studied or used by the abductors. In fact, there is little difference in the folklore tales handed down to us from a number of ancient cultural sources and the current tales of UFO abductions recounted by Budd Hopkins's victims, or the other classic cases such as that of Betty and Barney Hill, Calvin Parker and Charles Hickson, or Travis Walton.

In fact, in each and every one of the classic abduction cases there are anomalies, flaws, and facts which cast grave doubt on their authenticity (Klass, *UFO Abductions: A Dangerous Game*). In the case of Betty and Barney Hill, for example, it did not occur to Betty that she had been abducted until she read Donald Keyhoe's book along with other UFO tracts, and then had a number of dreams involving being abducted. A careful analysis of Mrs. Hill's testimony under hypnosis clearly indicates the unreality, i.e., the dreamlike character, of the entire experience. Moreover, there are a number of amusing inconsistencies in Mrs. Hill's account of her encounters with the aliens that are, interestingly enough, very characteristic of dreams.

According to Dr. Simon, Betty and Barney Hill's psychiatrist, "At one point when Betty tried to explain why Barney had 'removable teeth,' she referred to people getting older. When the 'spacemen' didn't understand, Betty explained 'with the passage of time . . . ,' but the spaceman said he didn't understand what 'time' was because there was no such thing on their planet." (This is ridiculous on the face of it. According to Einstein's theory of relativity—time is a universal dimension.) Yet, a few moments later, as Betty and Barney Hill were about to depart, the *same* spaceman said, "Wait a minute," and the spaceman *did* want them to delay their departure.

In the case of Parker and Hickson, the investigations carried out by Philip Klass and others have convincingly established the purported abduction was a hoax. First of all, the alleged abduction took place beside a very busy highway at a time when motorists would surely have spotted a hovering spaceship had one been there. Second, a bridge attendant on duty near where the alleged abduction occurred saw nothing during the entire time though he was watching the area. Third, Hickson—the ringleader—changed the time of the purported abduction every time he was interviewed. Fourth, after "passing" a polygraph test administered by an untrained operator, Hickson refused to take any test administered by a qualified operator. Parker, the younger of the two alleged abductees, refused to answer questions about the incident on the grounds that he "fainted" and was, therefore, unconscious during most if not all of the time of the experience. There is now little doubt that the entire affair was staged to help Hickson solve his financial problems.

With regard to the Travis Walton affair, this was one of the more tawdry examples of "true-believer" chicanery, sensationalizing on the part of the media, and greedy men who tried to pull off a hoax that failed. In the summer 1987 issue of *The Skeptical Inquirer,* Jeff Wells, a former reporter for *The National Enquirer,* told what happened when he covered the story of Travis Walton's alleged abduction on 3 November 1975 near Heber, Arizona.

According to the story, a timber-cutting work crew consisting of twenty-two-year-old Travis and six co-workers was at work one afternoon when they spotted a strange light in the sky. Travis, who was nearest the light, started moving toward it and disappeared. Five days later Travis stumbled into town, phoned his cowboy brother, and claimed he had been kidnapped by the crew of an alien spaceship. Because local law-enforcement officers suspected Travis might have been a victim of foul play at the hands of his co-workers, most of the questions on the polygraph test dealt with whether Travis had been killed or injured. Five of the six passed this test with the sixth inconclusive. When these results were reported in the media, the tests were seen as validation of the existence of the UFO and Travis's abduction. After Travis was questioned, John J. McCarthy, the most experienced polygraph examiner in Arizona, was called in to test Travis on 15 November 1975. The test lasted an hour, and in Wells's own words,

The kid had failed the test miserably. The polygraph man said it was the plainest case of lying he'd seen in twenty years, but the office was yelling for another expert and a different result. To head that off we had the two psychiatrists (called in to calm Travis down) put the cowboy (Travis's protective older brother) and the kid through a long session of analysis. Their methods were unique. The next day the four of them disappeared into a room, and soon a waiter headed in there with two bottles of cognac. At the end of it the psychiatrists were rolling drunk, but they had their story and the brothers were crest-fallen. It seemed that Travis's father, who had deserted him as a child, had been a spaceship fanatic, and all his life Travis had wanted to ride in a spacecraft. He had seen something out there in the woods, some kind of an eerie light that had triggered a powerful hallucination that might recur at any time. There was no question of any kidnap by mushroom men. The kid (Travis) needed medical help and the cowboy swore solemnly that he would shield him from further harassment.

(Wells 1981, p. 51)

As for the witnesses, their polygraph tests supported the story that they had all seen a strange light, but nothing that could be called a spaceship. According to Wells, "It had been a lunatic experience from beginning to end, made more disturbing by the fact that on several occasions with coaxing from the professor (James A. Harder), I had almost believed that the story was real." (p. 52)

As seen in these three cases, we find similar patterns of misinterpretations, deceit, hallucinations, or delusions in each and every case of alien abduction that is carefully and intensively investigated. Unfortunately, in most cases of alleged abductions by aliens it is physically impossible to follow up on the event or to determine the truth or falsity of the claims. All of the abduction reports we have are exactly that—reports. We have yet to receive a piece of hardware from an alien craft or an alien souvenir of any kind. What so-called physical evidence there is of extraterrestrial spacecraft consists of crushed foliage, burn marks in the soil, and photographs of fuzzy lights or alleged metallic objects. The physical evidence to support abduction claims is even skimpier: there are no photos, no pieces of metal, and no souvenirs. What we do have are burn marks on the body, blemishes, and hitherto unnoticed scars. Though brain implants have been claimed, so far modern medical science has been unable to find any to analyze. There have also been claims of neurological, physiological, and psychological disturbances following these alleged abductions, but there is no proof that some other much more traumatic event might have been the true cause of the disturbance. In fact, the physical evidence is, and has always been, merely circumstantial and never so massive that it has ever become persuasive. For every item—be it a burn mark, an unnoticed scar, a fit of trembling, breathing difficulties, and so on—a perfectly natural or normal cause is as equally likely as the more unlikely alien abductor.

As for witnesses, it is most notable that they are lacking. John Rimmer argues this lack of corroborating witnesses is more than just an unfortunate coincidence. In those cases where there are two or more witnesses, we find there is confirmation only of the initial non-abduction parts of the story. In other cases, the victims are married or closely related, and in such circumstances there are many reasons why the couple confirms each other's stories. For one thing, there are many opportunities for the couple to discuss the event, and reinforce and influence each other's memories and conceptions. They will also tend to support each other to insure that their stories do not conflict and brand one or both as being deranged or a liar.

We must also deal with the variety of the kinds of aliens that the human abductees encounter. If we take the descriptions of all of the alien abductors into account—from beautiful golden supermen and superwomen to hideous dwarfs and robots—we would be tempted to assume that almost every abduction has been the work of a separate race of alien visitors. The one exception—if there is one—might be the small, thin, big-eyed, gray-skinned ETs made popular in the movie *Close Encounters of the Third Kind*. A number of recent abductions feature these aliens in the starring role.

No matter where we look, the evidence seems more and more convincing that all so-called alien abductions are a psychological phenomenon that offers the abductee-claimants rewards that are unavailable in other ways. We are referring here, of course, to those abductee cases that are hoaxes. There may well be a second category: cases made up of individuals who are mentally aberrant, who are mentally incapable of separating truth and fiction in this regard, and who, therefore, sincerely believe they have been, and will continue to be, abducted by supernatural or extraterrestrial forces. Finally, there may even be a third category of normal, mentally stable, socially well-adjusted individuals who, while under hypnotic regression (or who have had a hypnogogic or hypnopompic dream), are persuaded by an overly credulous UFOlogist that either the regression or the dream, or both, represents a real event. These three categories more than likely account for 99.9 percent of all abductee claims. Because of the high incidence of distorted perceptions and deliberate hoaxes, many UFO investigators agree with Dr. Allen Tough's statement, "In fact, no single (thoroughly studied) UFO case is highly convincing to most of the people who study it [them] carefully. I cannot think of any single case that I would want to defend vigorously in front of a group of well-informed skeptics." (Tough 1989, p. 270)

All in all when we consider the contradictions in the UFO and UFO abduction reports—the amazing reports received turn out to be amazing only because of poor investigation and bad reporting, i.e., reports that are filled with improbabilities, exaggerations, and outright lies—a strong case for skepticism can be made. Evans notes that while the older contactee cases were so filled with contradictions and absurdities that only the most credulous could accept them, the more recent abductee cases are much more plausible. Fowler's *The Andreasson Affair* (1979), Budd Hopkins's *Missing Time* (1981) and *Intruders* (1987), and Strieber's *Communion* (1987) are cited as good examples. Yet, according to Evans, doubt sets in when these tales are compared with each other. First, while there are many shared details in the kind of events reported, none of the spaceships are alike, none of the abductors are alike, they have different motives for their behavior, and so on. Second, although the abductees are taken aboard spaceships hovering overhead, no independent witness has ever confirmed this existence. Moreover, no one has ever reported seeing an abductee in the act of being abducted. Finally, the modern abductee tales bear a remarkable resemblance to the tales told by folklorists and anthropologists. The French investigator Bertrand Méheust has listed numerous parallels between the abduction reports and science fiction stories, folktales, and legends. In this regard, Martin Kottmeyer, in his brilliant paper "Gauche Encounters: Bad Films and the UFO Mythos" (1989), has shown in abduction case after abduction case that themes, content, ideas, and even dialogue had been borrowed directly from old science fiction movies, *Star Trek* episodes, and science fiction short stories and novels. Kottmeyer points out that Hopkins's idea, for example, that the aliens are conducting interbreeding and hybridization experiments on humans was preceded by a number of films and TV movies including Barbara Eden's 1974 TV film, *The Stranger Within,* and the movies *Night Caller From Outer Space* (1966), *Mars Needs Women* (1966), *Village of the Damned* (1960), and *The Mysterians* (1957). One can even go back to Eric Frank Russell's novel *Sinister Barrier* (1939), which has the plot theme about aliens indulging in artificial insemination, virgin births, and the creation of odd-looking hybrid humans.

It is also very curious that the Gulf Breeze UFOs photographed by Ed Walters bear a remarkable stylistic similarity to the alien supership featured in the TV series, *Greatest American Hero.*

Barney Hill's description of aliens with "wraparound eyes" did not show up in his hypnosis sessions with Dr. Simon until a session with Simon on 22 February 1964. It is curious indeed that aliens with "wraparound eyes" were featured in an *Outer Limits* episode titled, "The Bellero Shield," broadcast on 10 February 1964. Barney Hill also referred to the fact that "the alien's eyes were talking to me." In the "Bellero Shield" episode the Bifrost alien claimed to speak through its eyes. Obviously, since it showed up in the hypnotic session, it was another example of a pseudo-memory.

Like many cultural myths and urban legends, the sighting of a UFO, or better yet—being abducted by one—became so popular in the summer of 1987 that movie stars and other celebrities began to seize on the opportunity to gain a little more publicity by claiming UFO sightings and their belief in the alleged abductors. One of John Lennon's former girlfriends, May Pang, who reported seeing a UFO while in his company, told a *New York Times* reporter, "It's almost like a status symbol now in some cities.

You say you've seen a UFO and people say 'Oh, so have I.' It's very *in* right now!"

The fact that all of these UFO abduction stories are a part of a collective social mythology was clearly substantiated in 1977 by an experiment carried out by Drs. Alvin H. Lawson and W. C. McCall (1978). Dissatisfied with the incredible tales their hypnotic regressions of alleged abductees were providing, Lawson and McCall hypnotized volunteers who knew little or nothing about UFOs. Asking the volunteers to imagine being abducted, they modeled the sequence of their questions on their "real" cases and were very careful to avoid undue cueing. Their questions were as follows:

1. Imagine you see a UFO. Describe it.
2. Imagine you are aboard a UFO. How did you get there?
3. Describe the interior of the UFO.
4. Imagine there are entities in the UFO. Describe them.
5. Imagine you are given a physical exam by the entities. Describe it.
6. Imagine the entities communicate with you. What do they say and how do they say it?
7. Imagine you are back on the ground. How did you get there?
8. Imagine time has passed. Do you suffer any after effects?

Though they expected superficial accounts that were obviously taken from films and books, they were stunned when in answer to the questions the volunteers gave elaborately detailed narratives which were impossible to distinguish from those provided by the alleged abductees. Here, again, is evidence that the abductions are psychological events, while the results also show the unreliability of hypnotically obtained information.

After hearing about Lawson and McCall's work, out of our own curiosity we carried out a small replication with a few student volunteers. Following their procedures with four students, we also obtained detailed and elaborate accounts of bug-eyed, hairless aliens with ESP and levitation powers, operating-room equipment, etc., with one interesting exception. One of the students with strong religious beliefs saw the aliens as angelic creatures who were the emissaries of Christ and who examined her to see if she was worthy of being lifted into heaven at the time of the Rapture. It is also of interest to note that Lawson and McCall have found extensive parallels between imagery from the alleged abduction narratives and that from revivified birth memories. This, along with the persistent presence of birth imagery in numerous science fiction stories and films, e.g., Kubrick's *2001: A Space Odyssey, Close Encounters of The Third Kind, Aliens,* and *ET,* suggests that the presence of birth imagery in abduction reports is neither an aberration nor a result of one investigator's wild imagination. (Lawson 1985) It also indicates the presence of cryptomnesia—memories that emerge whenever the eliciting conditions are provided, in these instances: hypnotic suggestion.

UFOlogists who believe alien abductions are veridical frequently argue that many of the abductees are normal, ordinary people with no signs or symptoms of any mental disorders. Moreover, they are in no way psychotic. To all appearances, they are as normal and well-adjusted as me and thee. While this is undoubtedly true, those who have read the preceding chapters by now should be painfully aware of the many and various ways in which the mind of man can go awry, how often we deceive ourselves, and how easy it is to confuse fantasy with reality. Despite the UFOlogist's claims that hundreds—if not thousands—of ordinary people are being abducted daily (or nightly), abductees are still few and far between. Moreover, most well-adjusted, mentally stable, ordinary citizens are not abducted by aliens. Neither are most neurotics, alcoholics, drug-users, or mentally aberrant individuals in the general population of those classified as "disturbed."

In fact, there are many good reasons for believing that all of those individuals claiming to be victims of an alien abduction are, instead, victims of overzealous and sensationalistic actual, or would-be, therapists. While it might be an exaggeration to claim that *all* alleged abductions are *iatrogenic,* i.e., caused by the therapist, it is clearly evident that a very large proportion of the abduction stories are due to the suggestive influence of the therapist. If the therapist is a well trained, experienced professional rather than an untrained, naive UFO believer, most abduction claims would not surface.

Within the last year a number of therapists, led by a young overzealous psychiatrist, have attempted to create a new psychiatric category to accommodate those who claim to be victims of alien abduction. Labeling the claim as Experienced Anomalous Trauma (E.A.T.), these therapists have created a disorder that not only doesn't exist, but in light of our present knowledge of mental disorders is unnecessary and redundant. Then why do they do it? The reasons are obvious: for fame and for fortune. Not only will the creators become famous for discovering and labeling a new disorder (e.g., Korsakoff's psychosis—memory loss; Capgras syndrome—the impostor delusion; Ganser's syndrome—prison psychosis; or Cotard's syndrome—the delusion of negation), but other therapists will call for consultantships and lectures and as *the* recognized medical authorities on the disorder riches beyond imagination will accrue. To do this, the creators will first have to discount or ignore the fact that most clinicians when encountering someone who claims to have been abducted by aliens immediately suspect that: (1) they are fantasy-prone personalities; (2) they are suffering from delusions of persecution, so are overstressed; (3) they are lying and are seeking attention and sympathy; (4) they are mentally ill, i.e., psychotic, and suffering from a schizophrenic episode or one of the many sorts of dissociative disorders; or (5) like those individuals claiming abuse by satanic cults the abductees are, indeed, victims of trauma, but not a trauma due to either satanists or UFOs.

Most importantly, the assumption of a completely *new* type of mental aberration is totally unnecessary. Of the above assumptions the last two are the most relevant. The Cinderella disorder, schizophrenia, is diagnosed in approximately one percent of the population which means that one out of every hundred persons will, at some time or other, be diagnosed as schizophrenic. We also know that many times that number of people go undiagnosed. When this figure is multiplied by the number of people who come into significant contact with each schizophrenic, it should be clear that extensive social networks are affected. One schizophrenic suffering from a strong fixed delusion can cause an unbelievable amount of damage before the illness is discovered.

A recent sad example is the case of Judy Johnson, discussed earlier, who triggered the horrible McMartin child sex-abuse case in Manhattan Beach, California. Because of her pathology, she accused everyone in sight of abusing her child. Yet, not being able to diagnose or even recognize the symptoms of acute paranoid schizrenia, the local police and the District Attorney assumed Judy Johnson was telling the truth. So did Judy's neighbors and other mothers of the daycare-center children. The subsequent wave of hysteria and panic triggered the longest, most paranoid, and most expensive trial in American history and came close to convicting seven innocent victims. This witchhunt was due to a very sick woman with a fixed delusion, but who in every other way seemed quite normal. Fortunately, she was diagnosed as an acute paranoid schizophrenic a year or so after her original charge. Unfortunately, by this time the witchhunt was already well underway.

If this was the only case of its kind we could relax and dismiss it as just one of those occasional social anomalies. Sadly enough almost the same scenario was acted out in the Memphis, Tennessee, region in 1988. One schizophrenic mother suffered from the delusion that she was being persecuted by Satan and that Satanists were all around her, and told a group of mothers of local school children that a Satanic cult in their neighborhood was kidnapping and torturing their children. The rumor spread like wildfire, and before the panic subsided, approximately a dozen elderly women and school teachers were branded as Satanists. It took months of investigative work by the *Memphis Commercial Appeal* reporters, the local police, and the Tennessee State Police to scotch the rumors and prove there were no Satanists in that part of the state.

The problem is that there are hundreds of undiagnosed schizophrenics who are able to function quite normally most of the time. They can hold a job, take care of their personal needs, interact effectively with people around them, and appear, superficially, to be perfectly normal. They do, however, show one little abnormality which gives them away if they finally do come to the attention of a trained and qualified therapist. The case of Barbara O'Brien discussed earlier (see chapter 4) is a good example. Depending upon the individual, the one behavioral quirk may be: (1) a belief that Satan is watching every move they make; (2) aliens are pursuing them relentlessly with death rays; (3) they have just returned from Mars, Jupiter, Venus, and Saturn—as well as from some nice planets of distant stars in other galaxies; (4) a specific friendly bartender in their favorite bar is trying to poison them; (5) there is a horned demon-rapist living under her bed and he comes out and assaults her every night—this is why she has insomnia; (6) a dead man keeps coming into the dining room and sits down at the table across from her—this is why she has no appetite; (7) his secret invention for controlling time is wanted by every government on earth, and that's why all these people he meets are trying to kill him and steal this invention; and (8) she was aroused in the middle of the night by these three blue-skinned aliens who abducted and raped her, and so on, and so on. These eight examples are those that have come to my attention in my own work and from friends within the last year. It is also evident that whatever happens to be in the news, or that is threatening to life and limb, or that is the subject of the latest urban legend is also sure to show up as a central theme in the schizophrenic's delusion. Of course, many schizos have more than one delusion at a time and they change them, periodically, as well.

What is most disturbing, however, is that too many licensed and accredited psychotherapists fail to understand and appreciate the many ways in which the human mind can go awry, or they have other non-therapeutic axes to grind which are not in the best interests of either their patients or the society they are supposed to serve. By failing to recognize the abductees for what they are, they are helping to legitimize their claims and thus perpetuate the mythology. What is most disturbing is the failure of so many so-called professionals to understand the psychodynamics of either those claiming abuse by satanic cultists or by alien abductors.

By far the most likely explanation for these reports is confabulation during *hypnotic regression.* We can be very confident that the memories retrieved with hypnotic assistance are not accurate representations of real events in their lives. Memory even while awake and alert is also highly unreliable. *Source amnesia* is also common, i.e., we remember events but forget the true source or origin of the memories. Such amnesias serve as protection and shield us from the pain of highly traumatic events. Both satanic torture and alien abduction are examples of common confabulations. As discussed earlier, we do not remember things exactly. We recreate them and in doing so we change, rearrange, amplify, diminish, and distort the memories we have stored to better serve our needs and desires. Moreover, we, like nature, abhor a vacuum and we fill in the gaps and shape the past to make a more satisfactory or fulfilling story. If horrible or unpleasant things have happened to us in the past, and there are gaps in these memories, we will fill in these gaps with events that never happened or with events that did not happen the way we imagined. In order not to be overwhelmed and paralyzed by such painful experiences, we change the memories to make them more acceptable and less disturbing. In some people the resulting memory can be not only radically different, but even bizarre. In such cases, however, the disguise—the fantasy—serves to protect the individual from a painful reality which is unacceptable. Richard Noll (1990), among others, has suggested that:

> In order to live a healthy life and not go insane, children "rewrite" their experiences of abuse at the hands of their parents—whom they love—or other adults. This revision of memory may serve to protect them from the shattering pain of the truth. . . . We already know that child abuse leads to the development of multiple personalities, as one way of keeping the true memories of pain out of awareness.
>
> (p. 60)

The trauma, in a word, was not due to alien abduction, but to a deeper *hidden memory* vastly more traumatic. As long as the therapist naively assumes and accepts the reality of "flying saucers and satanists," he or she will never make any effort to look for the real, true cause of the Experienced Anomalous Trauma.

An even more serious therapeutic error is for the therapist to implant false memories of sexual, satanic, and/or alien abuse in the psyches of their clients via suggestion, thereby creating additional and more serious problems.

Besides their failure to be of any real help to victims of serious psychological problems caused by deep-seated emotional traumas, the abductee therapists create more problems than they solve.

UFOs, Religion, and Folklore

Barry Beyerstein has also called our attention to the similarities between religious fanaticism and UFO abductions.

> When accounts of sudden religious conversions in temporal-lobe epileptics are laid alongside the epiphanous revelations of the religious tradition, the

parallels are striking. The same is true of the recent spate of UFO abductees. Parsimony alone argues against involving spirits, demons, or extraterrestrials when natural causes will suffice.

(Beyerstein 1988, p. 255)

And with regard to such experiences as UFO abductions, encountering demons, etc., it is well known that we can put ourselves into a mental state where such experiences are more likely to occur. Persinger (1983) suggested that all these sorts of spiritual or other worldly experiences can be cultivated. We know that temporal lobe transients can be conditioned since they are, themselves, intrinsically rewarding experiences. In fact, Persinger argues that such mystical experiences can be looked at as learned microseizures brought on by a number of precipitating stimuli followed by a significant reduction in anxiety. People who are fantasy prone or good at self-stimulation would have a number of or repeated spiritual or mystical experiences.

Evans (1989) has observed that the most characteristic feature of extraterrestrial encounters is the claim of the witnesses that they have been entrusted with messages for the entire human race. Typically the aliens state that they come in peace, that they are here to enlighten the human race, that they are here to spread love and brotherhood and bring an end to war and the threat of nuclear war, and, finally, when the human race grows up, it can join the federation of intelligent galactic life. Evans notes that while it is by no means impossible that other worldly beings might be concerned about the Earth's welfare, it is highly improbable that we would have so many different messages, from different entities, from different parts of the universe, although in general agreement as to philosophy. Evans says, "I must have at least a hundred such collections of messages here on my shelves." (1989, p. 217) I, too, have a fairly good collection of my own. Anyone interested in collecting such messages would have little or no difficulty in amassing a sizeable and varied assemblage.

Bill Ellis, a folklore specialist at Penn State, has studied the UFO abduction literature and disagrees with Thomas Bullard, David Jacobs, Budd Hopkins, and the other UFO therapists. He sees Hopkins, Bullard, Jacobs, and company as creating a new folklore. Ellis notes that in many cultures, night-terrors, i.e., hypnopompic and hypnogogic dreams, are accepted as common experience:

In Italy it is called the Mourning and in Newfoundland the Old Hag. But in Anglo-American culture, the perception is considered too bizarre to talk about. Ellis also observes that the people coming to Hopkins lack the cultural tradition and the knowledge to understand the phenomena. They are, therefore, inadvertently swayed to believe the group's unprovable abduction hypothesis.

In Hopkins's work, Ellis also sees some sources of danger in that through his amateurish folk psychiatry he will keep some very disturbed people from receiving the expert clinical help they really need. In Ellis's words, "Less dramatic explanations will come out when the field attracts objective psychologists and folklorists who don't have a burning need to create a mythology for our time." (Ellis 1990, p. 73) These are wise words that all UFOlogists should ponder, and they remind us again of Philip Klass's message that UFO abductions are, indeed, a dangerous game!

Perhaps the easiest way to understand the alien abduction phenomena is to look at it in social psychological terms. Last year, Robert Hicks, in a brilliant analysis of the Satanic Cult conspiracy (1990), outlined exactly how people develop a belief that they were victims of abuse by satanic cults even though there is little or no evidence to support such a claim. Recently a large number of individuals have claimed they are suffering from a multiple personality disorder (MPD), caused by childhood abuse by satanic cult members. The growing number of alleged cult-survivor stories is taken by many people as proof that such violations did actually happen. Yet most of the cult survivors' stories are not only unverified, but unverifiable as well. There is, moreover, no physical evidence of any crime, and the stories that the alleged victims tell are hardly credible. The alleged victims can convincingly relate fantasies (See Jennifer's story in the Introduction) as fact and believe religiously the stories they tell. Hypnosis, for investigative purposes, results only in more elaborate and more incredible stories. It may well be that the victims did, indeed, suffer some type of abuse as children but that is not necessarily connected to Satanism. There is, nevertheless, another facet of the cult survivors' stories that lends them credibility in the public's eye; strangely enough, the cult survivors' stories of ritual abuse are almost identical even though the people come from hundreds or even thousands of miles apart. Many authorities see this as evidence of their truth despite the absence of any other supporting evidence. How can these things be explained?

First of all, the stories of Satanic cult abuse are a recent phenomenon. It is well known that cult survivors did not begin to appear on the talk show circuit and parade their claims until the 1980s. Similarly, the increase in cases of MPD has followed closely and paralleled the media attention given to the disorder within the past few years. There is good reason to believe that the alleged victims have borrowed the symbolism of satanic trappings from lurid novels, movies, and television. But here it is important to note that the rituals never involve historically accurate rites and proceedings—only the popularized version. These fantasies represent a fear deriving from an abused childhood, and they have taken a number of urban-legend themes and have woven these into their tales of suffering. Any study of this phenomena must, however, also include the therapists. According to Sherrill Mulhern, an anthropologist who has studied therapist-patient interactions in a number of cult-survivor cases:

> When one concentrates the research focus on discovering the specific ways in which the therapists come to believe in the reality of satanic/ritual abuse, one immediately uncovers a remarkable myth—making a network of therapists, patients and investigators blending together specific idiosyncratic data into one atemporal, analytic grid. I say this because, when one examines specific adult survivor stories, it becomes immediately apparent that initially patients were not saying the same things but came to say similar things over time.
>
> (1989)

Mulhern argues that, as a result, a mythic satanic model has emerged that now shows up everywhere that therapists, law enforcement officials, and cult survivors congregate, and it has come about through hours of networking among the various professionals, with the whole thing held together by deeply held fundamentalist beliefs.

Folklore theorists understand very well how such phenomena come about. It is well known that people tell improbable stories; they tell them for different reasons, to different audiences, and with different results. These "urban legends" are essentially prose narratives regarded by their tellers to be true. They frequently appear to be new at the outset when they begin to spread, but a little probing into the past will, in nearly all cases, uncover a very similar tale that made the rounds before. To those who are unfamiliar with such tales and who are unaware of the "urban legend phenomena," they do appear credible and are easy to believe.

Many of these tales also contain what Hicks calls a "subversion myth." Such myths reflect a high level of social tension and a threat to the individual's personal security. When these are coupled with a "collective readiness to believe," we find the myths presenting threats that menace not only the individual, but an entire society as well. Abduction by aliens in UFOs is a classic example. There is the description of a danger (hostile aliens from outer space); a group of conspirators and their evil motives (aliens conducting an intergalactic breeding experiment); a process by which conspirators manipulate the unwary to do their bidding (the aliens use hypnosis, ESP, mind control techniques, and implanted control devices); a threat to society (a UFO invasion is coming); and, finally, a remedy that citizens must pursue.

All the victims of abduction must be treated by therapists like Budd Hopkins and David Jacobs, and the public must act and do something about it! The parallels between claims of ritual satanic abuse and abduction by extraterrestrial aliens are too numerous and too close to ignore. There is little doubt that the same basic social and psychological forces are at work and that anyone naive or foolish enough to believe such claims is not only aiding and abetting the spread of a vicious, insidious, and socially disruptive superstition that is harmful and destructive in the end, but is, in no way, providing the therapeutic help the alleged victims deserve to receive. We have to remember that hard, cold reality, despite its shortcomings, always wins in the long run. As Martin Gardner notes, "realism is not a dirty word." Nor has it ever been.

Table 1. Behavioral Indicators and Claims of Alien Abductees and Their Therapists

Claims	*Most Likely Explanation*
1. Waking up paralyzed with fear and the sense of presence in room.	1. Sleep paralysis and hypnagogic and hypnopompic hallucinations.
2. Experiencing a period of "missing time"—a period of an hour or more in which one cannot remember what happened.	2. Common everyday behavior, woolgathering, fantasizing, loss of attention, and automatic behavior.
3. Feelings of floating or flying without knowing why or how.	3. Due to muscular relaxation and loss of proprioceptive inputs.
4. Seeing unusual lights or balls of light, faces, objects, or other things without knowing what is causing them; also hearing buzzing noises, etc.	4. Ishakower phenomenon—part of the hypnagogic experience (1938).
5. Having puzzling scars on one's body without memory of how they were caused.	5. Universally common, everyone has them. Nothing unusual.
6. Vague memories of being poked, probed, examined, and operated on by huge-eyed aliens.	6. Part of sleep paralysis and hypnagogic and hypnopompic experience. And also due to fear and panic.
7. Memories of sexual operations, e.g., sperm extraction, impregnation, breeding experiments, etc.	7. Due to reduced oxygen input to the brain; similar to autoerotic asphyxiation.
8. Feelings of having small material	8. Part of sleep paralysis and

objects (implants) inserted into various parts of one's body.

hypnagogic and hypnopompic experience; no implants have ever been found.

9. Feelings that aliens communicate via telepathic channels and have communicated vital messages. According to Swords the seven most often mentioned are: (1) colonization, (2) material gain and power, (3) threat at home planet, (4) threat here on earth, (5) galactic kinship, (6) religious conversion, and (7) curiosity and exploration (1989).

9. Fairly hallucinatory; hyperacusis also plays a part here. Messages that are communicated are all *human* motivations —not alien.

10. Under regressive hypnosis skilled therapists can uncover genuine memories of abductions by aliens, their behavior, and their motivation.

10. Confabulation is the result of all such efforts; hypnosis is a turning on of the imagination. Iatrogenic influences paramount here.

Anthropomorphism Revisited

Perhaps the biggest obstacle of all for the alien abduction believers stems from the well-established facts of evolutionary biology. Chris Boyce (1979), E. J. Coffey (1992), Stephen Jay Gould (1990), George Gaylord Simpson (1964), and Frank Tipler (1980), for example, have stressed that the number of chance events that went into the evolution of man is so vast that there is virtually no chance that man, as he exists here on Earth, exists anywhere else in the universe. Lifeforms evolving on other planets must go through an equally random number of events in their development. They would be unique in the cosmos just as we are. What we have in common with any extraterrestrial intelligence is our uniqueness, our singularity. We and all living beings have a profound and intimate relationship with our environment. We did not develop in a vacuum; therefore, we are products of our environment. All aliens will have this same sort of symbiotic relationship with their own environment.

As for the alien's physical appearance, it is highly unlikely, most improbable, that they exist as they have been described by the abduction victims in their small, gray, humanoid form—with no discernible reproductive organs. In a series of fascinating papers concerned with the human tendency to project human qualities upon the external world, E. J. Coffey (1992) reminds us that not only is there no incontrovertible evidence whatsoever that aliens exist, but evolution itself is not the ineluctable following of physical laws; instead, it is merely a chain of chance events, which easily could have been otherwise. Change any one of the many past events in our biological history—which is a cascade effect—and it will dramatically influence everything that follows. If, by some cruel stroke, the chordates had failed to survive millions of years ago, then neither vertebrates, mammals, nor humans would have evolved. We simply would not be here now. The Burgess shale fossils, representing a time just after the Cambrian explosion 570 million years ago, completely refute the anthropomorphic idea that diversity increased with time. Instead, the evolutionary pattern shows rapid diversification followed by decimation with perhaps as few as 5 percent surviving. In Coffey's words, "The survivors resemble the winners of a lottery rather than creatures better designed than the unlucky majority who do not survive." Stephen Jay Gould (1990) not only concurs, but points out that if we were to replay life's tape there is no reason whatsoever to assume that our particular type of self-conscious being would ever be expected to appear again. As Gould notes, our evolution is not a repeatable occurrence. If anything, we are the embodiment of contingency. What this means is that it is so highly improbable it approaches impossibility that there is any humanoid intelligence of any sort—albeit housed in different bodily frames—to be found anywhere else in the cosmos.

Coffey sums up our anthropomorphic fallacy quite succinctly:

> The evolutionary conclusion that humanoid intelligence elsewhere is improbable is not due to any anthropomorphic bias, but it is because of the deep understanding that evolution has no real goal other than adapting creatures to specific local environments. Neither we, nor our mode of intelligence, are the highpoint of evolution. The pathways of evolution are too circuitous for that to ever be the case.
>
> (1992, p. 28)

Little gray humanoids who bear a marked resemblance to human fetuses but who are able to communicate telepathically? Dragons, elves, and fairies are equally, if not more, probable. If the aliens come from any space at all it is from the "inner space" inside the human skull rather than "outer space" and the stars. It is also high time we realize that all of our scenarios of extraterrestrial life—from those of the SETI supporters to those of the "Star Trek" series—all are nothing but projections of ourselves! If, as the alien abduction believers insist, the aliens and alien technology are in our midst, why would NASA be playing with costly radio telescopes? According to

Coffey and many others, the hope for finding human intelligence elsewhere is a religious conviction: a belief. In his words, again: "It is religious in that it rests upon faith—not a rational comprehension of the message the evolutionary record cries out to us: of humans elsewhere there will be none forever" (1992, p. 28).

For many believers in alien visitations and abductions there is no doubt that their convictions are religious and are motivated by the same hopes and longings that motivate SETI scientists. Douglas Curran's beautifully illustrated book, *In Advance of the Landing: Folk Concepts of Outer Space* (1985) clearly shows that religious motives are behind most of the beliefs in saviors and in UFOs coming like angels from the skies. The therapist's argument that he must treat his clients' *belief* that they were abducted—whether or not they actually were abducted—will not hold water. The belief that they were spirited away, when reinforced and confirmed by a therapist, not only causes an increase in panic and anxiety since they're helpless to prevent future abductions, but having the therapist confirm their fear aggravates the initial trauma. If there was ever a tiny bit of doubt as to the reality of their prior experience, the therapist's authentication of their abduction removes all traces of conjecture. The result is that the helpless clients are now likely to have new nightmares about their original experiences. Now they are certain their waking-dreams were completely true alien abductions! *Elevating the victims' anxiety levels has never been, nor can it ever be in any conceivable way, therapeutic.*

In summary, what we have learned about aliens thus far tells us only one thing: they're not alien at all, they're human. They are popped out of the human imagination by human beings with human motives and human needs and desires. It is also motivated by the universal human need, it seems, to believe in entities—in fairies, demons, witches, elves, ETs, and gods—as well as their belief in their own egos, their own personal significance and importance in the scheme of things. The lack of scientific training and experience, analytical thinking, and respect for physical evidence leads, much too often, to the acceptance of folk beliefs, legends, half-truths, rumor, propaganda, and wishful thinking as substitutes for hard truth and common sense.

Therefore, everything alien when examined closely also turns out to be quite human. Stuart E. Guthrie, in his new book *Faces in the Clouds* (1993), shows that all religion is anthropomorphic and, like his gods, man also creates aliens in his own image. If one's vision of human nature is benign, then the aliens may well be the gentle, child-like creatures of Spielberg's *Close Encounters of the Third Kind.* On the other hand, if human nature is regarded as beastly and perverse, our aliens may be witches, old hags, hellions, or demons. It is perhaps of some comfort to remember that, according to a recent poll (Gibbs, *Time,* 27 December 1993), 69 percent of the American public not only believe in angels but 32 percent claim to have made personal contact with them. Given a choice between belief in either angels or aliens I would pick the angels every time. Not only are they prettier, warmer, gentler, have a better bedside manner, and never abduct their hosts, in many situations the guardian variety have even been known to save lives. Most importantly they have no desire to interbreed—with only one possible exception, which, according to legend, occurred about two thousand years ago. Over the years the entity who resulted from this encounter has brought a considerable amount of comfort and joy to those who believe in his supernatural powers and status. Like all these folk, if you have a need to believe in something extraterrestrial, by all means pick an angel.

9

Toward the Year 2000: A Modest Proposal

Even in the 1980s there were still a few men and women of science who had a sense of identification with science as a way of truth, civilization, morality and other constructive values and a high contempt for commercialism of any kind, much less mysticism, irrationalism and occultism. Many represent their generation's quota of irrepressible skeptics, hardheaded naysayers deviant enough to speak out in both the lab and a public forum to enlighten one part or another of the public. . . . But these surviving men and women of science were swamped numerically by other scientists who at most counted some sort of political or professional association work, that is, bureaucratic activity, as their service to science. Most likely, these "scientists" were in fact narrow technicians who did a job without a calling. In either case, such professionals did not struggle with other population elements for possession of the public mantle of science. Nor do they feel personally the obligation to pick a fight with other superstitions, pseudosciences or advertising. The chances were that they did not even know what civilization was or perhaps science as such. Few Americans of that era did. . . . Nowhere had the technical training, the education or the milieu of the technicians prepared them for an obligation to summarize, simplify or translate science for any non-specialist audiences. Indeed, in functional terms, science probably did not exist any longer on the popular level. Superstition did.

—John C. Burnham, *How Superstition Won and Science Lost*

One of the most depressing as well as one of the more important science books of our time was published a few years ago with little or no fanfare. The book, John C. Burnham's *How Superstition Won and Science Lost,* is a sobering account of how the scientific establishment lost the game to the purveyors of superstition and saw the cultural impact of both science and scientists frustrated and reduced. As difficult as it may be to believe, efforts to explain the work of scientists and findings from the laboratory in ways that the general public could understand and appreciate were more effective and successful in the nineteenth century than in the twentieth. Burnham's thesis is that, collectively, we have done a terrible job of popularizing science over the past several decades. In nearly every public medium, supernaturalism and the mystical and occult elements in modern society have dominated, stolen the thunder, and grabbed the prize, so to speak. Scientific reaction has been little more than a whimper.

According to Burnham, when everyone assumed that superstition and mysticism had been relegated to the past and science popularizers turned to other concerns, irrationalism and its agents disguised themselves and continued the fight. The result was a resounding victory for the occult. Not only did the science writers quit, they also isolated the products of research from the spirit and process of doing science. Moreover, the broadly educated and talented synthesizers also deserted and left the field to the public relations (PR) types. The outcome was, in Burnham's words, the abandonment of "interesting science-reporting which fits into a general world view and extends one's vision," for a type of "Gee Whiz science which excites irrelevant emotion and reinforces one's mysticisms."

Like most workers in the scientific laboratories, Burnham is perplexed by the "haunting paradox of how [our] culture ended up so little influenced by science when the products of both the natural and the health sciences so profoundly shaped everyday life and great events alike." Somehow or other science's negative paradigm against error, which proved to be so effective in the last part of the nineteenth century, wound up attenuated and derailed in the twentieth. Why? Perhaps one major reason was that the forms of superstition changed and hardly anyone recognized it for what it was. The new form adopted the standards of the all-powerful *media world.* Not only was this media world nonnaturalistic, but like superstition, it was actually competitive with the traditional world of popularized science. Furthermore, in the media world "the elements of sensationalism and disjointed segmentation of information were exactly the elements of superstition that early popularizers of science had attacked with skepticism and naturalism." Unfortunately, so completely did this new obscurantism—made up of sensationalism and iso-lated fact—dominate the media that magical thinking, suspension of in-credulity, and belief in mystic miracles were widely accepted. During the twentieth century, those scientists who saw science as a calling (with few exceptions) withdrew from all popularizing and left the task to the PR types and consumer economists. This is the major reason we find *The Globe, The Star,* the *Weekly World News,* and the *National Enquirer* at the check-out counters instead of *Discover* or *Scientific American.*

Burnham notes on another front that specialization and narrowness within scientific disciplines in the universities became so extreme that the scientist Conway Zirkle sarcastically suggested that students' diplomas should read:

The Johns Hopkins University
certifies that:
JOHN WENTWORTH DOE
Does not know anything but:
BIOCHEMISTRY

Please pay no attention to any pronouncement he may make on any other subject, particularly when he joins with others of his kind to save the world from something or the other. However, he worked hard for his degree and is potentially a most valuable citizen. Please treat him kindly.

(Burnham 1987, p. 251)

Among scientists themselves one finds a most curious mixture of modernism in a specialized field coupled with an intense adherence to medieval or primitive superstitions that are unworthy of them. A recent example of this is the flood of interest on the part of many psychiatrists in reincarnation, spirit possession, and alien abductions that were noted earlier.

As the twentieth century wore on, according to Burnham, not only did scientists suffer from a loss of passion and identity but, even more disturbing, what was most critically missing from popularization was skepticism. This, Burnham notes, was the one casualty in the war that proved to be decisive. Years earlier the popularizers managed to connect science's progress in solving nature's mysteries with traditional skepticism. In 1902 Joseph Jastrow, for example, described the scientific habit of mind "that makes one keen-scented for right beliefs and secure, not from error indeed, but from rash credulity." By contrast, the more recent science writers have not been able to convey even the most routine doubts of their investigations. By stressing only scientific products, they actually promote an askeptical way of thinking. What little skepticism there was, Burnham tells us, was often directed against science and medicine rather than against either folk or commercial error.

Burnham's message is that we need to devote more time and attention to scientific popularizing and that the best scientists need to devote more time and effort to the tasks of communication and education. They need to be aroused and motivated to enter the battle again. The war for the public mind is not over yet; there are many battles ahead, and if skeptics properly prepare and pool their resources, they will not lose them all. We also need to know our enemy as well as we know ourselves and our shortcomings. Burnham's book can be of great help with the latter, and skeptics, particularly, should read it carefully.

Nevertheless, in the eyes of the general public at the moment science as a career is not only highly unattractive and unappealing but leads quickly and remorselessly to terminal boredom.

Since science is, obviously, much too dull and difficult for the average student (as well as the average adult), and since what is popular, what is entertaining—and, consequently, what makes money—is of considerably more significance to the public and to the media than anything else—it is "high time" that the scientific establishment "get with it" and adapt. Burnham is correct; superstition has won. It was a fair fight, and science lost. We should, therefore, graciously concede and join the crowd. Pragmatists are well aware that in a society dominated by the marketplace, values such as truth, morality, and principle are passé if not wholly irrelevant! Though the time is short, if we keep our eye on the goal, feet on the ground, shoulders to the wheel, and get our antediluvian derrieres in gear we just might be able by the year 2000 to bring the brave new world of metapsychiatric metaphysics and the New Age of spiritualistic transcendence into full flower.

To do this we will, of course, have to make a number of sweeping changes in virtually every aspect of our reactionary "old fogyish" lives. While some slight adjustment problems are to be expected—caused by the radical transition from the old linear ways of thought—these will be more than compensated for by our newly acquired supernatural powers, and the veritable flood of love and joy that will fill our lives. To help forward this worthy endeavor, I would like to make the following modest proposal. To insure the success of the New Age and the coming social transformation, we should begin with education and the educational establishment. Since intuition and direct mind-to-mind communication will become essential survival skills in the coming New World, we should, of course, do away with reading and writing and replace them with classes in elementary, intermediate, and advanced divination including, of course, divination devices—Tarot cards, the *I Ching,* tea leaves, the crystal ball, and the Ouija board. Arithmetic and mathematics will also be unnecessary skills. In a world where love rules, money, prices and whatnot are meaningless. Numbers are for material things and have no relevance for spiritual matters. They all can be replaced by courses in numerology, bartering, and intuitive guessing. All classes in physics will be replaced by classes in psychotronics and paraphysics. Similarly, alchemy will be substituted for chemistry. Dowsing and the study of crystals and amulets will replace the older classes in geology. Curriculum substitutes for psychology will, of course, include palmistry, synchronicity, spiritualism, exorcism, past-lives regression, and future-lives progression. Courses in applied imagination, speculation, spiritual contacts, and channeling famous entities will take the place of philosophy. Astrology would take the place of astronomy, and other than a few professional astronomers, nobody would notice the change. Health and hygiene courses would be supported by psychic surgery, iridology, crystal healing, mental healing, and prayer. Courses in logic and advanced logic would be replaced with courses in basic and advanced stupidity. If these prove too difficult they can be supplemented with basic, intermediate, and advanced naiveté, or basic, intermediate, and advanced credulity.

Our medical schools would similarly alter their curricula to reflect the new times. Courses in medicine would be replaced by courses in psychic healing, imagery, crystals, color therapy, psychic surgery, magic, and witchcraft, as well as courses in amulets, spells, and prayer. Psychic healers and psychosurgeons would, of course, replace our current MDs and surgeons. Courses in history would all be replaced by actual time travel—past-lives regression to the historical times of choice, supplemented by conversations and interviews with all of the important but deceased historical personalities. Future-lives progression would substitute for all courses in mathematics, statistics, computers, and engineering predictions. If you *know* what the future holds, why bother to *estimate* it? The study of aeronautical engineering and aerodynamics would, logically, be replaced with intensive training in out-of-body experiences, astral travel, and levitation via Transcendental Meditation practices.

In fact, in the future New Age many of our old ways of living will be radically altered. Travel via automobiles, planes, ships, and trains will no longer be either necessary or desirable. Once we have managed astral or out-of-body travel, psychic projection, and remote viewing, the ends of the Earth as well as the farther reaches of the universe are open to us at no cost whatsoever. All we have to do is envision our journey's end, relax, concentrate, leave the body, go with the flow, and there we are—safe and sound and we don't even have to pack a bag! If you learn witchcraft, even out-of-body experiences are unnecessary. Just grab any broom that's handy and away you go!

Pain—of any sort whatsoever—will be no problem. Forget your pills and poultices. All one has to do is go into a self-induced trance, alter your state of consciousness, and "will" the hurt away. There are hundreds of ways to do it. If you have any problems, just contact your nearest friendly psychic or channel. If they are not readily available, then you can, of course, look within and select your own entity from the millions that have died and are now eagerly awaiting your summons. In case you aren't sure who you might want to contact, just consult the old Akashic Record.

As for entertainment, movies, plays, and TV will soon fade away once your powers of visualization have been maximized through training. (In case you don't know how to do this, check the classifieds in any issue of *Fate* magazine for qualified specialists and training institutes.) Your own fantasies and visions and visits to distant times and places—in both the past and the future—as well as trips to other worlds will far exceed in entertainment value anything that Hollywood or New York can offer.

Once the aliens here on earth have been befriended, we can scrap the work of NASA as well as the Space Shuttle, SETI programs, and the mission to Mars. We'll merely borrow or duplicate the UFO technology which will solve, in one fell swoop, not only all of our problems with space exploration and national defense, but we will also solve all of mankind's persistent problems with anything and everything as well. Knowledge that there are other intelligent races in the universe should help to unite all of mankind *against* an external foe (if they're hostile), or (in case they're friendly), to unite all of mankind *for* the exploration of distant worlds and strange civilizations and saucer trips where no man has ever gone before!

As silly as the foregoing scenario may sound, it is exceeded in silliness by far by most of the hundreds of New Age publications that promise their believers and adherents just such miracles and marvels if they will just believe and send cash—lots of cash. Let me assure the reader that none of these far-reaching and unsettling events will ever come to pass. If any of these psychic phenomena exist at all, they exist in such small, almost infinitesimal amounts, and are so incredibly weak—even in their strongest manifestations—as to cause even the most ardent of their champions to recognize their impact on the world of physical reality is somewhere between maximally insignificant and altogether unmeasurable. Colin Wilson recently stated:

> Spiritualism has ceased to be a challenge to science and has become little more than a harmless minority religion; in fact, it is perfectly obvious that it never was a challenge to science. We can also see that there was never any question of science being supplanted by superstition and old wives' tales, and that CSICOP is quite wrong to imagine that the success of Uri Geller heralds a return to the Middle Ages.

Wilson, unfortunately, must not believe his own words because he has long been a champion of the occult and a salesman for the supernatural (see Wilson 1981, and 1988), for many, many years. Wilson, Michael Crichton, Charles Berlitz, and other paranormal propagandists see any and all efforts of the rationalists and scientific-minded to counter their efforts as negative and reactionary. Individually and collectively, science and scientists have been accused of being overzealous and of adopting a religious-like stance in their efforts to defend their territory from attacks by the irrationalists. Crichton, for example, states a truism, "the scientific perception of reality is not reality itself. Even the most powerful scientific law is not a complete description of reality. There is always more to know. . . ." Thus far I cannot think of any scientist on earth who would disagree. Unfortunately, Crichton goes on to say, "We may each understand a part, an aspect of the whole, but, in any full or comprehensive sense, reality defies description. And if other modes of knowing are internal, subjective, and inherently unverifiable, that doesn't make them necessarily any less interesting or useful." (Crichton 1988, p. 413) Ah, Mr. Crichton, it most certainly does affect both their intellectual attractiveness and their utility. The contrast you have just stated is *the difference* between *public* knowledge (science) and *private* knowledge (religion), between the subjective and the objective. Unless human knowledge is external and verifiable, in no way can it be or has it ever been reliable or useful knowledge. The angels viewed in the context of the psychotic's hallucinations are of little or no use if our house is on fire. It is doubtful that even their advice, no matter how heavenly, is of any practical value in getting and holding a job, managing one's finances, or resolving an argument with one's spouse.

What Crichton fails to understand are the dangers inherent in the mystical, antirational, New Age mind-set and its attitude toward the world we inhabit. Besides his confusion of "science" with the cold, mechanical, reductionistic, anti-emotional, robotic world of "straw creatures" without either emotion or humane understanding he has crafted—beings that do not exist in reality—it is also obvious that Crichton has failed to see what belief in impossible things *can* lead to and *has* led to in the past. Pat Kehoe, the skeptic, recently provided a laundry list of the hazards of New Age thinking that all thoughtful persons, and Crichton, in particular, should read and remember:

HAZARDS OF THE MENTALITY OF NEW AGE AND THE PARANORMAL

- It lays the public open to fraud and exploitation by failing to provide either the means or the encouragement to evaluate unusual claims.

- It disseminates misinformation, stating as fact events and phenomena that are unproven or unprovable; lacking any system of checks and balances, it permits claims to be made without proof, challenge, or scrutiny.

- It encourages the belief that intuition and subjective experience are more valid avenues of knowledge than public, specifiable, observable and repeatable ways of verifying experience and inference.

- It encourages a belief in arbitrary and (often malevolent) supernatural forces.

- It reduces personal responsibility by attributing behavior to powers and influences beyond ordinary human experience and control.

- It implies that knowledge can be gained without effort, and that events can be predicted and controlled through powers that are supernaturally bestowed.

- It rejects and disparages critical thinking, analysis, and skepticism, which are fundamental to scientific reasoning.

- It encourages a belief in the quality of opinions, regardless of their foundations; since truth is subjective . . . your truth is as good as mine.

- It employs and therefore models explanatory devices (e.g., the hypothesis that cannot be refuted) that are counter-productive in the search for knowledge and understanding.

- Some claims can be actively harmful, such as by encouraging physically or psychologically dangerous practices; others can be passively harmful by discouraging an appropriate action, such as conventional medical treatment.

- Social policies may be developed on the basis of erroneous, unproven, pseudoscientific claims, Nazi racial theory being a classic example.

- It has special appeal to the naive and vulnerable (e.g. adolescents, the poorly educated, or the emotionally troubled), who are taken in by the claims of exotic, mysterious, and wonderful forces and powers, some of which can be acquired or used, and others of which are to be feared, marvelled at, or defended against.

- It distracts energy and resources from the legitimate search for knowledge.

(Kehoe 1990, p. 11)

Having carried out research on hypnosis and past-lives regression for a number of years, and having failed to find any evidence whatsoever of anything other than fantasy, imagination, and cryptomnesia within each and every one of the several hundreds of adult human beings studied, I reached the conclusion on the basis of this work that it is extremely unlikely that any human being's memories are attributable to any life other than the one he or she currently possesses. In every case where any careful, sustained, and systematic investigatory effort of any sort was made to determine the source of the so-called past-lives memories, the source was found to be firmly grounded in the past history of the person's *present* life—not in some other prenatal existence. The fact that we all have hidden memories (and many of them) in no way either establishes or supports the proposition that we have, indeed, lived before and reincarnation is a scientific fact. Other researchers, knowledgeable about the hypnotic fallacies, who have carried out past-lives regression studies (Spanos, et. al.), have reached similar conclusions. More telling is the fact that one of the most dedicated and famous reincarnationist researchers of all time, Ian Stevenson, also agrees. In Stevenson's words: "Although widely exploited by lay hypnotists and even by a few psychologists who should know better, hypnotic regression of 'previous lives' (with rare exceptions) generates only fantasies." (Stevenson 1984, p. 233)

To continue looking for the answers to our present problems in the alleged experiences of former lives is not only dishonest but patently irrational. Despite the claims of many past-lives therapists that their ministrations and explorations in the client's never-never-land were somehow or other "therapeutic," it is highly unlikely that a belief in the fact that in a previous life I was killed by a blow to the head is the reason why my unhit head in this lifetime is plagued with migraine headaches. Miraculously, once the knowledge of that fact is made known to one then all one's migraine headaches cease. Why? How does this knowledge shrink the cerebral arteries and arterioles? How does this truly remarkable event occur? What particular psychophysiological system and mechanisms are involved? Have any of these so-called and, indeed, most remarkable cures that are claimed to be due to insight and insight alone ever been subjected to any sort of controlled experimental tests in any laboratory on earth? Or are we supposed to accept hearsay or the patient's subjective reports as the sufficient and necessary evidence—all that is needed? Life is much too short and there are many many, too many, more important problems before us—both as individuals and as a society—than to continue to devote hundreds of hours and thousands of dollars of valuable scientific time merely to demonstrate how the human mind works, and to produce one more example of cryptomnesia. Certainly occult believers have produced enough examples and have staged enough demonstrations to last for a millennium. Here we need to emphasize the point made by David Marks in his review of Ray Hyman's *The Elusive Quarry: A Scientific Appraisal of Psychical Research* (1990). Trying to prove the existence of ESP is as futile as wasting time and effort in trying to invent a perpetual motion machine. As Marks states:

> I believe it would actually be irrational to continue the search for psi or to expend more than a modicum of effort reviewing the works of others, at least in this area at this time. . . . I question the rationality of continuing

the search for psi when the payoff has been so consistently poor over the 140 years of scientific study. Either psi exists or psi does not exist. I argue that the evidence Hyman and others have reviewed points much more strongly to the latter possibility than to the former. I therefore wonder how rational it is for Hyman to state . . . that he does not have "the faintest idea" whether psi exists. Surely, even the most patient and proper critic must have at least the faintest idea that the simple reason psi is so elusive is that it does not exist. On what evidence is any other conclusion justified? And even if it does exist, how could such an evanescent process possibly have any significant practical applications in the real world?

(p. 416)

Such questions are hard to ignore and they need to be answered. We do not need to lend credibility to what is *obviously* a discreditable and irrelevant fringe area of science. Lack of evidence for the existence of psi makes absolutely no difference to believers, and the fact that we have absolutely no proof whatsoever that reincarnation is possible also makes absolutely no difference to those who do believe in it. Ten thousand more years of demonstrations showing that the material dredged up from the amazing human brain was acquired in this lifetime and nowhere else would also make no difference whatsoever to the true believers in reincarnation. Asimov also has assured us this is so:

> In my opinion there are some beliefs that most individuals *must* have if they are to face life . . . there is the absolute refusal to accept the fact of death. We are the only species we know of, now or ever, that has discovered that death is inevitable for every individual. In reaction, the vast majority of us simply deny that death is death, and fervently believe in ghosts, in spirit worlds, in an afterlife, in the transmigration of souls. The evidence in favor of immortality of any part of ourselves is absolutely zero, but the will to believe easily overcomes that little matter.
>
> (1988, p. 11)

So why bother? Asimov says because if we are fortunate enough to be blessed with a bit of rationality, we have the obligation to use it. Furthermore, we may be able to lure some people who are teetering on the brink of sanity to tip our way. It is a sad fact of life that only skeptics or doubters read books such as this or if those on the other side read them, then it is only to reject and argue against the books' propositions. For the most part we are, indeed, preaching to the converted. But there is still one very important audience that is open-minded, curious, and eager for rational explanations of how the world works and why. These are the young people who manage to resist the brainwashing efforts of the deluded and who have a natural—almost instinctive talent—for sniffing out the fraudulent, the preposterous, and the irrational. No more noble cause is available to us than to aid and assist in the fight between science and superstition, and to do our best to insure that the long struggle against supernaturalism, religious fundamentalism, and primitivism—all the irrational fears that psychological flesh is heir to—will not end with our generation. We must not allow the world to reenter a new age of spiritualism, a return to the dark ages of occultism, and the brainless inanities of what the mentally lazy and aberrant call the New Age. Our children and their children deserve better than to be forced to live in a world where channelers, religious fundamentalists, people who talk with the dead, people who converse with aliens, people who run their lives by astrological charts, people who believe in creationism, people who believe in the abilities of psychics, and people who are ignorant of the laws of both science and human nature— are held up in front of the children of our generation as role models for admiration and emulation. Our children deserve more and better, and as long as we continue to promote the educational and scientific enterprise they will have it. We cannot afford to abandon this struggle. Not only is eternal vigilance the price of liberty—it is also the price we pay for the survival of truth and reason.

Raised on and conditioned by the media, once it informs us that something we would like to believe is true then, for most of us, it is TRUE. This is how urban legends are born. Once they become accepted as fact, they broaden, deepen, and become an established folk mythology. The folk mythology, in turn, is aided and abetted by secondary sensationalistic, money-grubbing, toadying, media sources that amplify and spread the myths. Thus is created a negative social force leading to such tragedies and disasters as the McMartin school fiasco—the most expensive and lengthy trial in United States history.

To consider these "folk mythologies" as mere entertainment for the masses at best, and as harmless idiosyncracies or irrelevances at worst, is to overlook the subtle and lasting damage that such mass attitudes and beliefs do to the efforts of educators and the entire educational establishment. Beliefs in ghosts, demons, dead spirits that talk, the psychokinetic powers of so-called psychics, and extraterrestrial aliens with unearthly abilities fosters attitudes and convictions that are not only contrary to the logic, principles, and even "the spirit of" every one of the natural sciences, but also these fictions undo and work directly against the efforts of science educators at all levels: in the grade schools, in the high schools, and in our colleges and universities.

If we are to grow and progress, not only as a nation but also as a race of intelligent and rational beings, it is imperative that we put all these sorts of primitive fears, senseless superstitions, and irrational beliefs behind us forever. If the race is, as H. G. Wells predicted long ago, a race between education and disaster, we had better recognize that disaster is gaining. We need to enlist the aid of an enlightened and socially responsible media, and to encourage them to take up this educational task. Their power is formidable, indeed, and it is high time that this power was enlisted to "work for us rather than against us." How they can be persuaded to adapt to and play such a new public educational role is a task that mainstream science and scientists have not yet attempted. The current tidal wave of misinformation and disinformation, the popularity of such TV programs as *Unsolved Mysteries,* occult and supernatural movies such as *Ghost,* pseudo-scientific book-series such as Time-Life's *Mysteries of the Unknown* and *Strange and Unusual Facts,* and the veritable flood of fear-based, supernatural fictions by Stephen King, Dean Koontz, et al., breed a variety of superstitious beliefs in demons, vampires, Satan, satanic powers, occult and unnatural forces, and supernatural evils beyond the ability of science and reason to deal with. Compare all of this with the few and far-between books, films, TV programs, newspaper space, etc., aimed at making science, reason, naturalism, humanism, and skepticism either appealing, exciting, admirable, or even respectable. Can anyone name a TV program or series aimed at a mass audience in which a scientist is cast as the hero in a sympathetic or nonhumorous light? With the exception of historical documentaries such as the development of the atomic bomb, or the stories of the astronauts, such "entertainments" are yet to be produced. Are scientists this dull, this bookish, this inhuman? I do not think so. In general, the class of human scientists as subjects worthy of admiration and emulation and science as a subject matter worthy of pursuit has been ignored as a subject matter deserving of popularization. To repair or even ameliorate this neglect is, indeed, a challenging task and one we should undertake without delay. Whether we will or not remains to be seen.

Postscript

In the epilogue to his 1984 book, written with John Fairley and Simon Welfare, the science-fiction writer and scientist Arthur C. Clarke created a scale with which to rate the validity of the paranormal and supernatural phenomena discussed in his book. The scale, cited below, runs from complete confidence to complete disbelief with zero meaning that Clarke was unable to make up his mind one way or the other. The scale is as follows:

+5	Certainly true
+4	Highly probable
+3	50:50 Chance of being true
+2	Possible—worth investigating
+1	Barely possible—not worth investigating
0	Don't know
−1	Very unlikely
−2	Almost certainly untrue
−3	Untrue beyond all reasonable doubt
−4	Certainly untrue

Clarke is aware his scale is asymmetric; though the ratings start at +5 they only go to −4. This is an inevitable consequence of the laws of logic. While we can prove that a phenomenon *does* occur, it is impossible to prove that it doesn't. In Clarke's words, "Human judgment must stop at −3; only God can go to −4."[1] Using Clarke's scale for the topics discussed in this book all of them must be rated at −3, i.e., untrue beyond all *reasonable doubt*. There is great emphasis here on the underlined word: *reasonable*. Unfortunately, there is a great deal of *unreason* surrounding all of these topics and when reason and unreason clash in the minds of human beings if unreason has wishful thinking as an ally, reason is "doomed to defeat." As Asimov notes:

> . . . in an uncertain world, with terror and disaster lurking unseen in the murk of the future; with misfortune ready to spring upon you in the very next moment; life would be unbearable if you could not find some way of easing matters—of being warned about the existence of specific monsters ahead, and how to thwart them. Why else would we turn to astrologers, palm-readers, dream analyzers, fortune-tellers and every other variety of palpable quack and enrich them in return for their phony advice. Nothing will wean the future-frightened public from them, for the belief seems universal that a false security is better than none.
>
> (1988, p. 10)

To the above list we should add spirit or demon possession, and salvation from the skies in the form of extraterrestrial space-ships who will transport the deserving and the true-believers to a far paradise among the stars. And, if by chance we are not worthy enough to be chosen for salvation by the Star People, we at least are important enough to be abducted by aliens and chosen for selective breeding in the intergalactic game of evolutionary development! In this vast human sea of faceless and egoless impersonality

---

[1]If as the New Agers tell me, "I am God," I am sorely tempted to rate them all as −4.

it's better to be wanted for murder than not to be wanted at all. Better a date with an alien than to remain all by oneself on the shelf. What are the ultimate human fears: extinction, loneliness, and death in a cold and loveless, uncaring, and unremembering universe? Is there any human terror greater than this? Has there ever been? Will there ever be? For some people, perhaps, the concept of the extinction of the human race itself holds a greater chill. For most, however, such a concept has no meaning. After all, what has posterity ever done for me? As Robert Heilbronner asked some time ago while he supplied his own rational answer: "Nothing, and most of us could care less if the human race is extinguished after we are gone." (1975, p. 169) The sun is gradually expanding and in 12 billion years the Earth will be swallowed up anyway. One hundred years from today, more than likely, I will have been dead for three quarters of a century. My children will also be dead and my grandchildren will be senile. What difference could it possibly make to me now whether they or the rest of the human race manages to survive beyond a hundred years from today? The future simply isn't real to most of us, and there's very little that concerns us beyond our own narrow ken. We will hoard and conserve for our own use and the use of our children, but for mankind at large? This is another matter, as every conservationist knows. Maybe humanity would be better off dead. But few of us are so inhuman that we *are* willing to kiss off all the rest of the unborn generations. Because we are human we cannot help but be concerned, we cannot help but care, we cannot help but feel some small measure of responsibility. Yet, if it is true that this measure of personal responsibility cannot be brought about except through personal experience, and that there can and will be no personal commitment unless the individual human being encounters death and destruction first hand, and has a chance to fully understand and appreciate the preciousness of life—then we can earnestly hope that all future generations will encounter famine, war, and other life-threatening disasters, i.e., in Heilbronner's words, "A glimpse into the void of a universe without man." (1975, p. 176) Maybe this is required in order to insure there *will be* a posterity, and that man will not only survive but prosper. The crucial question, however, is: Are such extreme lessons truly *necessary* for such an intelligent and humane race of beings? They won't be if intelligence and reason triumph. They will be if superstition and fear prevail. You can bet on it!

Recapitulation: Questions and Answers

Q: You've discussed a large number of complex topics and issues in the foregoing pages and I'm not quite sure that I have fully understood everything you've been saying. Is it all right if I ask a few questions?

A: By all means, be my guest.

Q: In the first part of the book you seem to suggest that everyone is a little "crazy" now and then and that this is, in a sense, quite "normal." Then you go ahead and argue that the clinicians and mental health experts also see the entire human population as mentally ill but you're opposed to this. Aren't you contradicting yourself?

A: No, not really. The points being made are first, unusual behavior that is rare or aperiodic or infrequent—occasional hallucinations or delusions that are temporary and that can be traced specifically to some specific source such as stress, alcohol, drugs, fatigue, etc.—are much more common in the general population than most people assume. Such individual sufferers are not permanently crazy, insane, or psychotic. Fortunately, the number of serious mental "diseases" disorders that require medical intervention and treatment are very few in number. Most of the clinician's business and most of his or her time is taken up by people suffering from problems of living. Such problems can be dealt with by any number of caring and loving individuals: a wise or older friend or relative, a minister, a counselor, a social worker, or a teacher. Individuals with these problems (and this includes most of us) are, in no way, "mentally ill" and in need of a psychiatrist. Unfortunately, when people with such problems go to a psychiatrist with their anxiety or "nerves," they are given a tranquilizer and advised to relax. Most psychiatrists have neither the time nor the professional skill to deal with the individual's fundamental existential concerns. Too many psychiatrists, and clinical psychologists as well, tend to see every human being as neurotic and in need of their professional ministrations. They are also prone to see every minor human problem—even cases of overt sexual and racial discrimination—as something in need of their professional expertise. Sadly enough, neither their training nor their background experience qualifies them to play God. At the moment, there is great concern over the demand on the part of the clinical psychologists to be allowed to prescribe a limited number of psychoactive drugs. Psychiatrists, as expected, are adamantly opposed and argue heatedly that psychologists aren't trained to do this. On the other hand, the psychologists could make a good case for denying psychiatrists the right to practice psychotherapy on the same grounds, i.e., inadequate training.

Another very serious problem is that too many people who are mentally, physically, or both mentally and physically unable to care for themselves are not being attended to by anyone. They make up the bulk of our so-called "street people." Though, technically, they are not mentally ill and shouldn't be institutionalized simply because they are unable to cope, an enlightened and sophisticated society ought to be smart enough and humane enough to provide a place for them. A few years ago they were cared for in our state mental hospitals until financial concerns became more important than humane concerns. Moreover, the population most in need of psychiatric treatment, i.e., people in the state mental institutions, are not receiving it and the population that needs it least, i.e., the wealthy and upper middle class, receive the most treatment and concern.

Q: Although I hate to say this, I'm still not sure I understand how the human brain works and what cryptomnesia is. Could you help me here?

A: Well, at the moment, no one fully understands how the human brain-mind works. It's much too complex. But we do know a few things about some of its operations and specifically we have learned some very interesting things about memory. First of all, the human brain-mind is a gland and it is never still. Even when we're sleeping it is always active, always working putting older earlier experiences together in new permutations and combinations, forming new patterns we call "thoughts." The human brain-mind is basically creative and re-creative—especially when we're asleep. The two most common examples of cryptomnesia are found in our dreams and in the so-called past-lives regression memories. Quite often, in our dreams, we will encounter people we've never met or seen before, go places we've never been before, read books that don't exist, see pictures that have never been painted, or do things we've never done before, build marvelous buildings, make love to strangers, etc. and etc., living lives we've never had or ever will have in the real world. Where do these experiences—these dreams—come from? Certainly not out of the blue! They come from the always active, never still, restless and patterning human brain using all of our prior sensory experiences to form slightly new variations—new patterns—that we perceive on the screen of awareness as MEMORIES. The only difference between our "dreams" and past-life regression memories and our "real" memories is that in the latter case we can specifically remember and recall their source. In the case of our dreams, daydreams, past-life regressions, and *deja-vu* experiences, we cannot remember their source, i.e., the specific time and place or places they came from. But, as you can see, the mental mechanism is exactly the same. The significant difference is that in the case of veridical memories we are aware of their source and in the case of pseudo-memories we are physically and mentally relaxed, letting the permuting and combining brain (imagination) run free and uninhibited. With a little stimulation supplied in the form of a few "real" stored images or some powerful, externally supplied suggestions, nothing else is needed to unleash complete scenarios of people, places, and events that are entirely imaginary. The "suggestions" whether supplied externally or by one's self are all that is necessary to put the brain's pattern-making mechanism into high gear. The fact that "real" memories and false memories are quite often confused is also understood when we bring human emotion and motivation into the picture. We all want to live forever. We all want to be immortal. We all want to believe in reincarnation.

Q: Then we have to always take into consideration human needs and desires when we look at claims made by people who strongly believe in paranormal phenomena. Are you saying that people who flock to channels, believe in the healing power of crystals, demon possession, phone calls from the dead, and all such things are actually victims and more to be pitied then censured?

A: In many senses of the word this is certainly true. The need for transcendent and redemptive experiences is a powerful force in the general population. Equally powerful is the need for novel and transformative stimulation. These needs are usually met by our vicarious enjoyment of novels, drama, movies, TV, music, art, or our daydreams and fantasies. We need to escape from ourselves and too many of us do it to excess through drugs and intoxicants. Years ago orthodox religion managed to meet and satisfy these needs just as it still does for many people in the world today. Many others, however, are not satisfied with the older religious myths and look to the distant stars for salvation in the form of alien spaceships.

Q: Well, if UFOs, alien spaceships, and alien abductions are all modern myths and delusions, why do so many people all across the planet report these things?

A: Well, skeptics deal with this issue in terms of what we call the "ET or Extra-Terrestrial Hypothesis." Why is it, for example, when people go outside at night, look up, and see an unusual or strange floating or flying object overhead, do they immediately assume that it is an alien spaceship piloted by extraterrestrials? Why, instead, don't they ask themselves, "I wonder what unusual, *natural* aerial phenomena it is that I just witnessed?" Or why don't they ask, "I wonder what new experimental type of man-made aircraft or balloon that thing was?" The reason they do not ask such questions is very simple: people see what they expect to see and for the last 43 years the media across the entire planet has pumped and primed the public to see alien spaceships in our earthly skies. Instead of informing the public that of the three explanations for any bizarre or strange aerial phenomenon the possibility of an alien spaceship is by far the most unlikely and, in fact, extremely improbable, we get instead banner headlines and front-page stories suggesting that ET is here. Science fiction novels and movies for the last 50 years have convinced nearly everyone who can see or read that we are not alone in the universe. More recently pseudo-science fictions works like Strieber's *Communion* and *Transformation* and Budd Hopkins's fantasies have convinced the credulous we are, indeed, surrounded by intelligent aliens. Both television and the popular press have created an ET mythology, an ET folklore that many people believe in with a religious fervor. During the November-December 1990 TV season, for example, four major, prime time series featured programs dealing with and looking favorably upon the ET hypothesis (*MacGyver, Carol & Company, Guess Who's Coming For Christmas* with Richard Mulligan, and *Unsolved Mysteries*). Little wonder that every man and every woman now believes that if the Space Brothers are not already here, they are, at least, on the way.

Q: What do you see as a solution to these modern superstitions, things like channeling, past lives, alien abductions, crystal power, and so forth?

A: We need to improve science education in our schools at all levels and we need to win the media over to our side. We desperately need their help to both create and sell the antidote to the occult and superstitious nonsense now flooding the bookstores, newsstands, screens, and airwaves.

Q: But modern science and scientists are all so literal, so sober, and so deadly serious! Isn't there an important role in life for play, for humor, for fantasy and romanticism?

A: Certainly, there is a very important role for humor, imagination, and vision in science. Many very serious scientists both read and write science fiction and many are poets as well. There are even several academic journals devoted exclusively to scientific humor and satire.

Q: But we seldom ever hear much about this side of science. The public doesn't perceive the scientist as playing the part of a dreamer.

A: True, but you must remember that as Oscar Wilde once said, "We're all lying in the gutter but some of us are looking at the stars." You should also remember there are two types of stargazers. First, we have the scientist who got up a long while ago and has worked diligently to turn his dreams and visions into realities. Then we have the romantic who continues to lie there and dream. Which of the two, in your opinion, is the more admirable?

Reference List

Introduction

Flanagan, Dennis. 1989. *Flanagan's Version.* New York: Vintage Books, A. A. Knopf, 220–221.

Hopkins, Budd. 1987. *Intruders: The Incredible Visitations at Copley Woods.* New York: Random House (Ballantine ed., 1988).

Huyghe, Patrick. 1988. "'UFO Update." *Omni* (June 1988): 99.

Klawans, Harold L. 1989. *Toscanini's Fumble, And Other Tales of Clinical Neurology.* New York: Bantam Books, 137.

Lilly, John C. 1978. *The Scientist.* New York: Lippincott.

Pasquarello, Tony. 1984. "Proving Negatives and the Paranormal." *Skeptical Inquirer* (Spring 1984): 259–270.

Peters, Jennifer. 1990. "This Long Ascent Into the Light." *Matrix: Monthly Feminist Forum* (January 1990): 6–7.

Platt, Charles. 1980. *Dream Makers.* New York: Berkeley Books.

Randle, Kevin D. 1988. *The October Scenario.* Iowa City, Iowa: Middle Coast Pub., 53.

Siegel, Ronald K. 1988. "Long Day's Journey Into Fright." *Omni* 11 (3) (December 1988): 86–146.

Strieber, Whitley. 1987. *Communion: A True Story.* New York: Beach Tree Books, William Morrow Co.

———. 1988, *Transformation.* New York: William Morrow Co.

Chapter 1

American Psychological Association. 1991. *The Suggestibility of Children's Recollections,* Washington, D.C.

Anderson, James. 1989. Interview with Jeremy Campbell cited in Campbell, Jeremy, *The Improbable Machine*, 212.

Bergland, Richard. 1985. *The Fabric of Mind.* New York: Viking Penguin, Inc.

Bergler, Edmund. 1986. *The Writer and Psychoanalysis,* 2nd ed. Madison, Conn.: International University Press.

Bowers, Kenneth. 1984. "On Being Unconsciously Influenced and Informed." In *The Unconscious Reconsidered,* edited by Kenneth S. Bowers and Meichenbaum. New York: John Wiley and Sons.

Campbell, Jeremy. 1989. *The Improbable Machine.* New York: Simon and Schuster.

Carlson, Margaret. 1990. "Six Years of Trial by Torture." *Time* (29 January 1990): 26–27.

Ceci, S. J., M. P. Toglia, and D. F. Ross, eds. 1987. *Children's Eyewitness Memory.* New York: Springer-Verlag.

Ceci, S. J., D. E. Ross, and M. P. Toglia. 1987. "Age Differences in Suggestibility," in *Children's Eyewitness Memory.* New York: Springer-Verlag.

Cramer, Jerome. 1991. "Why Children Lie In Court." *Time* (March 4, 1991): 76.

Crewdson, John. 1988. *By Silence Betrayed.* Boston, Mass.: Little, Brown, 127.

Ekman, Mary Ann Mason. 1989. "Kids Testimony in Court: The Sexual Abuse Crisis." In *Why Kids Lie: How Parents Can Encourage Truthfulness.* New York: Charles Scribner's Sons.

Ekman, Paul. 1989. *Why Kids Lie: How Parents Can Encourage Truthfulness.* New York: Charles Scribner's Sons, 15.

Ellenberger, Henri. 1970. *The Discovery of the Unconscious.* New York: Basic Books.

Ellis, Bill. 1988. "The Varieties of Alien Experiences." *Skeptical Inquirer* 12(3) (Spring 1988): 263–269.

Faust, David, and Jay Ziskin. 1988. "The Expert Witness in Psychology and Psychiatry." *Science* 241: 312.

Fodor, Jerry. 1989. Interview with Jeremy Campbell in Campbell, Jeremy, *The Improbable Machine*, 182.

Gardner, Richard A. 1991. *Sex Abuse Hysteria: Salem Witch Trials Revisited.* Philadelphia, Pa.: Center for Applied Psychology.

Harding, C. M., et al. 1987. "The Vermont Longitudinal Study of Persons with Severe Mental Illness." *Am J. Psychiatry* 144: 727–735.

Horowitz, A. N. 1991. *The Clinical Detective: Techniques in the Evaluation of Sexual Abuse.* New York: W. W. Norton Co.

Hoyt, Michael F. 1978. "Secrets in Psychotherapy: Theoretical and Practical Considerations." *International Review of Psychoanalysis* 5: 223–241.

Jastrow, Joseph. 1935. *Wish and Wisdom: Episodes in the Vagaries of Belief.* New York: D. Appleton Century Co., ix.

Kihlstrom, John. 1987. "The Cognitive Unconscious." *Science* 237: 1445–1452.

King, M., and J. Yuille. 1987. "Suggestibility and the Child Witness." In *Children's Eyewitness Memory,* edited by S. J. Ceci, M. P. Toglia, and D. F. Ross. New York: Springer-Verlag.

Klein, D. B. 1977. *The Unconscious: Invention or Discovery of Historico-Critical Inquiry.* Santa Monica, Calif.: Goodyear Pub. Co. Inc.

Lashley, Karl S. 1963. *Brain Mechanisms and Intelligence.* New York: Dover Pub., Inc.

Lewis, Aubrey. 1949. "Philosophy and Psychiatry." *Philosophy* (October 24): 99–117.

Lewis, Michael, Catherine Stanger, and Margaret Sullivan. N.D. "Deception in Three-Year-Olds." Unpub. Manuscript, Institute for Child Development, University of Medicine and Dentistry, New Jersey.

Libet, B., E. Wright, B. Feinstein, and D. Pearl. 1979. "Subjective Referral of the Timing for a Conscious Sensory Experience." *Brain* 102: 193.

Lindsay, S., and M. Johnson. 1987. "Reality Monitoring and Suggestibility: Children's Ability to Discriminate Among Memories from Different Sources." In *Children's Eyewitness Memory,* edited by S. J. Ceci, M. P. Toglia, and D. F. Ross. New York: Springer-Verlag.

Loftus, Elizabeth. 1979. *Eyewitness Testimony.* Cambridge, Mass.: Harvard University Press.

McConnell, R. A. 1983. "On the Malpractice of Medicine." In *An Introduction to Parapsychology in the Context of Science.* Bio-Sciences Dept., Pittsburgh, Pa.: University of Pittsburgh.

Medawar, Peter. 1972. *The Hope of Progress.* London: Methuen.

Modrow, John. 1992. *How to Be a Schizophrenic: The Case Against Biological Psychiatry.* Everett, Wa.: Apollyon Press.

Mulhern, Sherrill. 1991. "Satanism and Psychotherapy: A Rumor in Search of an Inquisition." In *The Satanism Scare,* edited by James T. Richardson, Joel Best, and David Bromley. New York: Aldine de Gruyter.

Nicol, J. Fraser. 1979. "Never Too Young to Cheat." *Fate* 32 (12): 45–52.

Oldenburg, Don. 1991. "Dark Memories: Adults Confront Their Childhood Abuse." *The Washington Post* (June 20, 1991): p. D5.

Penfield, Wilder. 1975. *The Mystery of Mind.* Princeton, N.J.: Princeton University Press.

Piaget, Jean. 1969. *Judgment and Reasoning in the Child.* London: Routledge, Kegan and Paul, 98.

Podvall, Edward M. 1990. *The Seduction of Madness.* New York: HarperCollins.

Popper, Karl. 1962. *Conjectures and Reflections.* New York: Basic Books.

Rosenhan, D. L. 1973. "Being Sane in Insane Places." *Science* 179: 250–258.

Sarbin, Theodore, and James C. Mancuso. 1980. *Schizophrenia: Medical Diagnosis or Moral Verdict?* New York: Pergamon Press.

Schmeing, J. 1937. Cited by Hilary Evans in *Alternate States of Consciousness.* Wellingborough, Northamptonshire, England: The Aquarian Press, 1989, 122–123.

Searl, John. 1988. Quotation cited by Richard M. Restak in *The Mind.* New York: Bantam Books, 26.

Shevrin, Howard. 1988. Work cited by Richard M. Restak in *The Mind.* New York: Bantam Books.

Spiegel, Lawrence D. 1986. *A Question of Innocence.* Parsippany, N.J.: Unicorn Pub. House.

Storr, Anthony. 1968. "The Concept of Cure." In *Psychoanalysis Observed,* edited by C. Rycroft. London: Penguin Books.

Szasz, Thomas. 1961. *The Myth of Mental Illness.* New York: Harper & Row.

Thompson, Tracy. 1991. "Delayed Lawsuits of Sexual Abuse on the Rise." *The Washington Post* (August 14, 1991): pp. B1 and B9.

Thornton, Elizabeth M. 1983. *The Freudian Fallacy.* New York: Dial Press, Doubleday.

Whyte, Lancelot L. 1960. *The Unconscious Before Freud.* New York: Basic Books.

Wilson, Cedric. 1968. *Pharmacological and Epidemiological Aspects of Adolescent Drug Dependence.* New York: Pergamon Press.

Wilson, S. A. K. 1978. *Modern Problems in Neurology,* 2 vols. London: Edward Arnold.

Wood, Garth. 1987. *The Myth of Neurosis.* New York: Harper & Row.

Chapter 2

Adams, G. 1980. *Perception, Consciousness, Memory: Reflections of a Biologist.* New York: Plenum Press, 212.

Alcock, James. 1981. "Psychology and Near Death Experiences." In *Paranormal Borderlines of Science,* edited by Ken Frazier. Buffalo, N.Y.: Prometheus Books.

Bartlett, Fredericks. 1964. *Remembering: A Study in Experimental and Social Psychology.* Cambridge: Cambridge University Press.

Campbell, Jeremy. 1989. *The Improbable Machine.* New York: Simon and Schuster, 163–164.

Edelman, Gerald M. 1986. "Neural Darwinism, Population Thinking, and Higher Brain Function." In *How We Know,* edited by Michael Shafto. New York: Harper & Row.

Erdellyi, M. H., and B. Goldberg. 1979. "Let's Not Sweep Repression Under the Rug: Toward a Cognitive Theory of Repression." In *Functional Disorders of Memory,* edited by J. F. Kihlstrom and F. J. Evans. Hillsdale, N.J.: Lawrence Erlbaum and Associates Publishers.

Flournoy, Theodore. 1911. *Spiritism and Psychology.* New York and London: Harper & Bros. Pub.

———. 1963. *From India to the Planet Mars.* New Hyde Park, N.Y.: University Books (originally published in 1901).

Freud, Sigmund. 1915. *Complete Works of Sigmund Freud,* edited by J. Strochey. London: Hogarth Press, 105.

———. 1915. *The Interpretation of Dreams.* In *Complete Works of Sigmund Freud,* edited by J. Strachey. London: Hogarth Press.

Gloor, Pierre, et. al. 1982. "The Role of the Limbic System in Experimental Phenomena of Temporal Lobe Epilepsy." *Annals of Neurology* 12: 140–162.

Harris, Melvin. 1986. *Investigating the Unexplained* Buffalo, N.Y.: Prometheus Books.

Jones, Lewis. 1990. Personal communication, London.

Jung, Carl. 1973. *Memories, Dreams, Reflections.* New York: Pantheon, 117–118.

Kampman, Reima. 1976. "Hypnotically Induced Multiple Personality: An Experimental Study." *Int. J. Clin. & Exp. Hypnosis* 29 (3): 215–227.

Kline, Milton V. 1956. *A Scientific Report on "The Search For Bridey Murphy."* New York: Julian Press.

Mountcastle, Vernon B. 1978. "Cortical Columnar Organization." In *The Mindful Brain,* edited by G. M. Eidelman and V. B. Mountcastle. Cambridge, Mass.: MIT Press.

Netherton, Morris, and Nancy Shiffrin. 1979. *Past Lives Therapy.* New York: Ace Books.

Penfield, Wilder. 1975. *The Mystery of the Mind.* Princeton, N.J.: Princeton University Press.

Pazder, Lawrence, and Michelle Smith. 1980. *Michelle Remembers.* New York: St. Martin's Press.

Prince, Morton. 1908. "The Unconscious." *J. of Abnormal Psychology* 3 (Oct. 1908): 265.

Reed, Graham. 1988. *The Psychology of Anomalous Experience,* rev. ed. Buffalo, N.Y.: Prometheus Books.

Rosenfield, Israel. 1988. *The Invention of Memory.* New York: Basic Books, 10.

Sacks, Oliver. 1989. *Seeing Voices: A Journey Into the World of the Deaf.* Berkeley: Univ. of California Press, 22.

Schultz, Ted. 1989. "Voices from Beyond." In *The Fringes of Reason,* edited by Ted Schultz. New York: Harmony Books, Crown Pub., 54–65.

Woolger, Roger. 1987. *Other Lives, Other Selves.* New York: Doubleday.

Zolik, Edwin S. 1958. "An Experimental Investigation of the Psychodynamic Implications of the Hypnotic Previous Existence Fantasy." *J. Clinical Psychol.* 14: 179–183.

Chapter 3

Adamski, George, and Desmond Leslie. 1952. *Flying Saucers Have Landed.* New York: British Book Center.

Adamski, George. 1955. *Inside the Space Ships.* New York: Abelard-Schuman, Inc.

Condon, Richard. 1959. *The Manchurian Candidate.* New York: McGraw-Hill Book Co.

Davis, Andrew Jackson. 1847. *The Principles of Nature: Divine Revelations and a Voice to Mankind,* 8th edition. New York: S. S. Lyon and Wm. Fishbough.

Eastabrooks, George. 1957. "Hypnotism in Warfare." In *Hypnotism,* 2nd ed.

Evans, Hilary. 1984. *Visions—Apparitions—Alien Visitors: A Comparative Study of the Entity Enigma.* Wellingborough, Northamptonshire, England: Sterling Pub. Co., Aquarian Press.

———. 1987. *Gods, Spirits—Cosmic Guardians.* Wellingborough, Northamptonshire, England: The Aquarian Press.

Fair, Charles. 1974. *The New Nonsense: The End of the Rational Consensus.* New York: Simon and Schuster.

Flournoy, Theodore. 1963. *From India to the Planet Mars.* New Hyde Park, N.Y.: University Books.

Harris, Thomas Lake. 1858. *Celestial Arcane.* New York: New Church Pub. Association.

Harrison, Eva. 1916. *Wireless Messages From Outer Worlds.*

Hoagland, Richard C. 1986. *The Monuments of Mars: A City on the Edge of Forever.* Berkeley, Calif.: North Atlantic Books.

Lindner, Robert. 1955. *The Fifty-Minute Hour.* New York: Rinehart & Co.

Marchetti, Victor, and John D. Marlos. 1974. *The CIA and the Cult of Intelligence.* New York: Alfred A, Knopf.

Marks, John. 1979. *The Search for the Manchurian Candidate: The CIA and Mind Control.* New York: Quadrangle Books.

McRae, Ron. 1984. *Mind Wars.* New York: St. Martin's Press.

Mundo, Laura. 1982. *The Mundo UFO Report.* New York: Vantage Press, 92–93, 109–110, 120.

Norman, Ruth, and Thomas Miller. 1989. *Mars Underground: Cities Discovered by Cosmic Visionaries.* El Cajun, Calif.: Norman-Miller Pub. Co.

O'Brien, Barbara. 1958. *Operations and Things: The Inner Life of a Schizophrenic.* New York: Arlington Books, Inc., A. S. Barnes & Company.

Reiser, Martin, L. Luburg, Susan Saxe, and C. Wagner. 1979. "An Evaluation of the Use of Psychics in the Investigation of Major Crimes." *J. Police Sci. & Administration.*

Rogo, D. Scott. 1977. *The Haunted Universe.* New York: Signet, 113.

Scheflin, Alan W., and Edward M. Opton. 1978. *The Mind Manipulators.* New York and London: Paddington Press.

Swedenborg, Emanuel. 1976. *Heaven and Hell.* New York: Pillar Books.

Woodrew, Greta. 1981. *On a Slide of Light: A Glimpse of Tomorrow.* New York: Macmillan Pub. Co.

———. 1988. *Memories of Tomorrow: One Woman's Cosmic Connection.* New York: Dolphin Books (Doubleday).

Chapter 4

Baker, Robert A. 1988. "The Aliens Among Us: Hypnotic Regression Revisited. *Skeptical Inquirer* 12 (2): 148–162.

———. 1990. *They Call It Hypnosis.* Buffalo, N.Y.: Prometheus Books.

Barber, Theodore X. 1969. *Hypnosis: A Scientific Approach.* New York: Van Nostrand and Reinhold.

———. 1982. "Hypnosuggestive Procedures in the Treatment of Clinical Pain." In *Handbook of Health Care in Clinical Psychology,* edited by T. Milton, C. J. Greene, and R. B. Meagher, New York: Plenum Press.

Barber, T. X., and R. W. J. Hahn. 1962. "Physiological and Subjective Responses to Pain-producing Stimulation under Hypnotically-suggested and Waking-imagined 'Analgesia.' " *J. Abnormal & Soc. Psychol.* 65: 411–418.

Barber, T. X., N. P. Spanos, and J. F. Chaves. 1974. *Hypnosis, Imagination and Human Potentialities.* New York: Pergamon Press.

Bernstein, Morey. 1956. *The Search for Bridey Murphy.* Garden City, N.Y.: Doubleday & Co.: Pocket Books Edition, 1978.

Beyerstein, Barry. 1989. "The 10% Solution." *The Rational Enquirer* 3 (2) (Oct. 1989):12–14.

Chaves, John F. 1989. "Hypnotic Control of Clinical Pain." In *Hypnosis: The Cognitive-Behavioral Perspective,* edited by N. P. Spanos and J. E. Chaves. Buffalo, N.Y.: Prometheus Books.

Christie-Murray, David. 1981. *Reincarnation: Ancient Beliefs and Modern Evidence.* London: David and Charles, Newton Abbot.

Coe, William C. 1989. "Posthypnotic Amnesia: Theory and Research." In *Hypnosis: The Cognitive-Behavioral Perspective,* edited by N. P. Spanos and J. F. Chaves. Buffalo, N.Y.: Prometheus Books.

———. 1989. "Hypnosis: The Role of Sociopolitical Factors in a Paradigm Clash." In *Hypnosis: A Cognitive-Behavioral Perspective,* edited by N. P. Spanos and J. F. Chaves. Buffalo, N.Y.: Prometheus Books.

D'Eon, Joyce. 1989. "Hypnosis in the Control of Labor Pain." In *Hypnosis: The Cognitive-Behavioral Perspective,* edited by N. P. Spanos and J. F. Chaves. Buffalo, N.Y.: Prometheus Books.

Edwards, Paul. 1986–1987. "The Case Against Reincarnation." *Free Inquiry,* 4 Parts: Fall 1986, Winter 86–87, Spring 87, Summer 87.

Evans, M. B., and G. L. Paul. 1970. "Effects of Hypnotically Suggested Analgesia on Physiological and Subjective Response to Cold." *J. Consult. & Clinical Psychol.* 35: 362–37 1.

Fiore, Edith. 1978. *You Have Been Here Before.* New York: Coward, McCann & Geoghegan, Inc. (Ballantine edition 1979).

Goldberg, Bruce. 1982. *Past Lives, Future Lives.* New York: Newcastle Pub. Co. Inc. (Ballantine editon 1989).

Gribbin, John. 1980. *Time Warps.* New York: Delta Books, Den Pub. Co.

Harris, Melvin. 1986. *Investigating the Unexplained.* Buffalo, N.Y.: Prometheus Books.

Hilgard, Ernest R. 1977. *Divided Consciousness: Multiple Controls in Human Thought and Action.* New York: John Wiley & Sons.

Hilgard, E. R., and Josephine R. Hilgard. 1983. *Hypnosis in the Relief of Pain,* 2nd ed. Los Altos, Calif.: Wm. Kaufman Pub.

Hilgard, Josephine. 1979. *Personality and Hypnosis: A Study of Imaginative Involvement.* Chicago: University of Chicago Press.

Holmes, David S. 1990. "The Evidence for Repression: An Examination of Sixty Years of Resarch." In *Repression and Dissociation: Implications for Personality Theory, Psychopathology and Health,* edited by J. Singer. Chicago: University of Chicago Press, 89–102.

Hoyt, I. F., and J. F. Kihlstrom. 1986. "Posthypnotic Suggestion and Waking Instruction." Paper presented at DPA meeting in Washington, D.C.

Iverson, J., and A. Bloxham, A. 1977. *More Lives Than One.* London: Pan Books.

Jay, C. E. 1977. *Gretchen, I Am.* New York: Wyden Books (Avon edition 1979).

Juhasz, J. B., and T. R. Sarbin. 1966. "On the False Alarm Metaphor in Psychophysics." *Psychological Record* 76: 323–327.

Kampman, R., and R. Hirvonoja. 1976. "Dynamic Relation of the Secondary Personality Induced by Hypnosis to the Present Personality." In *Hypnosis at Its Bicentennial,* edited by F. G. Frankel and H. S. Zaransky. New York: Plenum Press.

Kline, Milton V. 1951. "Hypnosis and Age Progression: A Case Report." *J. Genetic Psychol.* 78: 195–206.

———. 1952. "A Note on Primate-like Behavior Induced through Hypnosis." *J. Genetic Psychol.* 81: 125 131.

———. 1956. *A Scientific Report on the Search For Bridey Murphy.*

Levy, Jerry. Cited by Ed Dolnick in *Omni* 45: (December 1998).

Macready, R. 1980. *The Reincarnation of Robert Macready.* New York: Zebra Books.

Melzack, R., and P. D. Wall. 1988. *The Challenge of Pain,* 2nd edition. New York: Penguin Books.

Mersky, H. 1983. "The Psychological Treatment of Pain." In *Relief of Intractable Pain,* edited by M. Swerdlow. Amsterdam, Netherlands: Elsevier Pub. Co.

Netherton, Morris, and N. Shiffrin. 1978. *Past Lives Therapy.* New York: William Morrow Co.

Orne, Martin T. 1966. "Hypnosis, Motivation, and Compliance." *Am. J. Psychiatry* 122: 721–726.

Penfield, Wilder. 1975. *The Mystery of the Mind.* Princeton, N.J.: Princeton University Press.

Perky, C. W. 1910. "An Experimental Study of Imagination." *Am. J. Psychol.* 21: 422–452.

Pope, H. G., and J. I. Hudson. 1994. "Can Memories of Childhood Sexual Abuse Be Repressed?" Unpublished paper in press. See also "Recovered Memories: Recent Events and Review of Evidence." An Interview with Harrison G. Pope. *Currents In Affective Illness* 15 (7): 5–12.

Ready, W. B. 1956. "Bridey Murphy: An Irishman's View." *Fantasy & Science Fiction* 11 (2) (August): 81–88.

Rinn, Joseph F. 1950. *Sixty Years of Psychical Research: Houdini and I Among the Spiritualists.* New York: Truth Seeker Co.

Rodney, J. 1959. *Explorations of a Hypnotist.* London, England: Elek Publications.

Rubenstein, Rand, and R. Newman. 1954. "The Living Out of 'Future' Experiences under Hypnosis." *Science* 119: 472–473.

Sarbin, T. R. "Attempts to Understand Hypnotic Phenomena." In *Psychology in the Making: Histories of Selected Research Problems,* edited by L. Postman. New York: Alfred A. Knopf, 745–785.

Sarbin, T. R., and M. L. Andersen. 1967. "Role Theoretical Analysis of Hypnotic Behavior." In *Handbook of Clinical & Experimental Hypnosis,* edited by Jesse E. Gordon. New York: Macmillan Company.

Sarbin, T. R., and W. C. Coe. 1972. *Hypnosis: A Social Psychological Analysis of Influence Communication.* New York: Holt, Rinehart & Winston.

Segal, Sidney J. 1971. *Imagery: Current Cognitive Approaches.* New York: Academic Press.

Silverman, P. S., and P. L. Retzlafaff. 1986. "Cognitive Stage Regression through Hypnosis: Are Earlier Cognitive Stages Retrievable?" *Int. J. Clin. Exp. Hypnosis* 34: 192–204.

Sinclair-Greben, A. A. C., and D. Chamlmers. 1959. "Evaluation of Treatment of Warts by Hypnosis." *Lancet* 2: 480–482.

Snow, Chet B. 1989. *Mass Dreams of the Future.* New York: McGraw-Hin Pub. Co.

Spanos, N. P. 1971. "Goal-directed Fantasy and the Performance of Hypnotic Test Suggestions." *Psychiatry* 34: 86 96.

———. 1982. "Hypnotic Behavior: A Cognitive Social Psychological Perspective." *Research Communications in Psychology, Psychiatry and Behavior* 7: 199–213.

Spanos, N. P., and John F. Chaves. 1989. *Hypnosis: The Cognitive-Behavioral Perspective.* Buffalo, N.Y.: Prometheus Books.

Spanos, N. P., and J. D. McPeake. 1977. "Cognitive Strategies: Goal-directed Fantasy and Response to Suggestion in Hypnotic Subjects." *Am. J. Clin. Hypnosis* 20: 114–123.

Spanos, N. P., and E. C. Hewitt. 1980. "The Hidden Observor in Hypnotic Analgesia: Discovery or Experimental Creation." *J. Person. and Social Psychol.* 39: 1201–1214.

Spanos, N. P., Gwynn, and Stam. 1983. "Instructional Demands and Ratings of Overt and Hidden Pain during Hypnotic Analgesiac." *J. Abnormal Psychol.* 92:479–488.

Spanos, N. P., and J. L. D'Eon. 1980. "Hypnotic Amnesia, Disorganized Recall and Inattention." *J. of Abnormal Psychol.* 89: 744–750.

Spanos, N. P., and H. I. Radtke. 1982. "Hypnotic Amnesia as a Strategic Enactment: A Cognitive, Social-psychological Perspective." *Res. Comm. in Psychol. Psychiatry and Behavior* 7: 215–231.

Spanos, N. P., and D. R. Gorassimi. 1984. "Structure of Hypnotic Text Suggestions and Attribution of Responding Involuntarily." *J. Person. & Social Psychol.* 46: 688–696.

Spanos, N. P., and M. DeGroh. 1984. "Effects of Active and Passive Wording on Response to Hypnotic and Nonhypnotic Instructions for Complete and Selective Forgetting." Unpub. manuscript, Carleton University.

Spanos, N. P. 1987–1988. "Past-life Hypnotic Regression: A Critical Review." *Skeptical Inquirer* 12 (2) (Winter): 174–180.

Stam, J. J. 1984. "Hypnotic Analgesia and the Placebo Effect: Controlling Ischemic Pain." *Dissertation Abstracts International* 44: 2286B.

Sutcliffe, J. P. 1961. " 'Credulous' and 'Skeptical' View of Hypnotic Phenomena." *J. Abnormal and Social Psychol.* 62 (2): 189–200.

Wambach, Helen. 1978. *Recalling Past Lives.* New York: Harper & Row.

———. 1979. *Life Before Life.* New York: Bantam Books.

Weisman, Azan. 1979. *We Immortals.* New York: Pocket Books.

Wheeler, John. 1979. "Point of View: Drive the Pseudos Out." *Skeptical Inquirer* (3) (Spring): 12–13.

Zolik, Edwin. 1958. "An Experimental Investigation of the Psycho-dynamic Implications of Hypnotic 'Previous Existence.' " *J. Clin. Psychol.* 14 (2): 179–183.
———. 1962. "Reincarnation Phenomena in Hypnotic States." *Intl. J. of Parapsychology* 4 (3): 66–78.

Chapter 5

Alli, Autero. 1989/90. "New Age Casualties: Meditation Monsters and Kundalini Krack-Ups." *Critique* 30.
Allison, Ralph B., with T. Schwarz. 1980. *Minds in Many Pieces.* New York: Rawson, Wade Publishers.
Bander, Peter. 1973. *Voices from the Tapes.* New York: Drake Pubs.
Bliss, E. L. 1986. *Multiple Personality, Allied Disorders and Hypnosis.* New York: Oxford University Press.
Braun, Bennett. 1983. "Psychophysiological Phenomena in Multiple Personality and Hypnosis." *Am. J. of Clinical Hypnosis* 26: 124–137.
Coons, Philip, Victor Milstein, and Carma Marley. 1982. "EEG Studies of Two Multiple Personalities and a Control." *Arch. of Gen. Psychiatry* 39: 823–825.
Christie-Murray, David. 1978. *Voices From the Gods: Speaking with Tongues.* London: Routledge & Kegan Paul.
Crabtree, Adam. 1985. *Multiple Man: Explorations in Possession and Multiple Personality.* New York: Praeger.
Estep, Sarah W. 1988. *Voices of Eternity.* New York: Fawcett Good Medal.
Fiore, Edith. 1977. *You Have Been Here Before.* New York: Coward-McCann.
———. 1982. *The Unquiet Dead.* New York: Doubleday and Co.
Fuller, John G. 1981. *The Ghost of 29 Megacycles.* New York: New American Library.
Ganaway, George K. 1989. "Historical versus Narrative Truth: Clarifying the Role of Trauma in MPD and its Variants." *Dissociation* 2 (4): 205–220.
Goodman, Felicitas D. 1988. *How About Demons.* Bloomington, Ind.: Indiana University Press.
Guirdham, Arthur. 1982. *The Psychic Dimensions of Mental Health.* Wellingborough, England: Thurston Press.
Hilgard, E. R. 1977. *Divided Consciousness: Multiple Controls in Human Thought and Action.* New York: John Wiley & Sons.
Hines, Terence. 1988. *Pseudoscience and the Paranormal: A Critical Examination of the Evidence.* Buffalo, N.Y.: Prometheus Books.
Huxley, Aldous. 1952. *The Devils of Loudon.* New York: Harper and Brothers.
Johnson, M. K., and C. L. Raye. 1981. "Reality Monitoring." *Psychol. Review* 88: 67–85.
Johnson, M. K. 1988. "Reality Monitoring: An Experimental Phenomena—Analogical Approach." *J. Exp. Psychol. General* 117: 480–494.
Kastenbaum, Robert. 1969. "Death and Bereavement in Later Life." In *Death and Bereavement,* edited by A. H. Kutscher. Springfield, Ill.: C. C. Thomas, 28–54.

Holenberg, R. J. 1973. "Behavioristic Approach to Multiple Personality: A Case Study." *Behavior Therapy* 4: 137–140.

Leighton, Alexander. 1965. "Discussion" in A. V. S. De Rueck and R. Porter, eds. *Transcultural Psychiatry.* Boston, Mass.: Little, Brown & Co.

Ludwig, Arnold M., et. al. 1972. "The Objective Study of Multiple Personality." *Archiv. of Gen. Psychiatry* 26: 298–310.

Montgomery, Ruth. 1981. *Strangers Among Us.* New York: Fawcett Crest Books.

Osterreich, T. K. 1966. *Possession: Demonical and Others.* Secaucus, N.J.: Citadel Press.

Parkes, C. M. 1972. *Bereavement.* New York: International Universities Press.

Peck, M. Scott. 1978. *The Road Less Traveled.* New York: Simon and Schuster.

———. 1983. *People of the Lie.* New York: Simon and Schuster.

———. 1984. "A Psychiatrist's View of Exorcism." *Fate* 37 (9) (September 1984): 87–96.

Peterson, Terence. 1987. "Spiricom or Spiricon." *Fate* 40 (1) (January 1987): 92–97.

Raudive, Konstantine. 1970. *Breakthrough.* New York: Taplinger Pub. Co.

Rawcliffe, D. H. 1959. *Illusions and Delusions of the Supernatural and the Occult.* New York: Dover Pub.

Rees, W. D., and S. G. Lutkins. 1976. "Mortality of Bereavement." *British Med. Journal* 4: 13–25.

Rogo, D. Scott. 1987. *The Infinite Boundary.* New York: Dodd Mead.

Rogo, D. Scott, and Ray Bayless. 1979. *Phone Calls from the Dead.* Englewood Cliffs, N.J.: Prentice-Hall.

Rogo, D. Scott. 1977. "Paranormal Tape-recorded Voices." In *Future Science,* edited by John White and Stanley Kriffner. New York: Anchor Books.

Robin, Jeff. 1990. *The Spirits of America.* New York: Pocket Books.

Sargant, William. 1957. *Battle for the Mind.* Garden City, N.Y.: Doubleday.

Slater, E. 1966. "Diagnosis of Hysteria." *British Medical Journal* 29: 1395–1399.

Smith, Susy. 1977. *Voices of the Dead.* New York: New American Library.

Spanos, N. P. 1983. "Demonic Possession: A Social Psychological Analysis." In *Compliant Behavior,* edited by Max Rosenbaum. Human Sciences Press, 149–199.

———. 1989. "Hypnosis, Demonic Possession and Multiple Personalities." In *Altered States of Consciousness and Mental Health,* edited by C. A. Ward. Newbury Park, Calif.: Sage Pubs.

Spanos, N. P., and E. C. Hewitt. 1979. "Glossolalia: A Test of the 'Trance' and Psychopathology Hypothesis." *J. Abnormal Psychol.* 88: 427–434.

Spanos, N. P., and E. C. Hewitt. 1980. "The Hidden Observor in Hypnotic Analgesia: Discovery or Experimental Creation." *J. Person. & Social Psychol.* 39: 1201–1214.

Spanos, N. P., Wendy Cross, Mark Lepage, and Marjorie Coristine. 1986. "Glossolalia as Learned Behavior: An Experimental Demonstration." *J. Abnormal Psychol.* 95 (1): 21–23.

Spanos, N. P., E. Menary, N. J. Gabora,, S. C. DuBrenil, and B. Dewhurst. 1990. "Secondary Identity Enactments During Hypnotic Past Life Regression." Unpublished manuscript. Dept. of Psychology, Carleton University, Ottawa.

Spiegel, David, S. Cutcomb, C. Ren, and K. Pribram. 1985. "Hypnotic Hallucination Alters Evoked Potentials." *J. Abnormal Psychol.* 94: 249–255.

Sutcliffe, J. P., and J. Jones. 1962. "Personal Identity, Multiple Personality and Hypnosis." *Int. J. Clin. & Exp. Hypnosis* 10: 231–269.

Thigpen, C. H., and H. M. Cleckley. 1957. *Three Faces of Eve.* New York: McGraw-Hill Book Co.

Thorne, S. D., and P. Hemestein. 1984. "The Role of Suggestion in the Perception of Satanic Messages on Rock-and-Roll Recordings." *J. of Psychology* 116: 245–248.

Vokey, John R., and J. D. Read. 1985. "Subliminal Messages: Between the Devil and the Media." *American Psychologist* 40 (11) (November 1985): 1231–1239.

Weinberger, Julius. 1977. "Apparatus Communication with Discarnate Persons." In *Future Science,* edited by John White and Stanley Krippner. New York: Anchor Books.

Welch, William A. 1975. *Talks with the Dead.* New York: Pinnacle Books.

Wickland, Carl. 1924. *Thirty Years Among the Dead.* Hollywood, Calif.: Newcastle Pubs.

Wilson, Ian. 1982. *All in the Mind.* Garden City, N.Y.: Doubleday & Co.

Chapter 6

Alcock, James E. 1983. "Psychology and the Out-of-Body Experience." *Skeptical Inquirer* 8: 75–77.

Alli, Autero. 1989–90. "New Age Casualties: Meditation Monsters and Kundalini Krack-Ups." *Critique* 32 (October-January 1989–90).

Bassoir, Jean-Noel. 1988. "Astral Travel." *New Age Journal* 5 (6) (November/December 1988).

Bear, David M., and Paul Fedio. 1977. "Quantitative Analysis of Interical Behavior in Temporal Lobe Epilepsy." *Archives of Neurology* 34 (Aug. 1977): 454–467.

Beyerstein, Barry L. 1988. "The Brain and Consciousness: Implications for Psi Phenomena." *Skeptical Inquirer* 12 (2): 163–173.

Blackmore, Susan. 1988. "Visions From the Dying Brain." *New Scientist* (May 1988): 43–46.

Blackmore, Susan. 1993. *Dying to Live.* Buffalo, N.Y.: Prometheus Books.

Bond, Frederick Bligh. 1921. *The Gate of Remembrance.* Oxford: Basic Blackwell.

Christie-Murray, David. 1978. *Voices from the Gods: Speaking with Tongues.* London: Routledge & Kegan Paul.

Coleridge, Samuel T. *Biographia Literaria.* Everyman Library Edition. London: Dent, 58–60.

Drab, K. J. 1981. "The Tunnel Experience: Reality or Hallucination?" *Anabiosis* 1: 126–152.

Edwards, Harry. 1989. "Calling All Spirits." *The Skeptic* 9 (4) (Summer 1989): 59–63.

Ehrenwald, J. 1974. "Out-of-Body Experiences and the Denial of Death." *J. Nerv. & Mental Diseases* 159 (4): 227–233.

Flammarion, Camille. 1906. *Mysterious Psychic Forces: An Account of the Author's Investigations in Psychical Research.* Boston: Small, Maynardo Co.

Fodor, Nandor. 1966. *Encyclopedia of Psychic Science.* New York: University Books.

Francuch, Peter D. 1982. *Principles of Spiritual Hypnosis.* Santa Barbara, Calif.: Spiritual Advisory Press.

Freeborn, H., and C. A. Mercier. 1902. "Temporary Reminiscence of a Long Forgotten Language During Delirium." *J. Soc. for Psychical Research* and the *Lancet* (1902): 279–283.

Gabbard, Glen O., and Stuart W. Twenlow. 1984. *With the Eyes of the Mind: An Empirical Analysis of Out-of-Body States.* New York: Praeger.

Gardner, Martin. 1989. "Glossolalia." *Free Inquiry* 9 (2) (Spring 1989): 46–48.

Goodwin, James, and Jean Goodwin. 1987. "Impossibility in Medicine," ch. 4. In *No Way: The Nature of the Impossible,* edited by Philip J. Davis and David Park. New York: W. H. Freeman Co.

Gregory, Richard L. 1966. *Eye and Brain: The Psychology of Seeing.* New York: McGraw Hill.

Greyson, B. 1983. "The Psychodynamics of Near-Death Experiences." *J. Nerv. Mental Diseases* 171: 376–381.

Gurney, Edmund. 1886. *Phantoms of the Living.* F. W. H. Myers and F. Podmore, 2 vols. London: Trubner.

Hallinan, Timothy. 1989. *The Four Last Things.* New York: NAL, Penguin Books.

Hammond, W. A. 1876. *Spiritualism and Allied Causes and Conditions of Nervous Derangement.* New York: G. P. Putnam's Sons, 292–293.

Holzer, Hans. 1990. "Channeling and Past Lives: The Real Story." *Fate* 43 (6) (June 1990): 74–86.

Horton, Lydeard. 1981.

Hyman, Ray. 1986. Quoted in Lynn Smith, "The New Chic or Mark Pheniner Metaphysical Fad of Channeling." *Los Angeles Times,* 5 December 1986.

Inglis, B. 1983. "Power Corrupts: Skepticism Corrodes." *A.S.P.R. Newsletter* 9 (1): 1–3.

James, William. 1961. *The Varieties of Religious Experience* (Modern Library). New York: Collier Books.

Klimo, Jon. 1987. *Channeling: Investigations on Receiving Information from Paranormal Sources.*

Leuba, James H. 1925. *The Psychology of Religious Mysticism.* New York: Harcourt Brace Co..

Lilly, John. 1978. *The Scientist.* Philadelphia: J. P. Lippincott Publishers.

Lukianowicz, N. 1958. "Autoscopic Phenomena." *AMA Archives of Neurology and Psychiatry* 80: 199–220.

McConnell, R. A. 1983. *An Introduction to Parapsychology in the Context of Science,* Bio-Sciences Dept., Pittsburgh, Pa.: University of Pittsburgh.

MacLaine, Shirley. 1985. *Dancing in the Light.* New York: Bantam Books.

Monroe, Robert. 1971. *Journeys Out of the Body.* New York: Anchor Books, Doubleday.

Monroe, Robert. 1985. *Far Journeys*. New York: Doubleday.

Morse, Melvin. 1990. *Closer to the Light*. New York: Villard Books.

Neder, Andrew. 1980. *The Psychology of Transcendence*. Englewood Cliffs, N.J.: Prentice-Hall.

O'Donnell, Bernard. 1955. "The Masked Medium Spoof." In *Grand Deception*, edited by Alexander Klein. New York: Ballantine Books.

Osis, Karlis, and E. Haraldson. 1977. *At the Hour of Death*. New York: Avon Books.

Palmer, John. 1978. "The Out-of-Body Experience: A Psychological Theory." *Parapsychology Review* 9: 19–22.

Preisinger, John, Jr. 1990/1991. "My Near-Death Experience." *Free Inquiry* 11 (1) (Winter 1990/1991): 52.

Randi, James. 1986. "On Channeling." Letter to Jeremy P. Tarcher, December 8, 1986.

Ridall, Kathryn. 1988. *Channeling: How to Reach Out to Your Spirit Guides*. New York: Bantam Books.

Ring, Kenneth. 1992. *The Omega Project: Near-Death Experiences, UFO Encounters, and Mind at Large*. New York: William Morrow and Company, Inc.

Roberts, Glenn, and John Owen. 1988. "The Near-Death Experience." *Brit. J. Psychiatry* 153: pp. 607–617.

Rogo, D. Scott. 1978. *Mind Beyond the Body*. New York: Penguin Books, Ltd.

———. 1990. "Is Religion In The Brain?" *Fate* 43 (11) (November 1990): 80–92.

Samarin, William. 1972. *Tongues of Men and Angels*. New York: Macmillan.

Schucman, Helen C. 1976. *A Course in Miracles*. 3 volumes. Tiburon, Calif.: Foundation For Inner Peace.

Schultz, Lea. 1988. "Samuel." *Phoenix Newsletter* 6 (2) (Fall 1988): 13 and 20.

Siegel, Ronald K. 1991. "Remember Rogo." *Omni* 13 (4) (January 1991): 73.

Sinnett, A. P. 1901. *Nature's Mysteries*. London, England: Theosophical Pub. Society.

Spanos, N. P., Wendy P. Gross, Mark Lepage, and Marjorie Coristine. 1986. "Glossolalia as Learned Behavior: An Experimental Demonstration." *J. Abnormal Psychol.* 95 (1): 21–23.

Sperrill, J. L. 1965. *They Speak with Other Tongues*, ch. 9. London: Hodder & Stoughton.

Tobin, Simon. 1988. "The Out-of-Body Experience: It's All In the Mind." *The Skeptic* 8 (3) (Spring 1988): 23–27.

Waxman, Stephen, and Norman Geschwind. 1974. "Hypergraphics in Temporal Lobe Epilepsy." *Neurology* 24 (July 1974): 629–636.

Zollner, Johann. 1880. *Transcendental Physics*. London: Haworth.

Chapter 7

Barber, T. X. 1970. "Hypnosis, Suggestions, and Auditory-Visual Hallucinations: A Critical Analysis." In *Origin and Mechanisms of Hallucinations*, edited by W. Kemp. New York: Plenum Press.

Barber, T. X., and D. S. Caverly. 1964. "An Experimental Study of Hypnotic (Auditory and Visual) Hallucinations." *J. Abnormal & Social Psychol.* 63: 13–20.

Billig, Otto. 1982. *Flying Saucers: Magic in the Skies.* Cambridge, Mass.: Schenkman Publishing Company.

Bowers, K. S. 1967. "The Effect of Demands for Honesty of Reports of Visual and Auditory Hallucinations." *Int. J. Clin. & Exp. Hypnosis* 15: 31–36.

Chapman, Loren J., and Jean P. Chapman. 1988. "The Genesis of Delusions." In *Delusional Beliefs,* edited by T. F. Oltmanns and B. A. Maher. New York: John Wiley & Sons.

Esquirol, J. E. D. 1832. "Sur les Illusions des Sens chez les Aliénes." *Archives Generales de Medicine* 2: 5–23.

Evans, Hilary. 1989. *Alternate States of Consciousness.* Wellingborough, Northamptonshire, England: The Aquarian Press.

Fagan, B. M. 1984. *The Aztecs.* New York: W. H. Freeman Co.

Haught, James A. 1990. *Holy Horrors.* Buffalo, N.Y.: Prometheus Books.

Heise, David K. 1988. "Delusions and the Construction of Reality." In *Delusional Beliefs,* edited by T. F. Oltmanns and B. A. Maher. New York: John Wiley & Sons.

Johnson, M. K., and C. L. Raye. 1981. "Reality Monitoring." *Psychol. Review* 88: 67–85.

Kroll, J., and B. Backrack. 1982. "Medieval Visions and Contemporary Hallucinations." *Psychological Medicine* 12: 209–222.

Laing, R. D., and A. Esterson. 1964. *Sanity, Madness and the Family,* vol. 1. New York: Basic Books.

Langer, E. J. 1975. "The Illusion of Control." *J. Person. and Social Psychol.* 32: 311–528.

McKellar, P. 1968. *Experience and Behavior.* Harmondsworth: Penguin Press.

Maher, Brendan A. 1988. "Anomalous Experience and Delusional Thinking: The Logic of Explanations." In *Delusional Beliefs,* edited by T. F. Oltmanns and B. A. Maher. New York: John Wiley & Sons.

Mallcolm, Andrew L. 1971. *The Pursuit of Intoxication.* Arf. Ed. (Canada), 1971; New York: Simon and Schuster, 1972.

Mauromatis, Andreas. 1987. *Hypnagogia.* London and New York: Routledge and Kegan Paul.

Morrock, Richard. 1986. "A Heady Quest for Transcendence." *Skeptical Inquirer* 10 (3) (Spring 1986): 277–280.

Oltmanns, Thomas F. 1988. "Approaches to the Definition and Study of Delusions." In *Delusional Beliefs,* edited by T. F. Oltmanns and B. A. Maher. New York: John Wiley & Sons.

Parish, Edmund. 1897. "The International Census of Waking Hallucinations." In *Hallucinations and Delusions: A Study of the Fallacies of Perception.* London: Walter Scott Pubs.

Perky, C. W. 1910. "An Experimental Study of Imagination." *Am. J. of Psychol.* 21: 422–452.

Posey, T. B., and M. F. Losch. 1983. "Auditory Hallucinations of Hearing Voices in 375 Normal Subjects." *Imagination, Cognition, and Personality* 2: 99–113.

Rehm, Stanley R. 1991. "Sleep Paralysis and Nocturnal Dyspnea." Paper presented at Advances in Pulmonary and Critical Care Medicine, International Symposium, Vienna, Austria, 1991.

———. "Sleep Paralysis in the Salem Witchcraft Trials: A Physiological Basis for 'Spectral Evidence' " (in press).

Roszak, Theodore. 1981. "In Search of the Miraculous." *Harpers* (Jan. 1981): 54–62.

Segal, S. J. and S. Nathan. 1964. "The Perky Effect: Incorporation of an External Stimulus under Placebo and Control Conditions." *Percept. Motor Skills* 18: 469–480.

Segal, S. J. 1968. "Patterns of Response to Thirst in an Imagery Task (Perky Technique) as a Function of Cognitive Style." *J. of Personality* 36: 574–588.

Segal and Glicksman. 1967. "Relaxation and the Perky Effect: The Influence of Body Position on Judgments of Imagery." *Am. J. Psychol.* 80: 257–262.

Sidgewick, H. A., et. al. 1894. "Report of the Census of Hallucinations." *Proceedings of the Society of Psychical Research* 26: 259–394.

Siegel, Ronald K. 1992. *Fire in the Brain: Clinical Tales of Hallucination.* New York: Dutton and Penguin Books.

Slade, Peter D., and R. P. Rentall. 1988. *Sensory Deception: A Scientific Analysis of Hallucination.* Baltimore: Johns Hopkins University Press.

Spanos, N. P. and T. X. Barber. 1968. " 'Hypnotic' Experiences as Inferred from Subjective Reports: Auditory and Visual Hallucinations." *J. Exp. Research in Personality* 3: 136–150.

Sorokin, Patrimi. 1957. *Social and Cultural Dynamics.* Boston: Porter Sargant.

Starker, Steven. 1986. *Parathink: The Paranoia of Everyday Life.* New York: New Horizons Press, Macmillan.

Strieber, Whitley. 1988. *Communion: A True Story.* New York: Avon Books.

Tart, Charles, ed. 1972. *Altered States of Consciousness.* Garden City, N.Y.: Doubleday Auction Books.

Taylor, Shelly E. 1989. *Positive Illusion: Creative Self-Deception and the Healthy Mind.* New York: Basic Books.

West, D. J. 1948. "A Mass Observation Questionnaire on Hallucinations." *J. Soc. Psychical Research* 34:187–196.

Chapter 8

Berlitz, Charles, and William Moore. 1980. *The Roswell Incident.* New York: G. P. Putnam's Sons.

Beyerstein, Barry. 1988. "Neuropathology and the Legacy of Spiritual Possession." *Skeptical Inquirer* (Spring 1988): 255–265.

Blum, Howard. 1990. *Out There.* New York: Simon and Schuster.

Boyce, Chris. 1979. *Extraterrestrial Encounter: A Personal Perspective.* Secaucus, N.J.: Chartwell Books.

Coffey, E. J. 1992. "The Anthropomorphic Fallacy." *J. British Interplanetary Society* 45: 23–29.

Curran, Douglas. 1985. *In Advance of the Landing: Folk Concepts of Outer Space.* New York: Abbeville Press.

Ellis, Bill. 1990. "A Mythology for Our Time." *Omni* 12 (12) (September 1990): 73.

Evans, Hilary. 1988. "The Case for Skepticism." In *Phenomenon: 40 Years of Flying Saucers.* New York: Avon Books.

———. 1989. *Alternate States of Consciousness.* Wellingborough, Northamptonshire, England: The Aquarian Press.

Fahy, Thomas A. 1988. "The Diagnosis of Multiple Personality Disorder: A Critical Review." *Brit. J. Psychiatry* 153: 597–606.

Festinger, Leon, H. Riechen, and Schacter, 1956. *When Prophecy Fails.* Minneapolis: University of Minnesota Press.

Fowler, Raymond. 1979. *The Andreasson Affair.* Englewood Cliffs, N.J.: Prentice-Hall (Bantam Books 1980).

Fry, Daniel. 1966. *The White Sands Incident.* Louisville, Ky.: Best Books.

Gibbs, Nancy. 1993. "Angels Among Us." *Time* (December 27, 1993): 56–65.

Gould, Stephen J. 1990. *Wonderful Life.* London: Hutchinson Radius.

Guthrie, Stuart E. 1993. *Faces in the Clouds.* New York: Oxford University Press.

Hicks, Robert. 1990. "The Satanic Conspiracy and Urban Legends." *Skeptical Inquirer* 14 (3 and 4) (Spring and Summer 1990).

Hopkins, Budd. 1981. *Missing Time.* New York: G. P. Putnam's Sons (Berkeley Books Ed. 1983).

———. 1987. *Intruders: The Incredible Visitations at Copley Woods.* New York: Random House (Ballantine Books Ed. 1988).

Ishakower, Otto. 1938. "A Contribution to the Psychopathology of Phenomena Associated with Falling Asleep." *International Psychoanalysis* 19: 331–345.

Janis, Irving L. 1972. *Victims of Groupthink.* Boston, Mass.: Houghton Mifflin.

Keyhoe, Donald E. 1950. *The Flying Saucers are Real.* New York: Fawcett Pub.

Klass, Philip. 1988. "The MJ–12 UFO Documents: Parts I and II." *Skeptical Inquirer* 12 (2 and 3) (Winter 1987–88, Spring 1988).

———. 1989. *UFO Abductions: A Dangerous Game.* Buffalo, N.Y.: Prometheus Books.

Kottmeyer, Martin. 1989. "Gauche Encounters: Bad Films and the UFO Myths." Unpublished Manuscript. Carlyle, Illinois, Rt. 3, Box 31.

Lawson, Alvin H., and W. C. McCall. 1978. "Hypnosis of Imaginary UFO Abductees." Paper read at the 1978 annual meeting of the American Psychological Association, Toronto, Canada.

Lawson, Alvin H. 1985. "UFO Abductions or Birth Memories?" *Fate* 38 (3) (March 1985): 68–80.

Merkowitz, William. 1967. "The Physics and Metaphysics of Unidentified Flying Objects." *Science* 157: 1274–1279.

MacRae, Ron. 1984. *Mind Wars.* New York: St. Martin's Press.

Montgomery, Ruth. 1985. *Aliens Among Us.* New York: G. P. Putnam's Sons.

Mulhern, Sherrill. 1989. "Therapist-Patient Interactions in Cult-Survivor Cases." Paper read at the National Conference on Child Abuse and Neglect, Salt Lake City, Utah, 1989.

Nickell, Joe, and John F. Fischer. 1990. "The Crashed-Saucer Forgeries." *Int. UFO Reporter* 15 (2) (March-April 1990): 4–16.

Noll, Richard. 1990. *Bizarre Diseases of the Mind.* New York: Berkeley Books.

Persinger, M. A. 1983. "Geophysical Variables and Human Behavior." *Perceptual & Motor Skills* 56: 184–188.

Roberts, Andy. 1989. "The Legend of the Crashed Saucers." In *Phenomenon: 40 Years of Flying Saucers.* New York: Avon Books.

Scully, Frank. 1950. *Behind the Flying Saucers.* (Popular Library Ed. 1951). New York: Henry Holt & Co.

Simpson, George Gaylord. 1964. *This View of Life: The World of an Evolutionist.* New York: Harbinger Books, chapter 13.

Spencer, John, and Hilary Evans, eds. 1989. *Phenomenon: 40 Years of Flying Saucers.* New York: Avon Books.

Strieber, Whitley. 1987. *Communion: A True Story.* New York: Beach Tree Books, William Morrow Co.

Tipler, Frank J. 1980. "Extraterrestrial Intelligent Beings Do Not Exist." *Quarterly J. Royal Astronomical Society* 21 (2): 267–280.

Tough, Allen. 1989. "Extraterrestrial UFOS: Yes or No." In *Phenomenon: 40 Years of Flying Saucers,* edited by John Spencer and Hilary Evans. New York: Avon Books.

Stang, Ivan. 1988. *High Weirdness by Mail.* New York: Simon and Schuster.

Swords, Michael D. 1989. "Science and the Extraterrestrial Hypothesis in UFOlogy." *J. UFO Studies* 1 (1): 67–102.

Victor, Jeffrey S. 1991. "Satanic Cult Survivor Stories." *Skeptical Inquirer* 15(3): 274–280.

Walters, Ed, and Frances Walters. 1990. *The Gulf Breeze Sightings.* New York: William Morrow Co.

Watson, Nigel. 1989. "The Great Airship Scare." In *Phenomenon: 40 Years of Flying Saucers,* edited by John Spencer and Hilary Evans. New York: Avon Books.

Wells, Jeff. 1981. "Profitable Nightmare of a Very Unreal Kind." *Skeptical Inquirer* (Summer 1981): 47–52.

Chapter 9

Asimov, Isaac. 1988. Foreword to Henry Gordon's *Channeling Into the New Age.* Buffalo, N.Y.: Prometheus Books, 10–1 1.

Berlitz, Charles. 1974. *The Bermuda Triangle Mystery.* Garden City, N.Y.: Doubleday.

Burnham, John C. 1987. *How Superstition Won and Science Lost.* New Brunswick, N.J.: Rutgers University Press.

Crichton, Michael, 1988. "Postscript: Skeptics at Cal-Tech." In *Travels.* New York: Alfred A. Knopf.

Farley, John, and Simon Welfare. 1984. *Arthur C. Clarke's World of Strange Powers.* New York: G. P. Putnam's Sons.

Heilbronner, Robert L. 1975. *An Inquiry Into the Human Prospect.* New York:W. W. Norton & Co.

Kehoe, Pat. "Hazards of New Age Thinking." *Rational Enquirer* 3 (1) (July 1989): 11.

Marks, David. 1990. Review of Hyman's *The Elusive Quarry: A Scientific Appraisal of Psychical Research. Skeptical Inquirer* 14 (4) (Summer 1990).

Spanos, N. P. 1987–88. "Past-Life Hypnotic Regression: A Critical Review." *Skeptical Inquirer* 12 (2): 174–180.

Stevenson, Ian. 1984. Quoted in *Arthur C. Clarke's World of Strange Powers,* by John Farley and Simon Welfare. New York: G. P. Putnam's Sons, 233.

Wilson, Colin. 1981. *Poltergeist! A Study in Destructive Hauntry.* New York: Wedeview/Perigee Books, G. P. Putnam's Sons.

———. 1987. *The Psychic Detectives: Solving Crimes by ESP.* New York: Berkeley Books.

Wilson, Colin, with Damon Wilson. 1988. *The Encyclopedia of Unsolved Mysteries.* Chicago, Ill.: Contemporary Books.

Index

Abuse. *See* sexual abuse
Adamski, George, 119–21
Alcock, James, 87
Alien abductions, 327–37
Aliens, UFO occupants, 324, 326–27
Allen, Kirk, hero of Lindner's "The Jet-Propelled Couch," 123–25
Alli, Antero, 253–54
Allison, Ralph B., 203–204
Arnold, Kenneth, 315
Asimov, Isaac, 355, 358
Automatic behavior, 56–57
Autoscopic phenomena, 265–66
Aztecs, 308

Backster, Cleve, 135
Balise, Harry, 15, 21
Bander, Peter, 182–86
Barber, Theodore X., 285
Bartlett, Frederic, 94
Basterfield, Keith, 19, 318
Beliefs, false, 291
Bender, Hans, 184
Bergland, Richard, 50–54
Bergler, Edmund, 72
Besharov, Douglas, 41
Beyerstein, Barry, 173–75, 270–71,

337–38
Black hole, 16, 21
Blackmore, Susan, 271, 275–78
Blavatsky, Helen, 227
Bloxham, Arnall, 156–57
Blum, Howard, author of *Out There*, 325
Bo and Peep, 319
Bowers, Kenneth, 60
Brain:
   as a computer, 92–95
   as a gland, 50–55
   hormones, 50–54
   left-right brain myth, 172–75
   organization of, 95–102
   triune brain, 49–50
Browning, Robert, 228
Buchanan, J. Rhodes, 229–30
Buckey, Raymond, of the McMartin case, 37–39
Bull, Titus, 230–31
Bullard, Thomas, 338
Burnham, John C., author of *How Superstition Won and Science Lost*, 346

Campbell, Jeremy, 58–61, 101
Carlson, Margaret, 43
Carrington, Heyward, 224, 233

Ceci, Stephan J., 46
Channeling, 88, 237–54
   how to do it, 251–54
Chapman, Loren J., and Jean P., 293–95
Charismatics, 258
Children's lies and lying, 42–46
Christie-Murray, David, 159, 210, 255, 256
CIA (Central Intelligence Agency), 139–40
Clarke, Arthur C., 357–58
Close Encounters of the Third Kind, 331
Clozaril, 55
Coleman, Lee, 48
Copernicus, 309
Countess Maud by Emily Holt, 79
Crabtree, Adam, 203
Crewdson, John, 39
Crichton, Michael, 351–52
Cryptomnesia, 24, 45, 78–110, 157–59
Cryptopsychisms, 83–85
Curran, Douglas, author of *In Advance of the Landing,* 320

Davis, Andrew Jackson, 117
Déjà vu phenomena, 103–107
Delirium tremens (DTs), 195, 217, 219
Delusions, 287–99
Demon possession, 196–217
Descartes, René, 63–64
Devils of Loudon, The, by Aldous Huxley, 196
Diagnostic and Statistical Manual (DSM) of the American Psychiatric Association, 55
Dick, Philip K., 13, 18
DNA and RNA, role in memory, 98–99
Doyle, Sir Arthur Conan, 202–203
Drab, K. J., 275
Dreams, 297
Duvall, Ed, 17, 22

Eccles, Sir John, 270
Edelman, Gerald, 97–99
Edwards, Harry, 249–51

Edwards, Paul, 163
Einstein, Albert, 26
Ekman, Mary Ann Mason, 38–40
Ekman, Paul, 38
Electronic visual phenomena, 190–93
Electronic voice phenomena, 181–93
Ellenberger, Henri, 63
Ellis, Bill, 338
Ellis, David, 184–85
Encyclopedia of Psychic Science by Nandor Fodor, 223
Epilepsy, 175–76, 271–72
ESP (extra-sensory perception), 225
Estabrooks, George, 137–38
Estep, Sarah Wilson, 189–90
Evans, Jane, 156–57
Exorcism, 205–206
Experienced Anomalous Trauma (E.A.T.), 334–35

Fair, Charles, 118, 136
Fifty Minute Hour, The, by Robert Lindner, 123
Fiore, Edith, 213–17
Flanagan, Dennis, 28–29
Flournoy, Theodore, 78, 81–87, 111–12
Fodor, Jerry, 60
Fodor, Nandor, 223
Folklore, 33, 340, 356
Frankel, Soviet psychic, 24
Frankl, Viktor, and logotherapy, 76
Freud, Sigmund, 31, 58–59, 61–77, 80, 96, 107–10
Freudian Fallacy, The, by E. M. Thornton, 61–63, 66–77
From India to the Planet Mars by Theodore Flournoy, 81–83
Fromm, Eric, 309
Fromm, Erika, 79
Fuller, John G., 190

Gabbard, Glen O., and Twenlow, Stuart, 264
Ganaway, George, 20, 208–209
Gardner, Martin, 258, 341

Gardner, Richard A., author of *Sex Abuse Hysteria*, 45
Ghosts, 282
Glossolalia, i.e., speaking in tongues, 209, 254–60
 how to become a glossolaliac, 259–60
Goldberg, Bruce, 163–64
Goodman, Felicitas, 211–13
Goodwin, James and Jean, 270
Gordon, Henry, 222
Gribbin, John, 162
Gurney, Edmund, 283

Haber, Ralph, 47
Hall, G. Stanley, 68
Hallinan, Timothy, author of *The Four Last Things*, 253
Hallucinations, 17–18, 281–88
 census by D. J. West, 284
 census by Peter McKellar, 284
 in normal individuals, 282–88
 International Census of Waking, 283
Hallucinogenic drugs, 220, 269
Hare, Robert, 231–32
Harris, Melvin, 89
Harris, Thomas Lake, 117
Harrison, Eva, 118
Haught, James A., author of *Holy Horrors*, 310
Head, Henry, 94
Heaven's Union, 135
Heilbronner, Robert, 359
Heise, David K., 306–10
Hemi-Sync (Robert Monroe), 261
Hicks, Robert, author of *In Pursuit of Satan*, 339
Hilgard, Ernest R., 144, 147
Hill, Betty and Barney, 328, 332
Hoagland, Richard C., author of *The Monuments of Mars*, 119
Holt, Emily, author of *Countess Maud*, 79
Holy Roller religious sect, 209
Holzer, Hans, 243–45
Home, D. D., 228

Hopkins, Budd, 9, 17, 331, 338, 341
Hormones, of the brain, 50–54
Houdini, 150–51
Hyman, Ray, 238, 354
Hypnogogic and hypnopompic imagery, 267, 338
Hypnosis, 70, 87–88, 137–39, 141–76, 263
 Erroneous beliefs, 149–50
 Hypnosis and epilepsy, 175–76
 Hypnotic amnesia, 145–51
 Hypnotic progression, 164–72
 Hypnotic regression, 152–64
Hyslop, James H., 224

Ideational and sensate mentalities, 305–306
Illusions, 299–313
Illusory beliefs, 302–305

Jacobs, David, 338, 341
James, William, 59, 63, 224, 264, 283
Janov, Arthur, 76
Januarius, Saint, 62
Jastrow, Joseph, 33–34, 348
Jennifer, 14, 20
Johnson, Judy (in McMartin sex abuse case), 37, 335
Johnson, M. K., 298–99
Jones, Lewis, 109–10, 150
Jonestown (Reverend Jim Jones' settlement), 199
Journeys Out of the Body by Robert Monroe, 261
Jung, Carl, 87–88
Jurgenson, Frederick, 181

Kampman, Reima, 91–92, 109–10, 158
Keech, Marian, of *When Prophecy Fails*, 318–19
Keel, John A., 314
Kehoe, Pat, 352–53
Kelly, Robert F., 43
Key, Bryan Wilson, 187–88
Keyhoe, Major Donald, 320

Kihlstrom, John, 60
Klass, Philip J., 315, 320, 325, 328, 339
Klawans, Harold L., 14
Klein, D. M., 63
Klein, Milton V., 162–63
Klimo, Jon, author of *Channeling*, 237–43
Knight, J. Z., and *Ramtha*, 237, 240, 243
Knowles, Faye, and family, 14, 19, 20, and 317–18
Korsakoff's psychosis, 219–20
Kottmeyer, Martin, 332

Lashley, Karl, 50–51
Lawson, Alvin H., and McCall, W. C. (simulated UFO abductions), 333–34
Lazaris, entity channeled by Jach Pursel, 243
L-Dopa, 14
Leighton, Alexander, 213
Les Miserables, 100–101
Leuba, James H., 272–73
Levy, Jerry, 172
Lewis, Aubrey, 74
Libet, Benjamin, 57
Lilly, John, 13–14, 19
Lindner, Robert, author of *The Fifty Minute Hour*, 123–25
Locke, John, 55
Lotus, Elizabeth, 42, 46

Maher, Brendan A., 292–93, 296
The Manchurian Candidate, by Richard Condon, 137–40
Markowitz, William, 315
Marks, David, 354–55
Martha Mitchell effect, 292
Masked medium spoof, 234
Mass Dreams of the Future, by Helen Wambach and Chet B. Snow, 166–72
MC–12 (Operation *Majestic*), 325
McConnell, R. A., 225
McMartin's sex abuse case, 37–40
McRae, Ron, author of *Mind Wars*, 132–

33, 136–37
Medawar, Peter, 75–76
Media and media relations, 347
Mediums, 226–37
Memory, 78–110
    Anomalies of, 92–95, 102–107
    DNA-RNA system, 98
    Hidden memories, 24–25
    Panoramic memories, 69–70
Mesmer and mesmerism, 69, 81–82, 176, 200
Miller, Neal, 225–26
Mind, the unconscious, 55–62, 67–77
Minnock, Tommy, 150–51
Modest proposal, 349–51
Monroe, Robert, 261–62
Montgomery, Ruth, of *Aliens Among Us*, 220
Monuments of Mars, by Richard Hoagland, 119
Moody, Raymond A., 274–75
Mountcastle, Vernon, 95
Mulhern, Sherrill, 340
Mundo, Laura, 121–23

Nagel, Ernest, 74
NASA, 118–19
Near death experiences (NDEs), 267–78
Neher, Andrew, 262–63
Netherton, Morris, 87
Neural Darwinism, 97–98
New Age, 23, 34, 76, 349, 356
Nickell, Joe, 325
Night terrors, 338
Noll, Richard, 337

O'Brien, Barbara, of *Operators and Things*, 125–27, 336
O'Donnell, Bernard, 234
Ogatta (Greta Woodrew), 128
Orne, Martin, 143
Oscan, grammar, 90, 158

Paladino, Eusapia, 224, 233
Paranormal powers, 27–28

Parathink, 303–305
Parish, Edmund, 283
Parker, Calvin, and Hickson, Charles (UFO abductees), 328
Pasquarello, Tony, 26
Past lives regressions, 158–64
Peck, C. Scott, 204–206
Penfield, Wilder, 69, 96–97, 108, 176
Pentagon paranoia, 130–34
Pentecostals and neo-Pentecostals, 255
Perceptual set and expectancy, 288
Perky, C. W., 142, 286
Personal control, 301
Phone calls from the dead, 193–95
Piaget, Jean, 46–47
Pierce, Claudette, 14, 19
Plagiarism, 72
Platt, Charles, 13
Polygraph test, 329–30
Popper, Karl, 74
Positive illusions, 300–302
Preconscious, 57
Preisinger, John, Jr., 274
Prince, Morton, 85
Prophet, Elizabeth Clare, 319
Proust, Marcel, 71
Psychic detectives, 134–35
Psychic research, 133–34
Psychokinesis, 225
Psychological projection, 186–89
Psychometry, 229
Pugh, Emerson, 49

Ramtha (J. Z. Knight's channeled entity), 244
Randi, James, 131–32, 240
Randle, Kenneth, 17
Raudive, Konstantin, 181–83
Reality discrimination errors, 286–87
Reality monitoring, 287, 298–99
Reed, Graham, 90, 269
Regardie, Francis I., 76
Reincarnation, case against, 163–64
Repression, 107–10
Restless legs, 14, 19

Reticular activating system (RAS), 56
Ridall, Kathryn, 252–53
Rinn, Joseph F., 150
Roberts, Andy, 323, 325–26
Roberts, Jane, 252
Roe, Ellen, 44
Rogo, D. Scott, 120, 193–94, 206, 264, 271–73
Romer, Fraülein, 117
Rosen, Harold, 90–91, 158
Rosenfeld, Israel, 97
Rosenhan's study of insanity, 35–36
Rovin, Jeff, 191–92
The Roswell Incident, 323–24
Roszak, Theodore, 311–13

Sacks, Oliver, 101–102
Samarin, William, 258–59
Samuel, 245–48. *See also* Lea Schultz
Sardon, Victorién, 117
Sargant, William, 200
Satanism and satanic cults, 14–15, 20, 335–36, 339
Schmeing and psychic abilities, 54
Schucman, Helen C., of *A Course in Miracles,* 239
Schultz, Lea and Samuel, 245–48
Schultz, Ted, 88
Scully, Frank, author of *Behind the Flying Saucers,* 324
Searl, John, 32
Selbit, P. T., 234–37
Sensate and ideational mentalities, 305–306
Sexual abuse of children, 37–49, 335
Shaeffer, Robert, 315
Shepanek, Mercedes, 189
Shevrin, Howard, 57–59
Siegel, Ronald K., 15–16, 20–21, 273–74
Silva, Jose, 118
Sleep paralysis, 19
Smead, Mrs., 117–18
Smith, Helene (Catherine Elise Muller), 81, 112–17

Smith, Michelle, 80–81, 86
Snow, Chet B., 165–72
Social currency, 307
Sorokin, Pitrim, 305–306
Spanos, Nicholas, 144–46, 161–62, 197–200, 204–208, 354
Speaking in tongues. See glossolalia
Sperry, Roger, 172–73
Spiegel, Lawrence D., 41
Spiricom (spirit communication), 192
Spirit guides, 237, 243–44
Sprinkle, R. Leo, 165, 170
Steinberg, Gene, 314
Stevenson, Ian, 354
Storr, Anthony, 68
Strieber, Whitley, 9, 16, 22
Subversion myths, 340
Suggestibility, 142
Swedenborg, Emmanuel, 111

Tabin, Simon, 271
Tabori, Paul, 111, 222
Tabula rasa (John Locke), 55
Thomason, Sarah, 246–48
Thornton, E. M., of The Freudian Fallacy, 66–77
Tolman, Ralph, 15, 20–21
Tough, Dr. Allen, 331
Tribrain theory, 49
Truth, 305

UFOs (Unidentified flying objects), 22, 314–41

Unconscious, before Freud, 63–67
Unconscious mind, 29, 63–77
Unconscious skepticism, 226

Varondeck, 39
VOCAL (Victims of Child Abuse Laws), 41
Vokey, John R., and Read, J. D., 187–89
Vomit therapy, 76
Voodoo, 201

Walk-ins (Strangers Among Us), 220–21
Walters, Ed and Frances (Gulf Breeze UFOS), 320–21, 332
Walton, Travis (UFO abductee), 328–30
Wambach, Helen, 162, 165–72
Weinberger, Julius (contact with dead via Venus Flytrap), 194
Wheeler, John, 171–72
Whyte, Lancelot L., 63–65
Wickland, Carl, 202
Wilde, Oscar, 89–90, 364
Wilson, Cedric (neurologist), 69–71
Wilson, Colin, 351
Wood, Garth, 72–76
Woodrew, Greta (Ogatta), 128–30
Woolger, Roger, 31, 78

Zars (Spirits), 201
Zolik, Edwin, 91, 155–56
Zoliner, Johann, 233